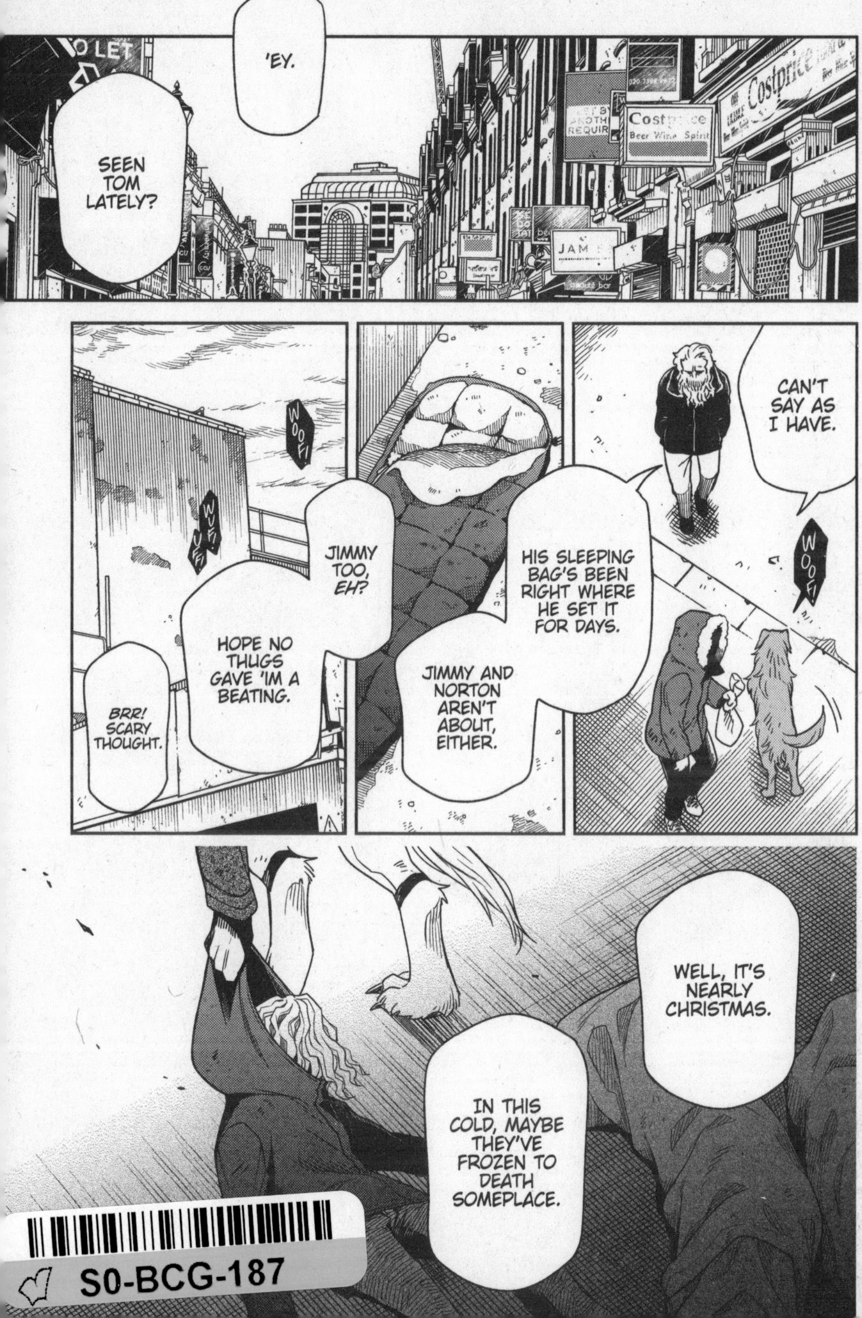
'EY.
SEEN TOM LATELY?
O LET
Costprice
Beer Wine Spirit
Costprice
CAN'T SAY AS I HAVE.
WOOF!
HIS SLEEPING BAG'S BEEN RIGHT WHERE HE SET IT FOR DAYS.
JIMMY AND NORTON AREN'T ABOUT, EITHER.
JIMMY TOO, EH?
HOPE NO THUGS GAVE 'IM A BEATING.
BRR! SCARY THOUGHT.
WOOF!
WUF! UF!
WELL, IT'S NEARLY CHRISTMAS.
IN THIS COLD, MAYBE THEY'VE FROZEN TO DEATH SOMEPLACE.

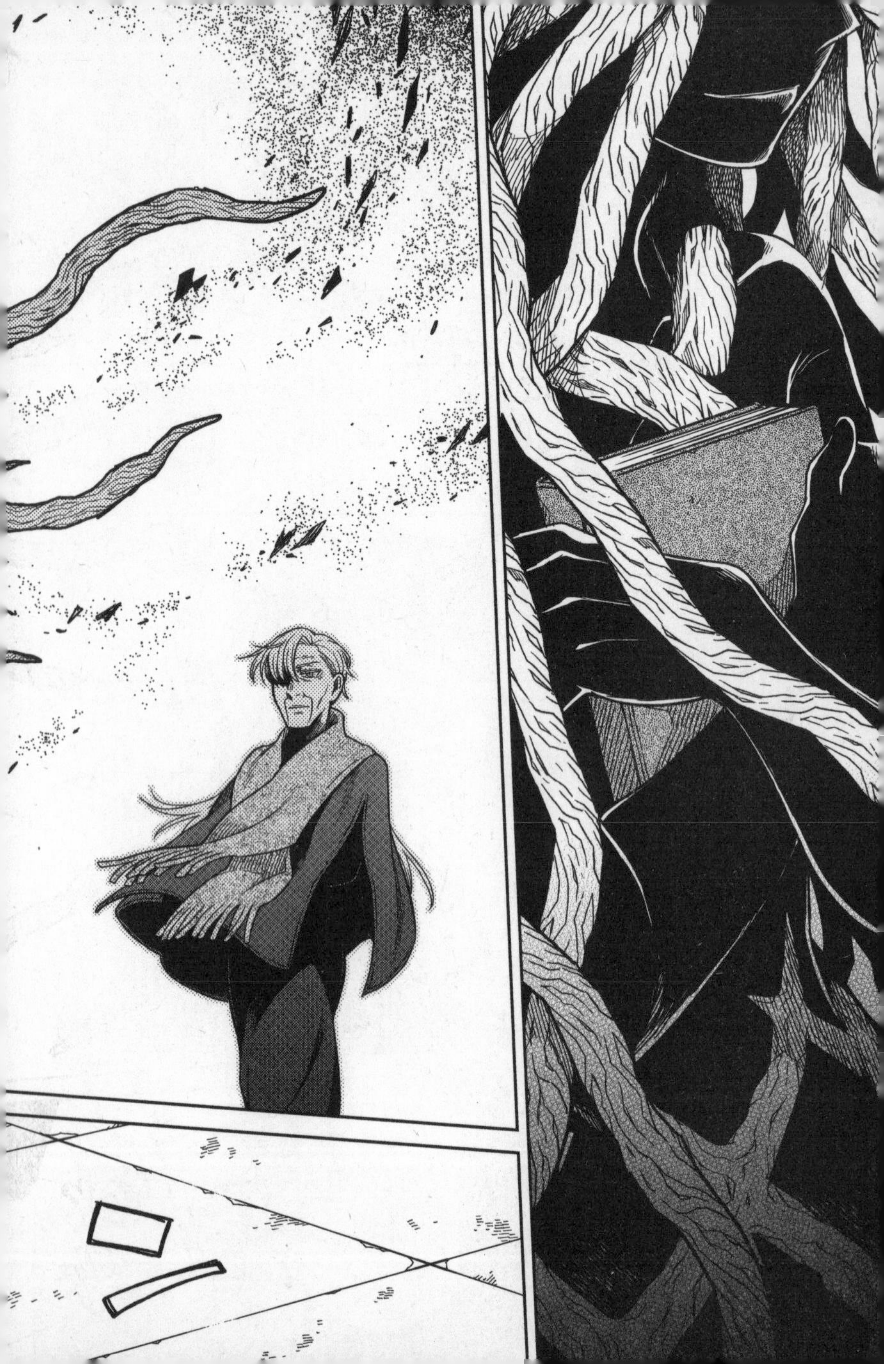

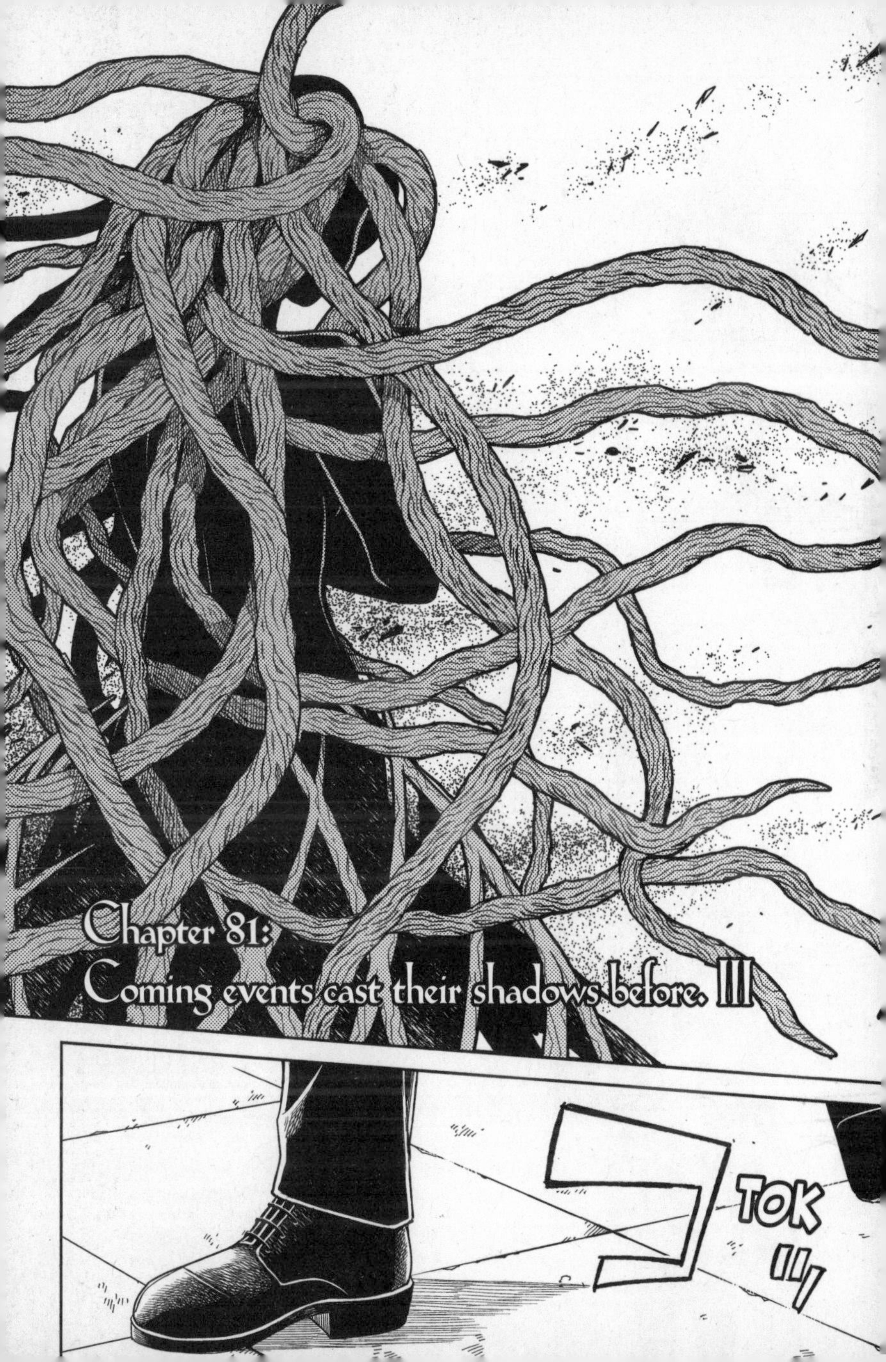
Chapter 81:
Coming events cast their shadows before. III
TOK

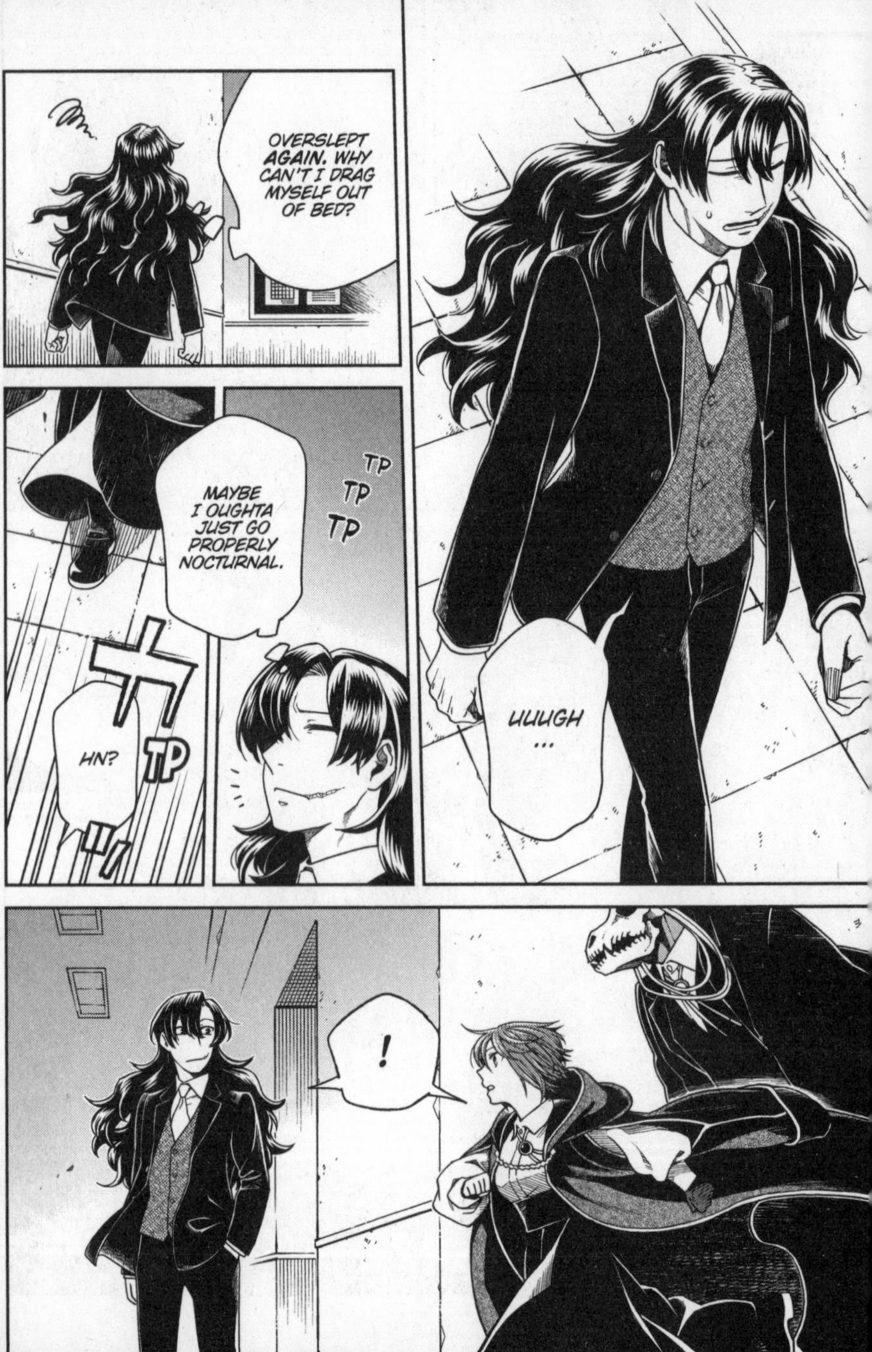
UUUGH ...
OVERSLEPT AGAIN. WHY CAN'T I DRAG MYSELF OUT OF BED?
TP TP TP
MAYBE I OUGHTA JUST GO PROPERLY NOCTURNAL.
HN?
TP
!

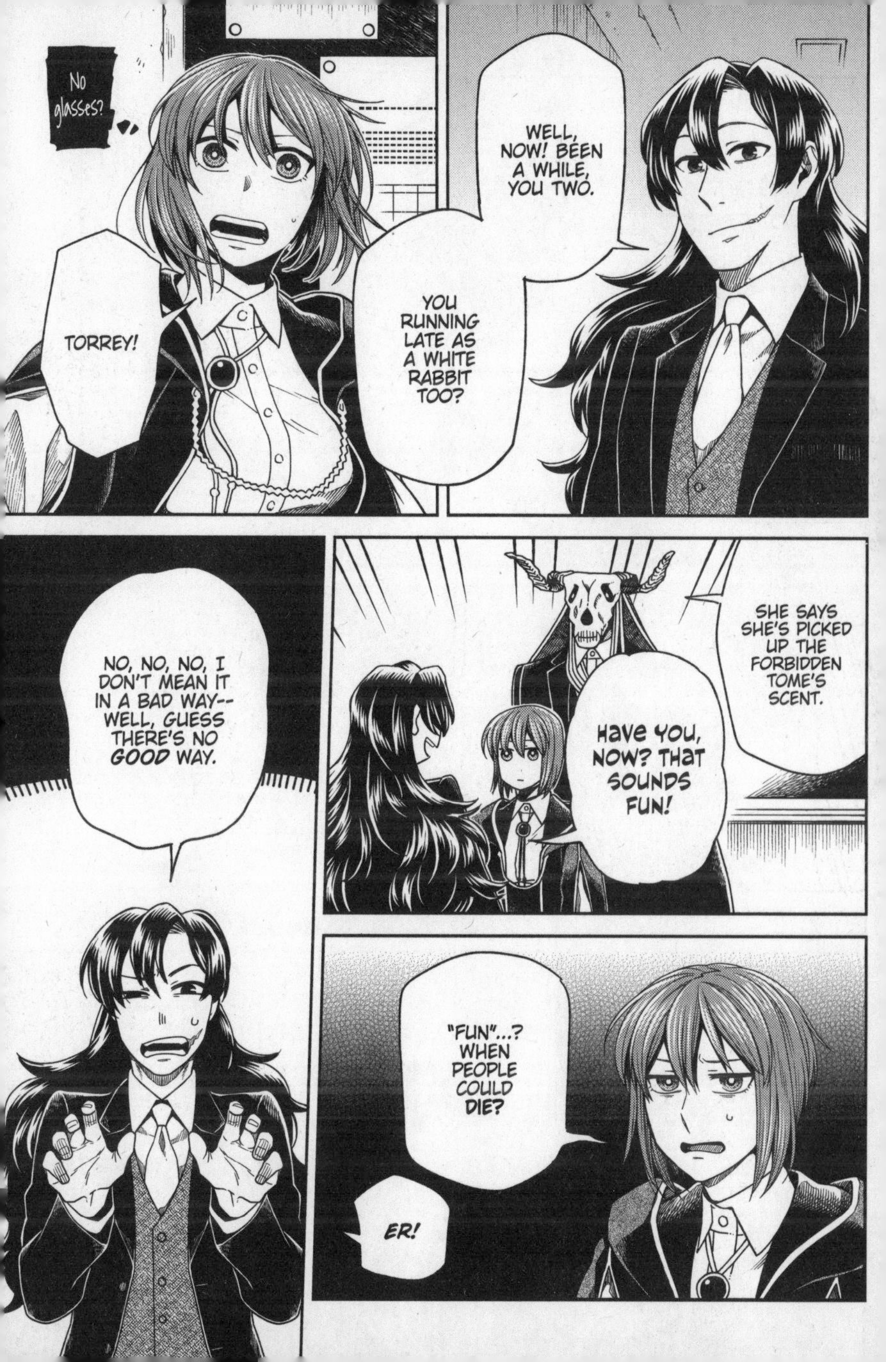
WELL, NOW! BEEN A WHILE, YOU TWO.
YOU RUNNING LATE AS A WHITE RABBIT TOO?
No glasses?
TORREY!
SHE SAYS SHE'S PICKED UP THE FORBIDDEN TOME'S SCENT.
Have you, now? That sounds fun!
"FUN"...? WHEN PEOPLE COULD DIE?
ER!
NO, NO, NO, I DON'T MEAN IT IN A BAD WAY-- WELL, GUESS THERE'S NO GOOD WAY.

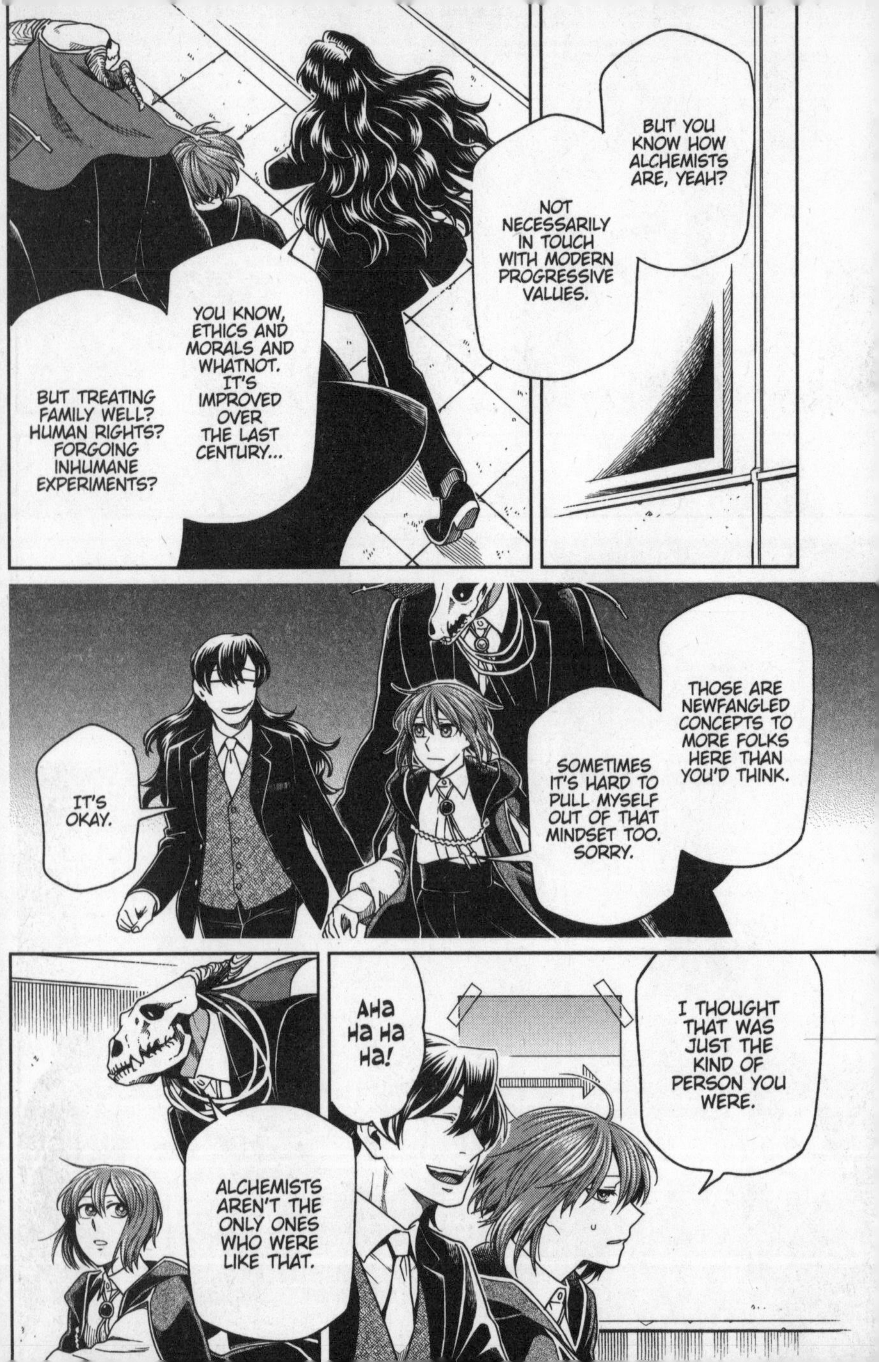
BUT YOU KNOW HOW ALCHEMISTS ARE, YEAH?
NOT NECESSARILY IN TOUCH WITH MODERN PROGRESSIVE VALUES.
YOU KNOW, ETHICS AND MORALS AND WHATNOT. IT'S IMPROVED OVER THE LAST CENTURY...
BUT TREATING FAMILY WELL? HUMAN RIGHTS? FORGOING INHUMANE EXPERIMENTS?
THOSE ARE NEWFANGLED CONCEPTS TO MORE FOLKS HERE THAN YOU'D THINK.
SOMETIMES IT'S HARD TO PULL MYSELF OUT OF THAT MINDSET TOO. SORRY.
IT'S OKAY.
I THOUGHT THAT WAS JUST THE KIND OF PERSON YOU WERE.
AHA HA HA HA!
ALCHEMISTS AREN'T THE ONLY ONES WHO WERE LIKE THAT.

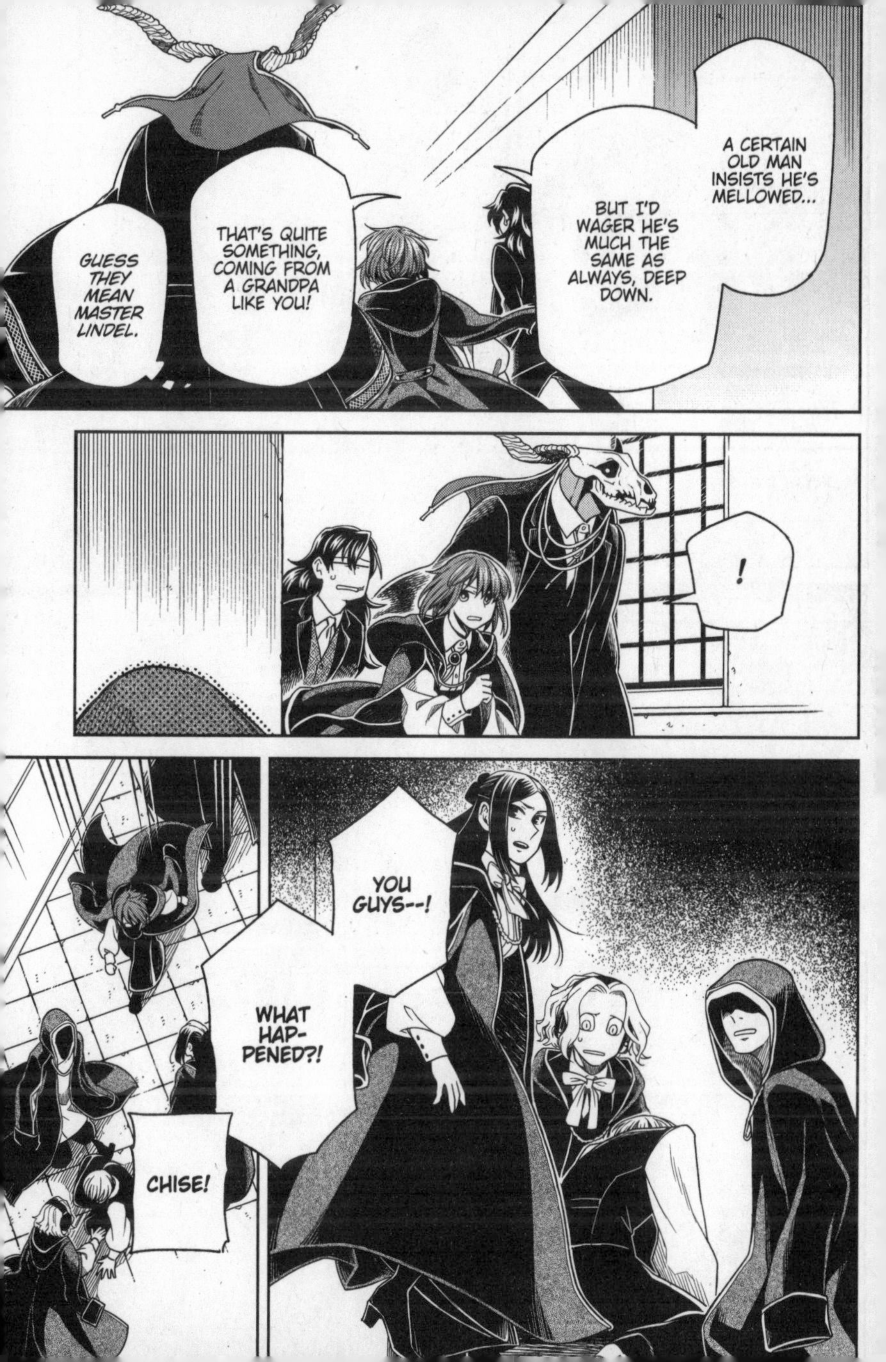
A CERTAIN OLD MAN INSISTS HE'S MELLOWED...
BUT I'D WAGER HE'S MUCH THE SAME AS ALWAYS, DEEP DOWN.
THAT'S QUITE SOMETHING, COMING FROM A GRANDPA LIKE YOU!
GUESS THEY MEAN MASTER LINDEL.
!
YOU GUYS--!
WHAT HAP-PENED?!
CHISE!

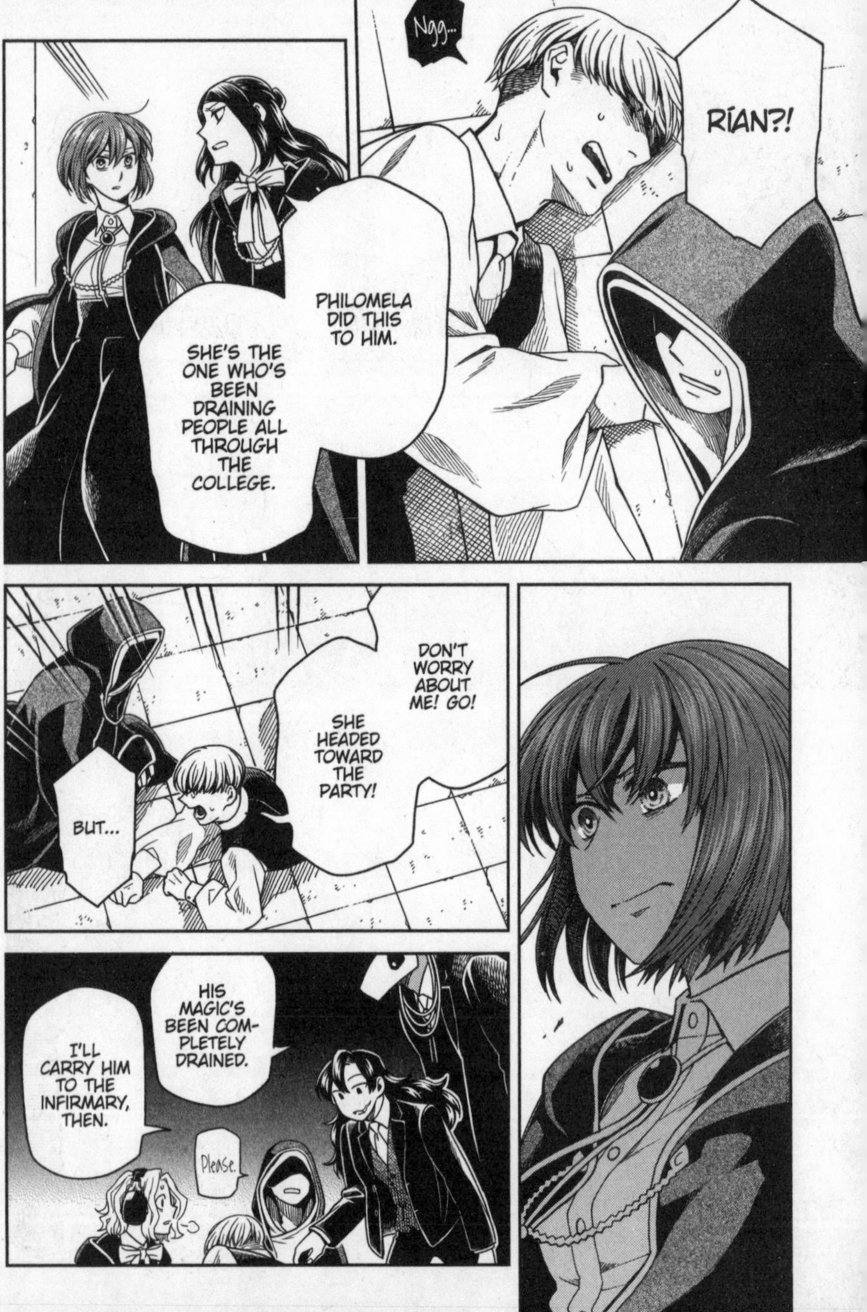
RÍAN?!
Ngg...
PHILOMELA DID THIS TO HIM.
SHE'S THE ONE WHO'S BEEN DRAINING PEOPLE ALL THROUGH THE COLLEGE.
DON'T WORRY ABOUT ME! GO!
SHE HEADED TOWARD THE PARTY!
BUT...
HIS MAGIC'S BEEN COM-PLETELY DRAINED.
I'LL CARRY HIM TO THE INFIRMARY, THEN.
Please.

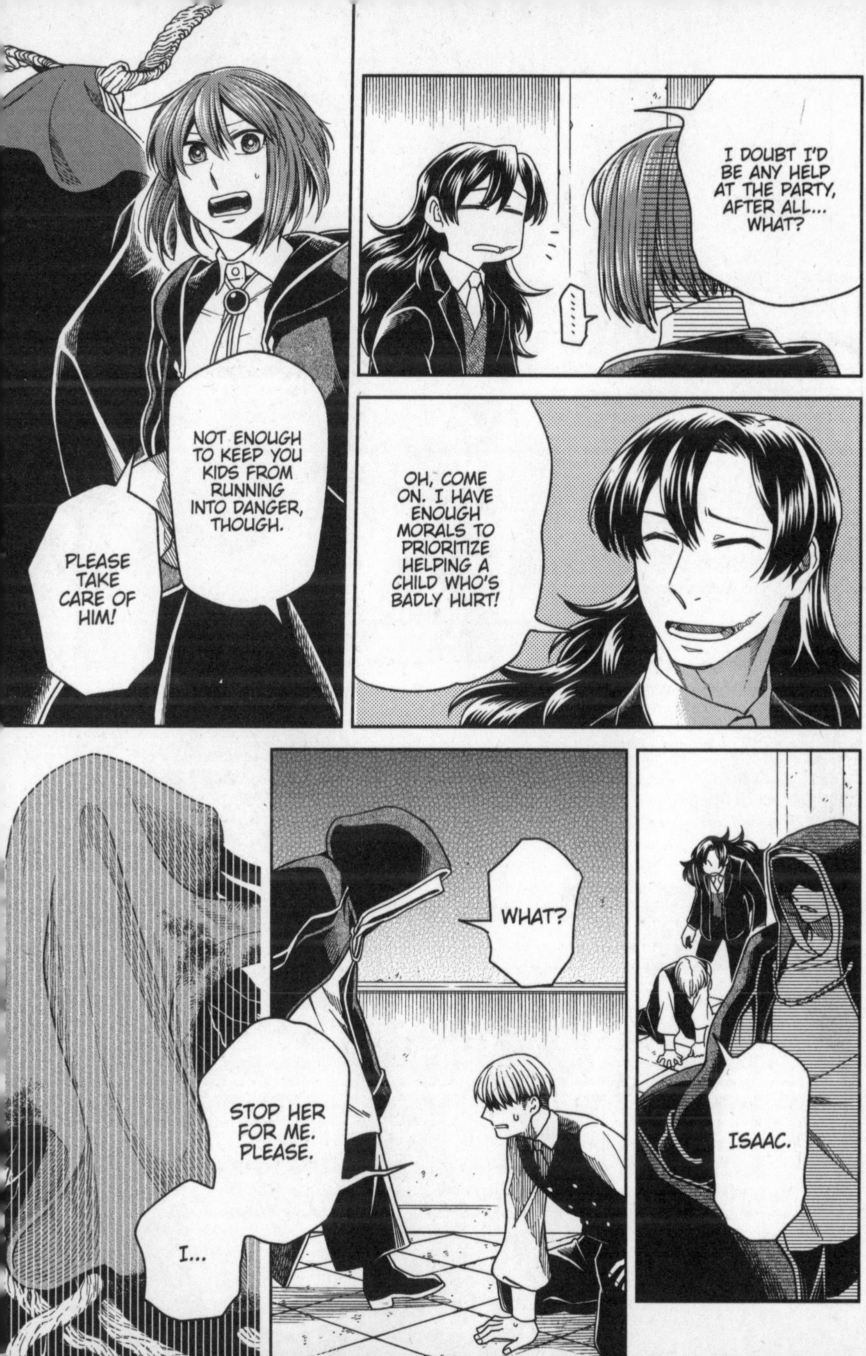
I DOUBT I'D BE ANY HELP AT THE PARTY, AFTER ALL... WHAT?
......
OH, COME ON. I HAVE ENOUGH MORALS TO PRIORITIZE HELPING A CHILD WHO'S BADLY HURT!
NOT ENOUGH TO KEEP YOU KIDS FROM RUNNING INTO DANGER, THOUGH.
PLEASE TAKE CARE OF HIM!
ISAAC.
WHAT?
STOP HER FOR ME. PLEASE.
I...

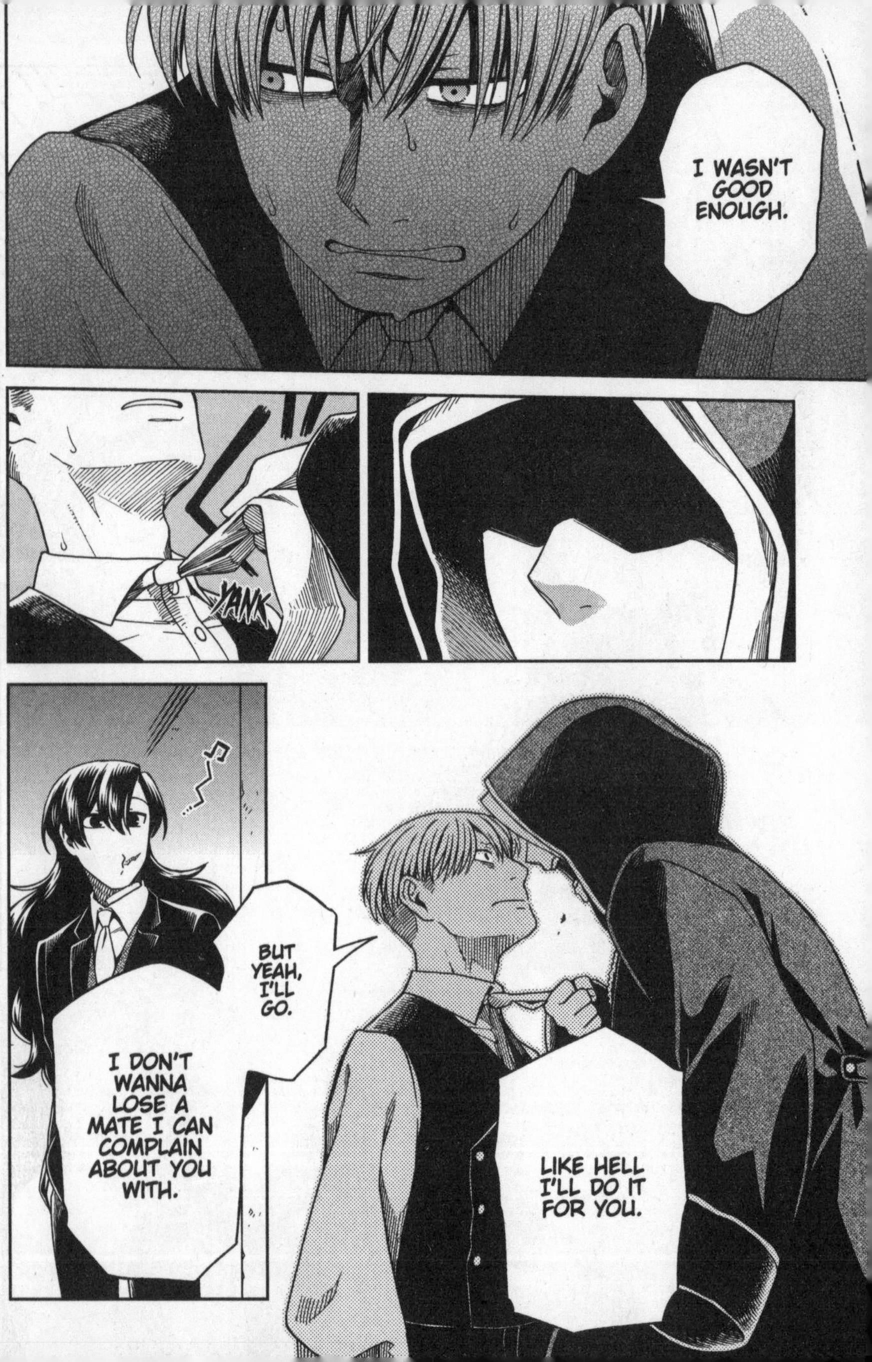
I WASN'T GOOD ENOUGH.
YANK
BUT YEAH, I'LL GO.
LIKE HELL I'LL DO IT FOR YOU.
I DON'T WANNA LOSE A MATE I CAN COMPLAIN ABOUT YOU WITH.

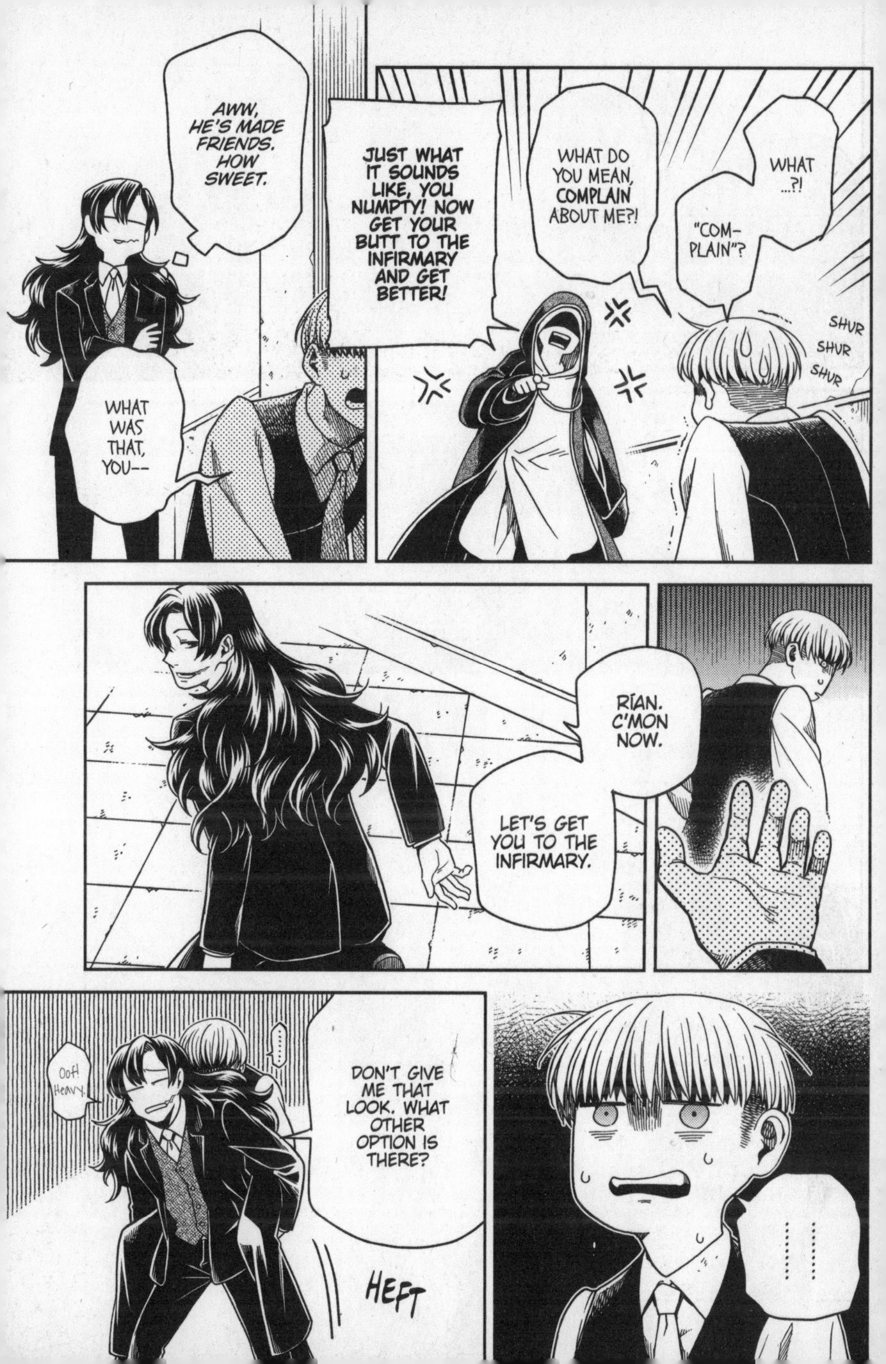
AWW, HE'S MADE FRIENDS. HOW SWEET.
WHAT WAS THAT, YOU--
JUST WHAT IT SOUNDS LIKE, YOU NUMPTY! NOW GET YOUR BUTT TO THE INFIRMARY AND GET BETTER!
WHAT DO YOU MEAN, COMPLAIN ABOUT ME?!
WHAT ...?!
"COM-PLAIN"?
SHUR
SHUR
SHUR
RÍAN. C'MON NOW.
LET'S GET YOU TO THE INFIRMARY.
......
Oof! Heavy.
DON'T GIVE ME THAT LOOK. WHAT OTHER OPTION IS THERE?
HEFT
......

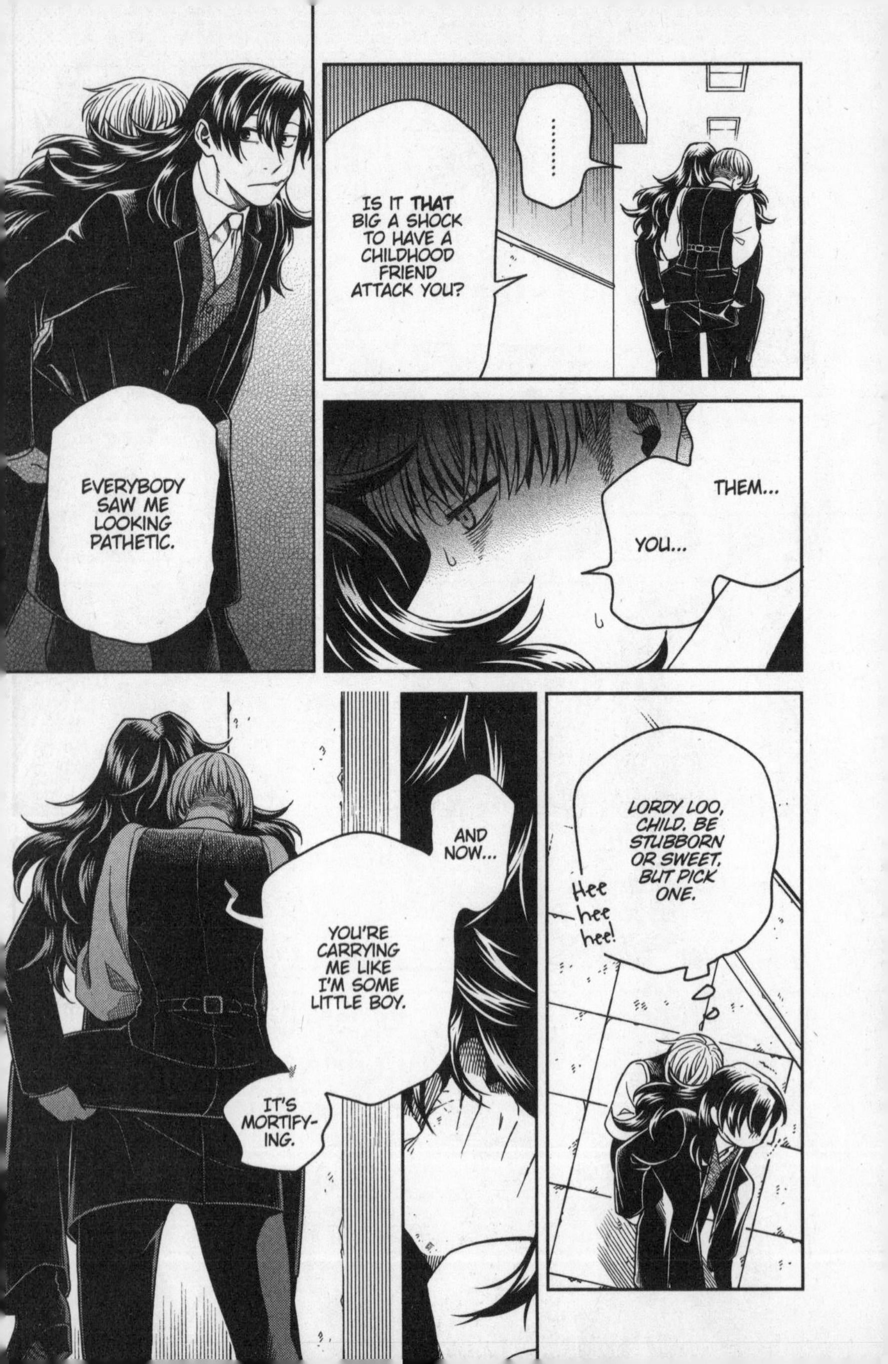
......
IS IT THAT BIG A SHOCK TO HAVE A CHILDHOOD FRIEND ATTACK YOU?
THEM...
YOU...
EVERYBODY SAW ME LOOKING PATHETIC.
LORDY LOO, CHILD. BE STUBBORN OR SWEET, BUT PICK ONE.
Hee hee hee!
AND NOW...
YOU'RE CARRYING ME LIKE I'M SOME LITTLE BOY.
IT'S MORTIFYING.

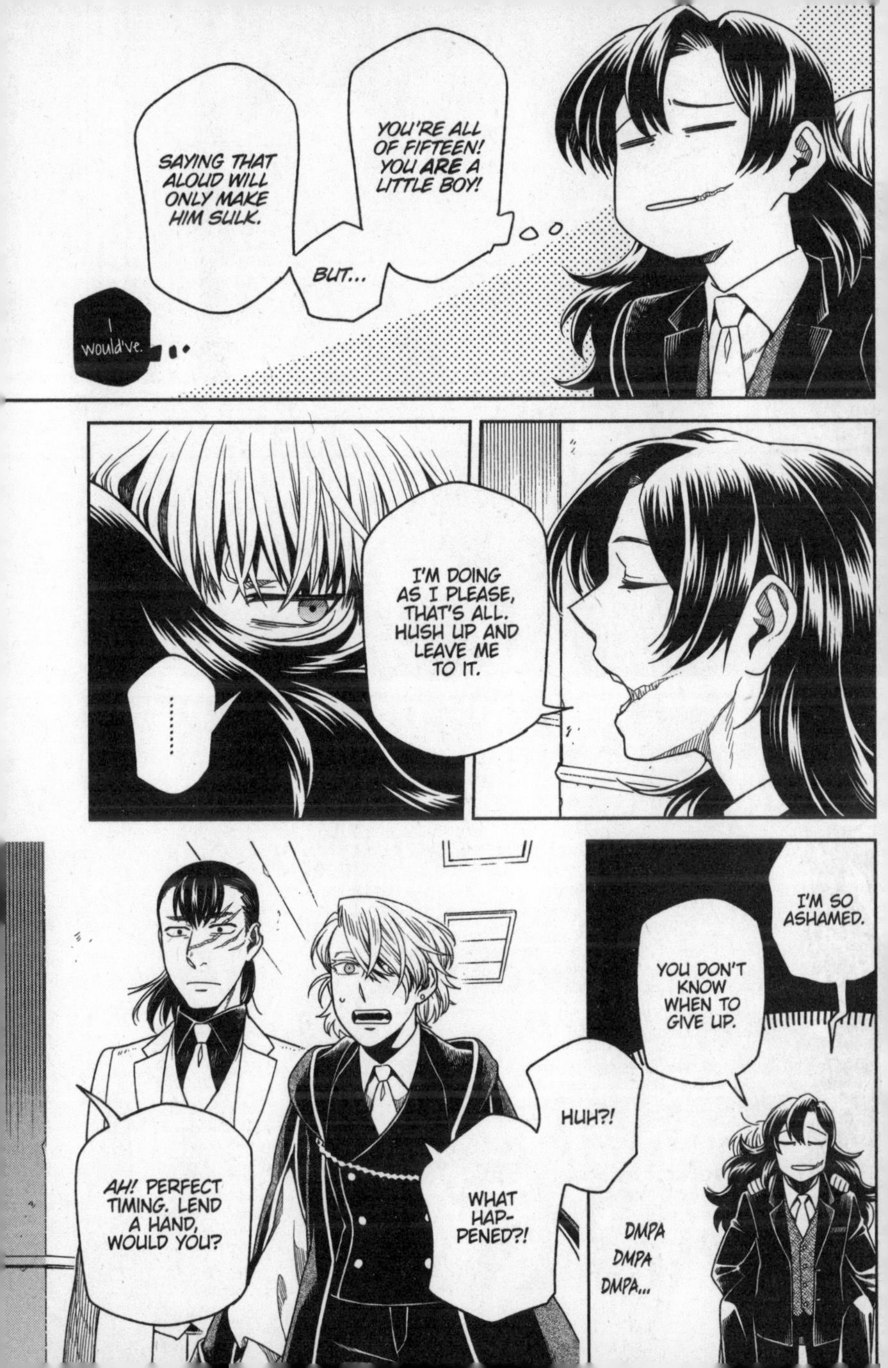
YOU'RE ALL OF FIFTEEN! YOU ARE A LITTLE BOY!
SAYING THAT ALOUD WILL ONLY MAKE HIM SULK.
BUT...
I would've.
I'M DOING AS I PLEASE, THAT'S ALL. HUSH UP AND LEAVE ME TO IT.
......
I'M SO ASHAMED.
YOU DON'T KNOW WHEN TO GIVE UP.
DMPA
DMPA
DMPA...
HUH?!
WHAT HAP-PENED?!
AH! PERFECT TIMING. LEND A HAND, WOULD YOU?

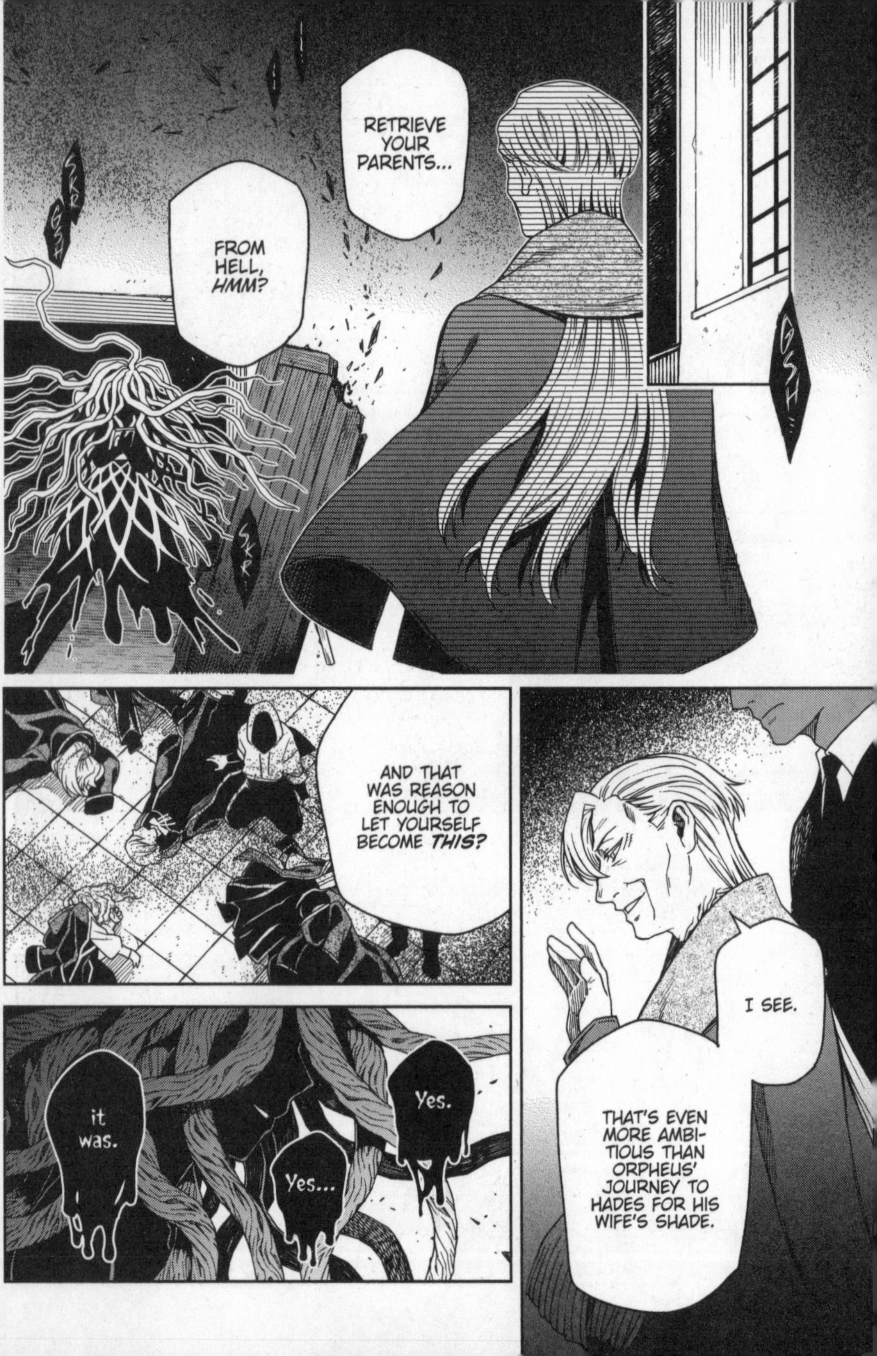

RETRIEVE YOUR PARENTS...
FROM HELL, *HMM?*
SKR GSH
GSH
SKR
AND THAT WAS REASON ENOUGH TO LET YOURSELF BECOME *THIS?*
Yes.
Yes...
it was.
I SEE.
THAT'S EVEN MORE AMBI-TIOUS THAN ORPHEUS' JOURNEY TO HADES FOR HIS WIFE'S SHADE.

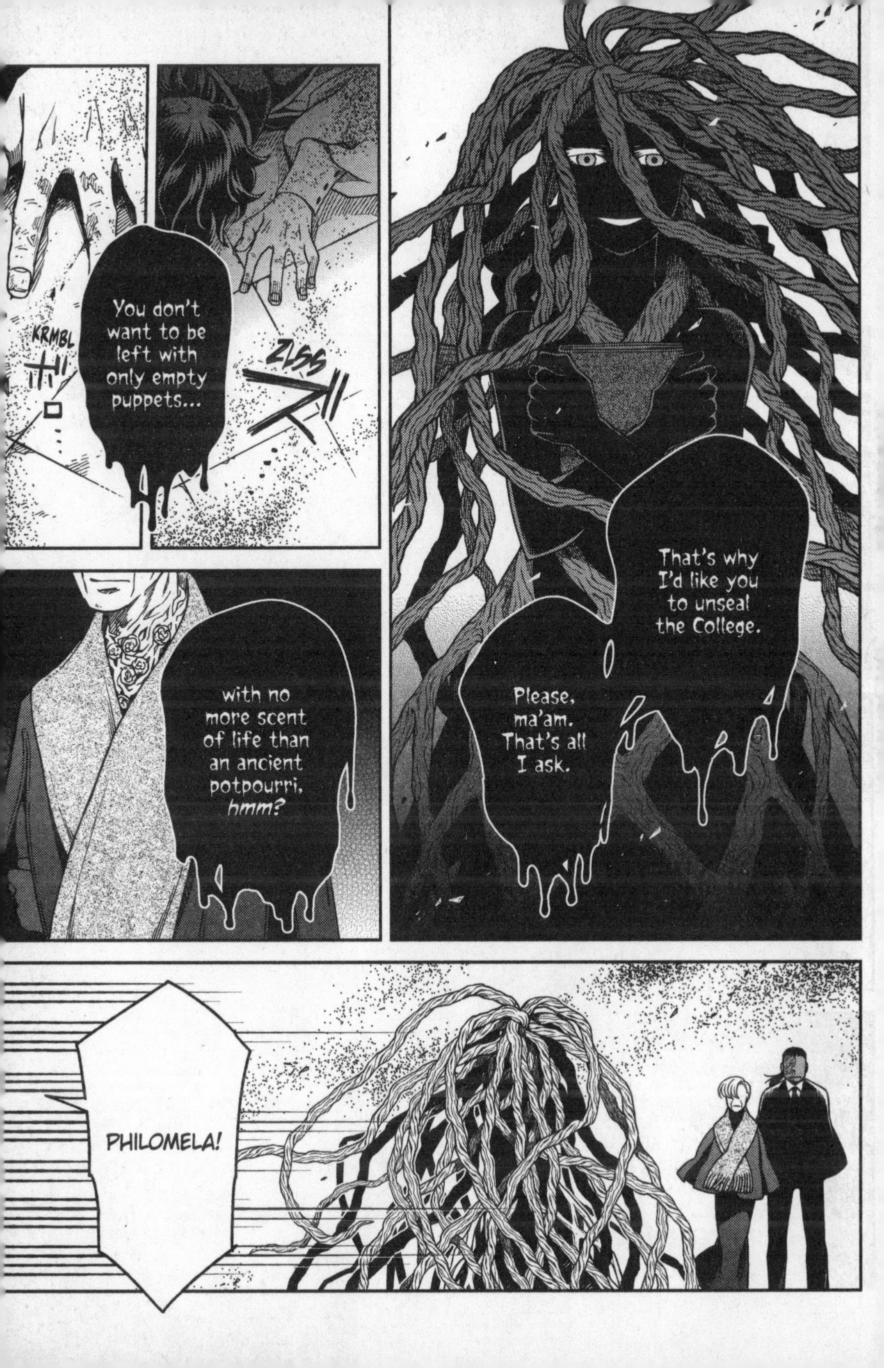
You don't want to be left with only empty puppets...
KRMBL
ZLSS
with no more scent of life than an ancient potpourri, *hmm?*
That's why I'd like you to unseal the College.
Please, ma'am. That's all I ask.
PHILOMELA!

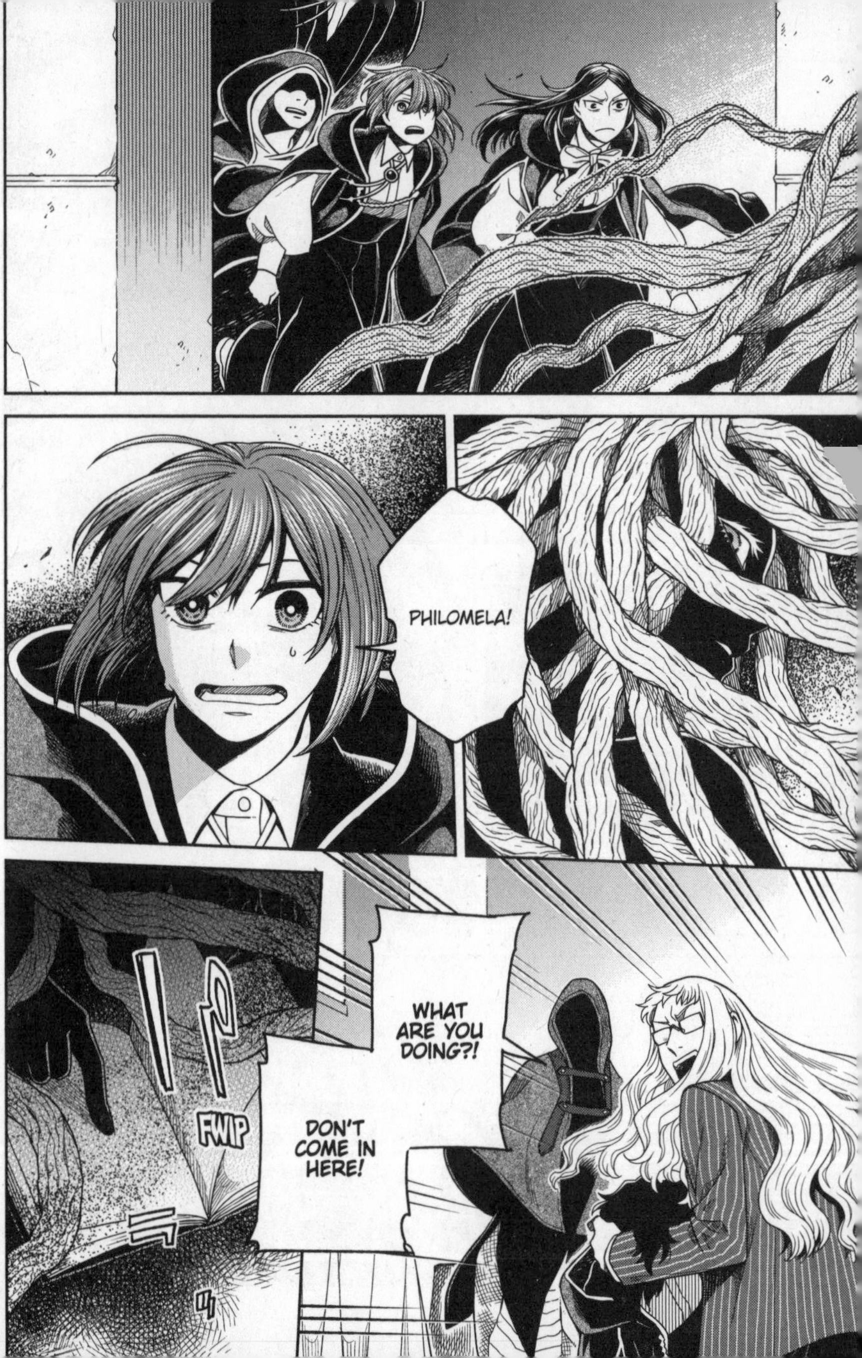
PHILOMELA!
WHAT ARE YOU DOING?!
DON'T COME IN HERE!
FWIP

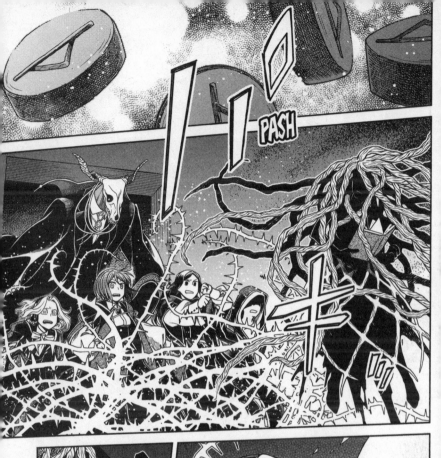

PASH

THE CHARMS?!

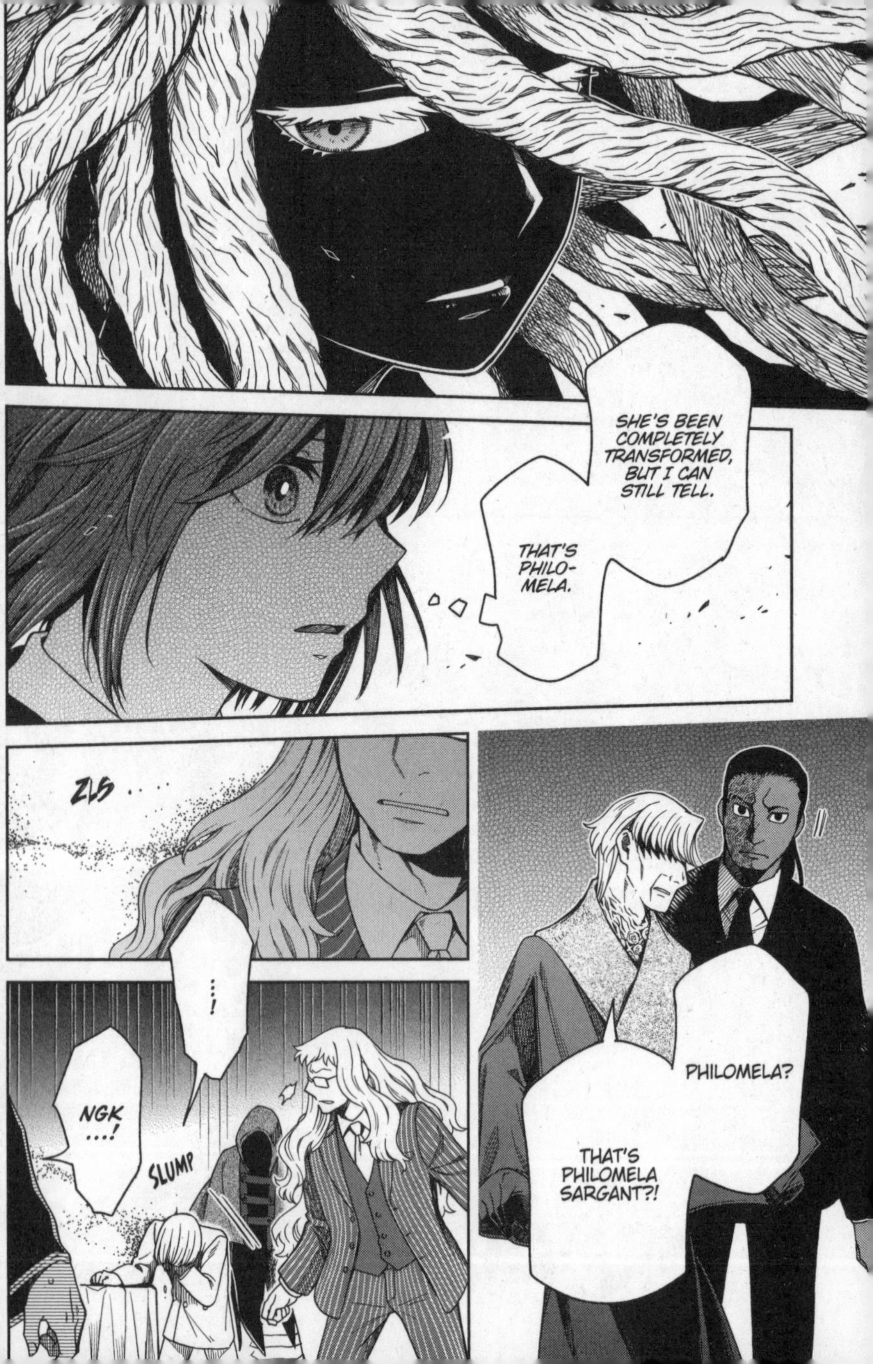

SHE'S BEEN COMPLETELY TRANSFORMED, BUT I CAN STILL TELL.
THAT'S PHILO-MELA.
ZLS...
...!
PHILOMELA?
THAT'S PHILOMELA SARGANT?!
NGK ...!
SLUMP

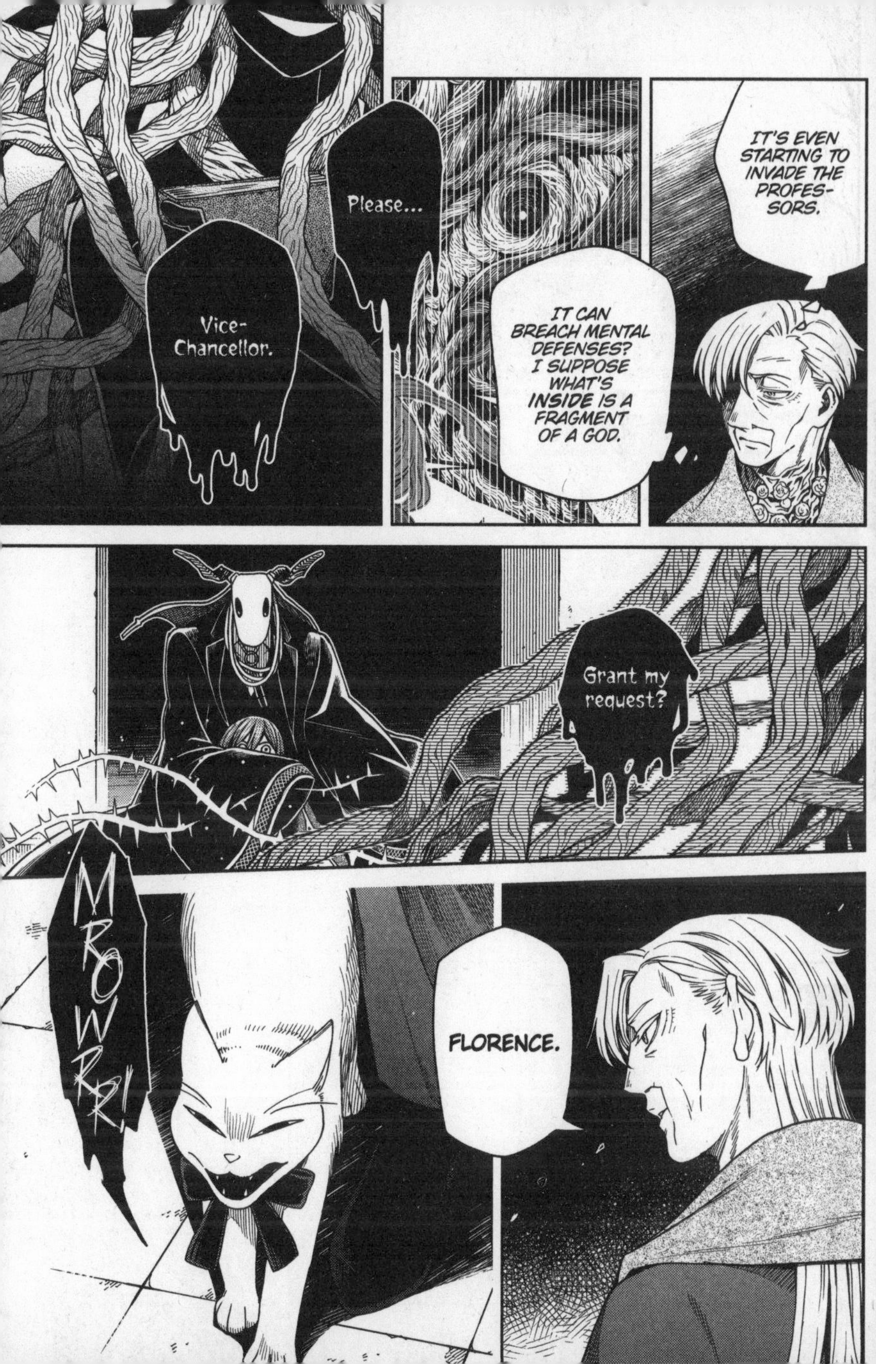
IT'S EVEN STARTING TO INVADE THE PROFES-SORS.
IT CAN BREACH MENTAL DEFENSES? I SUPPOSE WHAT'S INSIDE IS A FRAGMENT OF A GOD.
Please...
Vice-Chancellor.
Grant my request?
FLORENCE.
MROWRR!

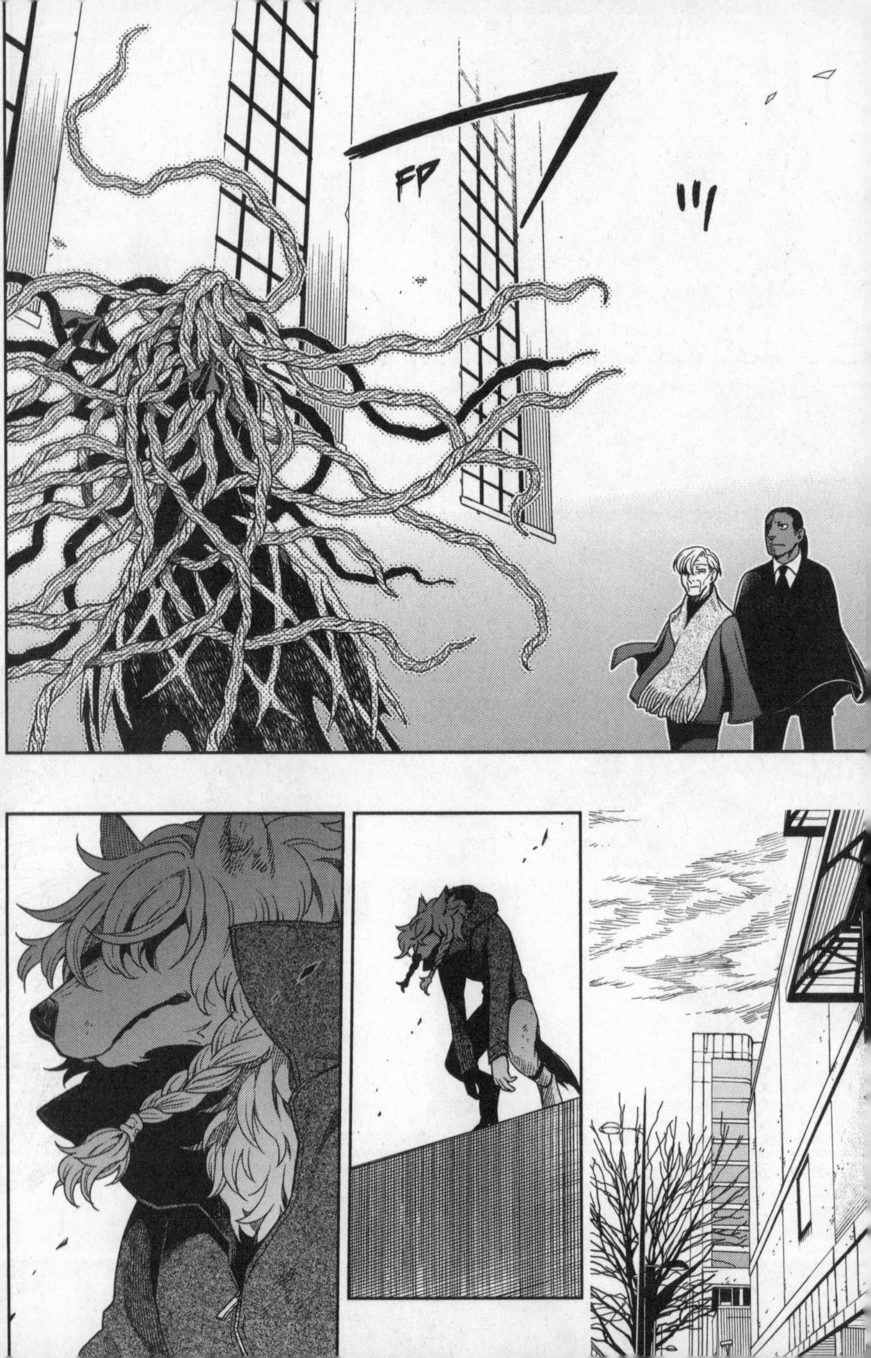
FP

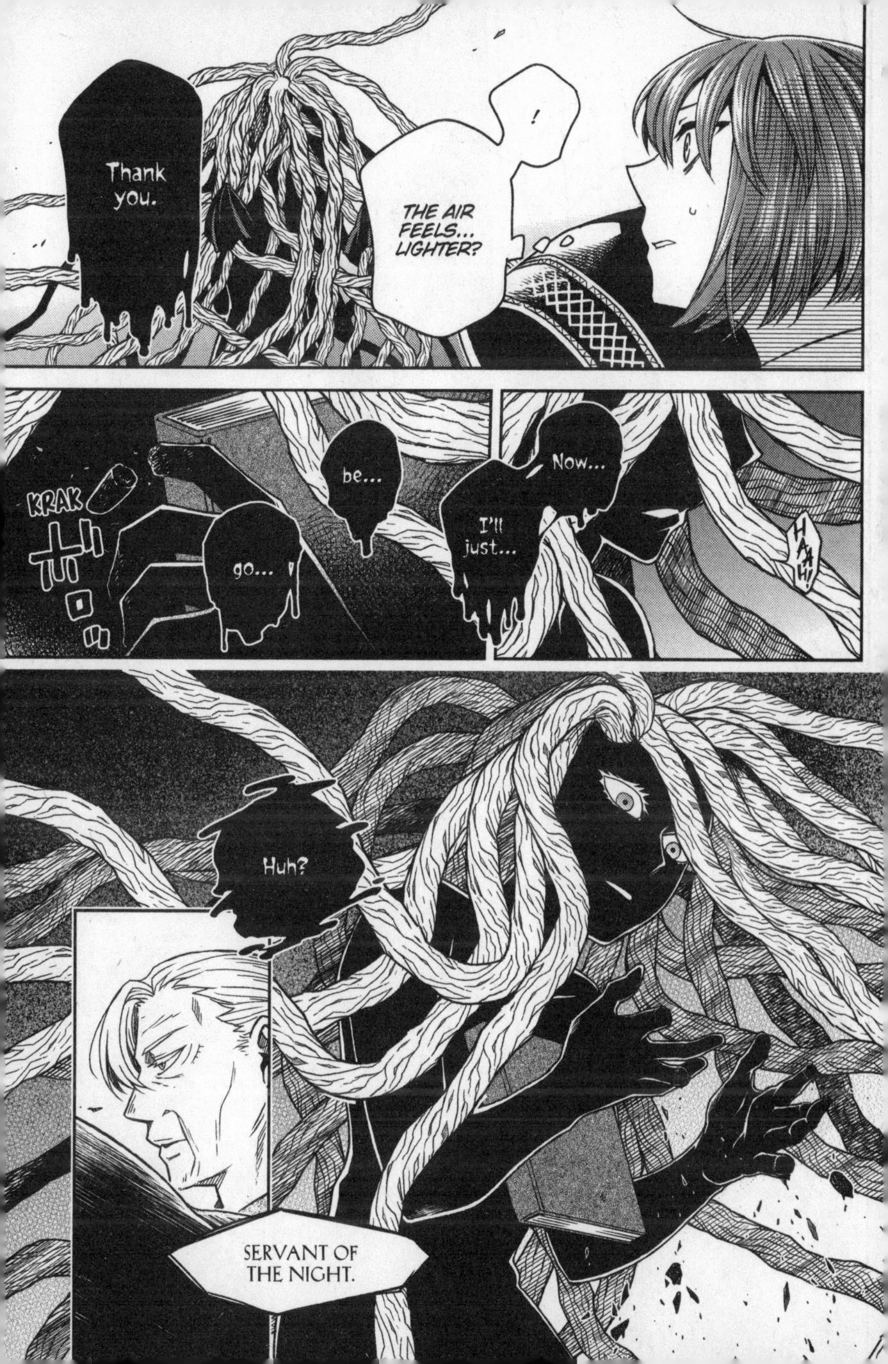
!
THE AIR FEELS... LIGHTER?
Thank you.
HAAAH!
Now...
I'll just...
be...
go...
KRAK
Huh?
SERVANT OF THE NIGHT.

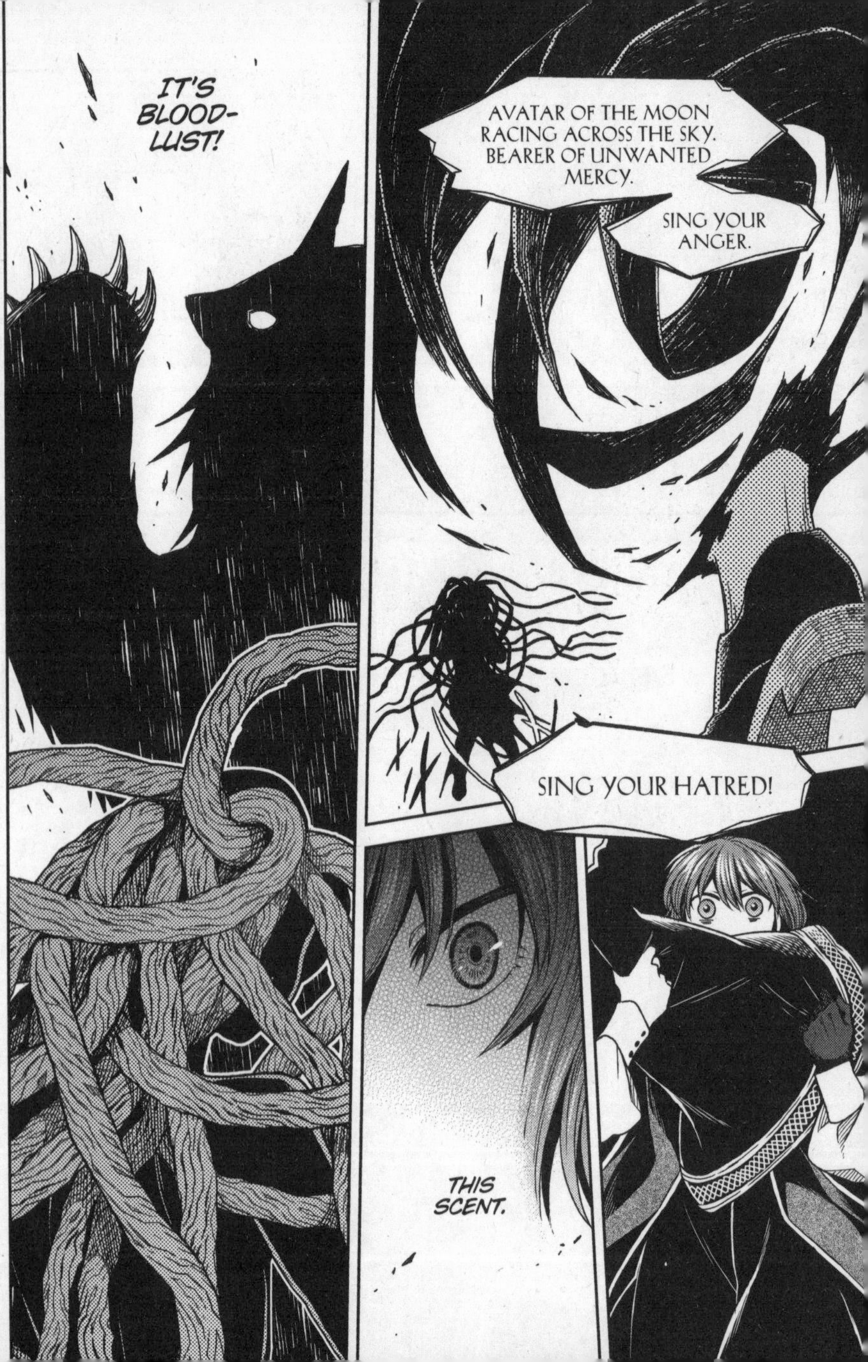
AVATAR OF THE MOON RACING ACROSS THE SKY. BEARER OF UNWANTED MERCY.
SING YOUR ANGER.
SING YOUR HATRED!
THIS SCENT.
IT'S BLOOD-LUST!

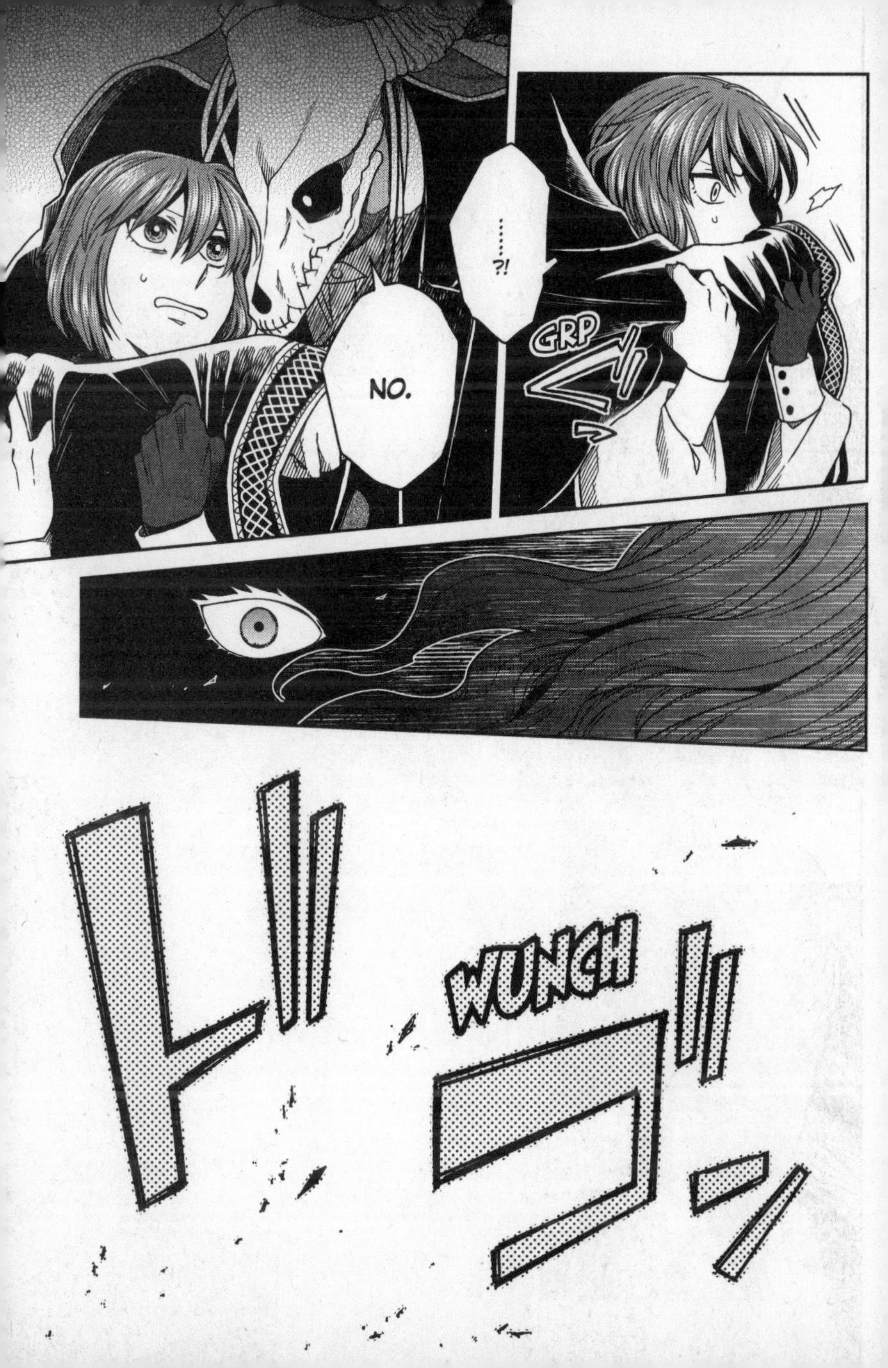

……?!
GRP
NO.
WUNCH

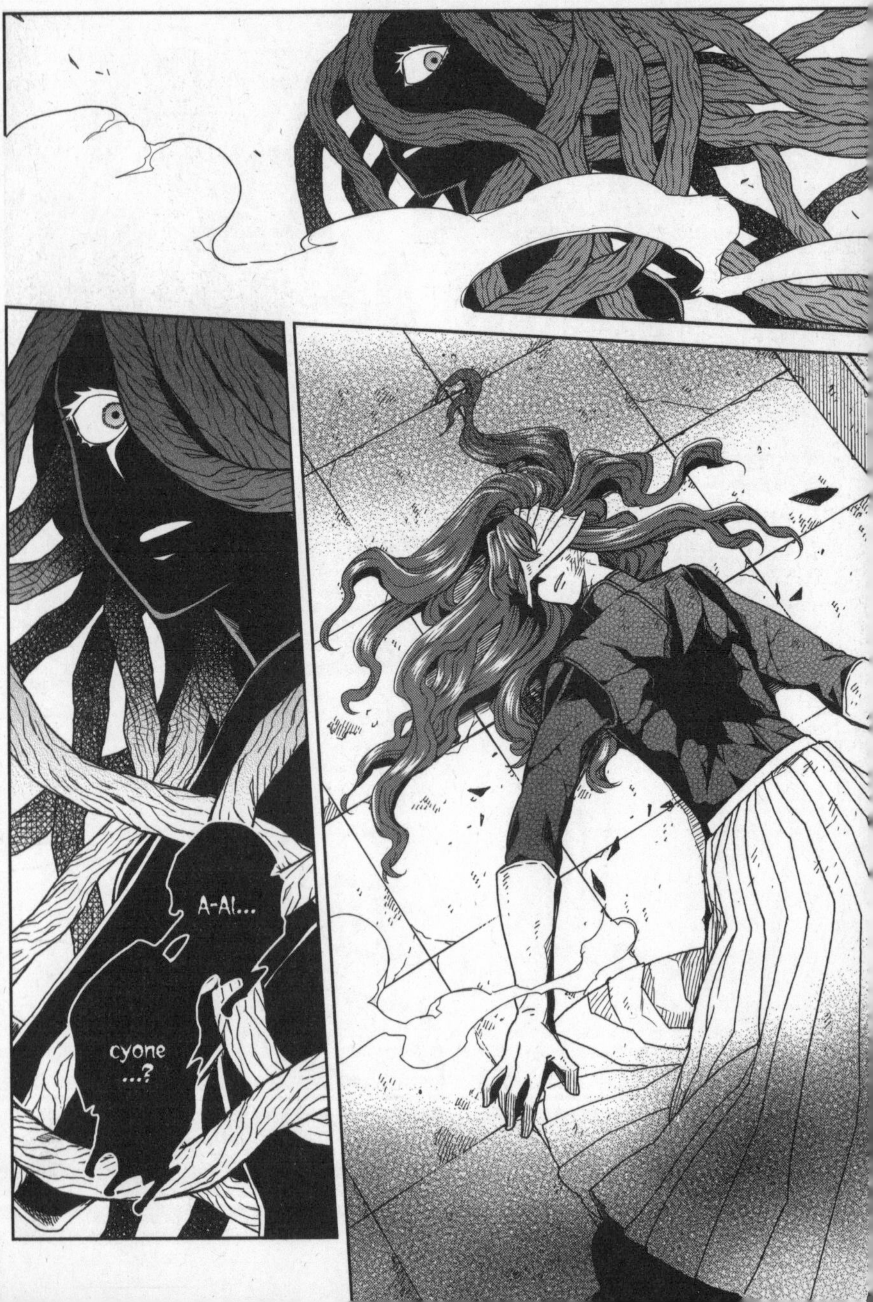
A-AI...
cyone
...?

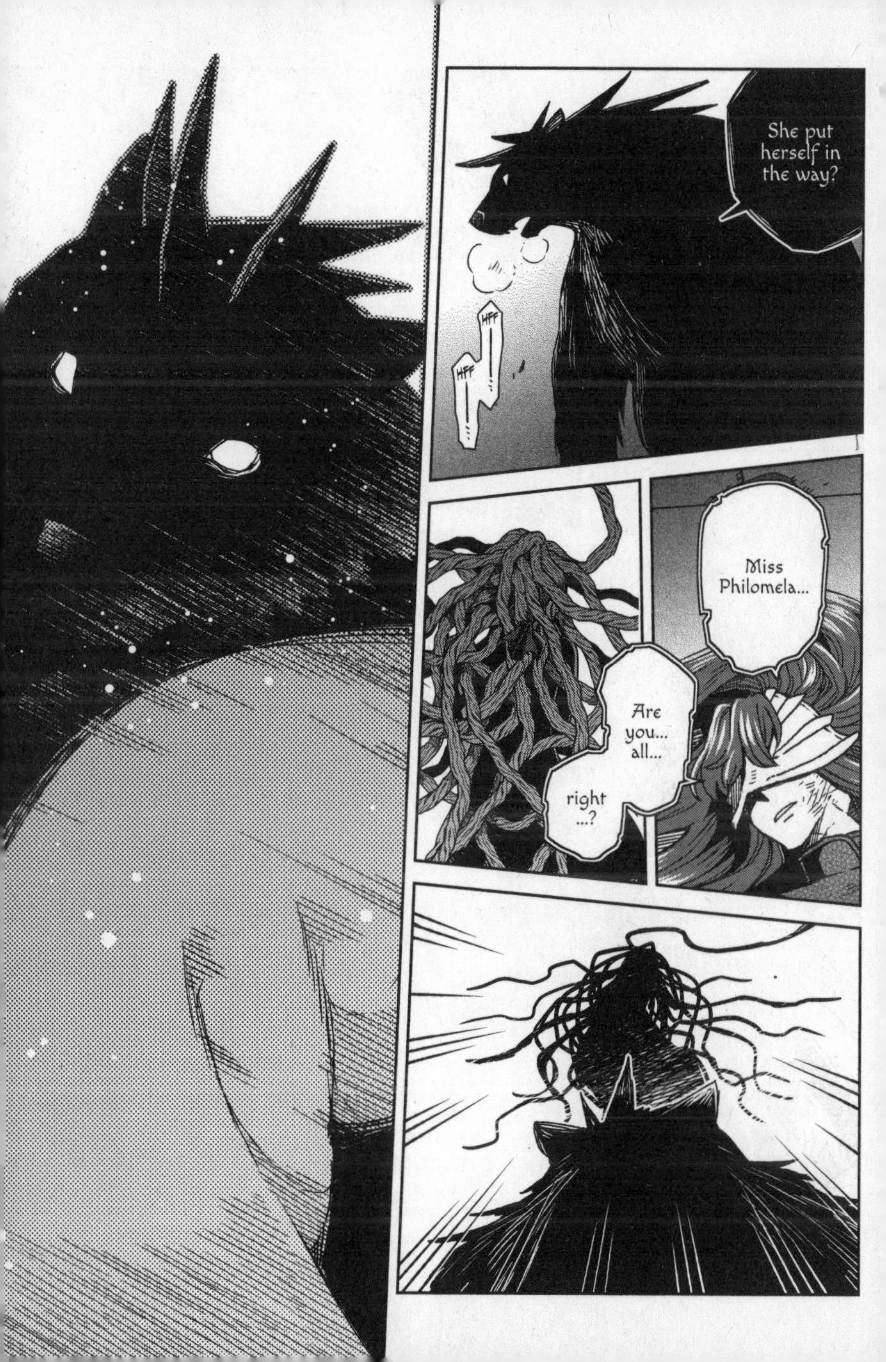
She put herself in the way?
HFF
HFF
Miss Philomela...
Are you... all...
right ...?

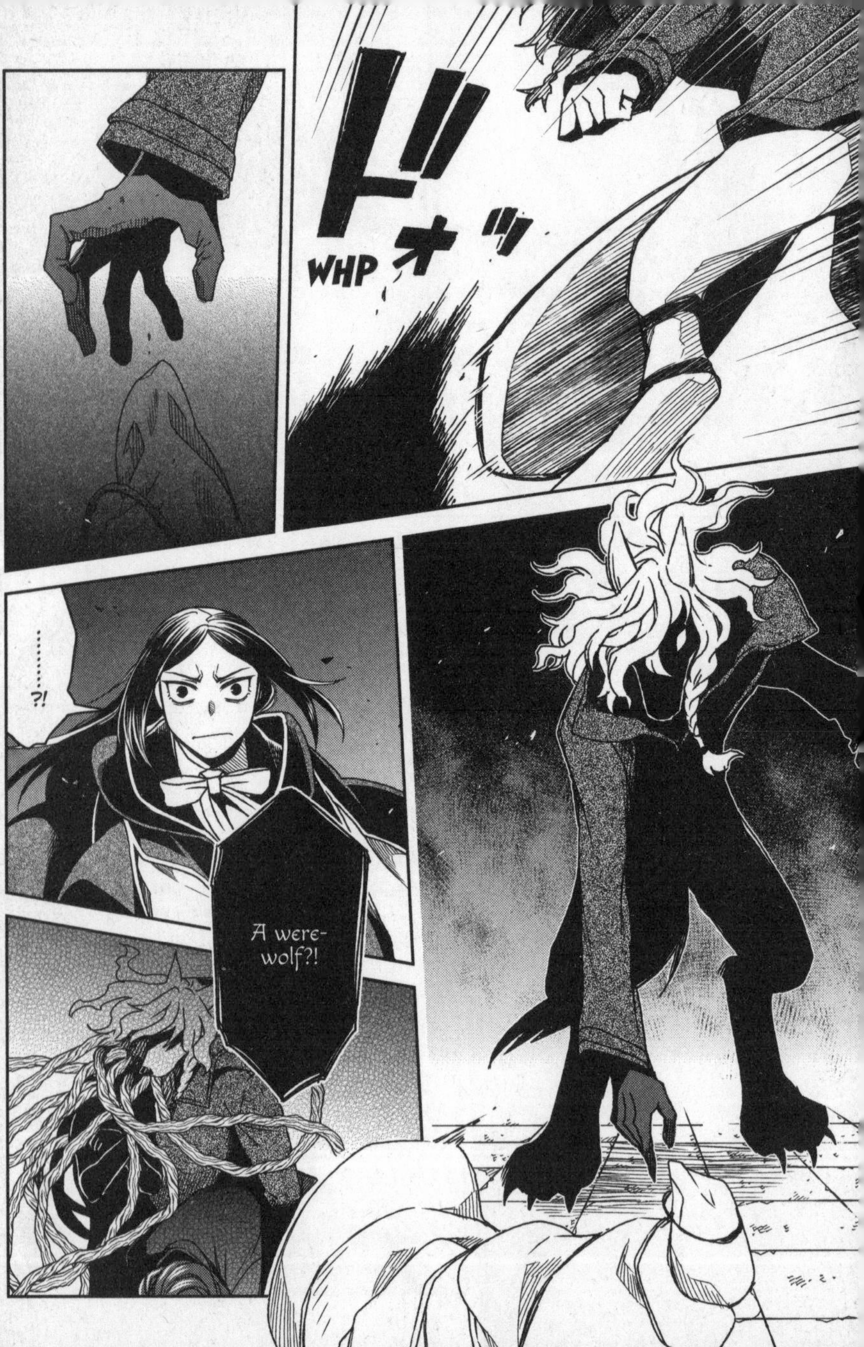
ドォッ
WHP
.........?!
A were-wolf?!

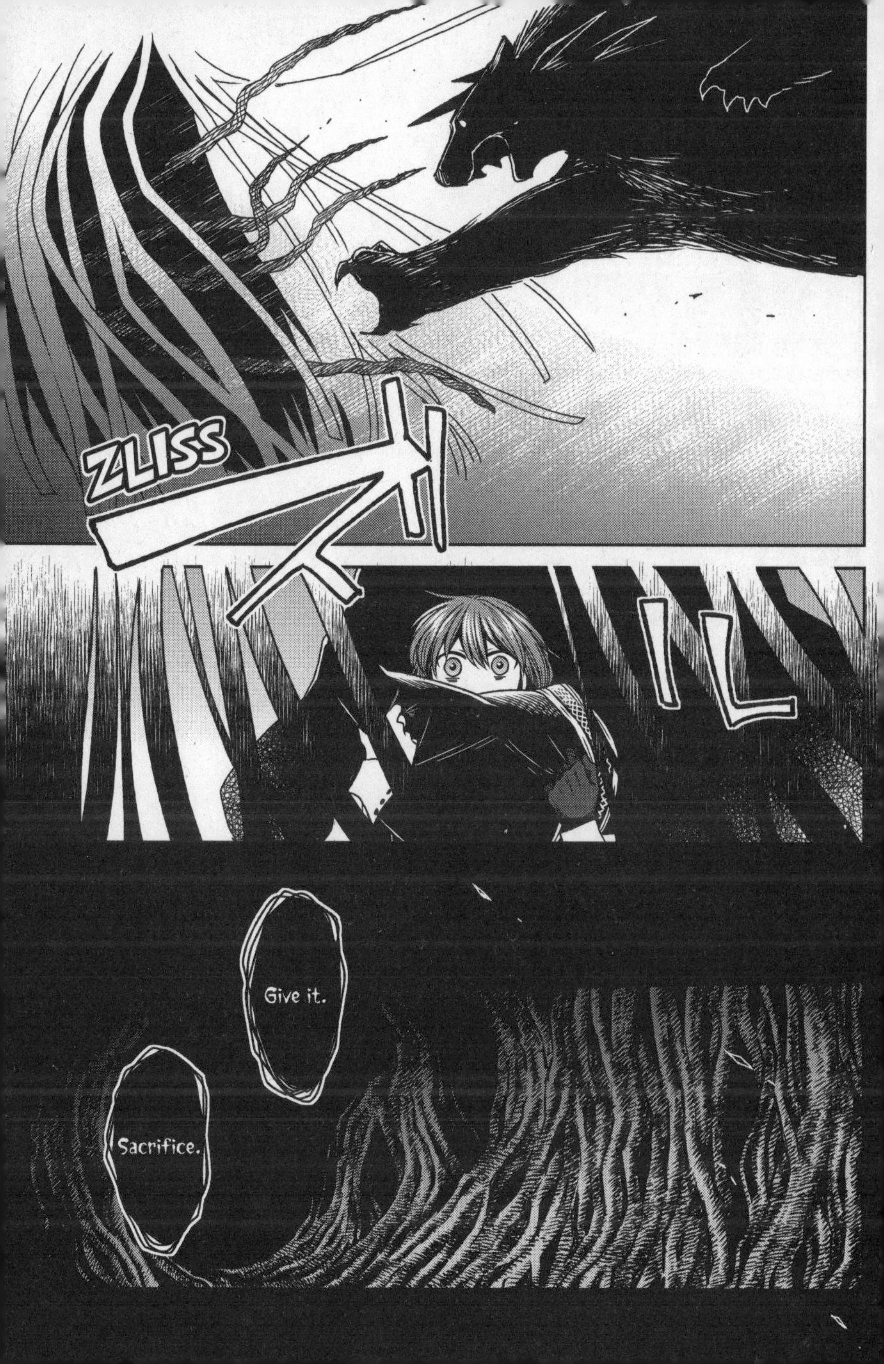
ZLISS
Give it.
Sacrifice.

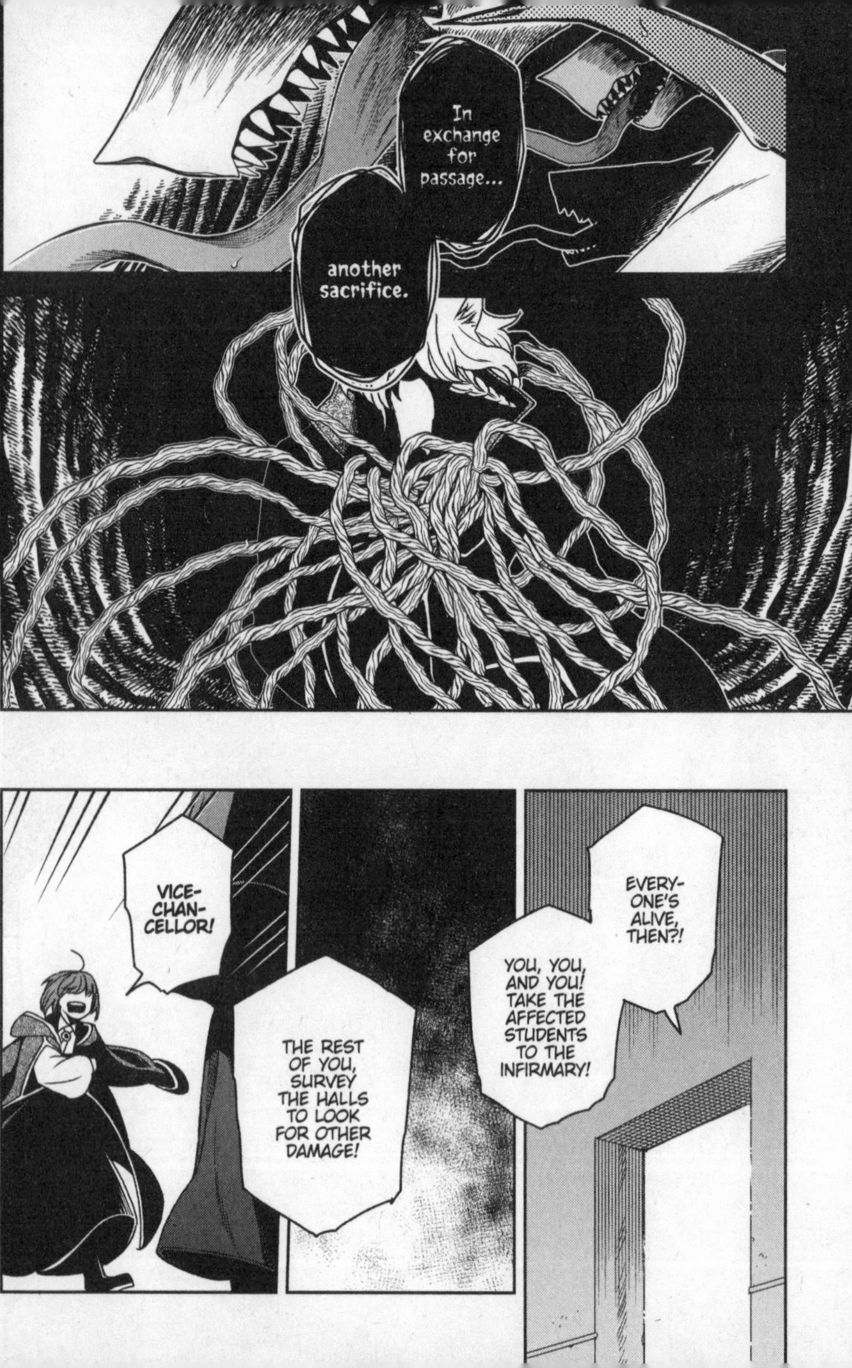
In exchange for passage...
another sacrifice.
EVERYONE'S ALIVE, THEN?!
YOU, YOU, AND YOU! TAKE THE AFFECTED STUDENTS TO THE INFIRMARY!
THE REST OF YOU, SURVEY THE HALLS TO LOOK FOR OTHER DAMAGE!
VICE-CHANCELLOR!

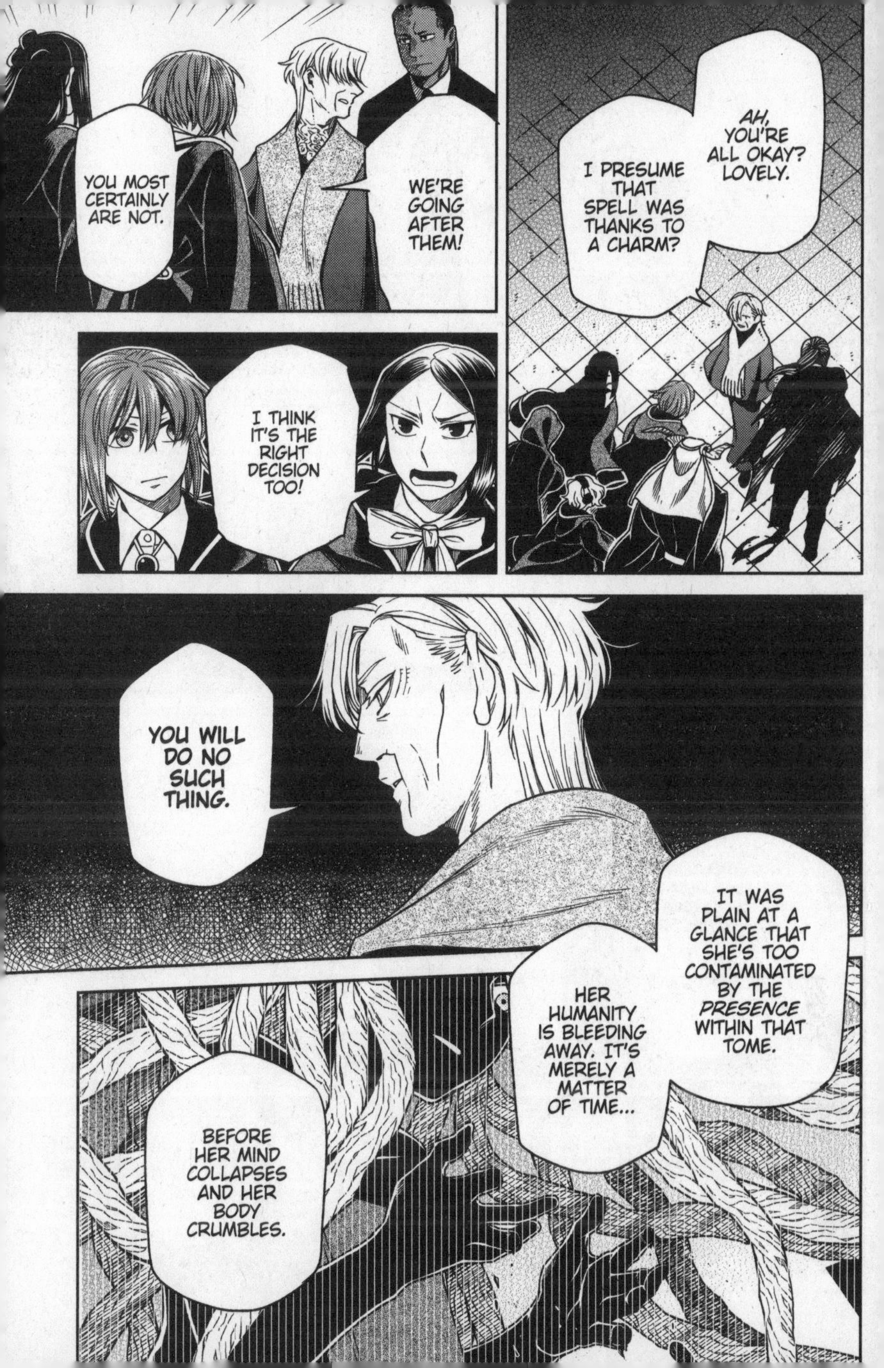
AH, YOU'RE ALL OKAY? LOVELY.
I PRESUME THAT SPELL WAS THANKS TO A CHARM?
WE'RE GOING AFTER THEM!
YOU MOST CERTAINLY ARE NOT.
I THINK IT'S THE RIGHT DECISION TOO!
YOU WILL DO NO SUCH THING.
IT WAS PLAIN AT A GLANCE THAT SHE'S TOO CONTAMINATED BY THE *PRESENCE* WITHIN THAT TOME.
HER HUMANITY IS BLEEDING AWAY. IT'S MERELY A MATTER OF TIME...
BEFORE HER MIND COLLAPSES AND HER BODY CRUMBLES.

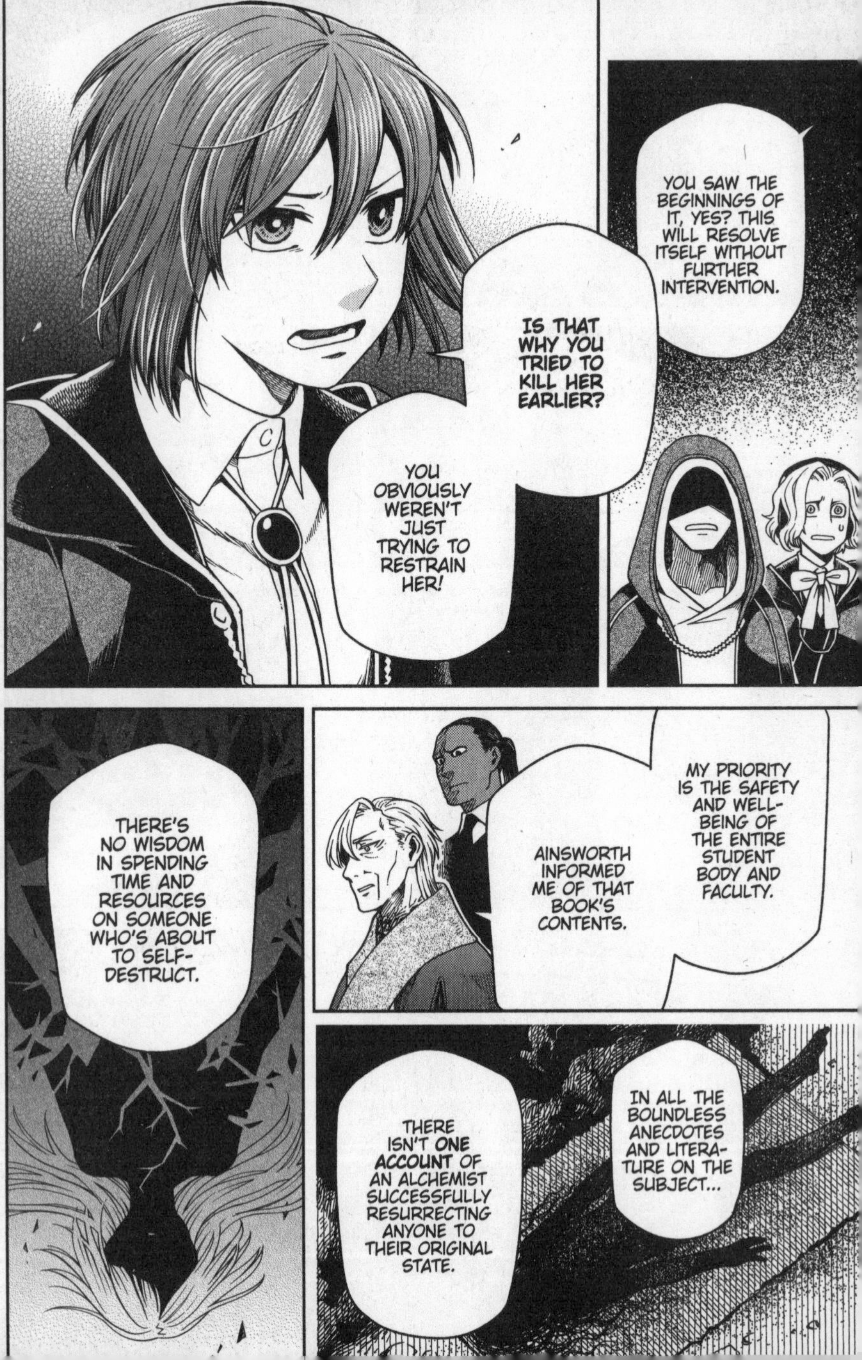
YOU SAW THE BEGINNINGS OF IT, YES? THIS WILL RESOLVE ITSELF WITHOUT FURTHER INTERVENTION.
IS THAT WHY YOU TRIED TO KILL HER EARLIER?
YOU OBVIOUSLY WEREN'T JUST TRYING TO RESTRAIN HER!
MY PRIORITY IS THE SAFETY AND WELL-BEING OF THE ENTIRE STUDENT BODY AND FACULTY.
AINSWORTH INFORMED ME OF THAT BOOK'S CONTENTS.
THERE'S NO WISDOM IN SPENDING TIME AND RESOURCES ON SOMEONE WHO'S ABOUT TO SELF-DESTRUCT.
IN ALL THE BOUNDLESS ANECDOTES AND LITERA-TURE ON THE SUBJECT...
THERE ISN'T ONE ACCOUNT OF AN ALCHEMIST SUCCESSFULLY RESURRECTING ANYONE TO THEIR ORIGINAL STATE.

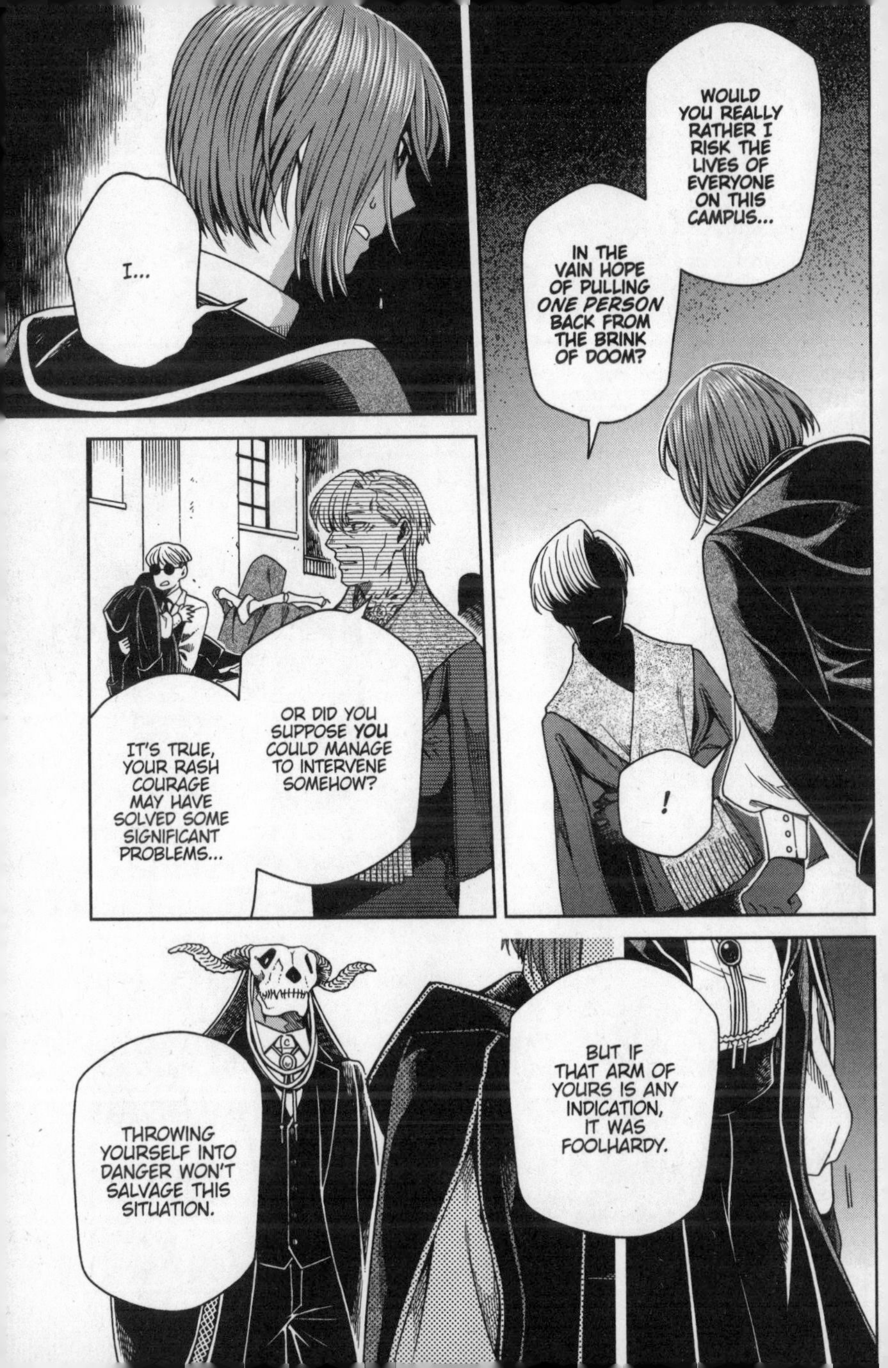

WOULD YOU REALLY RATHER I RISK THE LIVES OF EVERYONE ON THIS CAMPUS...
IN THE VAIN HOPE OF PULLING *ONE PERSON* BACK FROM THE BRINK OF DOOM?
I...
!
OR DID YOU SUPPOSE YOU COULD MANAGE TO INTERVENE SOMEHOW?
IT'S TRUE, YOUR RASH COURAGE MAY HAVE SOLVED SOME SIGNIFICANT PROBLEMS...
BUT IF THAT ARM OF YOURS IS ANY INDICATION, IT WAS FOOLHARDY.
THROWING YOURSELF INTO DANGER WON'T SALVAGE THIS SITUATION.

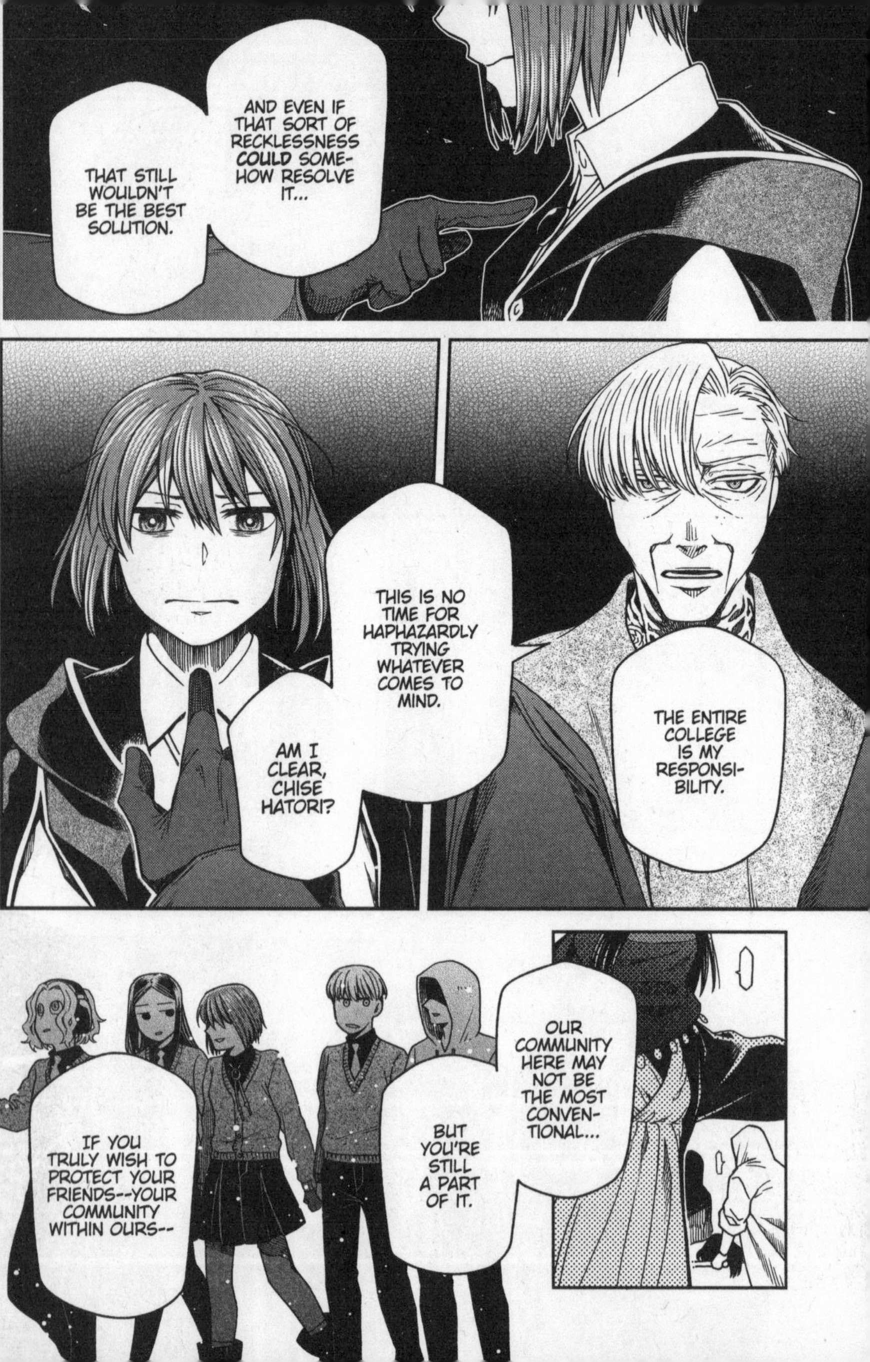
AND EVEN IF THAT SORT OF RECKLESSNESS COULD SOMEHOW RESOLVE IT...
THAT STILL WOULDN'T BE THE BEST SOLUTION.
THE ENTIRE COLLEGE IS MY RESPONSIBILITY.
THIS IS NO TIME FOR HAPHAZARDLY TRYING WHATEVER COMES TO MIND.
AM I CLEAR, CHISE HATORI?
OUR COMMUNITY HERE MAY NOT BE THE MOST CONVENTIONAL...
BUT YOU'RE STILL A PART OF IT.
IF YOU TRULY WISH TO PROTECT YOUR FRIENDS--YOUR COMMUNITY WITHIN OURS--

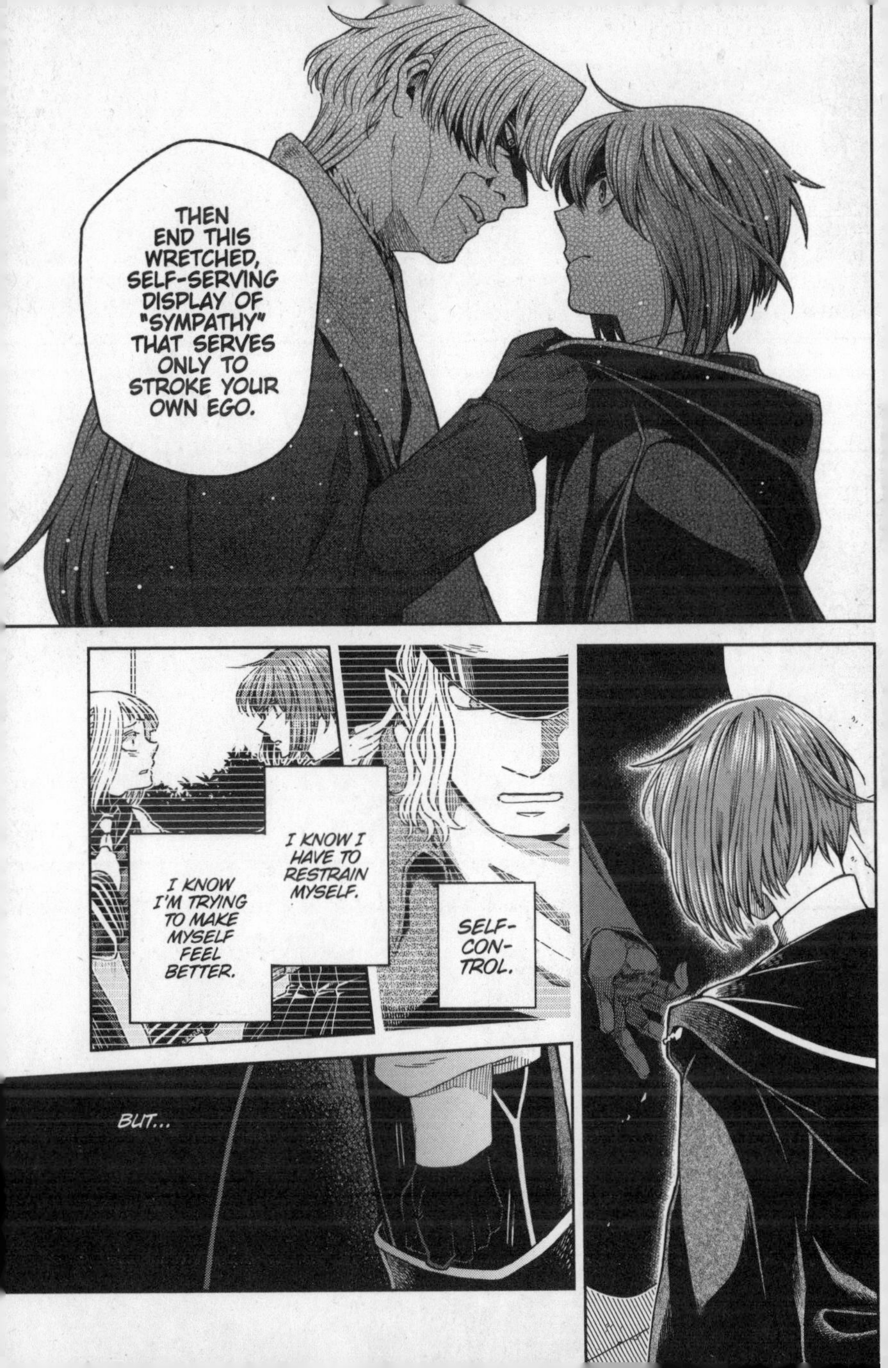
THEN END THIS WRETCHED, SELF-SERVING DISPLAY OF "SYMPATHY" THAT SERVES ONLY TO STROKE YOUR OWN EGO.
SELF-CONTROL.
I KNOW I HAVE TO RESTRAIN MYSELF.
I KNOW I'M TRYING TO MAKE MYSELF FEEL BETTER.
BUT...

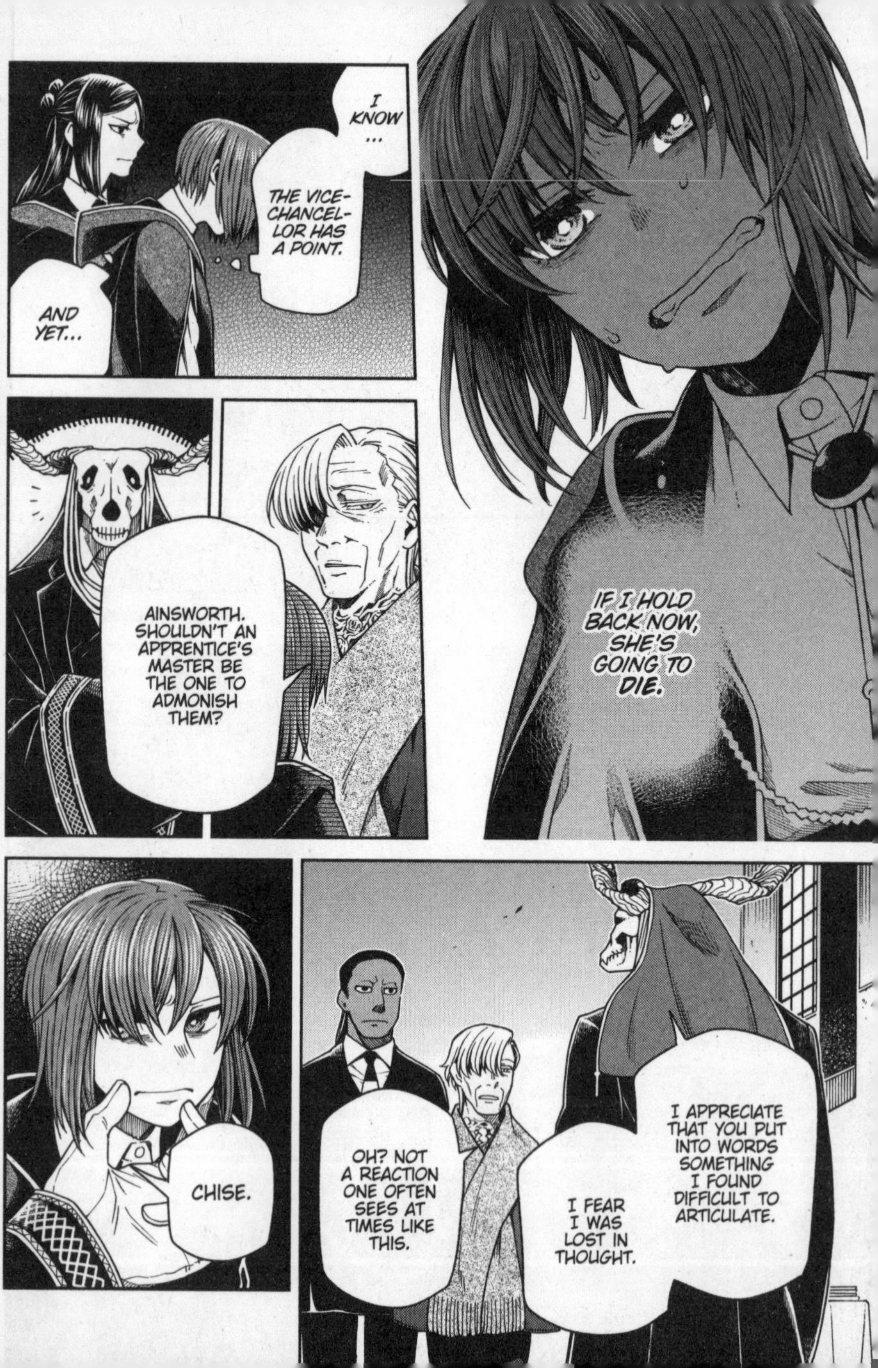
IF I HOLD BACK NOW, SHE'S GOING TO DIE.
I KNOW...
THE VICE-CHANCELLOR HAS A POINT.
AND YET...
AINSWORTH. SHOULDN'T AN APPRENTICE'S MASTER BE THE ONE TO ADMONISH THEM?
I APPRECIATE THAT YOU PUT INTO WORDS SOMETHING I FOUND DIFFICULT TO ARTICULATE.
I FEAR I WAS LOST IN THOUGHT.
OH? NOT A REACTION ONE OFTEN SEES AT TIMES LIKE THIS.
CHISE.

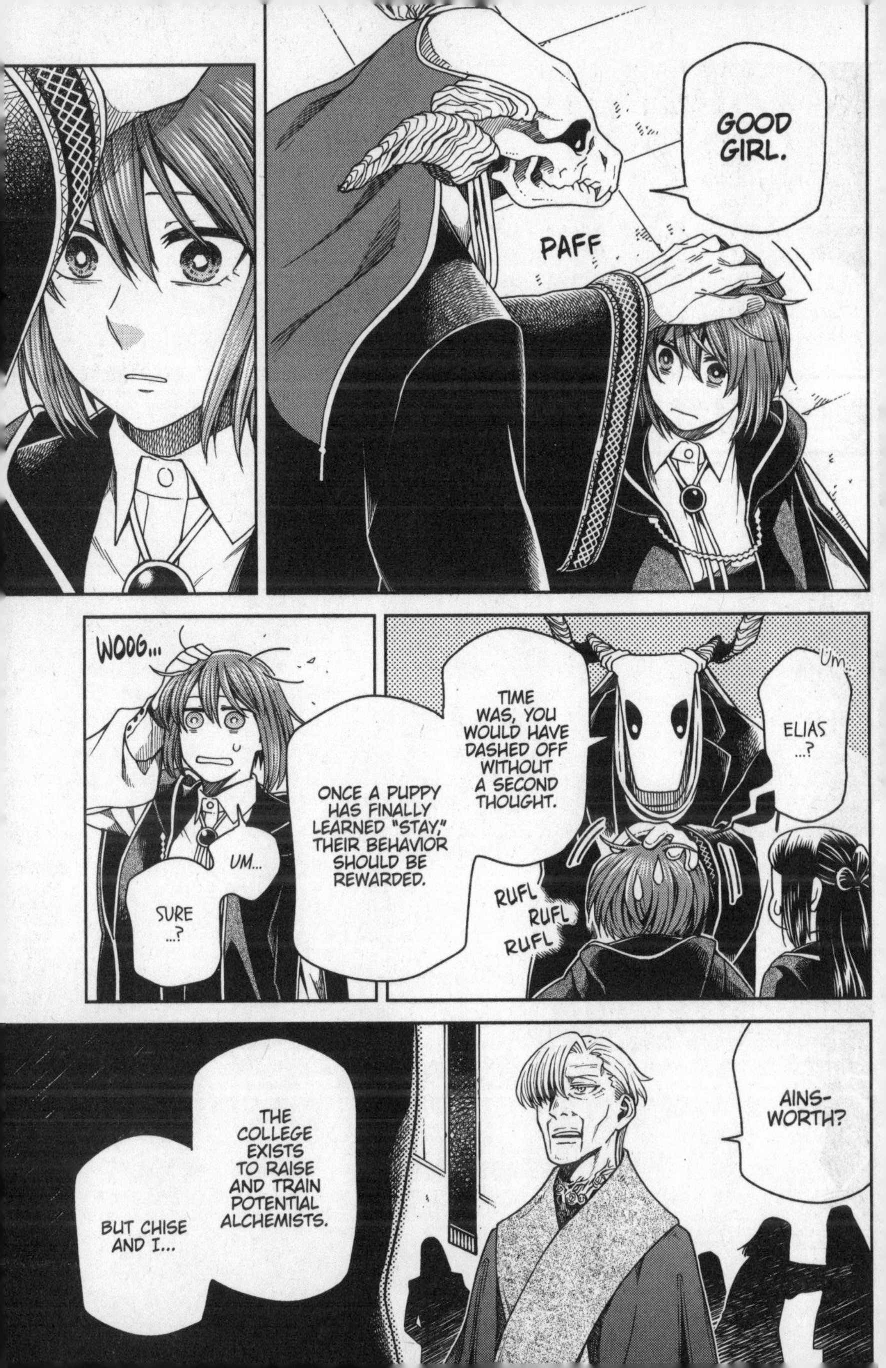
GOOD GIRL.
PAFF
Um...
ELIAS ...?
TIME WAS, YOU WOULD HAVE DASHED OFF WITHOUT A SECOND THOUGHT.
ONCE A PUPPY HAS FINALLY LEARNED "STAY," THEIR BEHAVIOR SHOULD BE REWARDED.
RUFL RUFL RUFL
WOOG...
UM...
SURE ...?
AINS-WORTH?
THE COLLEGE EXISTS TO RAISE AND TRAIN POTENTIAL ALCHEMISTS.
BUT CHISE AND I...

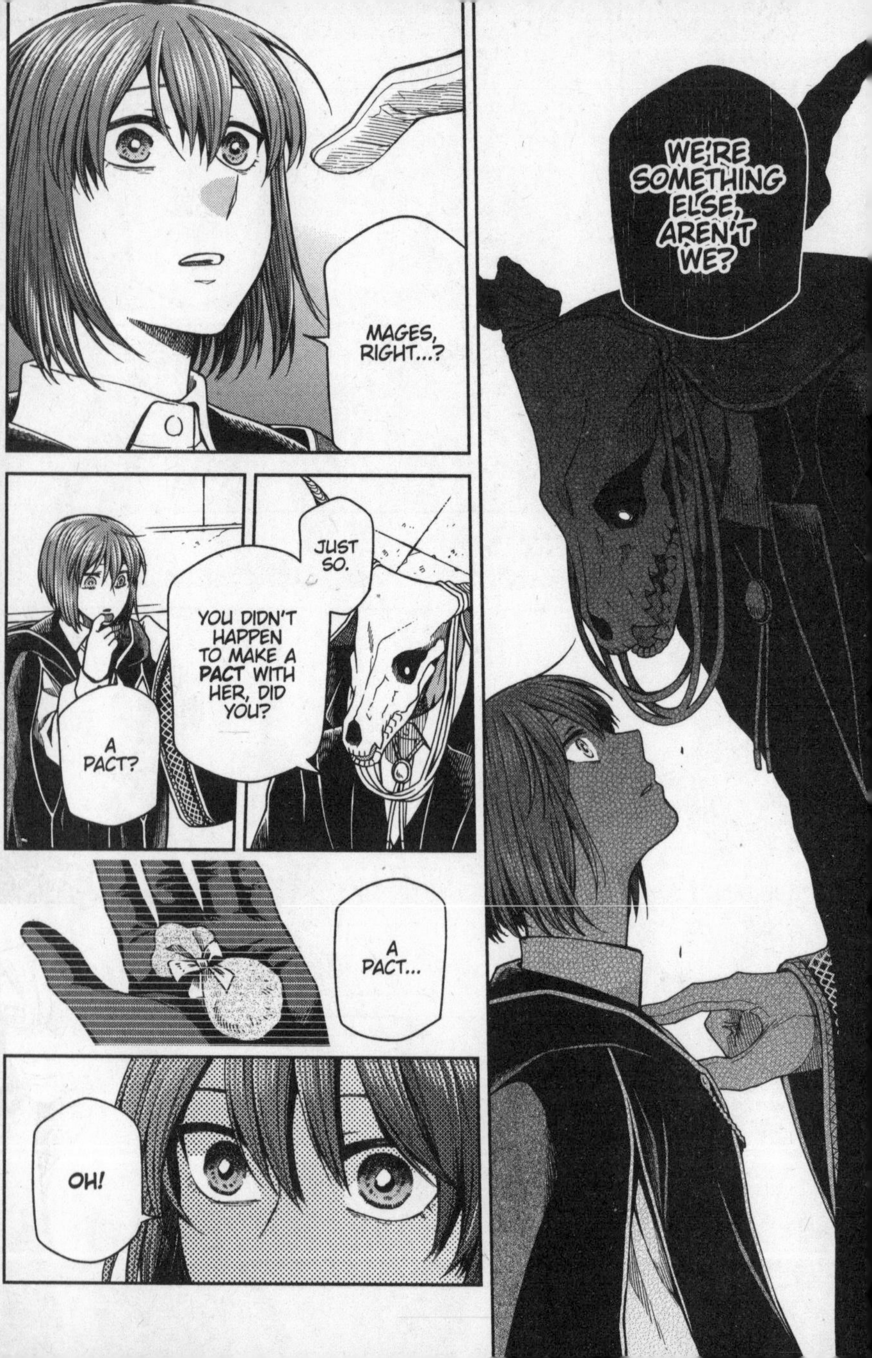
WE'RE SOMETHING ELSE, AREN'T WE?
MAGES, RIGHT...?
JUST SO.
YOU DIDN'T HAPPEN TO MAKE A PACT WITH HER, DID YOU?
A PACT?
A PACT...
OH!

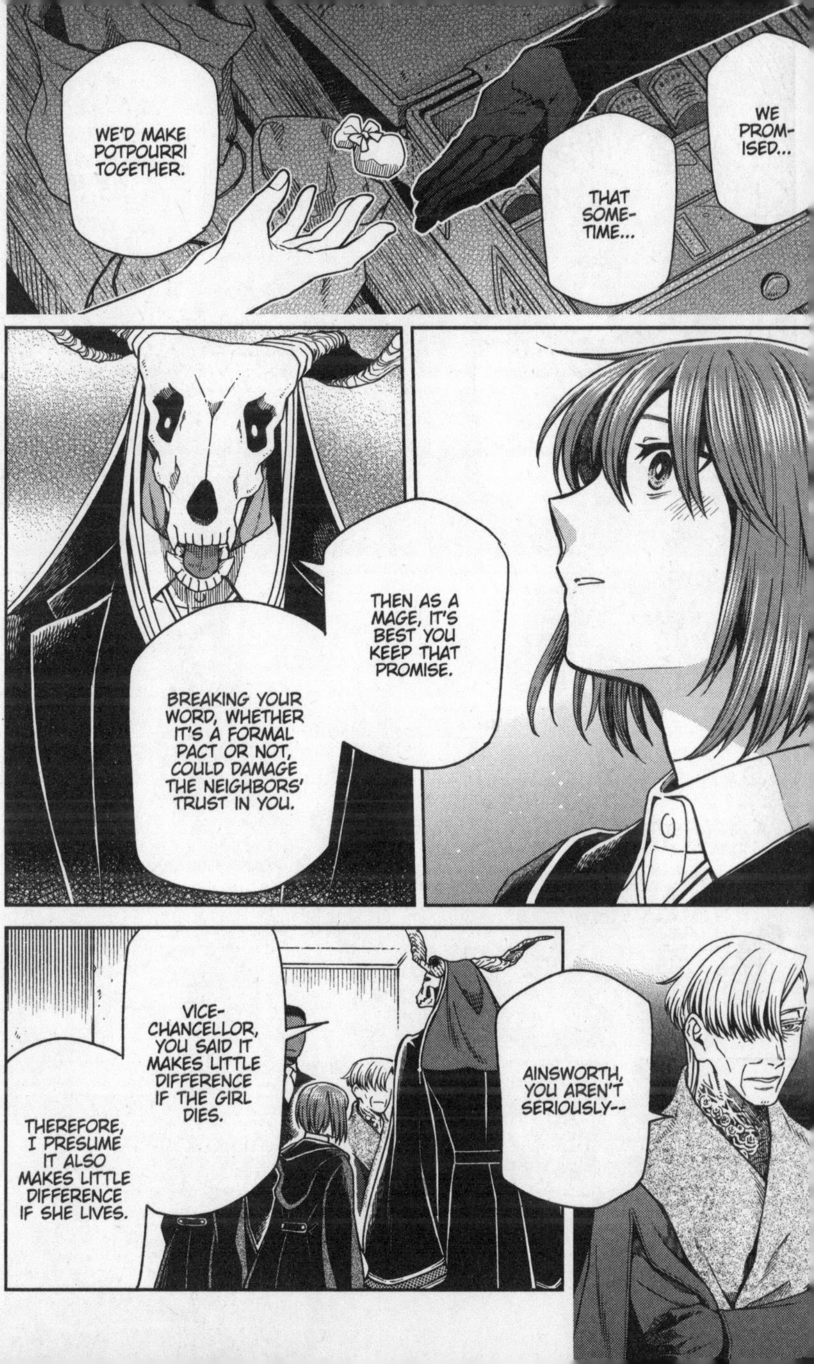
WE PROMISED...
THAT SOMETIME...
WE'D MAKE POTPOURRI TOGETHER.
THEN AS A MAGE, IT'S BEST YOU KEEP THAT PROMISE.
BREAKING YOUR WORD, WHETHER IT'S A FORMAL PACT OR NOT, COULD DAMAGE THE NEIGHBORS' TRUST IN YOU.
AINSWORTH, YOU AREN'T SERIOUSLY--
VICE-CHANCELLOR, YOU SAID IT MAKES LITTLE DIFFERENCE IF THE GIRL DIES.
THEREFORE, I PRESUME IT ALSO MAKES LITTLE DIFFERENCE IF SHE LIVES.

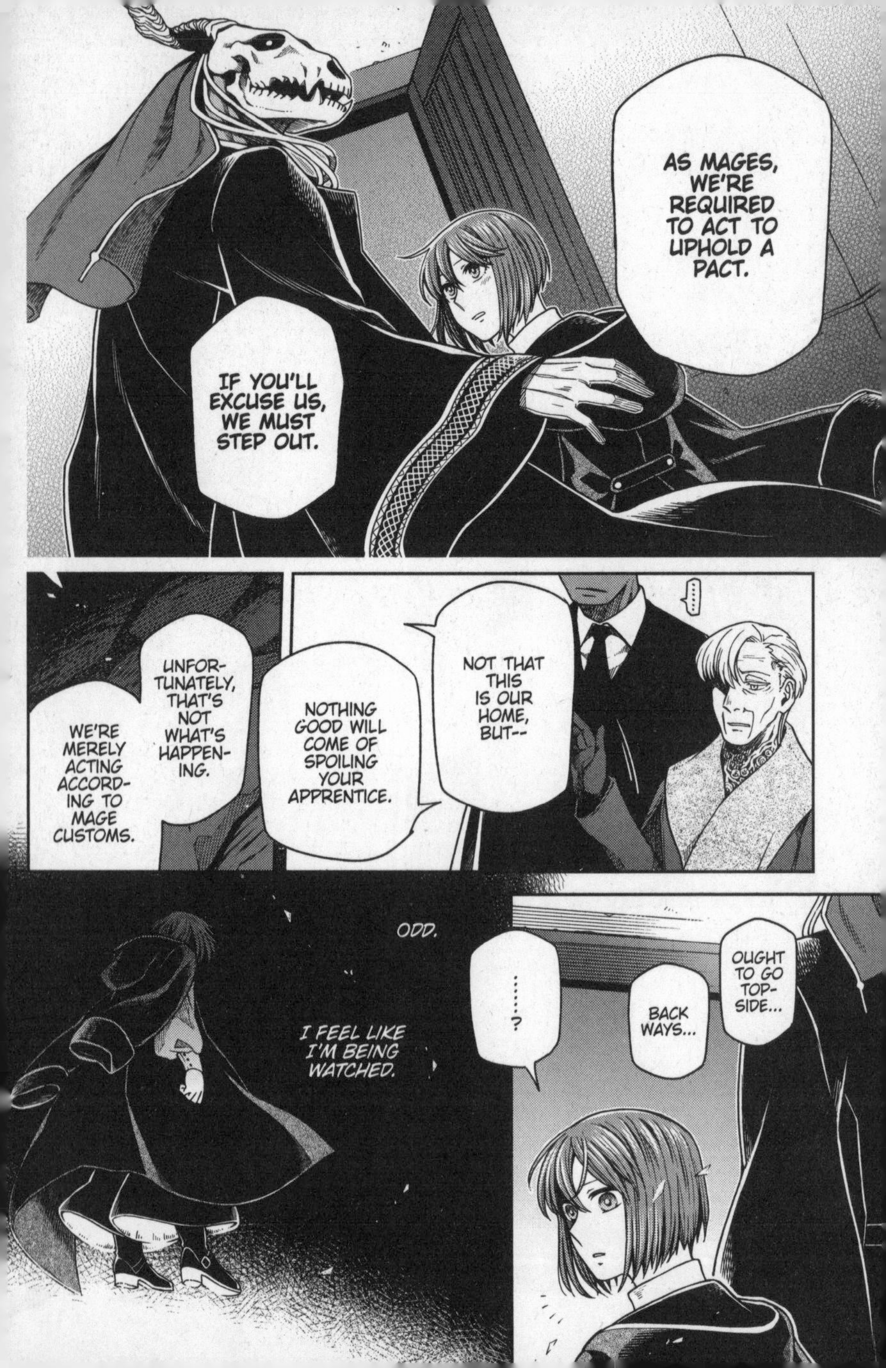
AS MAGES, WE'RE REQUIRED TO ACT TO UPHOLD A PACT.
IF YOU'LL EXCUSE US, WE MUST STEP OUT.
.....
NOT THAT THIS IS OUR HOME, BUT--
NOTHING GOOD WILL COME OF SPOILING YOUR APPRENTICE.
UNFORTUNATELY, THAT'S NOT WHAT'S HAPPENING.
WE'RE MERELY ACTING ACCORDING TO MAGE CUSTOMS.
OUGHT TO GO TOPSIDE...
BACK WAYS...
......?
ODD.
I FEEL LIKE I'M BEING WATCHED.

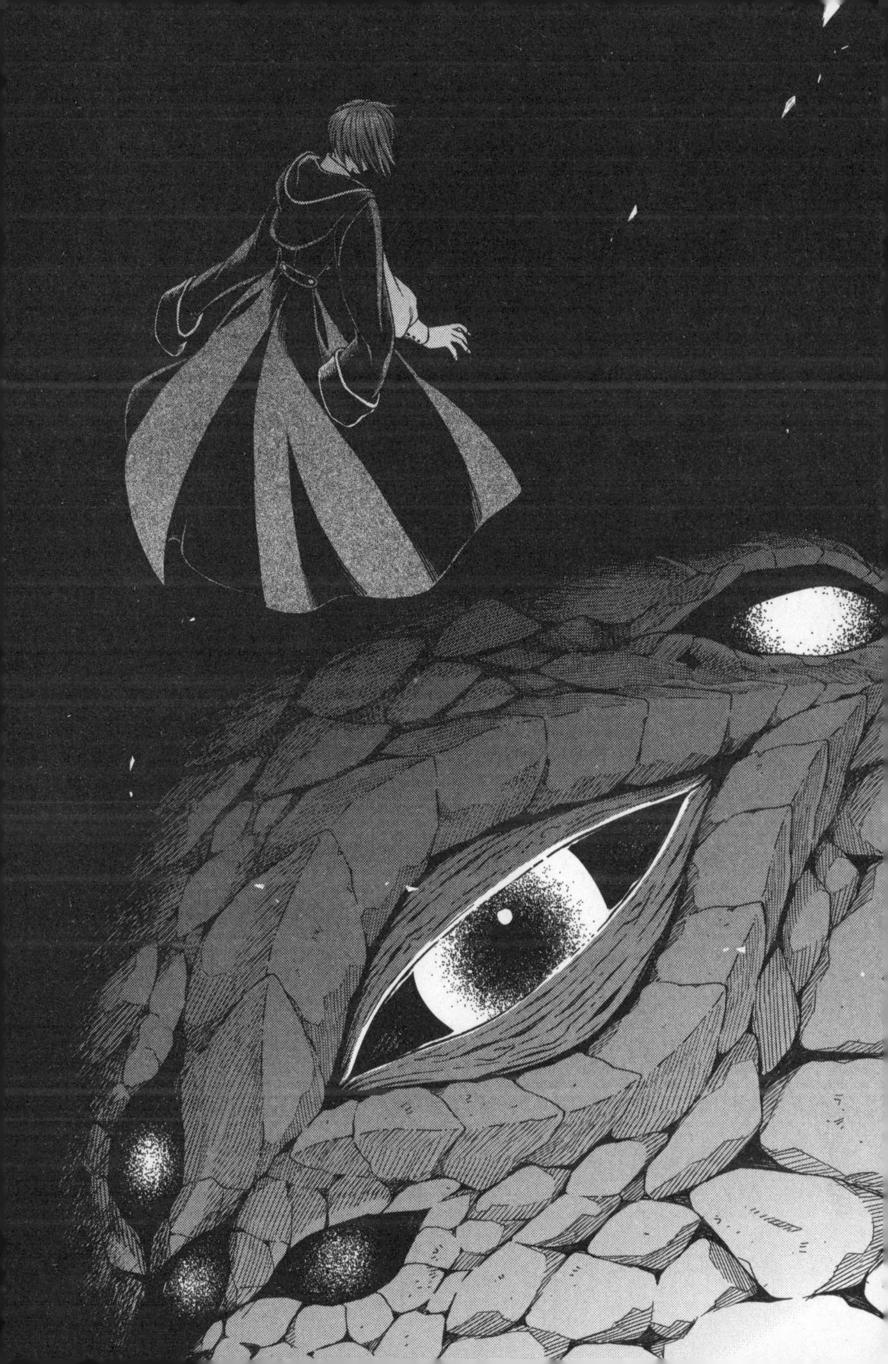

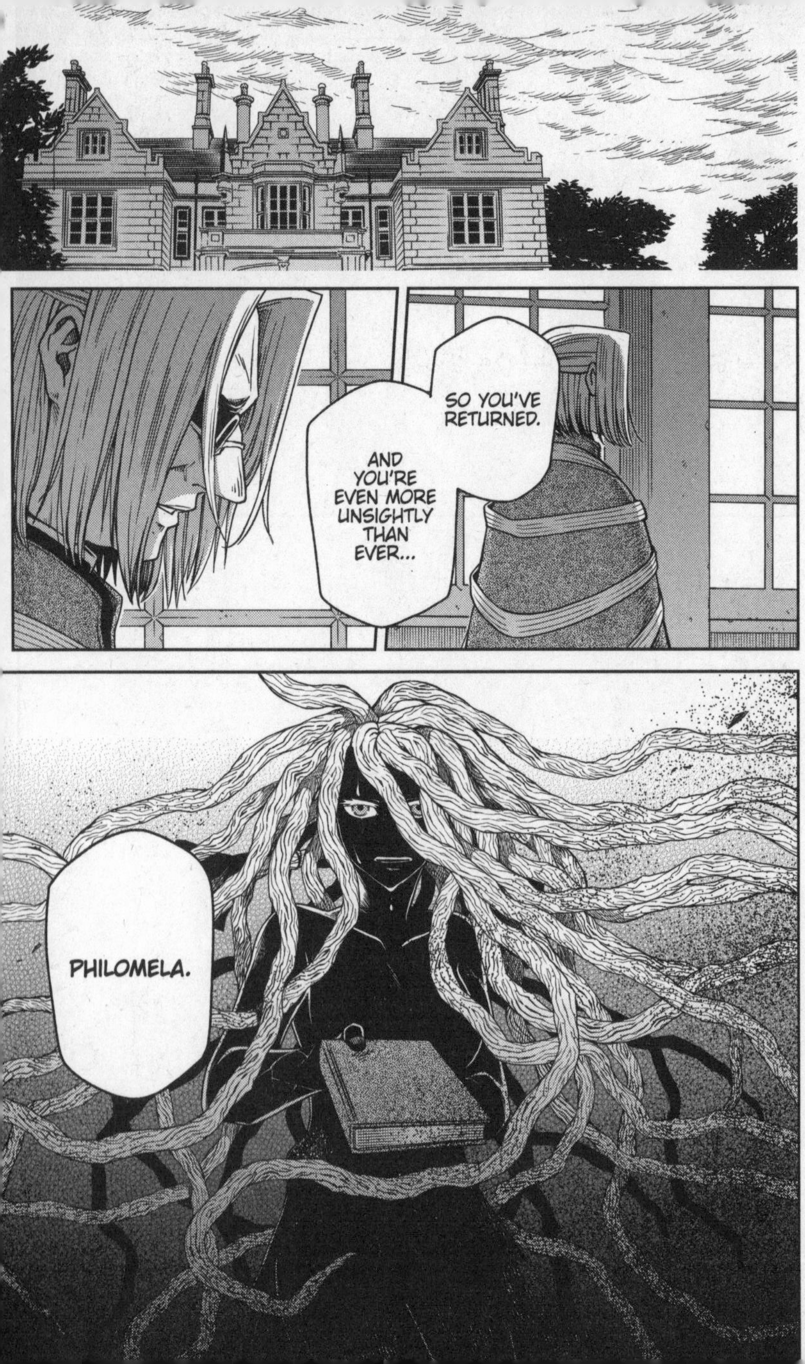
SO YOU'VE RETURNED.
AND YOU'RE EVEN MORE UNSIGHTLY THAN EVER...
PHILOMELA.

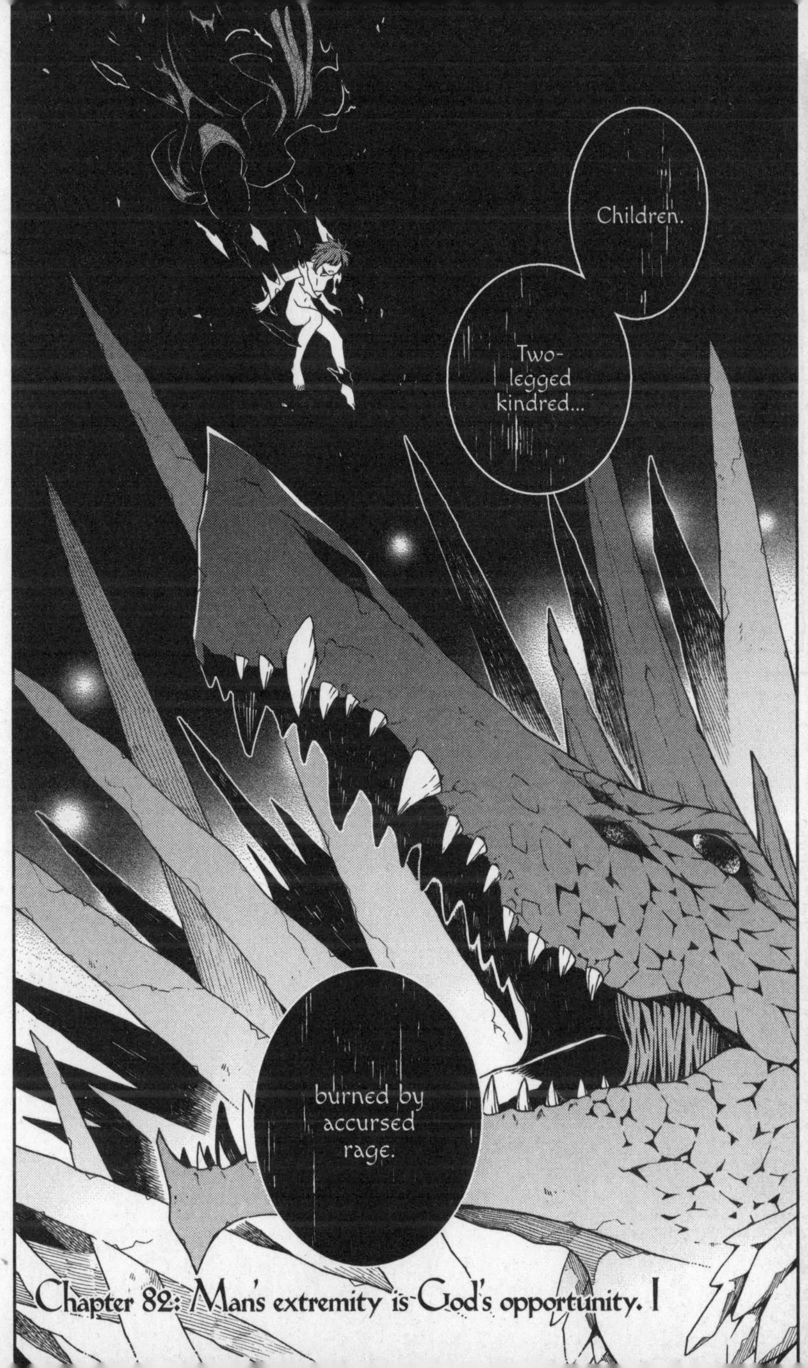
Children.
Two-legged kindred...
burned by accursed rage.
Chapter 82: Man's extremity is God's opportunity. I

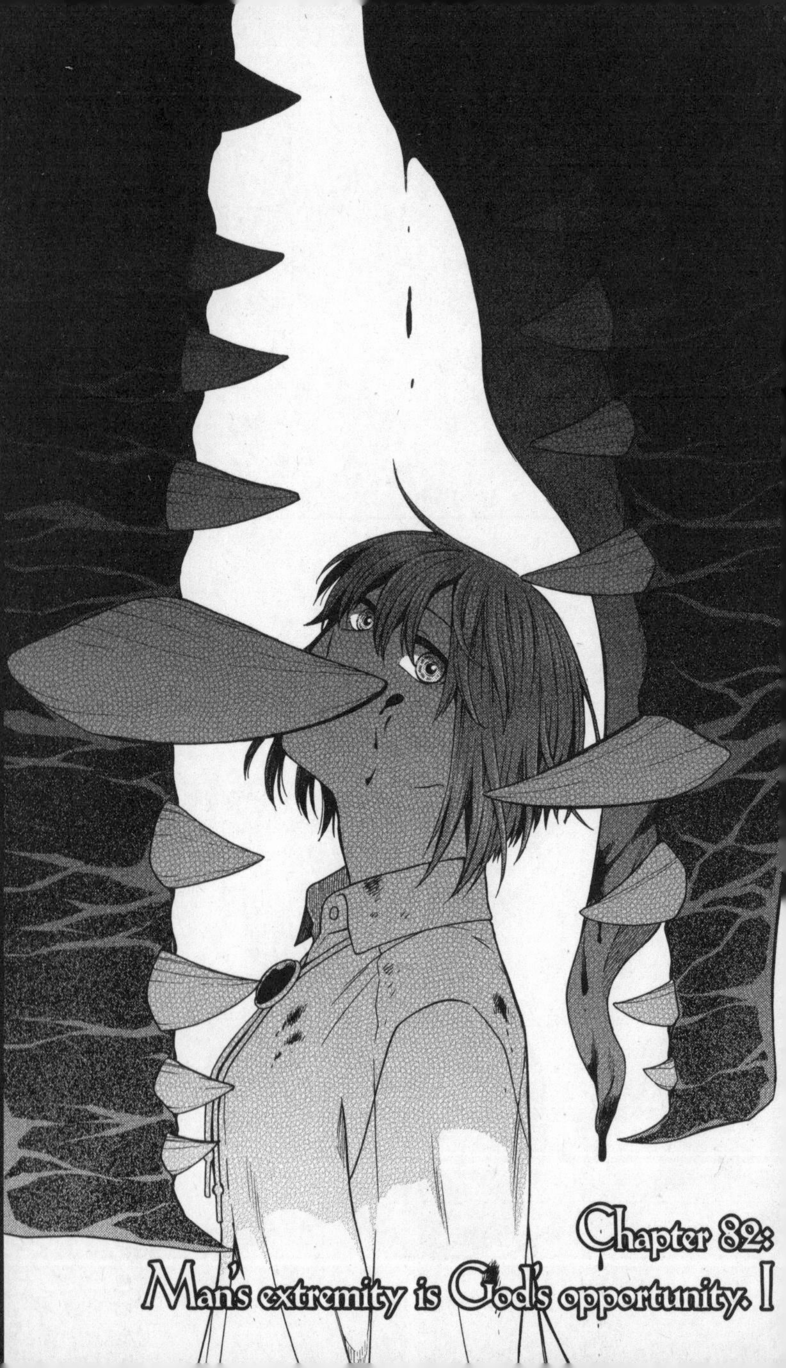

Chapter 82: Man's extremity is God's opportunity. I

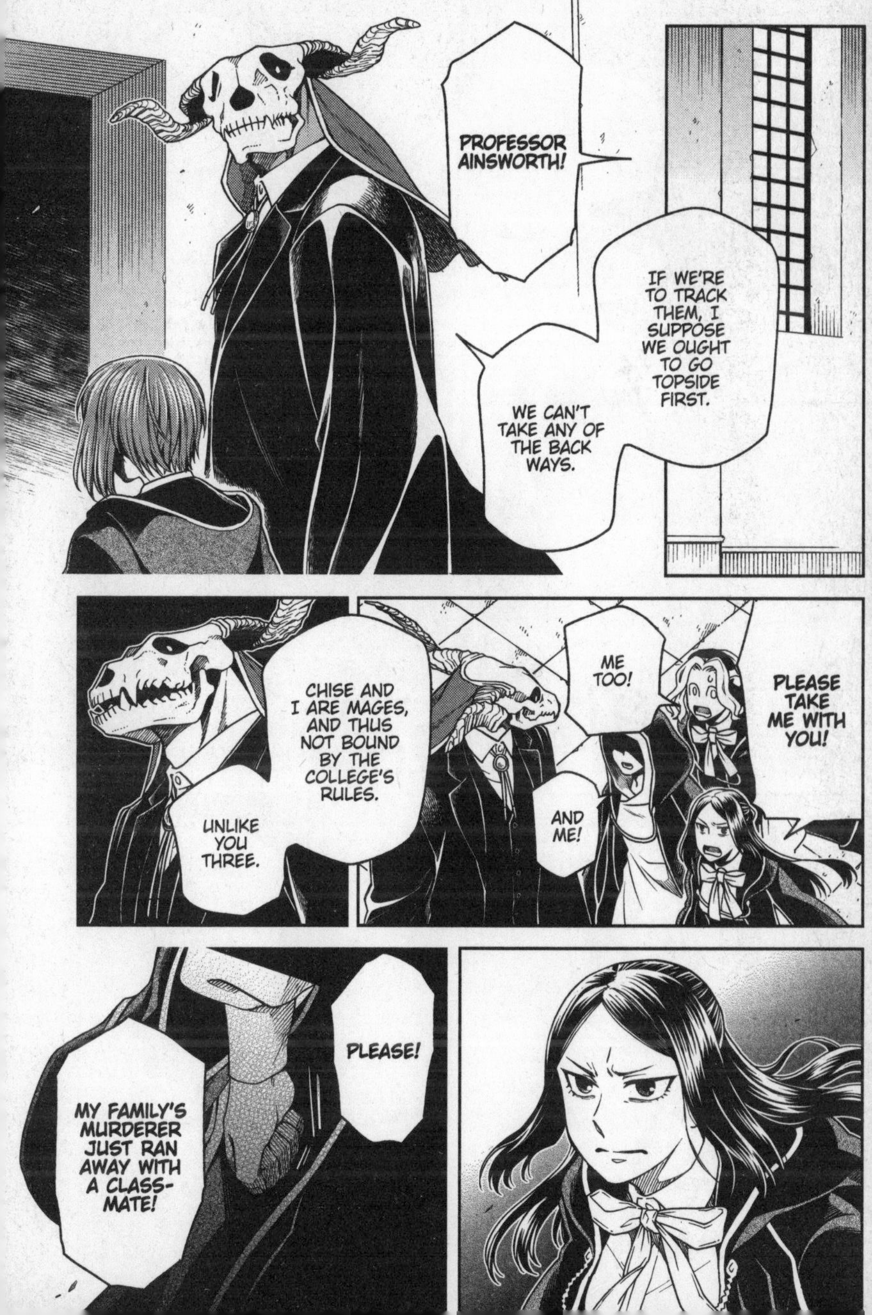
PROFESSOR AINSWORTH!
IF WE'RE TO TRACK THEM, I SUPPOSE WE OUGHT TO GO TOPSIDE FIRST.
WE CAN'T TAKE ANY OF THE BACK WAYS.
PLEASE TAKE ME WITH YOU!
ME TOO!
AND ME!
CHISE AND I ARE MAGES, AND THUS NOT BOUND BY THE COLLEGE'S RULES.
UNLIKE YOU THREE.
PLEASE!
MY FAMILY'S MURDERER JUST RAN AWAY WITH A CLASS-MATE!

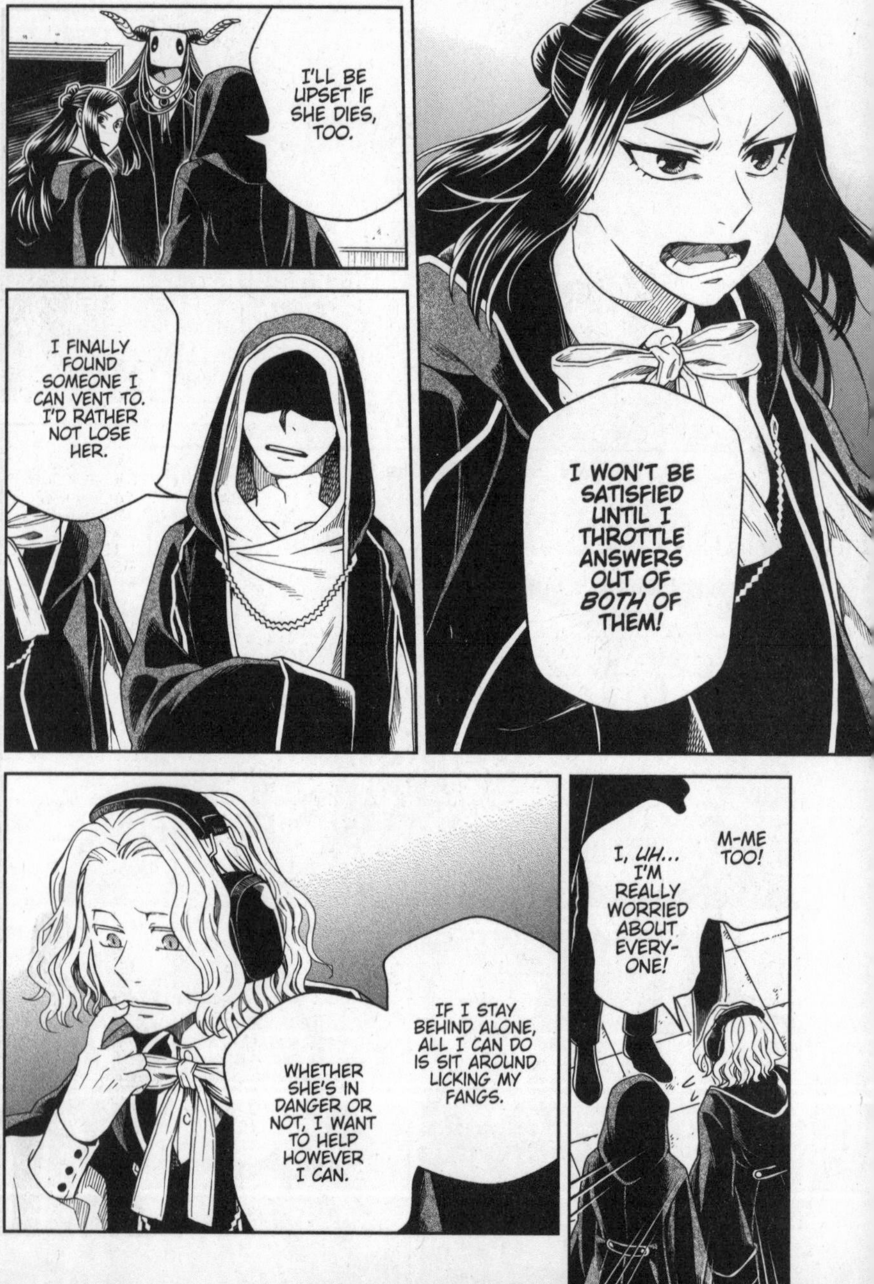
I WON'T BE SATISFIED UNTIL I THROTTLE ANSWERS OUT OF *BOTH* OF THEM!
I'LL BE UPSET IF SHE DIES, TOO.
I FINALLY FOUND SOMEONE I CAN VENT TO. I'D RATHER NOT LOSE HER.
M-ME TOO!
I, *UH*... I'M REALLY WORRIED ABOUT EVERY-ONE!
IF I STAY BEHIND ALONE, ALL I CAN DO IS SIT AROUND LICKING MY FANGS.
WHETHER SHE'S IN DANGER OR NOT, I WANT TO HELP HOWEVER I CAN.

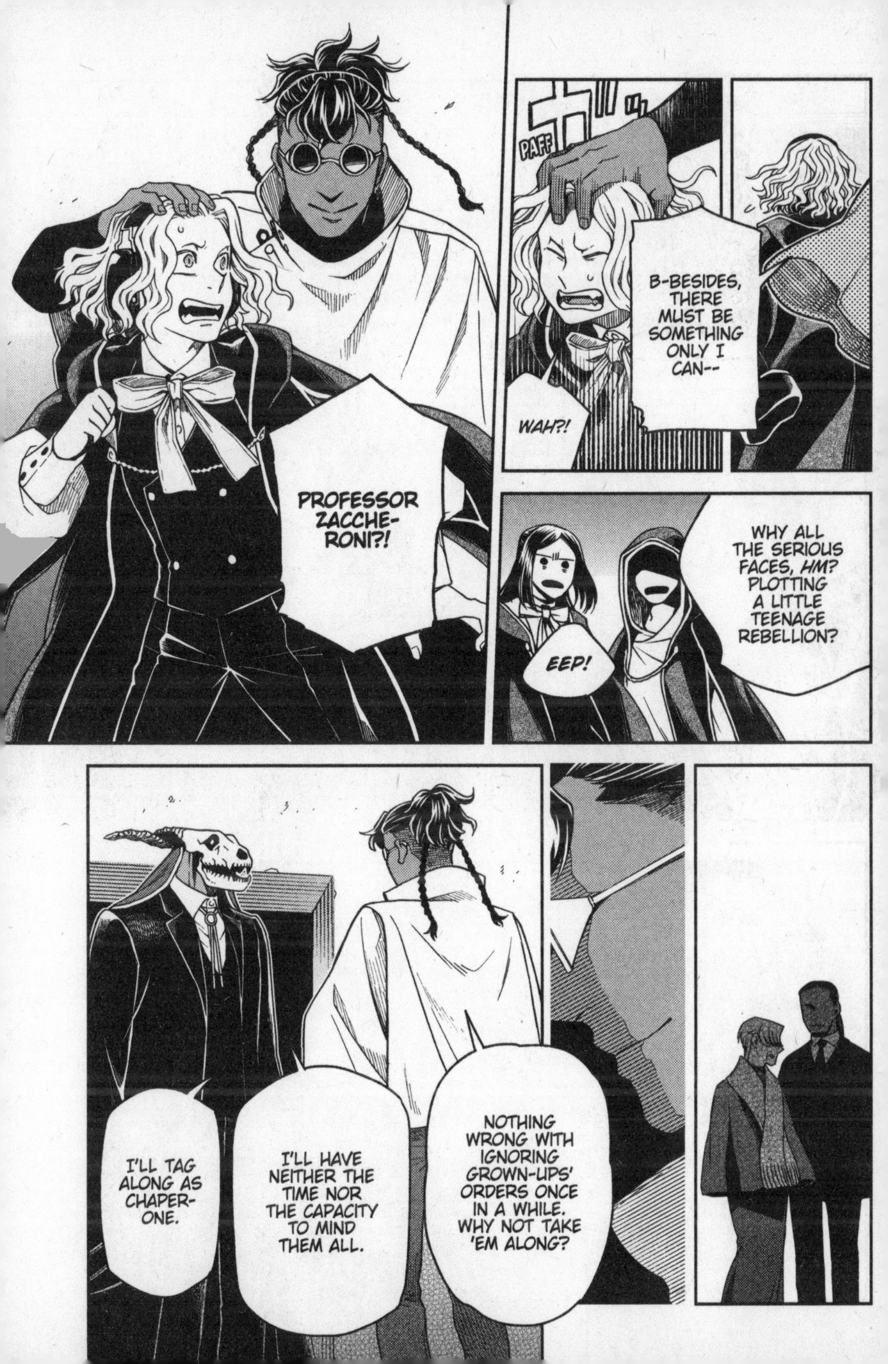
B-BESIDES, THERE MUST BE SOMETHING ONLY I CAN--
PAFF
WAH?!
PROFESSOR ZACCHE-RONI?!
WHY ALL THE SERIOUS FACES, *HM*? PLOTTING A LITTLE TEENAGE REBELLION?
EEP!
NOTHING WRONG WITH IGNORING GROWN-UPS' ORDERS ONCE IN A WHILE. WHY NOT TAKE 'EM ALONG?
I'LL HAVE NEITHER THE TIME NOR THE CAPACITY TO MIND THEM ALL.
I'LL TAG ALONG AS CHAPER-ONE.

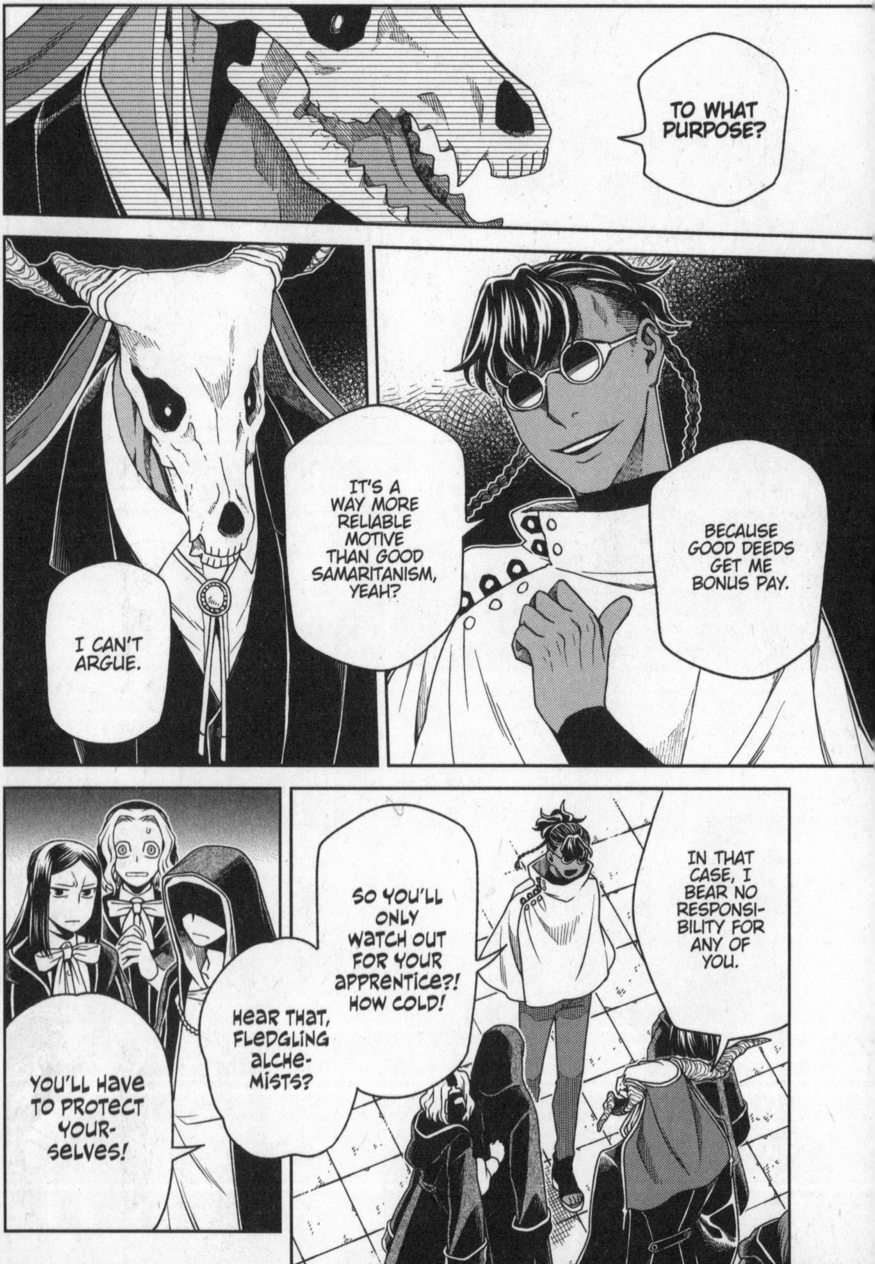
TO WHAT PURPOSE?
BECAUSE GOOD DEEDS GET ME BONUS PAY.
IT'S A WAY MORE RELIABLE MOTIVE THAN GOOD SAMARITANISM, YEAH?
I CAN'T ARGUE.
IN THAT CASE, I BEAR NO RESPONSIBILITY FOR ANY OF YOU.
SO YOU'LL ONLY WATCH OUT FOR YOUR APPRENTICE?! HOW COLD!
HEAR THAT, FLEDGLING ALCHEMISTS?
YOU'LL HAVE TO PROTECT YOURSELVES!

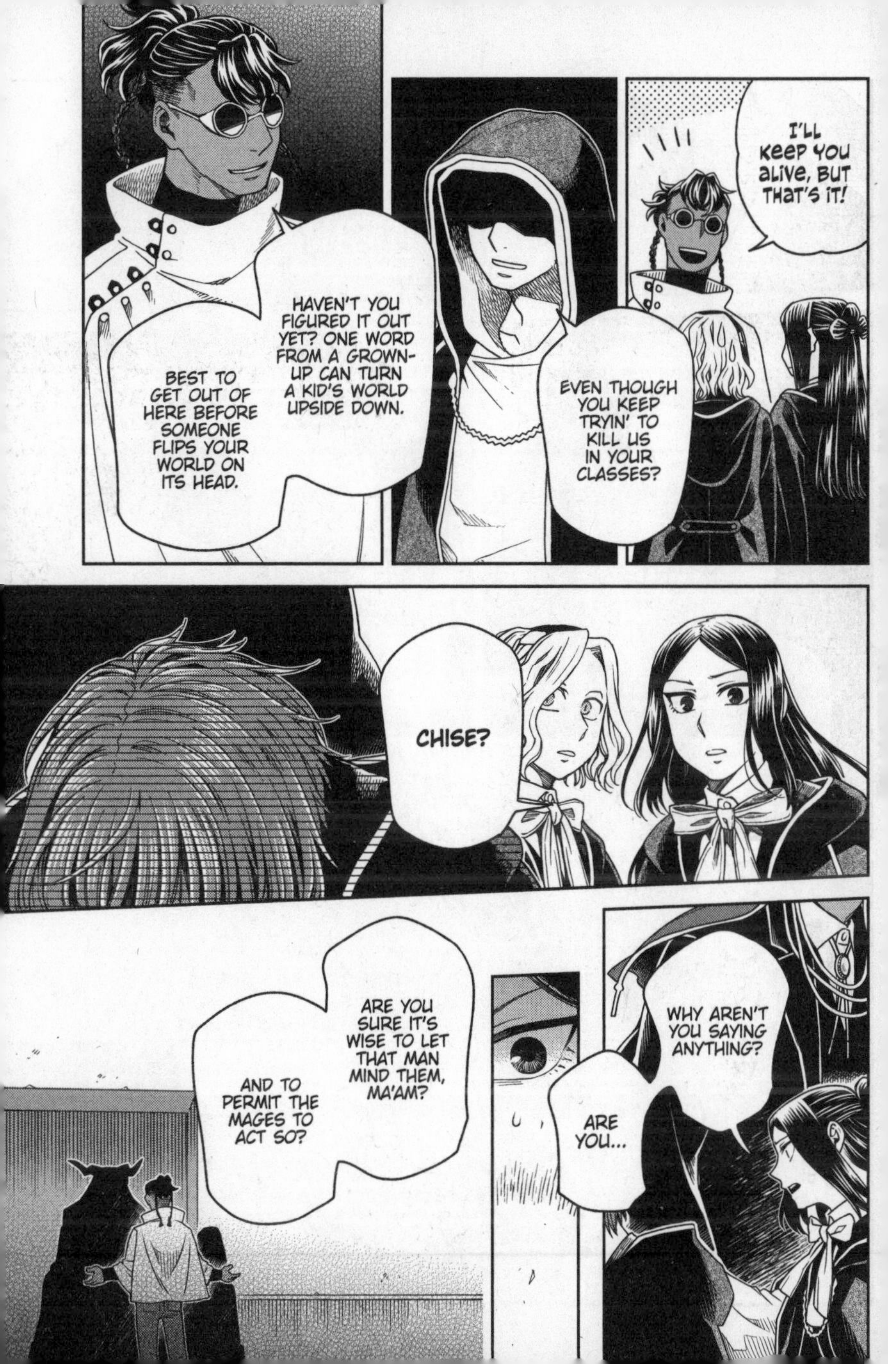
I'LL KEEP YOU ALIVE, BUT THAT'S IT!
EVEN THOUGH YOU KEEP TRYIN' TO KILL US IN YOUR CLASSES?
HAVEN'T YOU FIGURED IT OUT YET? ONE WORD FROM A GROWN-UP CAN TURN A KID'S WORLD UPSIDE DOWN.
BEST TO GET OUT OF HERE BEFORE SOMEONE FLIPS YOUR WORLD ON ITS HEAD.
CHISE?
WHY AREN'T YOU SAYING ANYTHING?
ARE YOU...
ARE YOU SURE IT'S WISE TO LET THAT MAN MIND THEM, MA'AM?
AND TO PERMIT THE MAGES TO ACT SO?

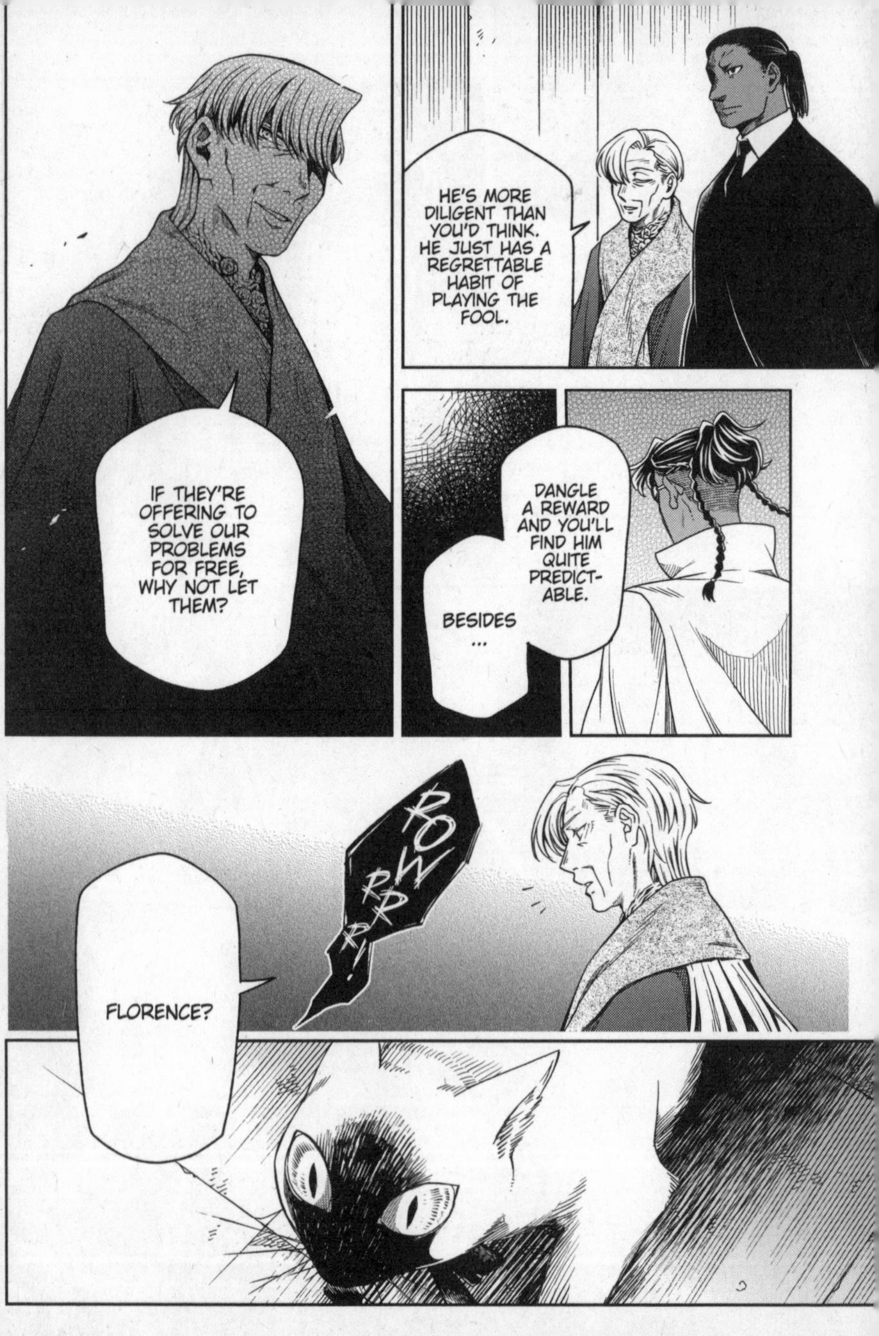
HE'S MORE DILIGENT THAN YOU'D THINK. HE JUST HAS A REGRETTABLE HABIT OF PLAYING THE FOOL.
DANGLE A REWARD AND YOU'LL FIND HIM QUITE PREDICT-ABLE.
BESIDES...
IF THEY'RE OFFERING TO SOLVE OUR PROBLEMS FOR FREE, WHY NOT LET THEM?
ROWRRR!
FLORENCE?

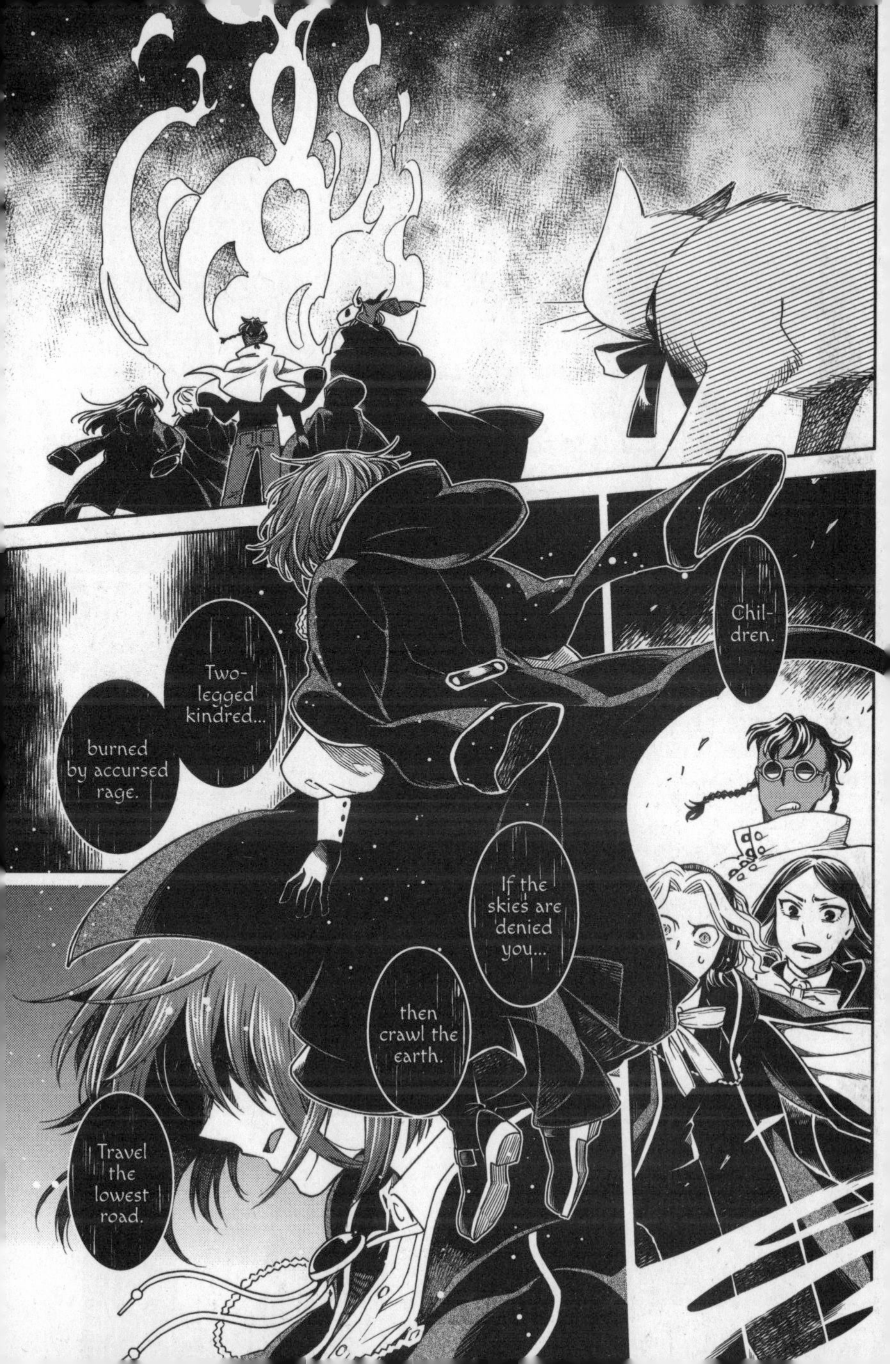
Chil-dren.
Two-legged kindred...
burned by accursed rage.
If the skies are denied you...
then crawl the earth.
Travel the lowest road.

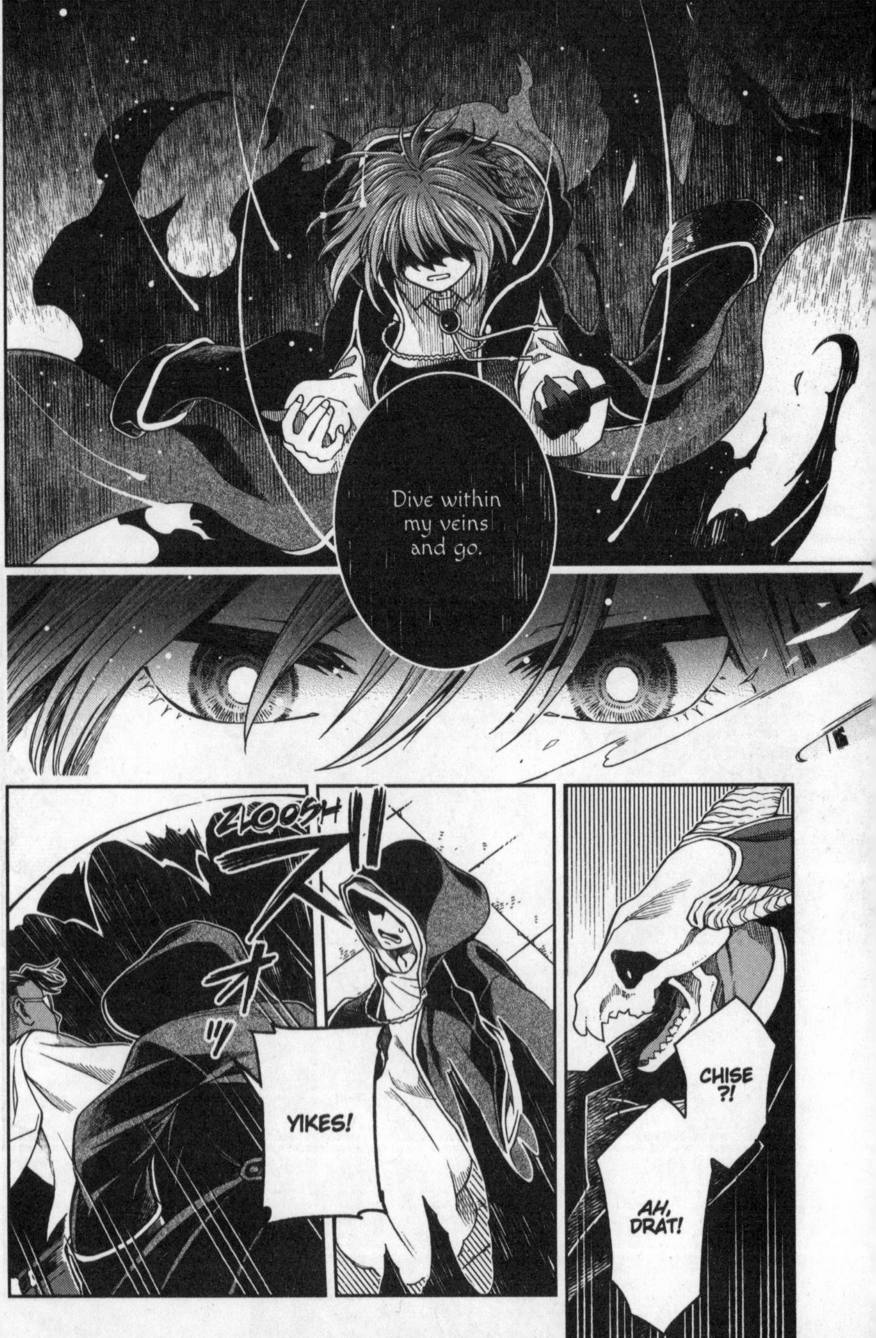
Dive within my veins and go.
ZLOOSH
CHISE ?!
AH, DRAT!
YIKES!

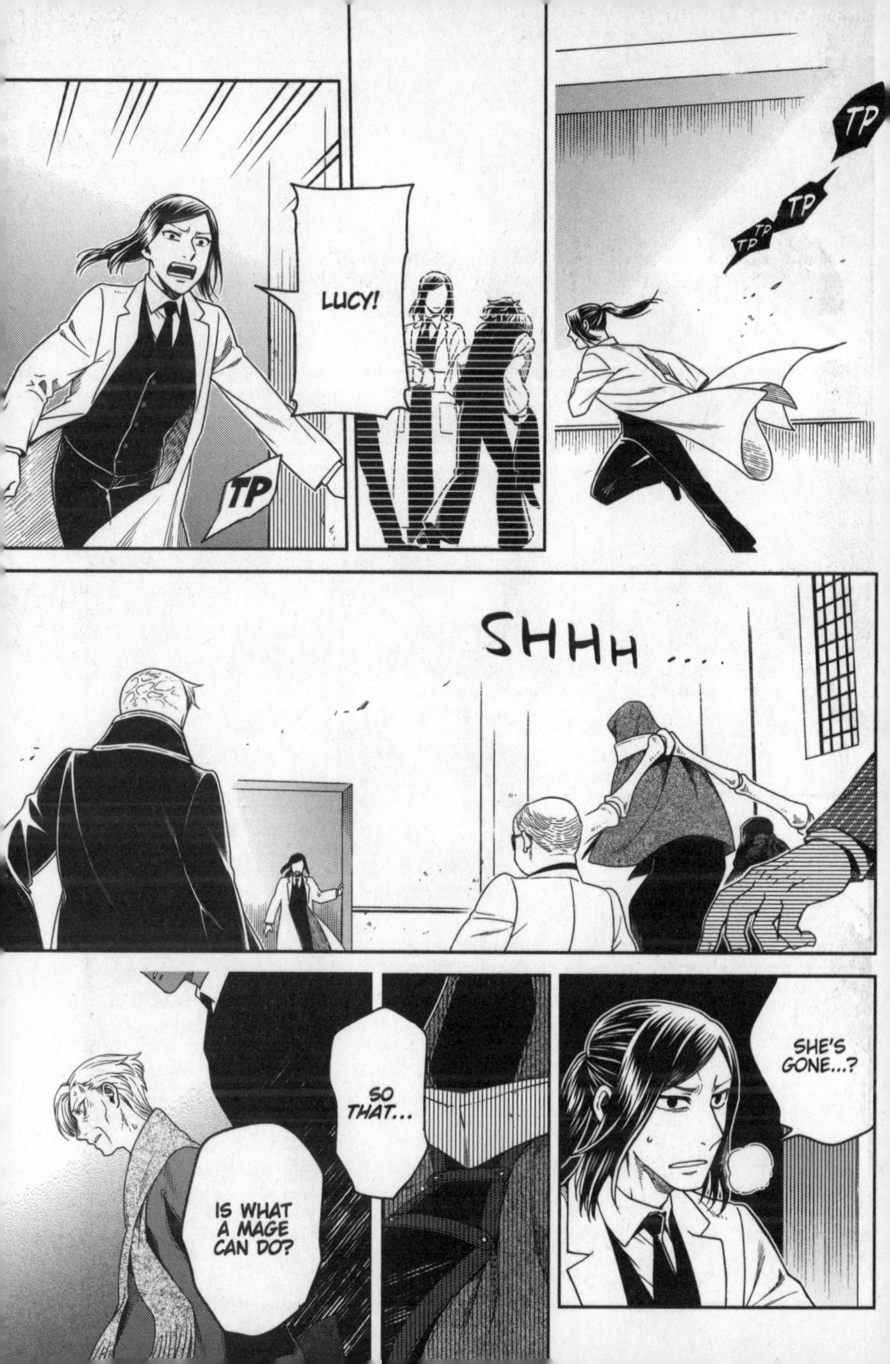
TP
TP
TP
TP
LUCY!
TP
SHHH....
SHE'S GONE...?
SO THAT...
IS WHAT A MAGE CAN DO?

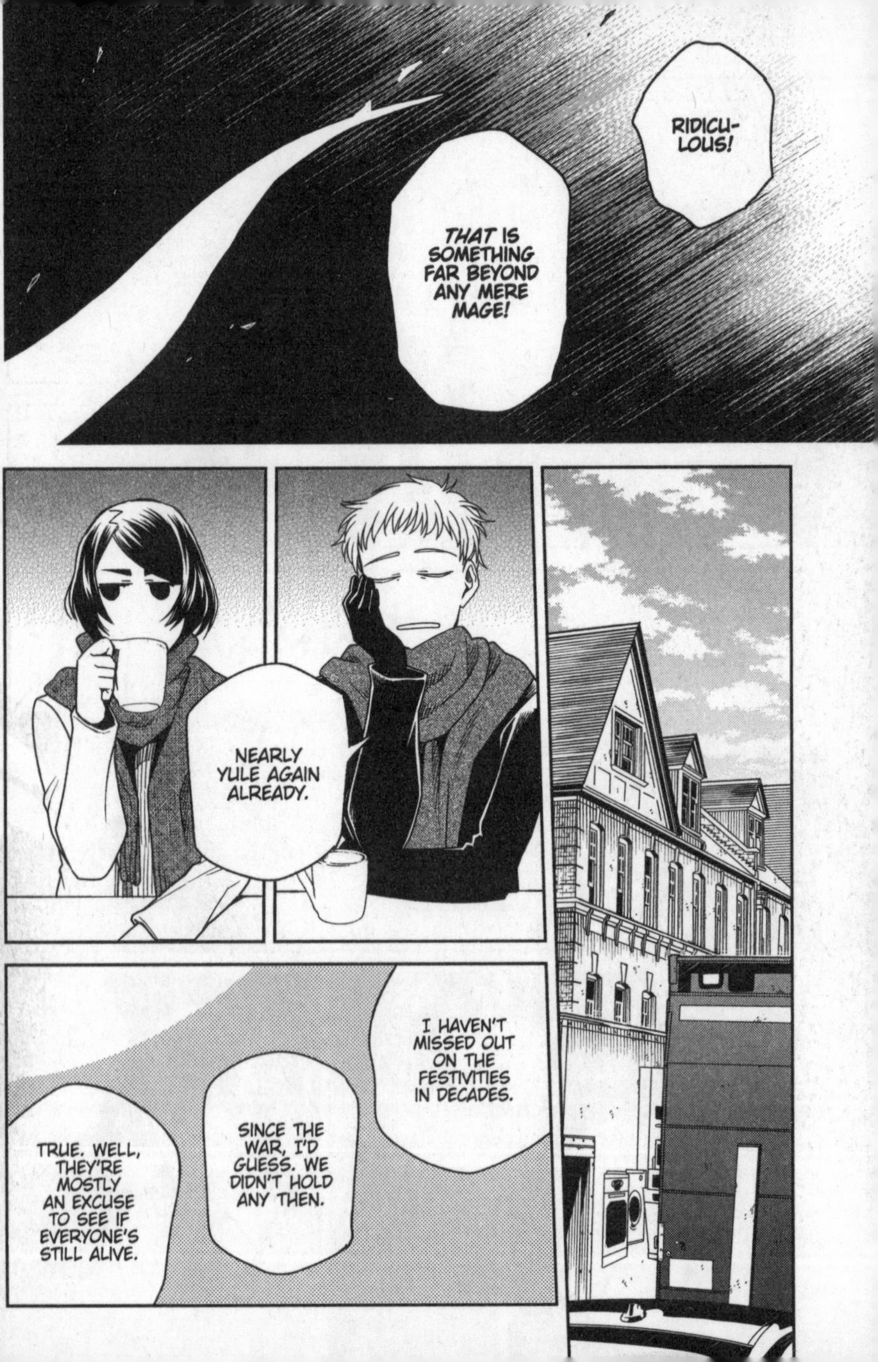
RIDICU-LOUS!
THAT IS SOMETHING FAR BEYOND ANY MERE MAGE!
NEARLY YULE AGAIN ALREADY.
I HAVEN'T MISSED OUT ON THE FESTIVITIES IN DECADES.
SINCE THE WAR, I'D GUESS. WE DIDN'T HOLD ANY THEN.
TRUE. WELL, THEY'RE MOSTLY AN EXCUSE TO SEE IF EVERYONE'S STILL ALIVE.

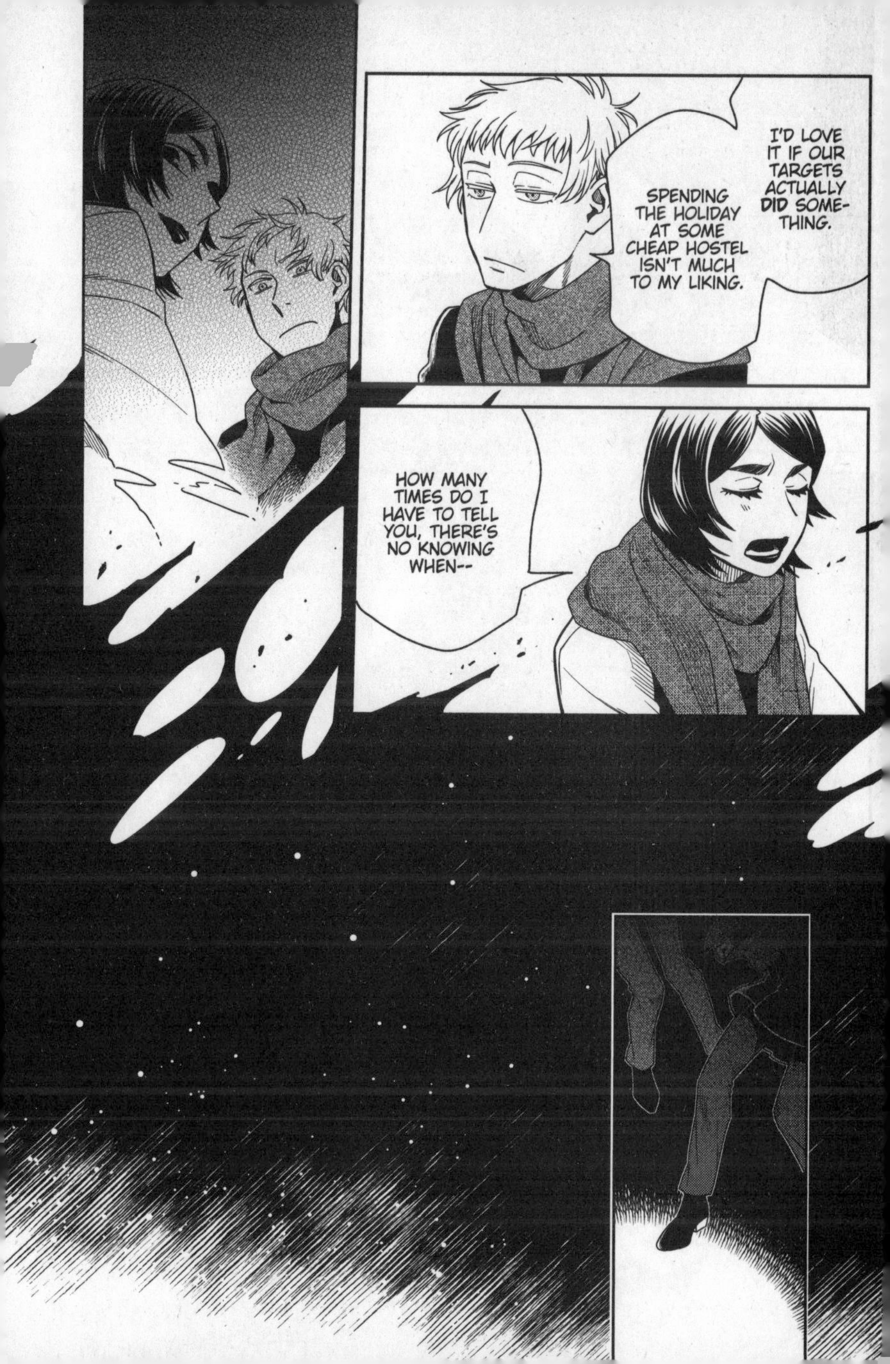
I'D LOVE IT IF OUR TARGETS ACTUALLY DID SOMETHING.
SPENDING THE HOLIDAY AT SOME CHEAP HOSTEL ISN'T MUCH TO MY LIKING.
HOW MANY TIMES DO I HAVE TO TELL YOU, THERE'S NO KNOWING WHEN--

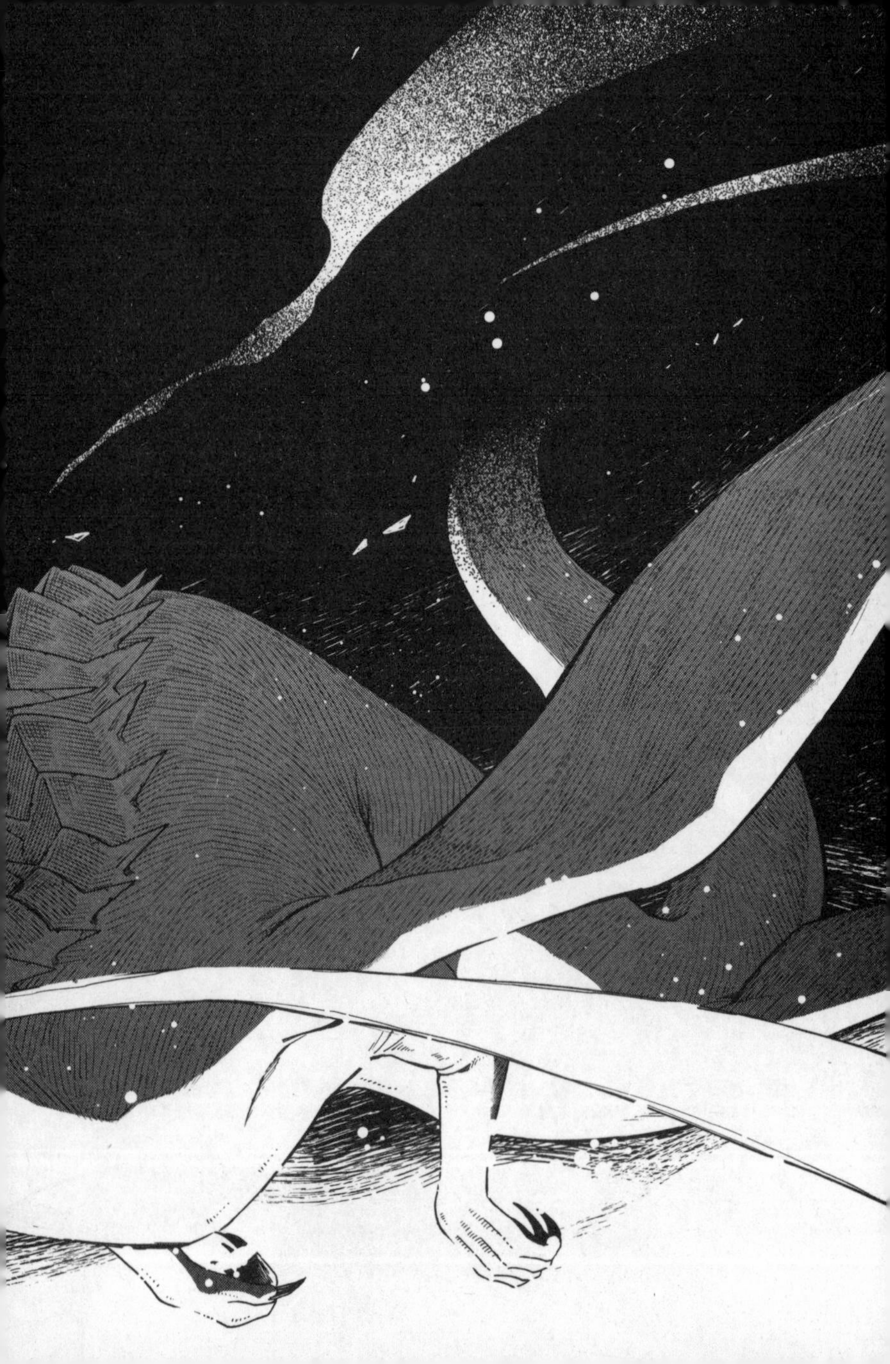

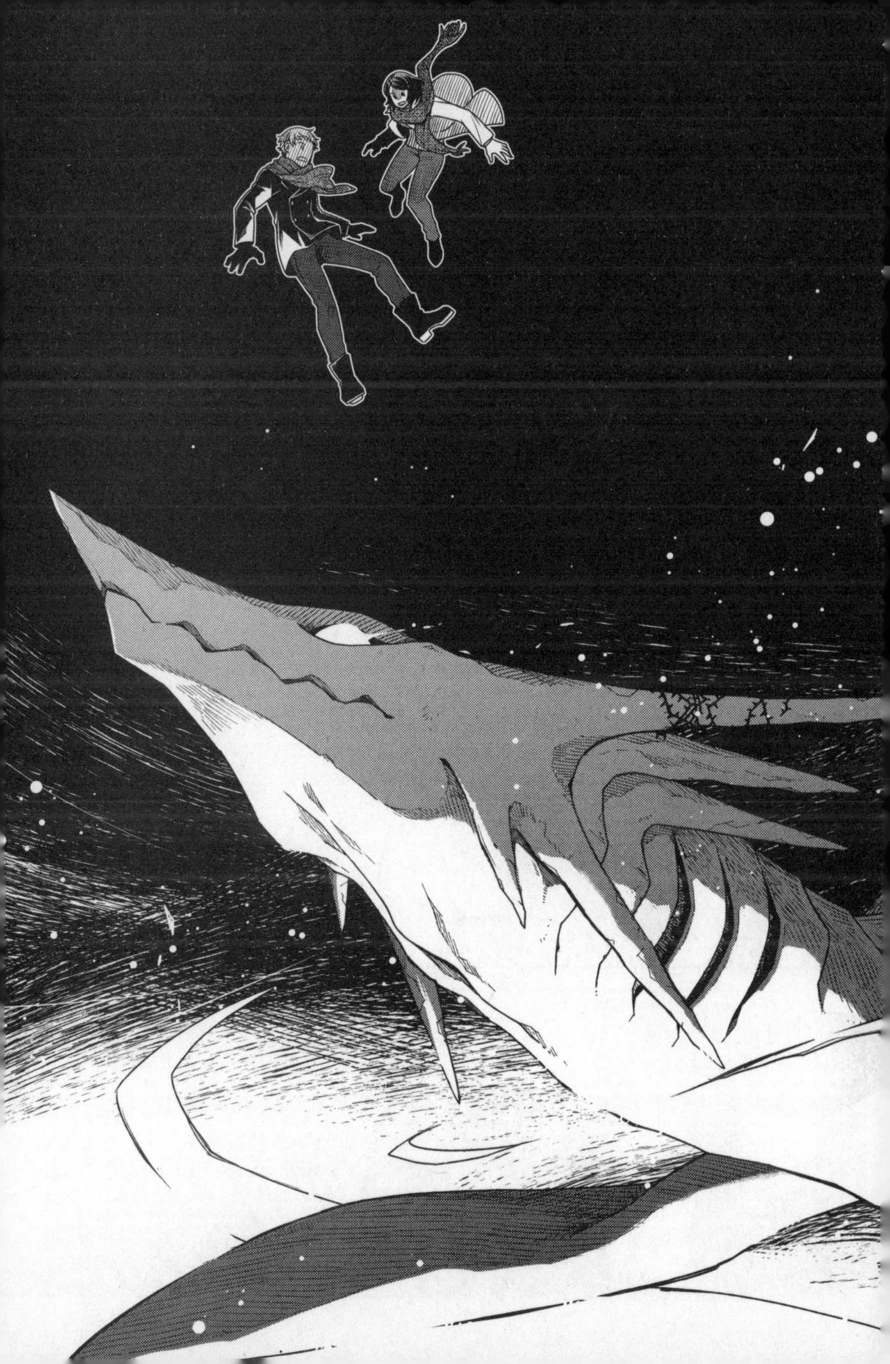

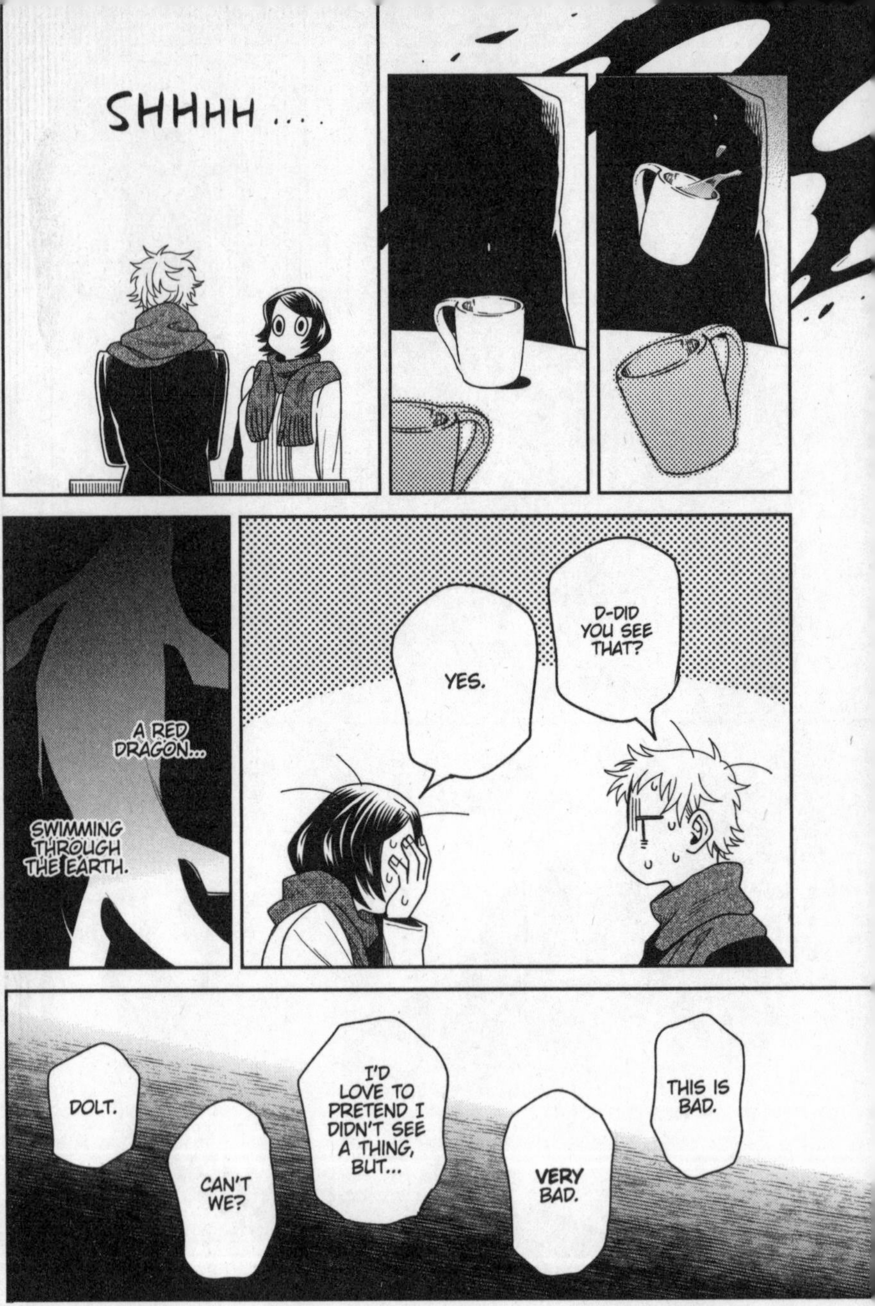
SHHHH....
D-DID YOU SEE THAT?
YES.
A RED DRAGON...
SWIMMING THROUGH THE EARTH.
THIS IS BAD.
VERY BAD.
I'D LOVE TO PRETEND I DIDN'T SEE A THING, BUT...
CAN'T WE?
DOLT.

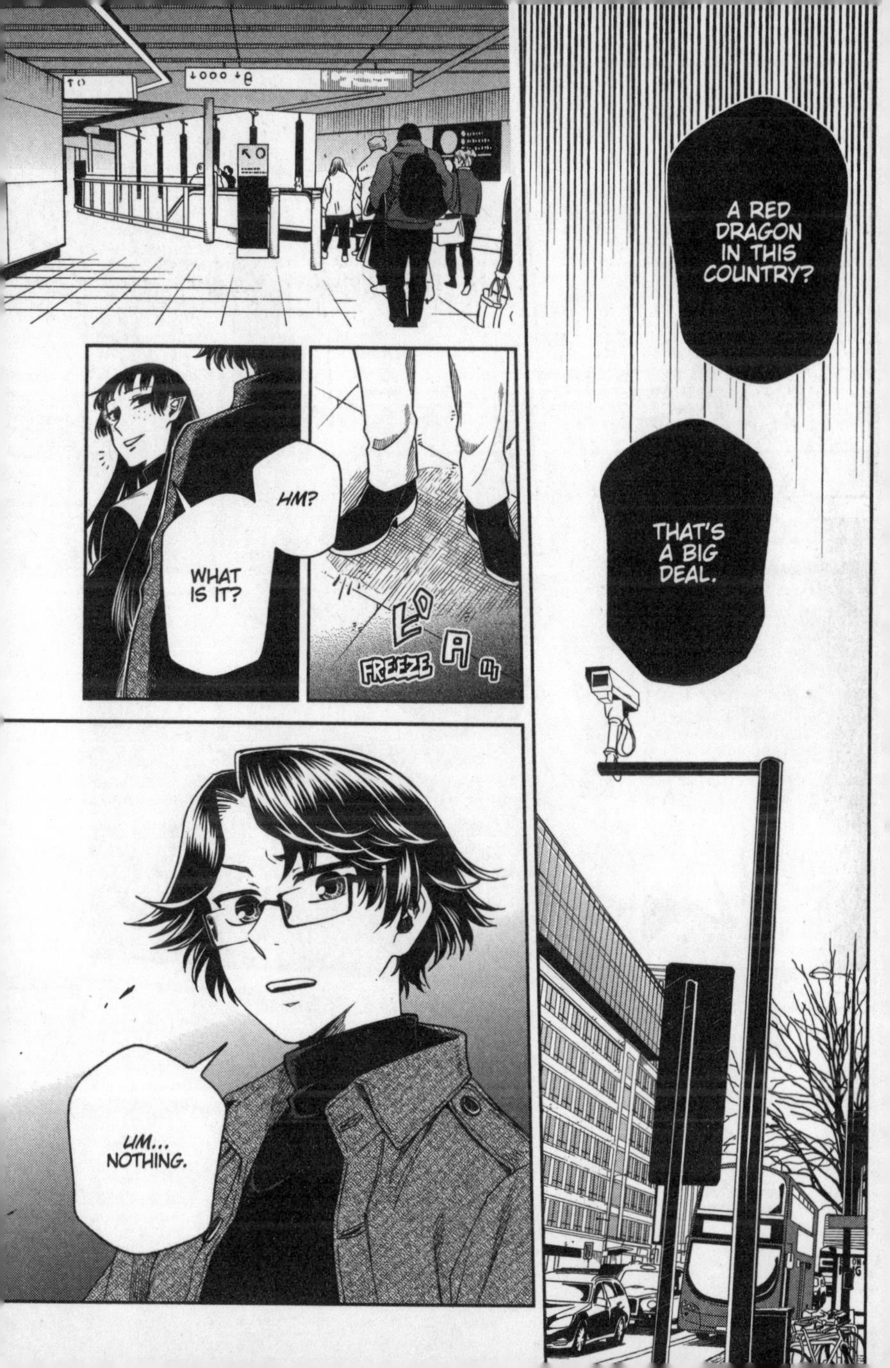
A RED DRAGON IN THIS COUNTRY?
THAT'S A BIG DEAL.
FREEZE
HM?
WHAT IS IT?
UM... NOTHING.

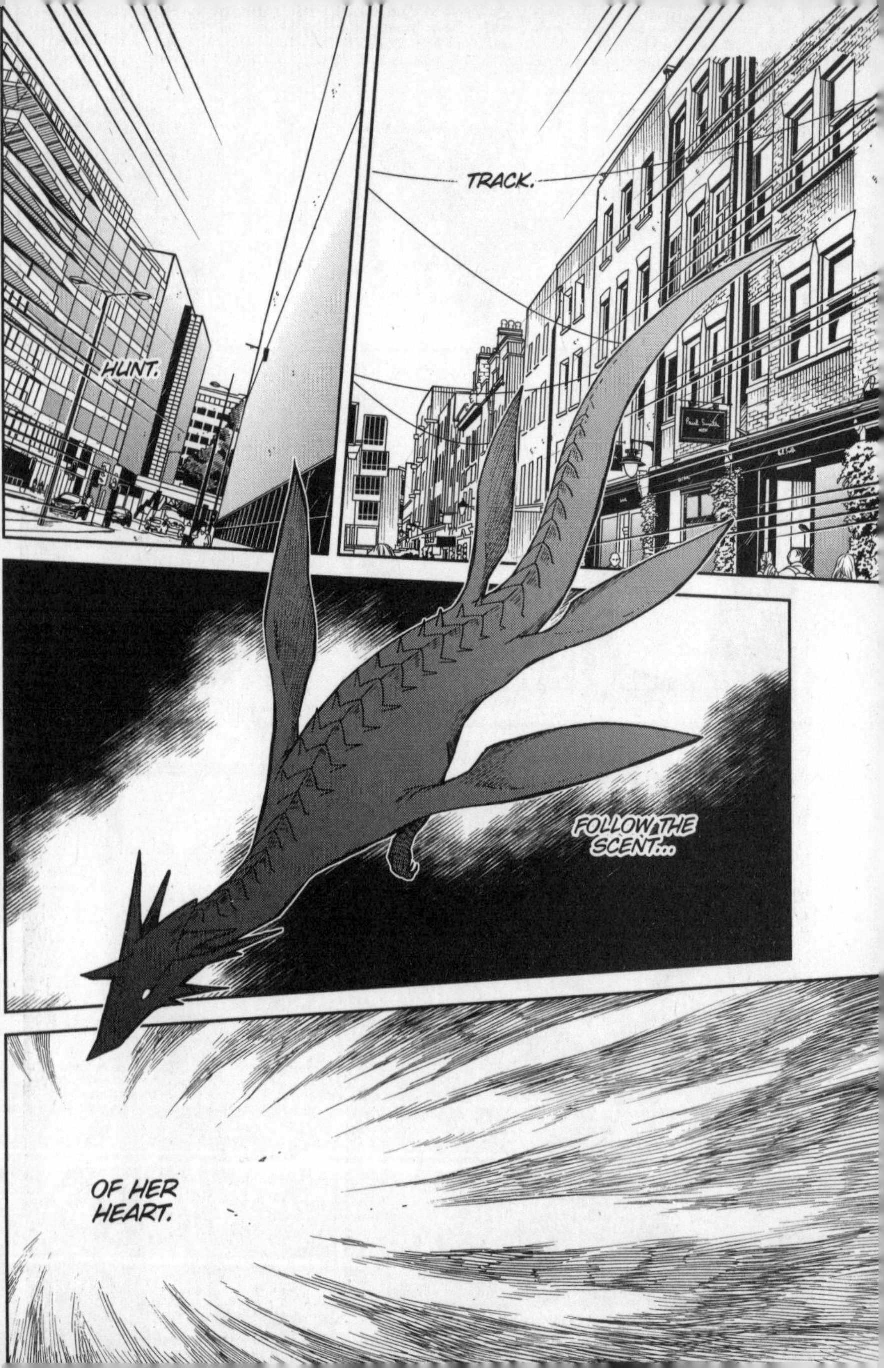
TRACK.
HUNT.
FOLLOW THE SCENT...
OF HER HEART.

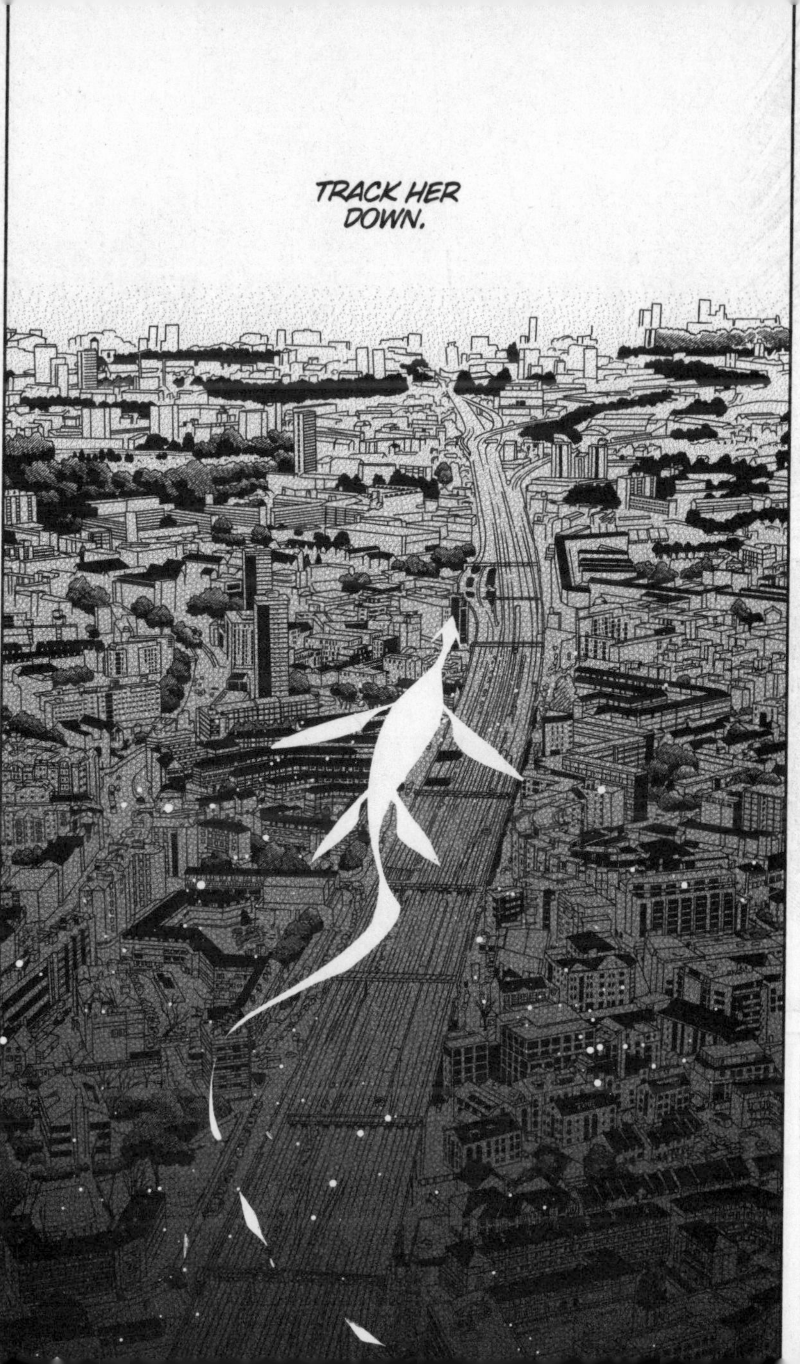
TRACK HER
DOWN.

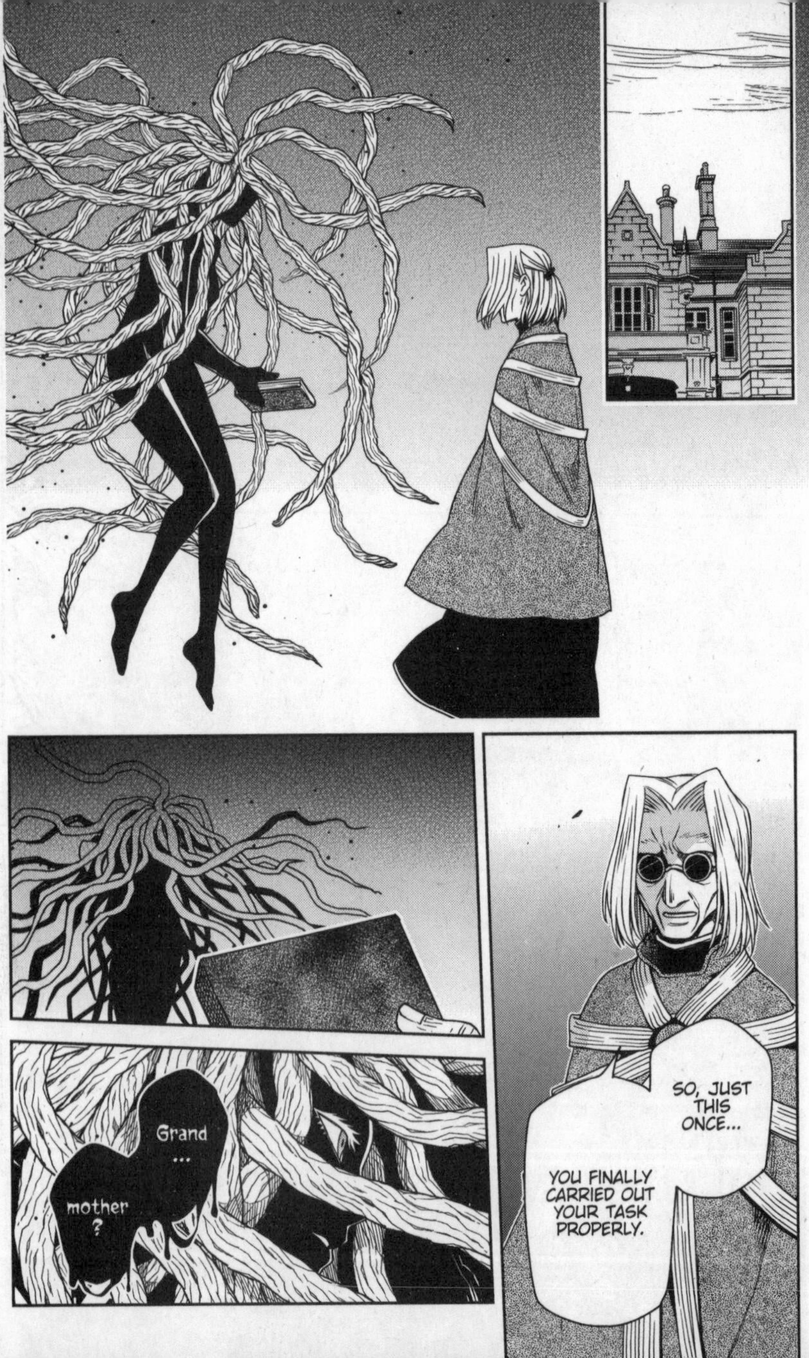
SO, JUST THIS ONCE...
YOU FINALLY CARRIED OUT YOUR TASK PROPERLY.
Grand... mother?

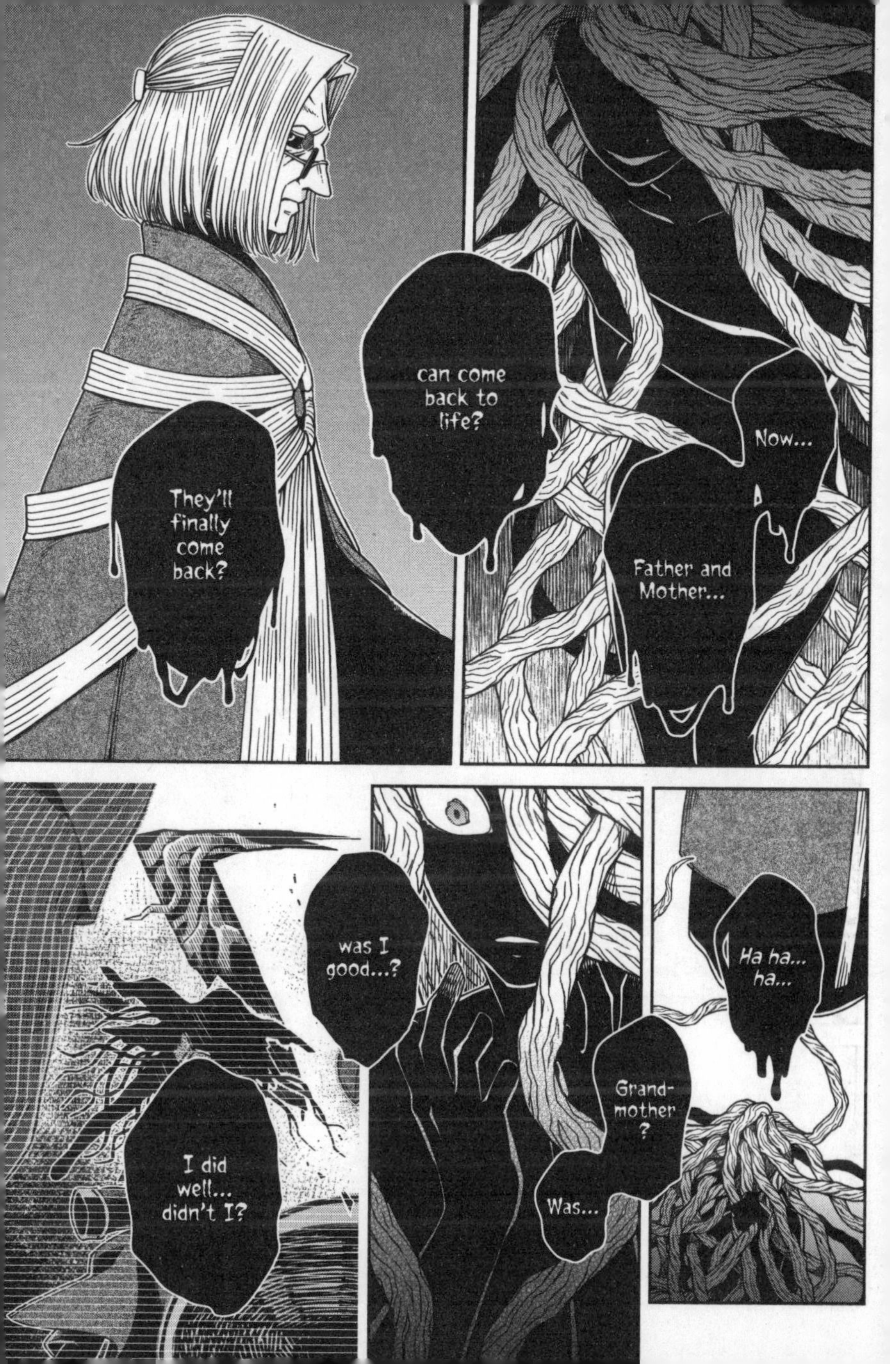
Now...
Father and Mother...
can come back to life?
They'll finally come back?
Ha ha... ha...
Grand-mother?
Was...
was I good...?
I did well... didn't I?

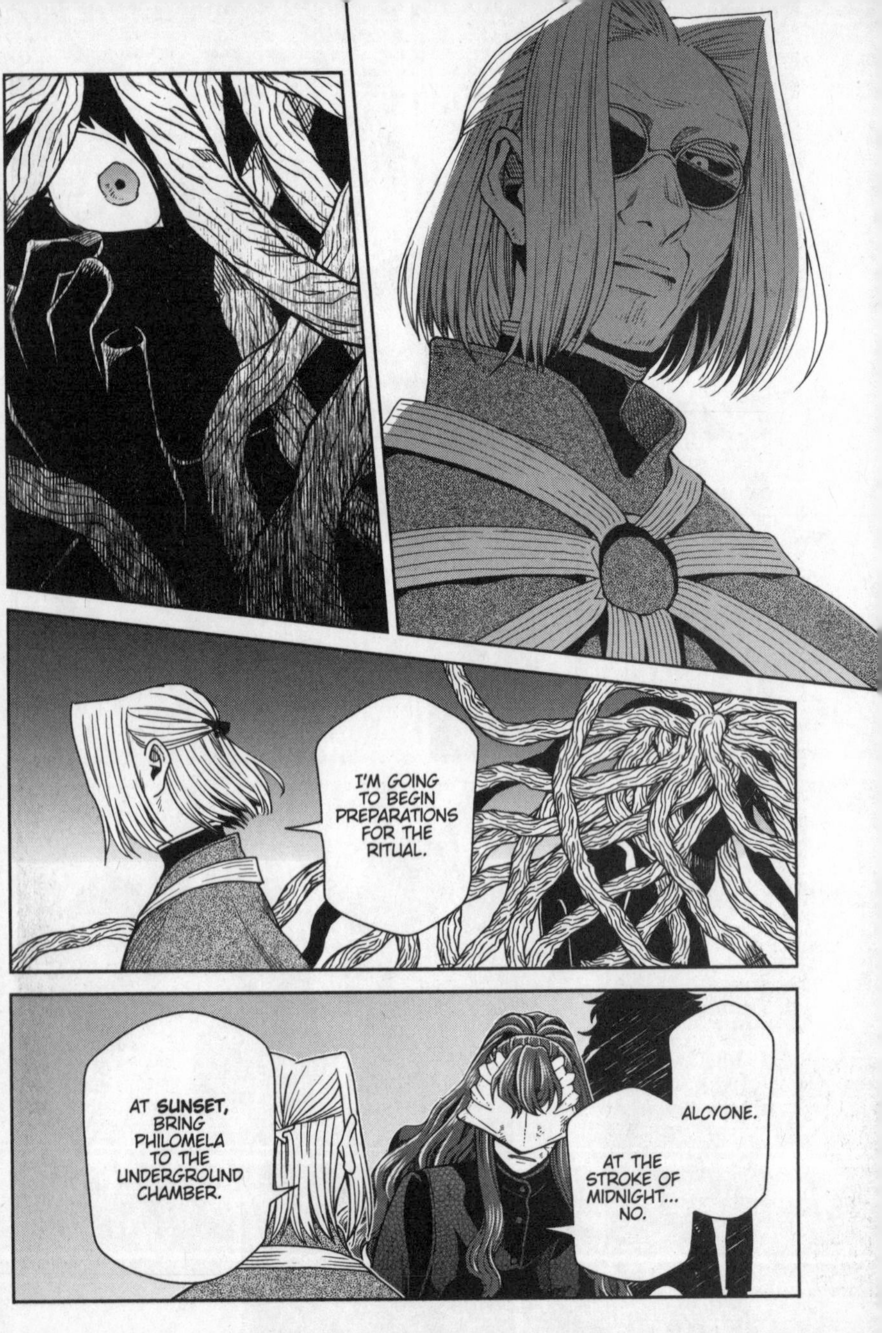
I'M GOING TO BEGIN PREPARATIONS FOR THE RITUAL.
ALCYONE.
AT THE STROKE OF MIDNIGHT... NO.
AT SUNSET, BRING PHILOMELA TO THE UNDERGROUND CHAMBER.

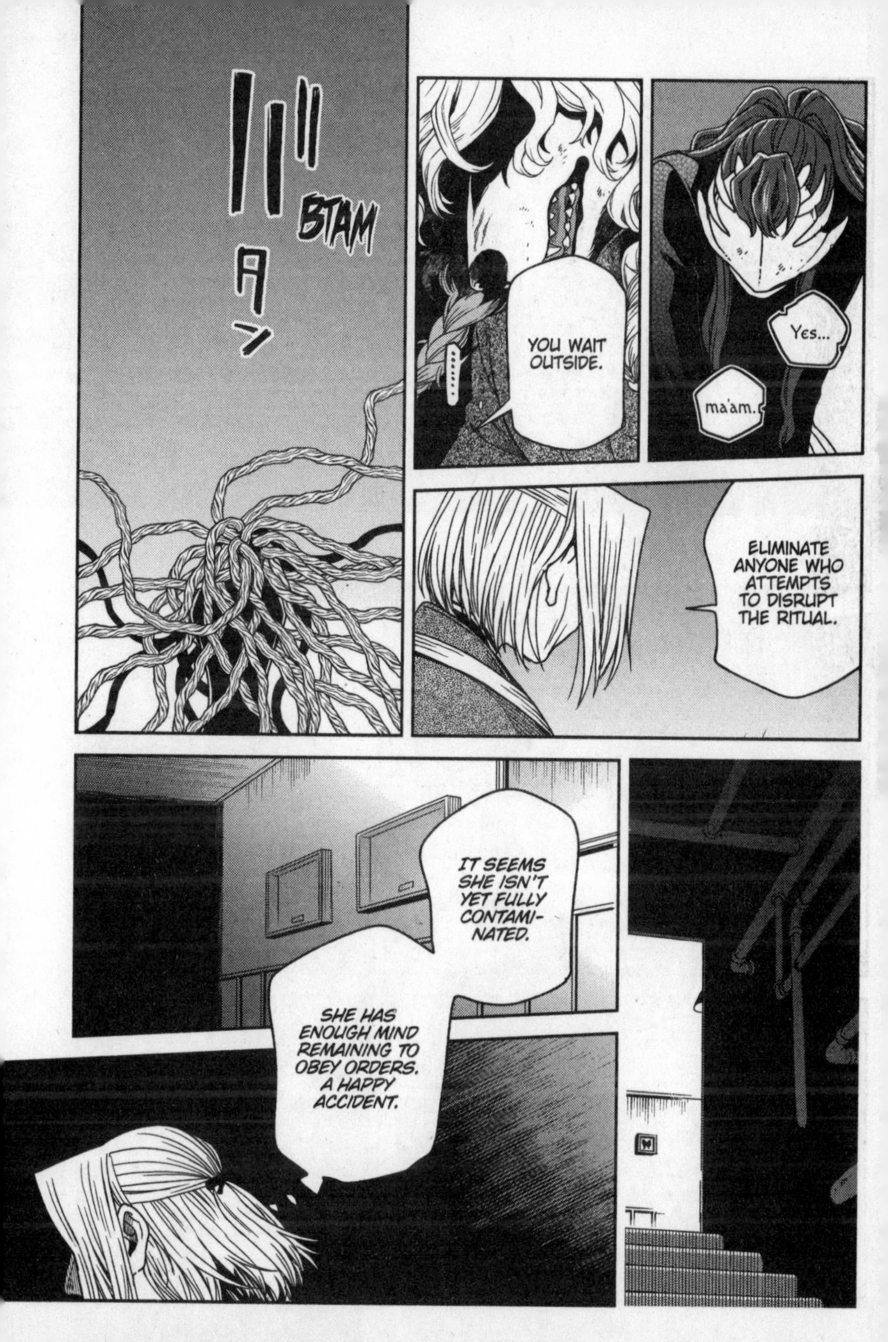
YOU WAIT OUTSIDE.
Yes...
ma'am.
ELIMINATE ANYONE WHO ATTEMPTS TO DISRUPT THE RITUAL.
バタン
BTAM
IT SEEMS SHE ISN'T YET FULLY CONTAMI-NATED.
SHE HAS ENOUGH MIND REMAINING TO OBEY ORDERS. A HAPPY ACCIDENT.

AFTER SO LONG...

I'LL SEE YOU AGAIN...

ADAM.

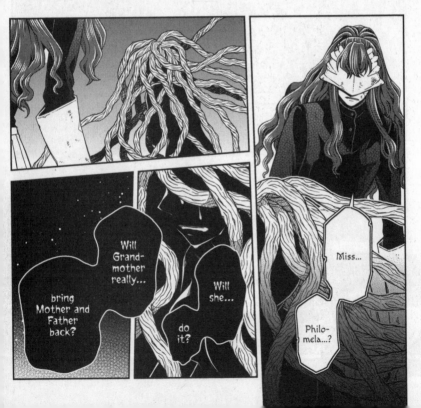

Will Grand-mother really...

Will she...

bring Mother and Father back?

do it?

Miss...

Philo-mela...?

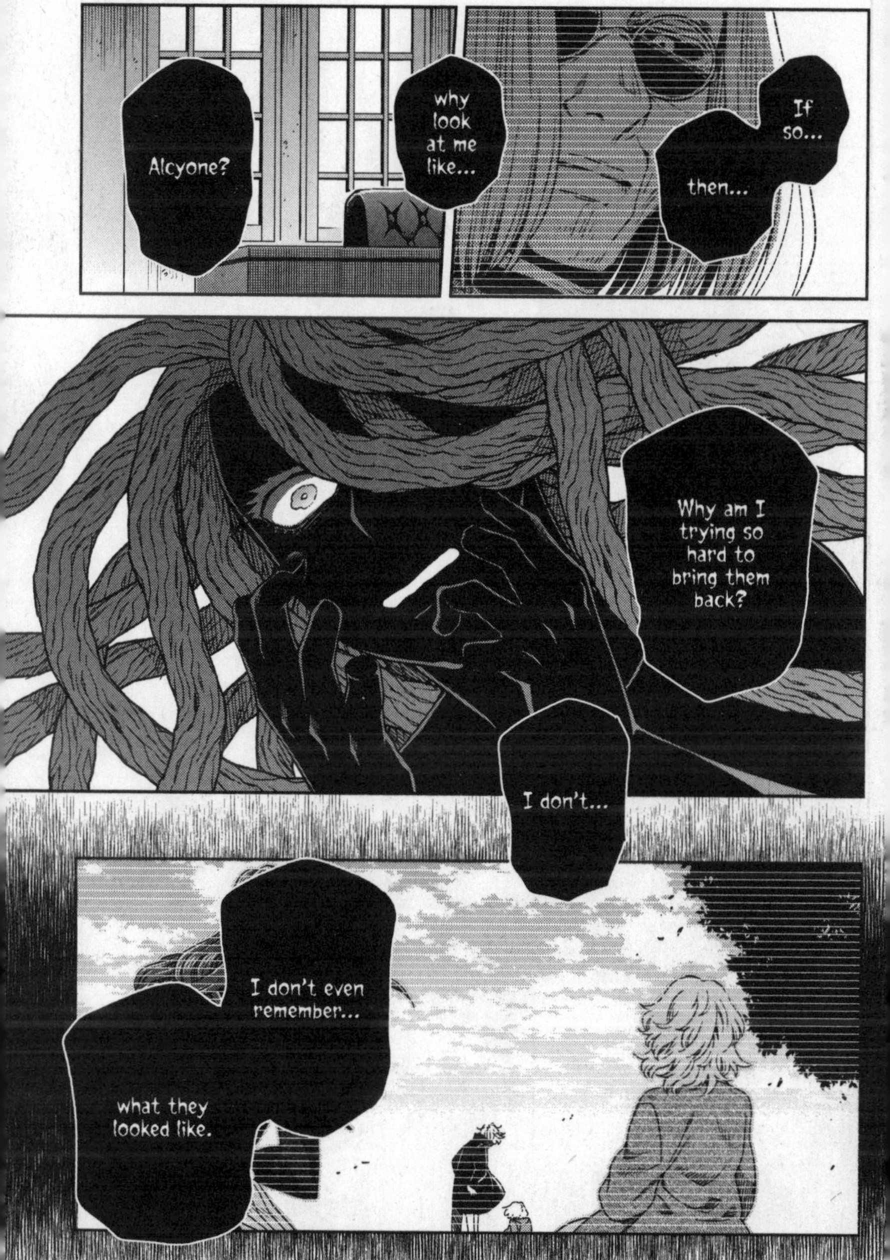
If so...
then...
why look at me like...
Alcyone?
Why am I trying so hard to bring them back?
I don't...
I don't even remember...
what they looked like.

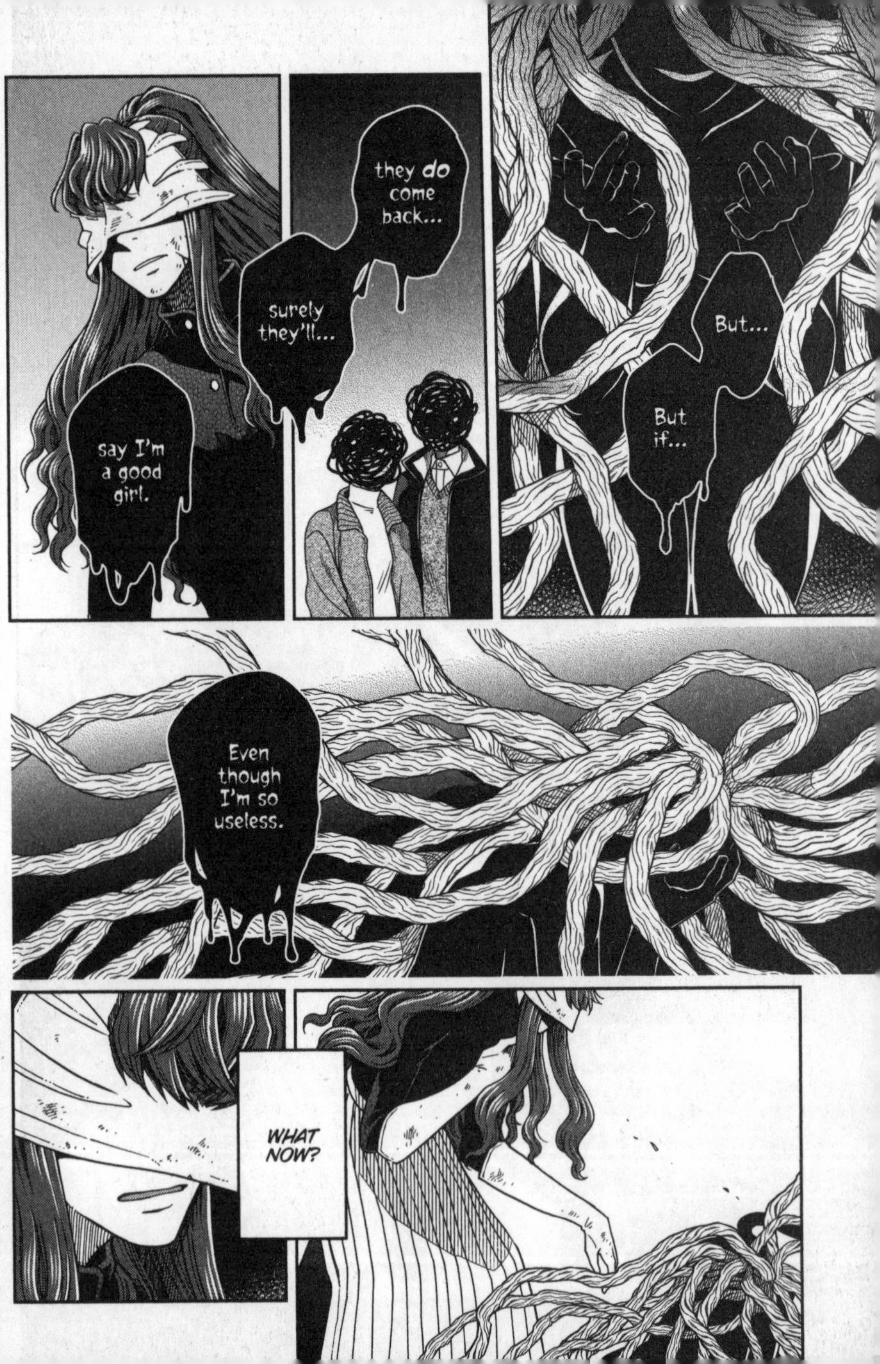

But...
But if...
they do come back...
surely they'll...
say I'm a good girl.
Even though I'm so useless.
WHAT NOW?

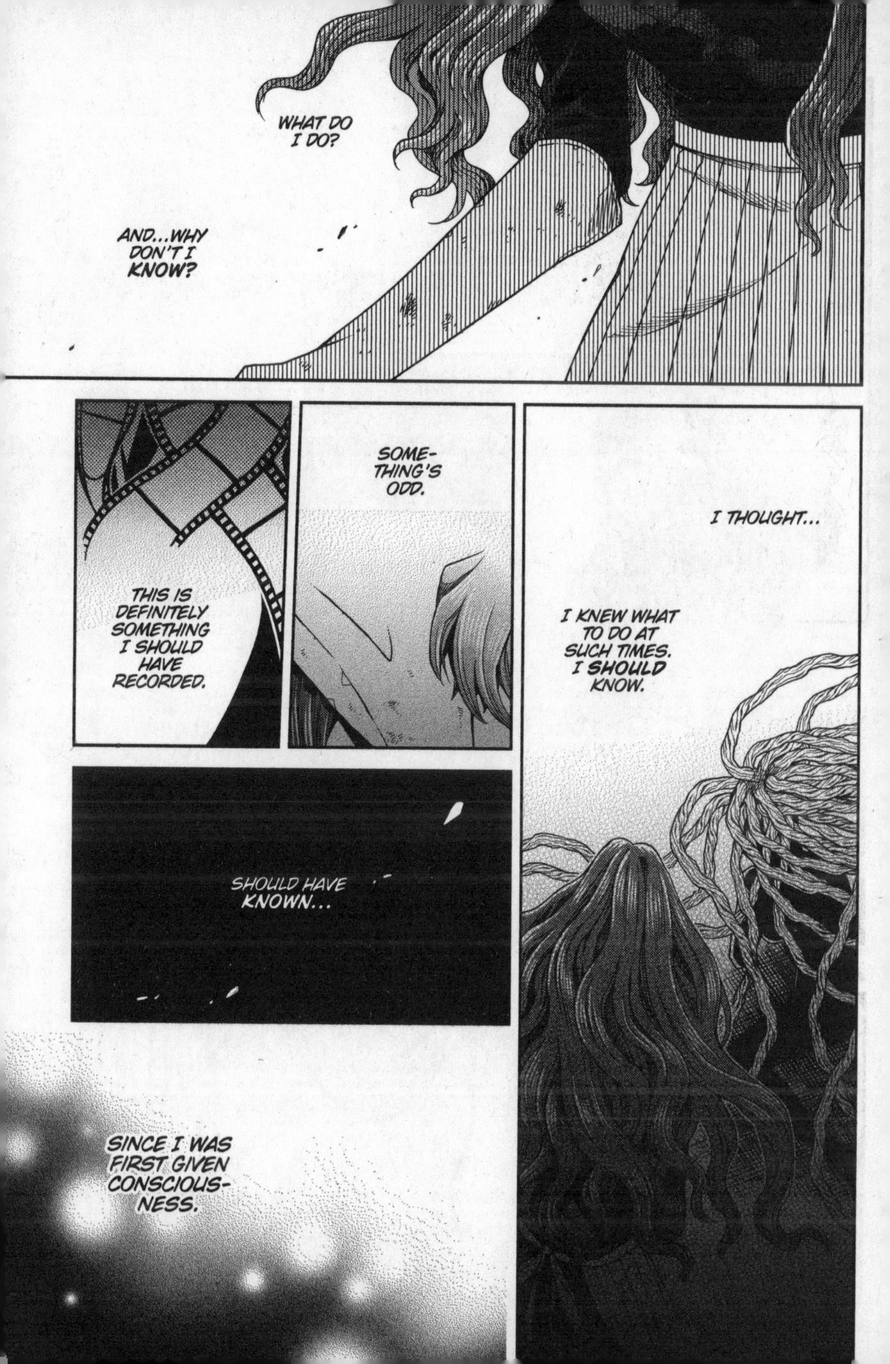
WHAT DO I DO?
AND...WHY DON'T I KNOW?
I THOUGHT...
I KNEW WHAT TO DO AT SUCH TIMES. I SHOULD KNOW.
SOME-THING'S ODD.
THIS IS DEFINITELY SOMETHING I SHOULD HAVE RECORDED.
SHOULD HAVE KNOWN...
SINCE I WAS FIRST GIVEN CONSCIOUS-NESS.

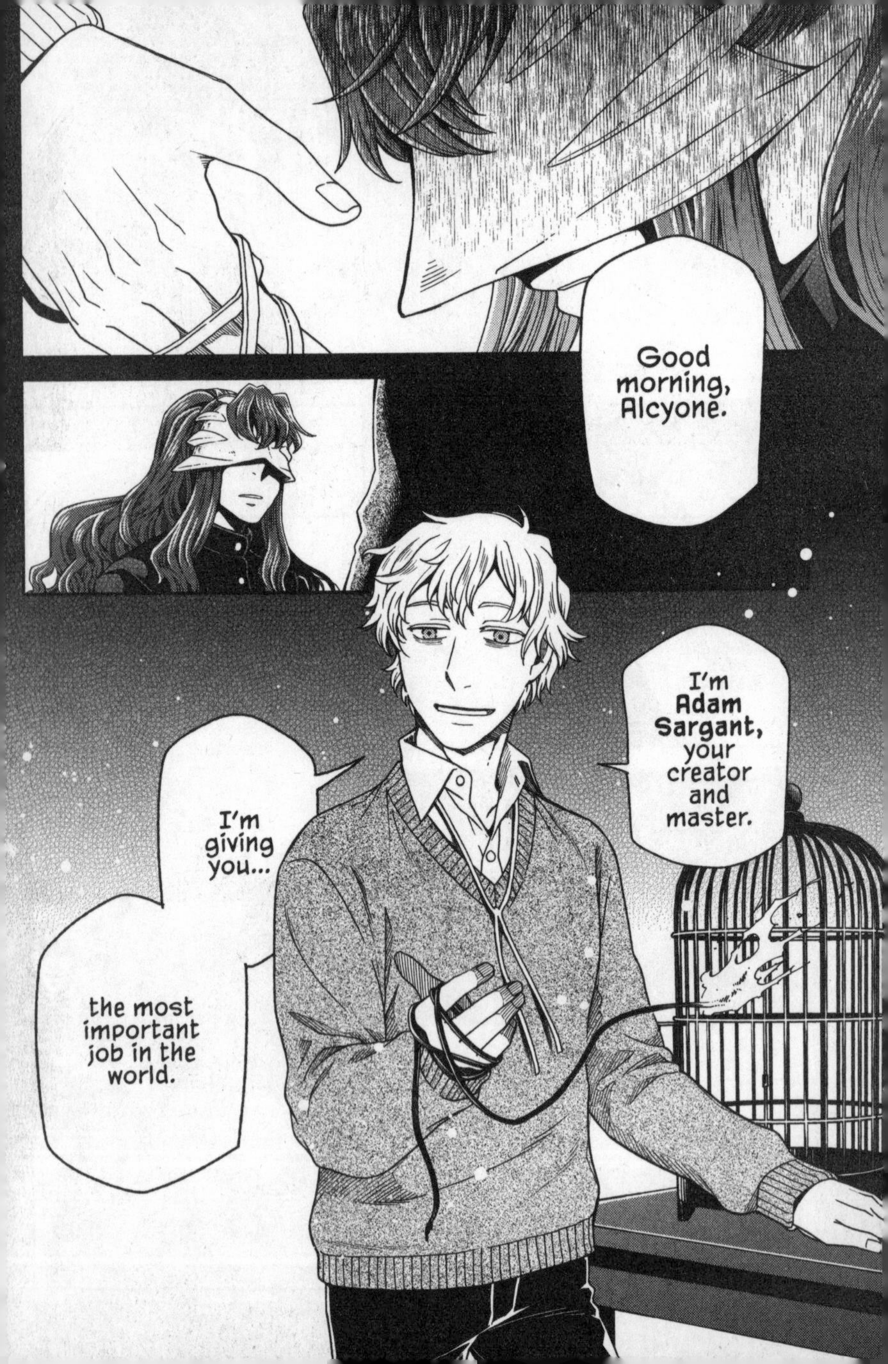
Good morning, Alcyone.
I'm Adam Sargant, your creator and master.
I'm giving you...
the most important job in the world.

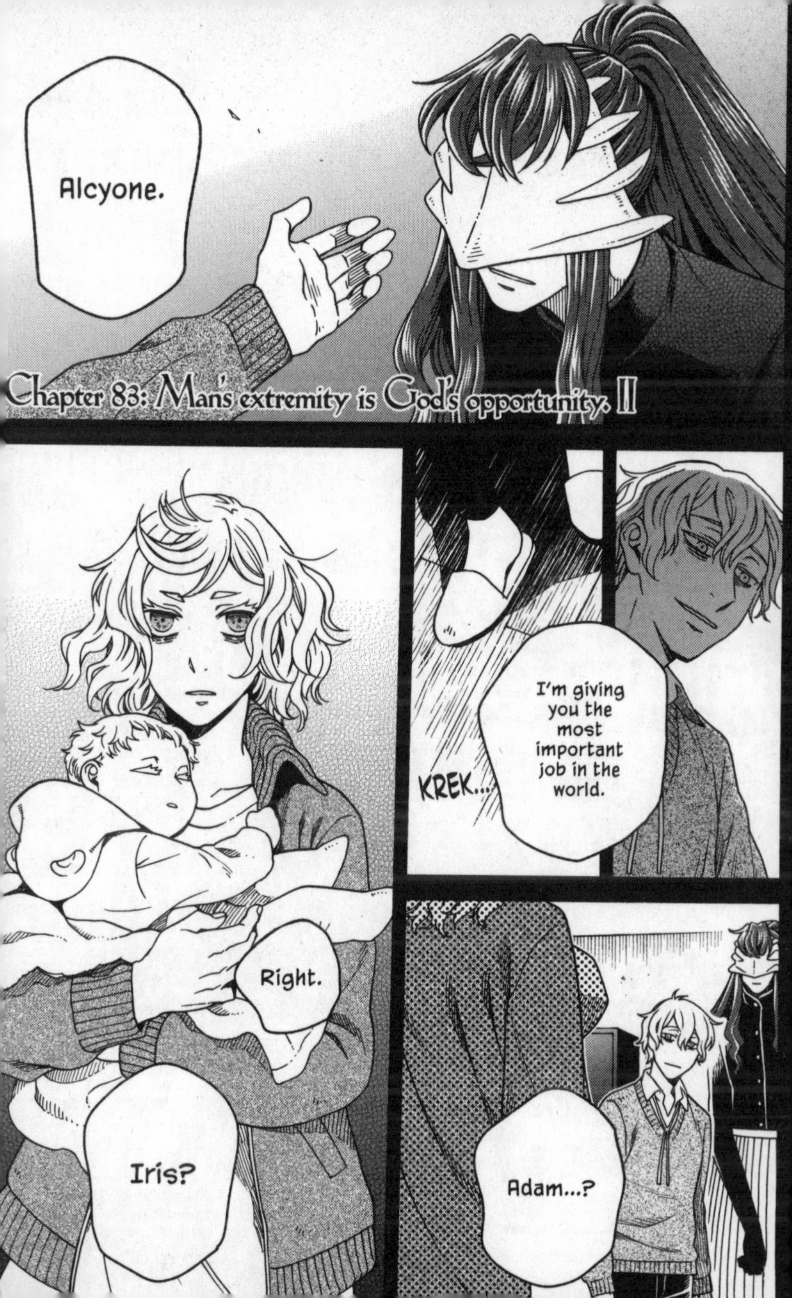
Alcyone.
Chapter 83: Man's extremity is God's opportunity. II
I'm giving you the most important job in the world.
KREK...
Right.
Iris?
Adam...?

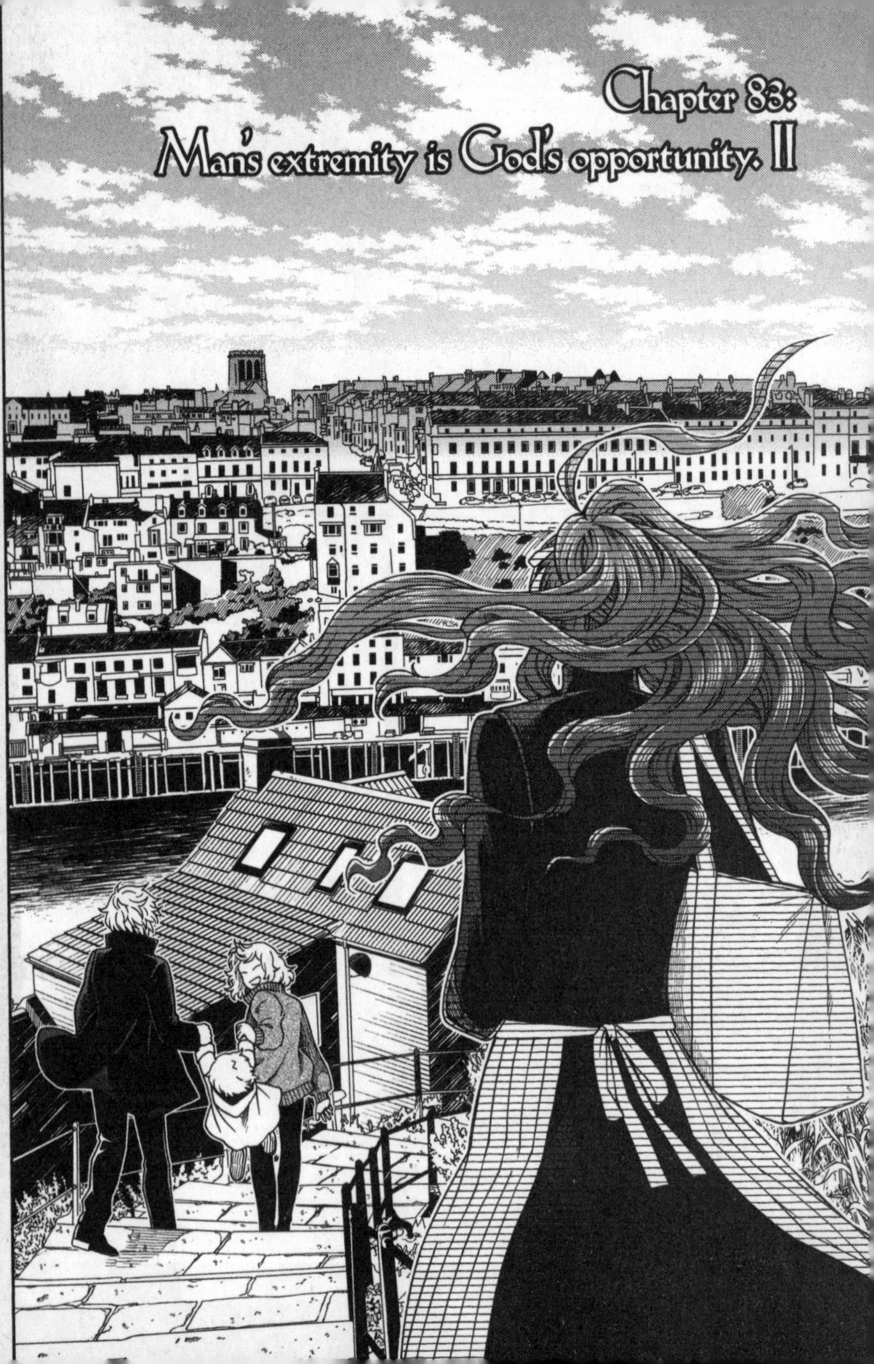

Chapter 83:
Man's extremity is God's opportunity. II

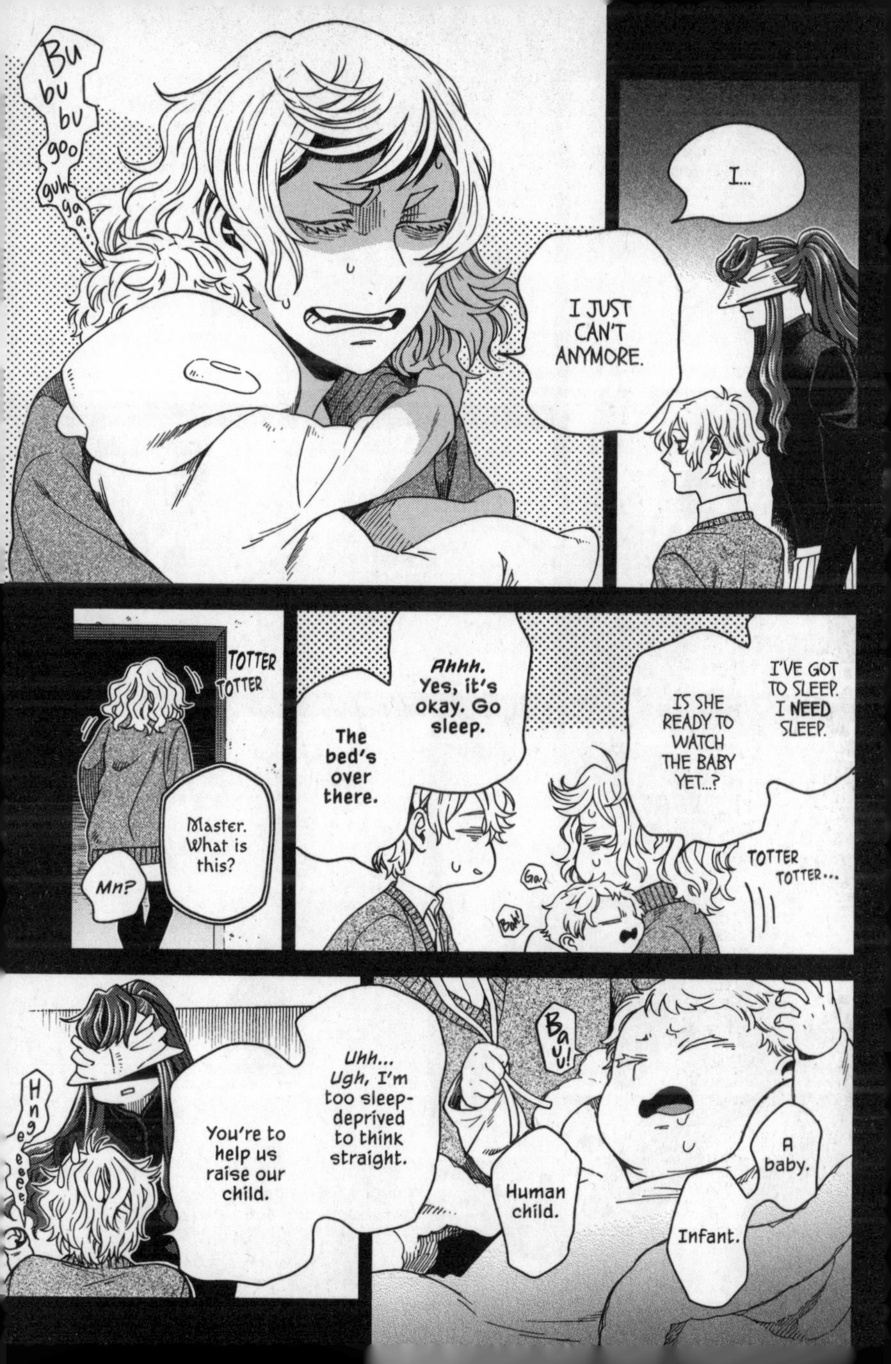
I...
Bu bu bu goo guh gaa...
I JUST CAN'T ANYMORE.
I'VE GOT TO SLEEP. I NEED SLEEP.
IS SHE READY TO WATCH THE BABY YET...?
TOTTER TOTTER...
Ahhh. Yes, it's okay. Go sleep.
The bed's over there.
TOTTER TOTTER
Master. What is this?
Mn?
Bau!
A baby.
Infant.
Human child.
Uhh... Ugh, I'm too sleep-deprived to think straight.
You're to help us raise our child.
Hngeeeee

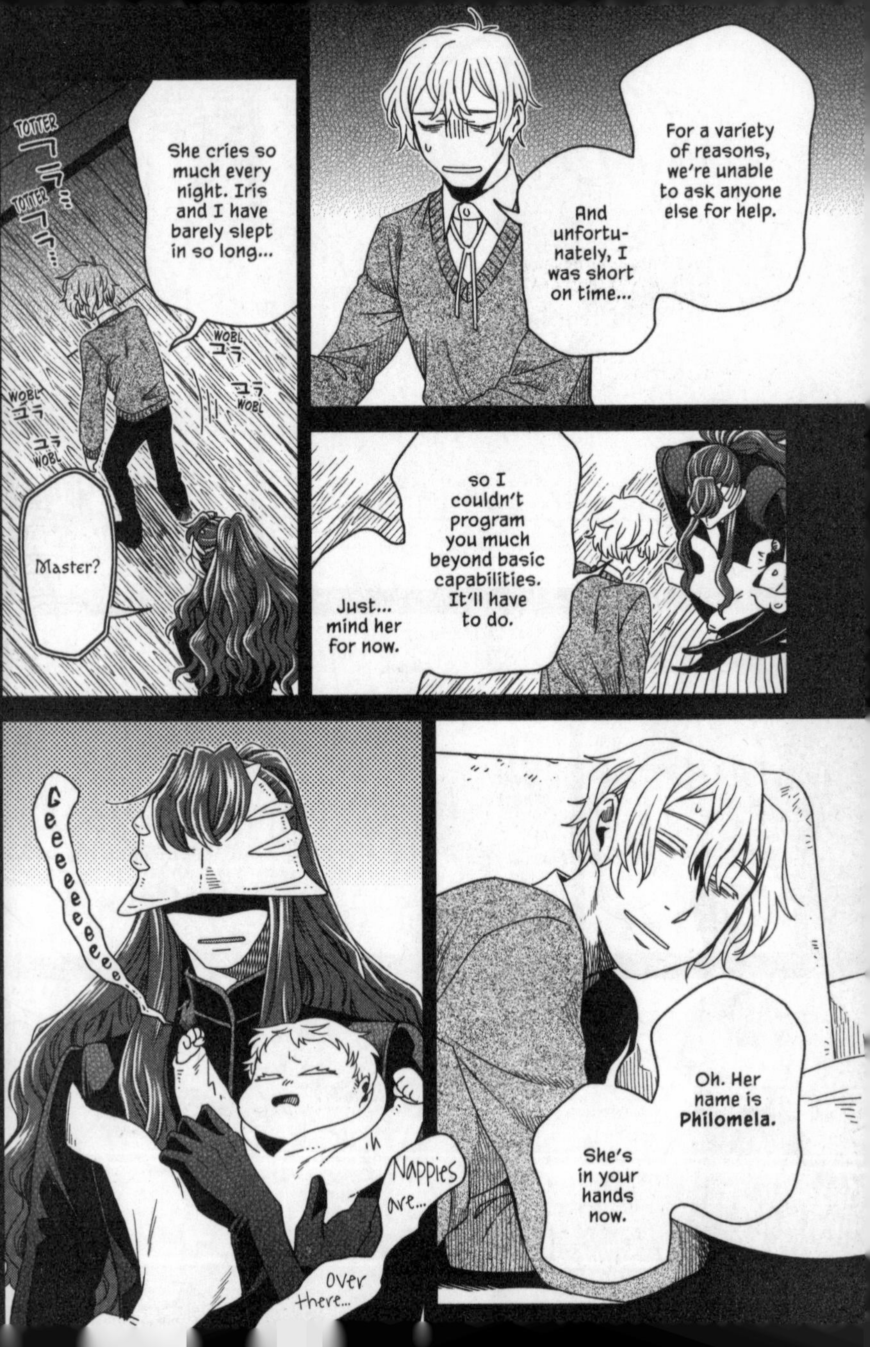
For a variety of reasons, we're unable to ask anyone else for help.
And unfortu-nately, I was short on time...
so I couldn't program you much beyond basic capabilities. It'll have to do.
Just... mind her for now.
She cries so much every night. Iris and I have barely slept in so long...
TOTTER
TOTTER
WOBL
WOBL
WOBL
WOBL
Master?
Oh. Her name is Philomela.
She's in your hands now.
Geeeeeeeeeee
Nappies are...
over there...

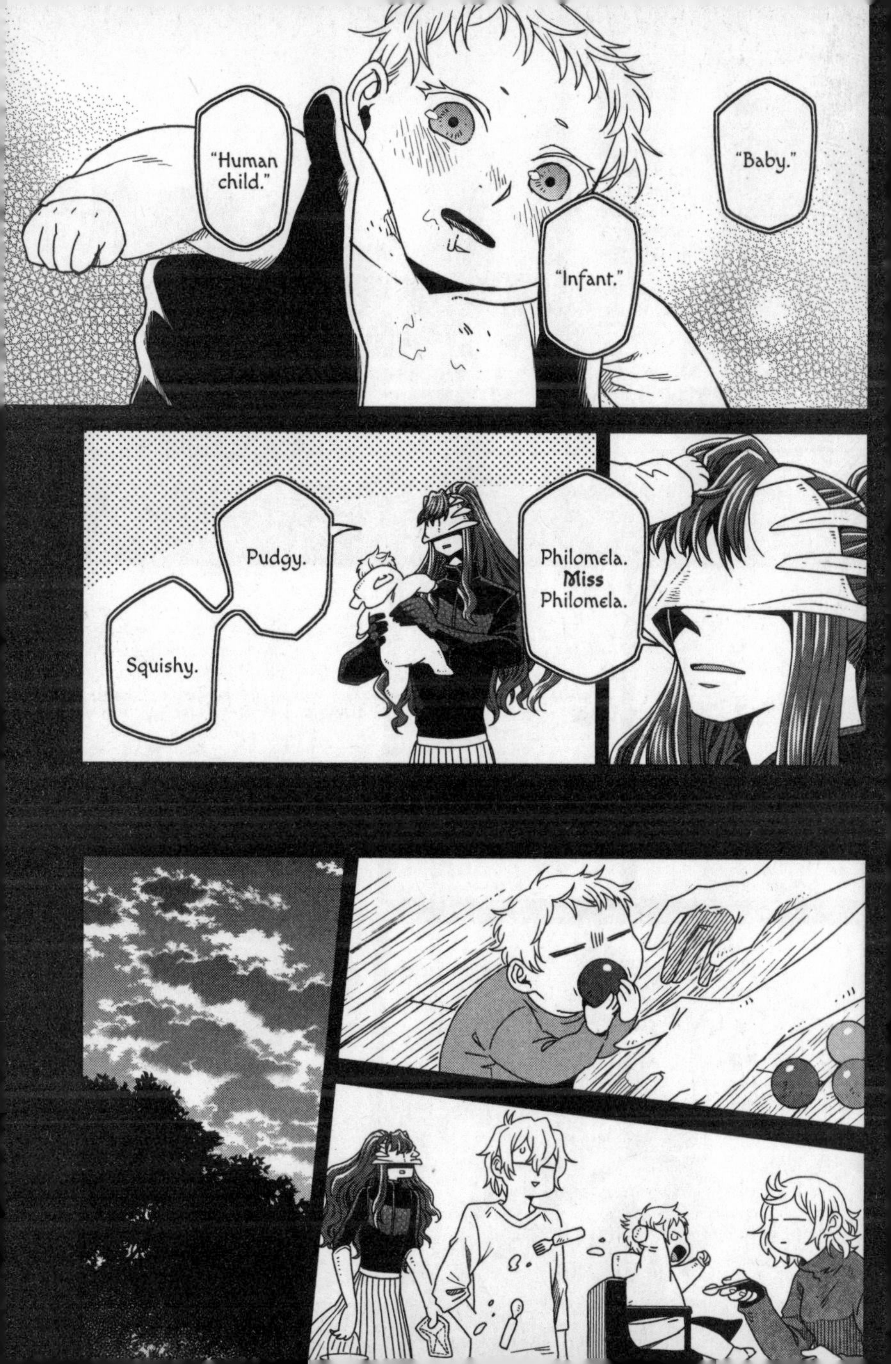
"Baby."
"Infant."
"Human child."
Philomela. Miss Philomela.
Pudgy.
Squishy.

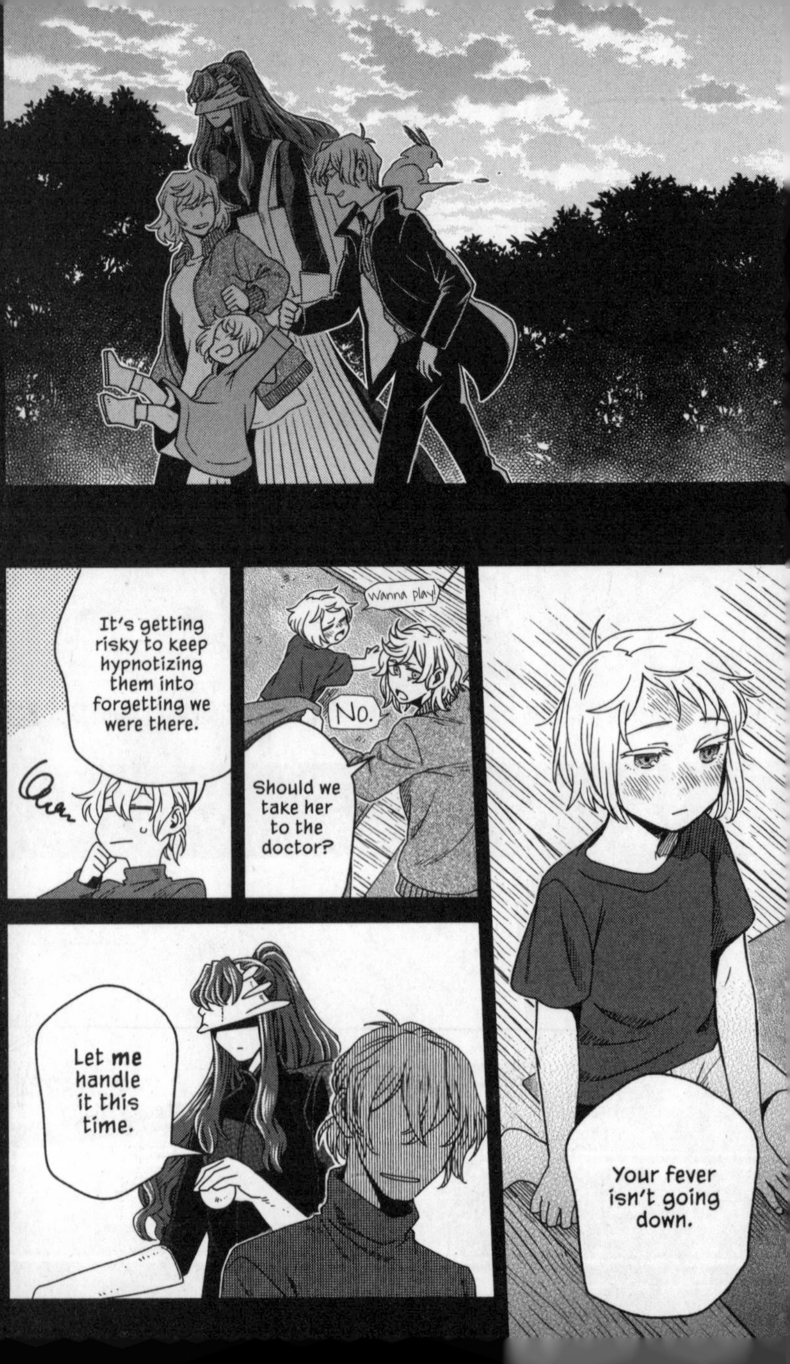
Your fever isn't going down.
Wanna play!
No.
Should we take her to the doctor?
It's getting risky to keep hypnotizing them into forgetting we were there.
Let me handle it this time.

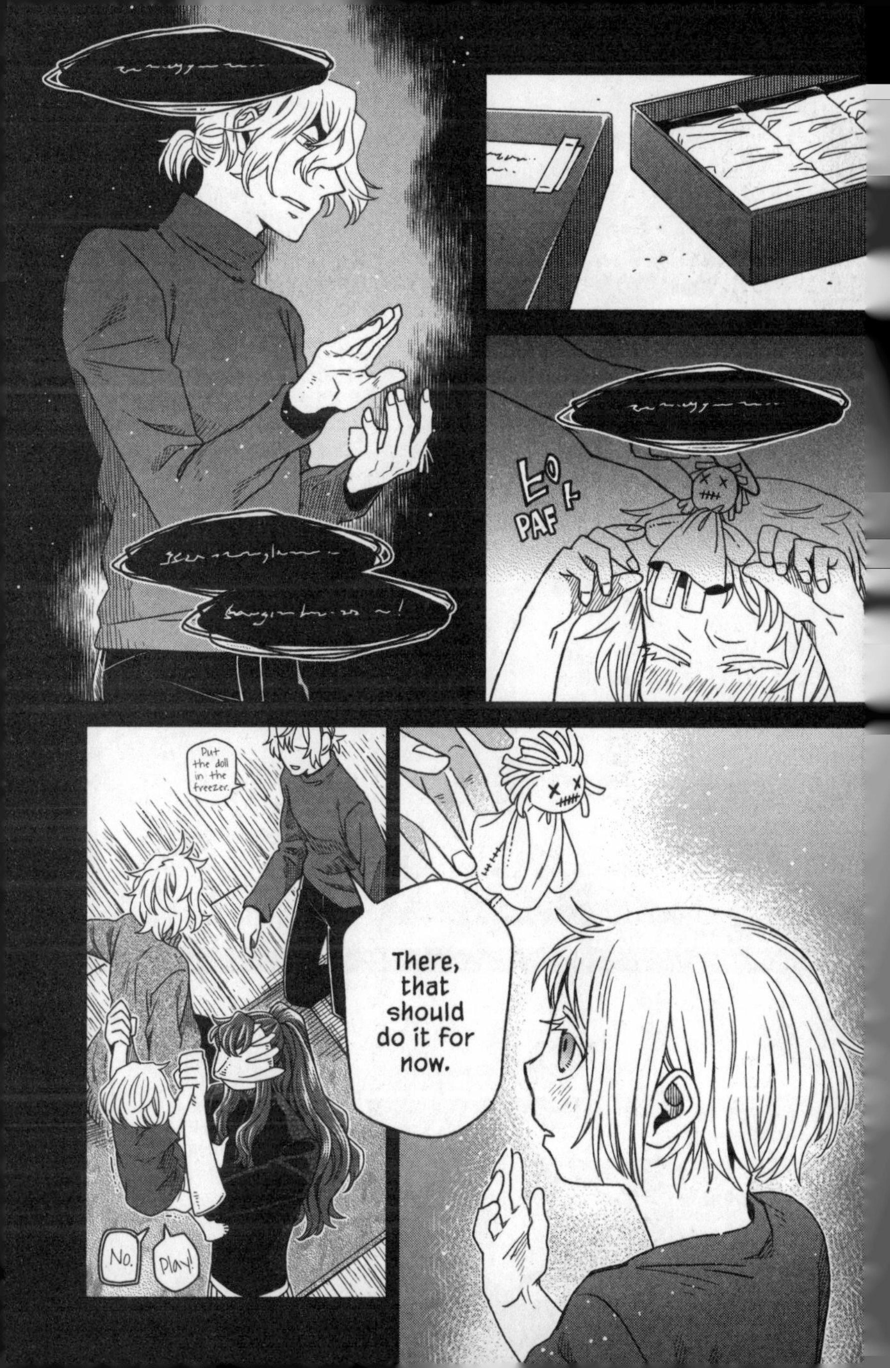

PAF
Put the doll in the freezer.
No.
Play!
There, that should do it for now.

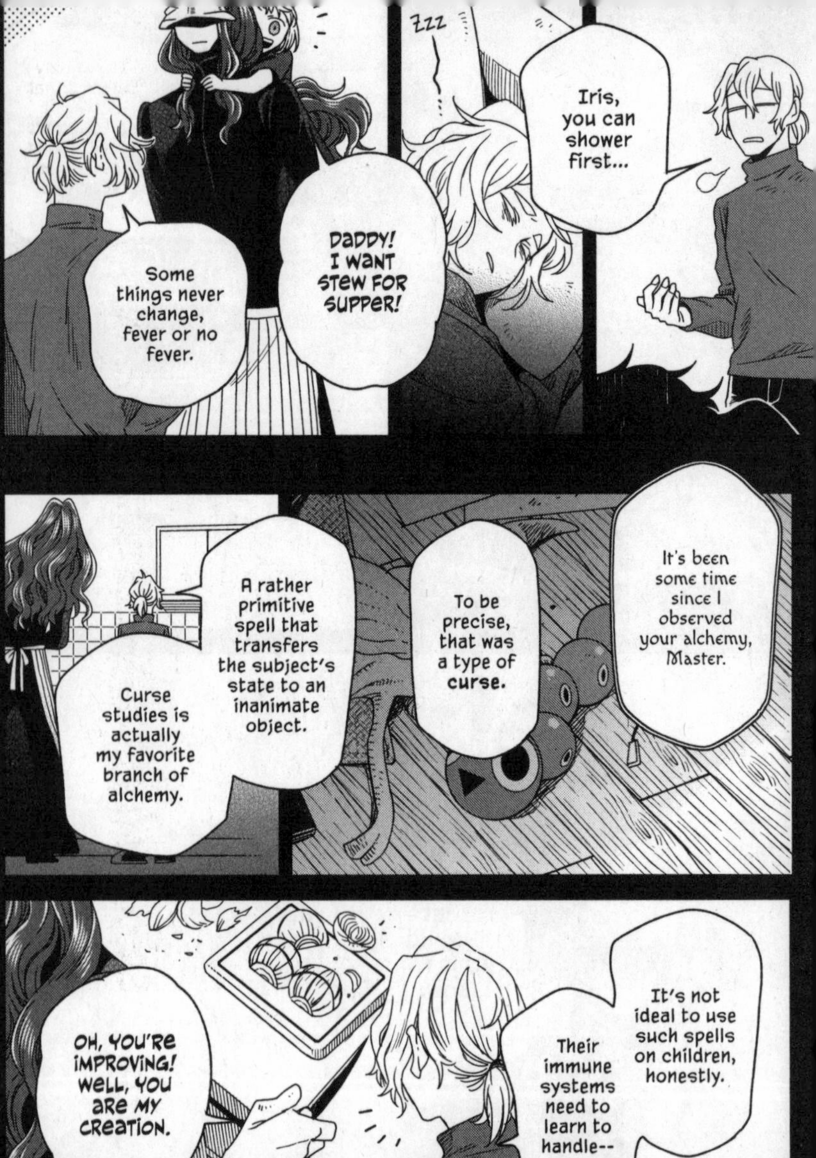

Iris, you can shower first...
Zzz
DADDY! I WANT STEW FOR SUPPER!
Some things never change, fever or no fever.
It's been some time since I observed your alchemy, Master.
To be precise, that was a type of **curse**.
A rather primitive spell that transfers the subject's state to an inanimate object.
Curse studies is actually my favorite branch of alchemy.
It's not ideal to use such spells on children, honestly.
Their immune systems need to learn to handle--
OH, YOU'RE IMPROVING! WELL, YOU ARE MY CREATION.

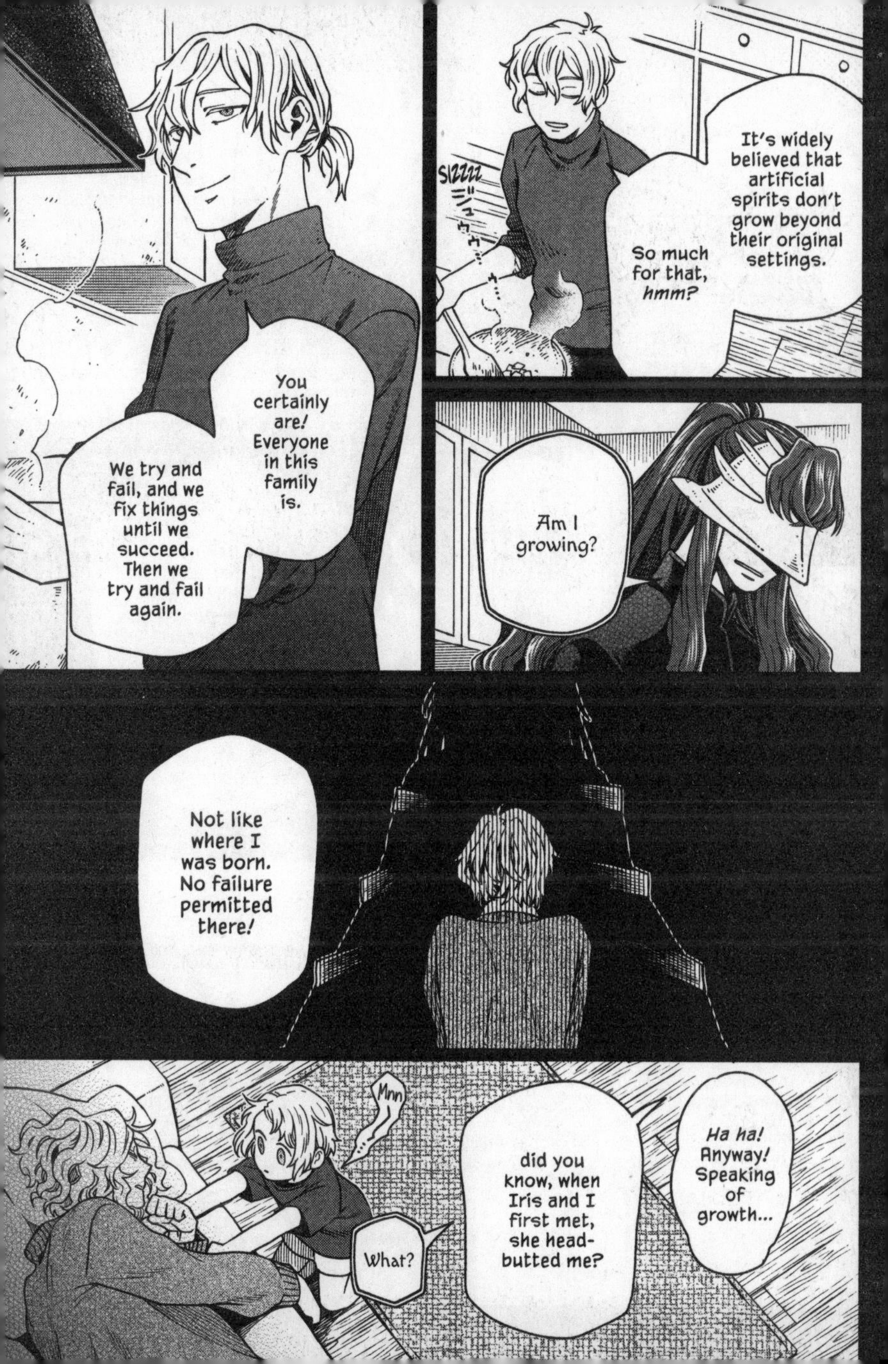
It's widely believed that artificial spirits don't grow beyond their original settings.
So much for that, *hmm?*
SIZZZZZ
ジュウウ…ウ…
Am I growing?
You certainly are! Everyone in this family is.
We try and fail, and we fix things until we succeed. Then we try and fail again.
Not like where I was born. No failure permitted there!
Ha ha! Anyway! Speaking of growth...
did you know, when Iris and I first met, she head-butted me?
What?
Mnn

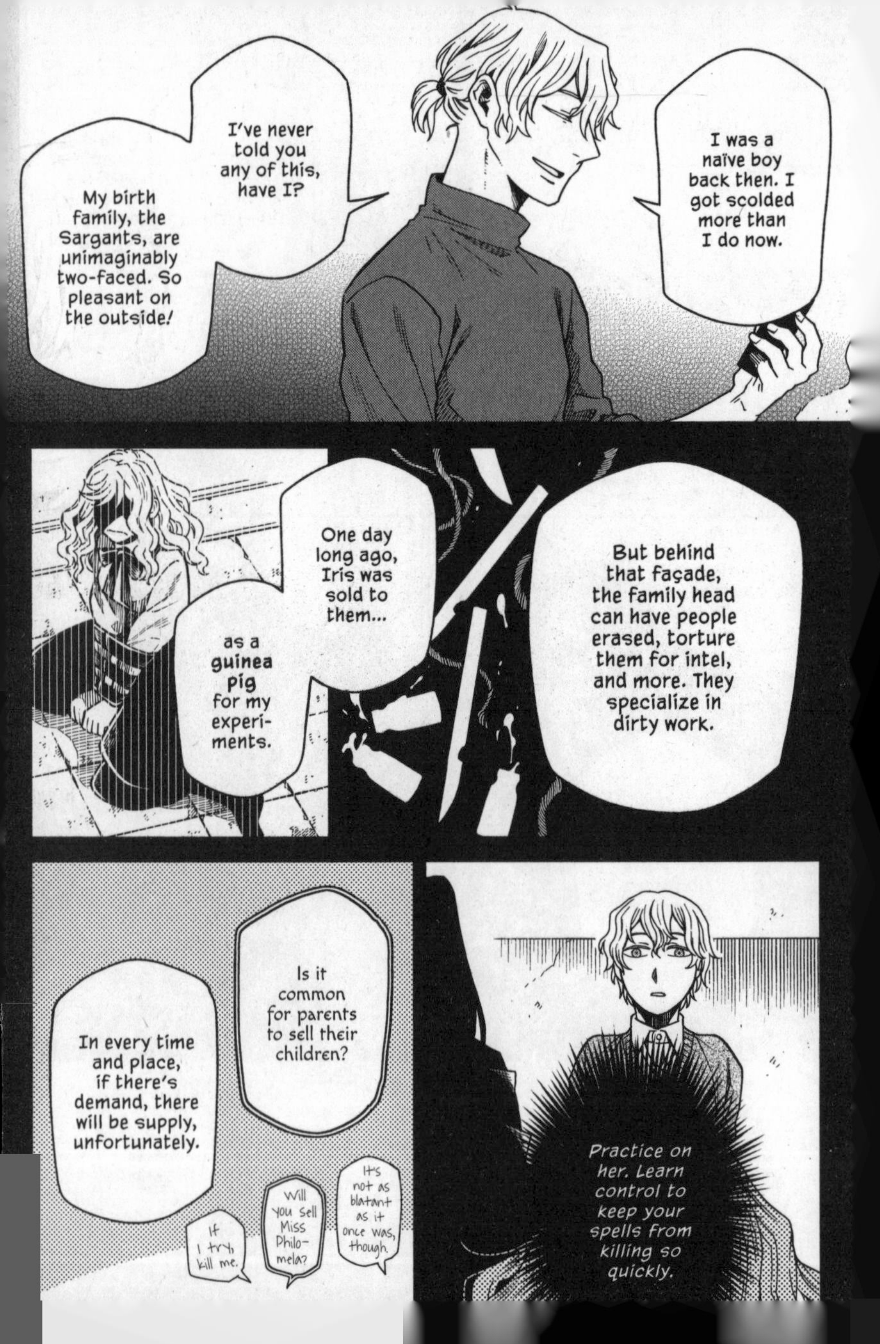
I was a naïve boy back then. I got scolded more than I do now.
I've never told you any of this, have I?
My birth family, the Sargants, are unimaginably two-faced. So pleasant on the outside!
But behind that façade, the family head can have people erased, torture them for intel, and more. They specialize in dirty work.
One day long ago, Iris was sold to them...
as a guinea pig for my experi-ments.
Practice on her. Learn control to keep your spells from killing so quickly.
Is it common for parents to sell their children?
In every time and place, if there's demand, there will be supply, unfortunately.
It's not as blatant as it once was, though.
Will you sell Miss Philo-mela?
If I try, kill me.

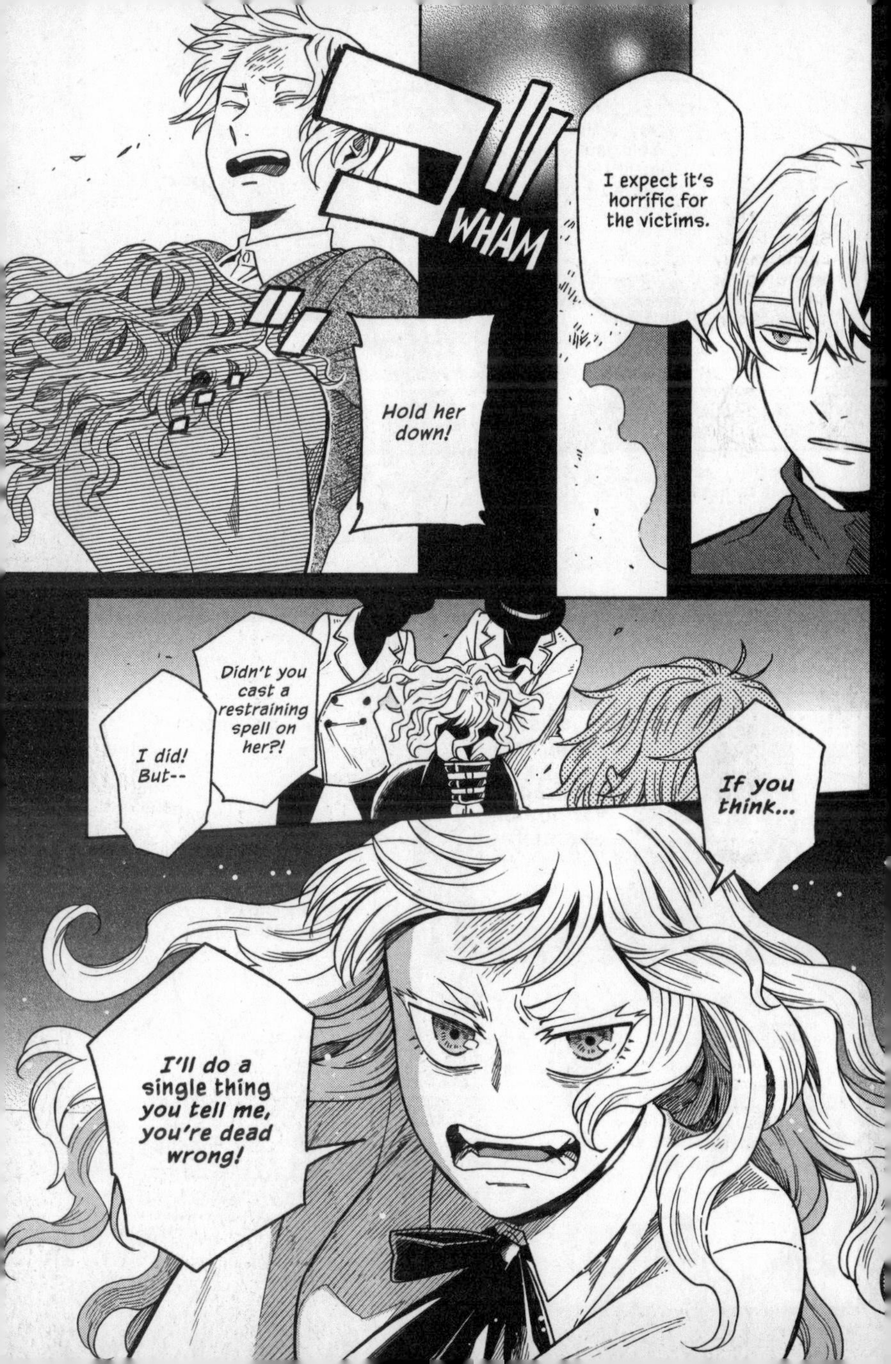
I expect it's horrific for the victims.
WHAM
Hold her down!
Didn't you cast a restraining spell on her?!
I did! But--
If you think...
I'll do a single thing you tell me, you're dead wrong!

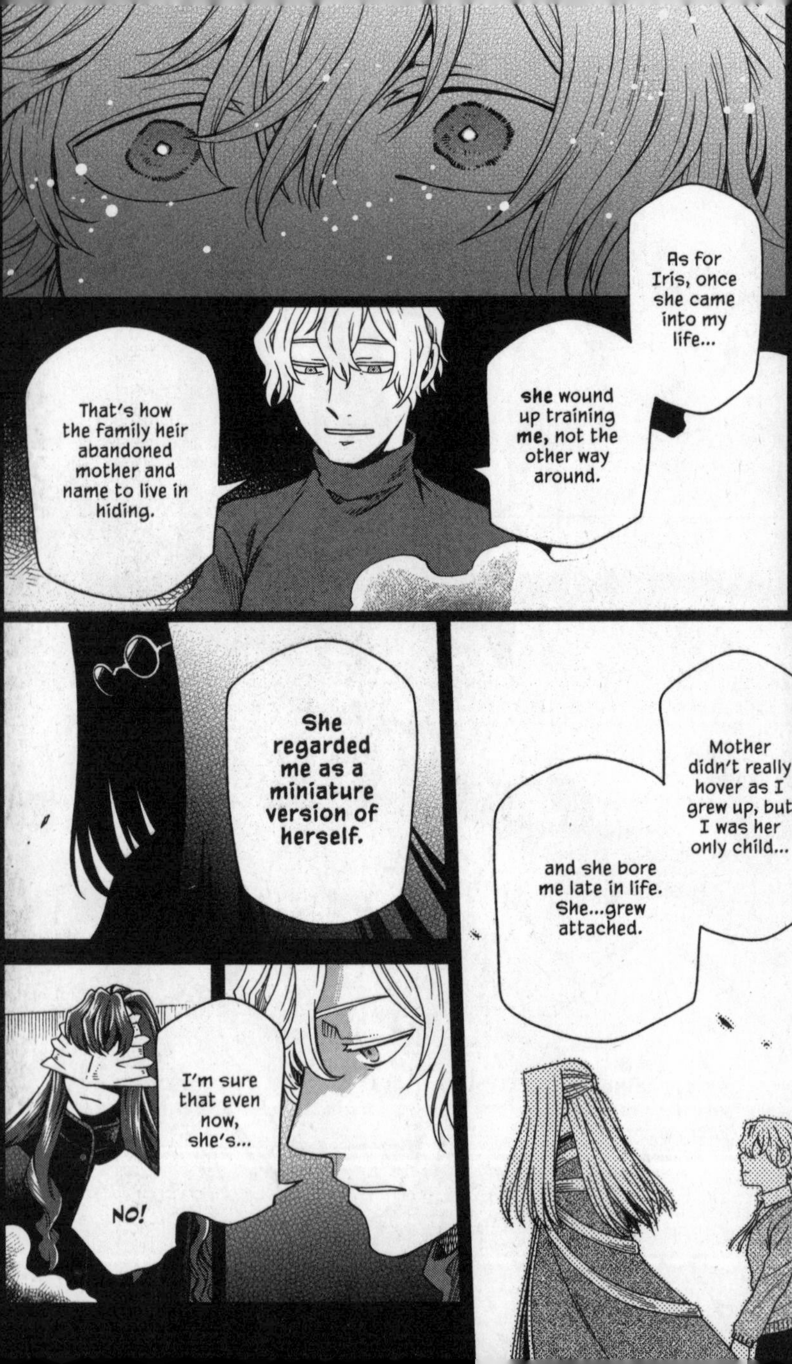
As for Iris, once she came into my life...
she wound up training me, not the other way around.
That's how the family heir abandoned mother and name to live in hiding.
Mother didn't really hover as I grew up, but I was her only child...
and she bore me late in life. She...grew attached.
She regarded me as a miniature version of herself.
I'm sure that even now, she's...
NO!

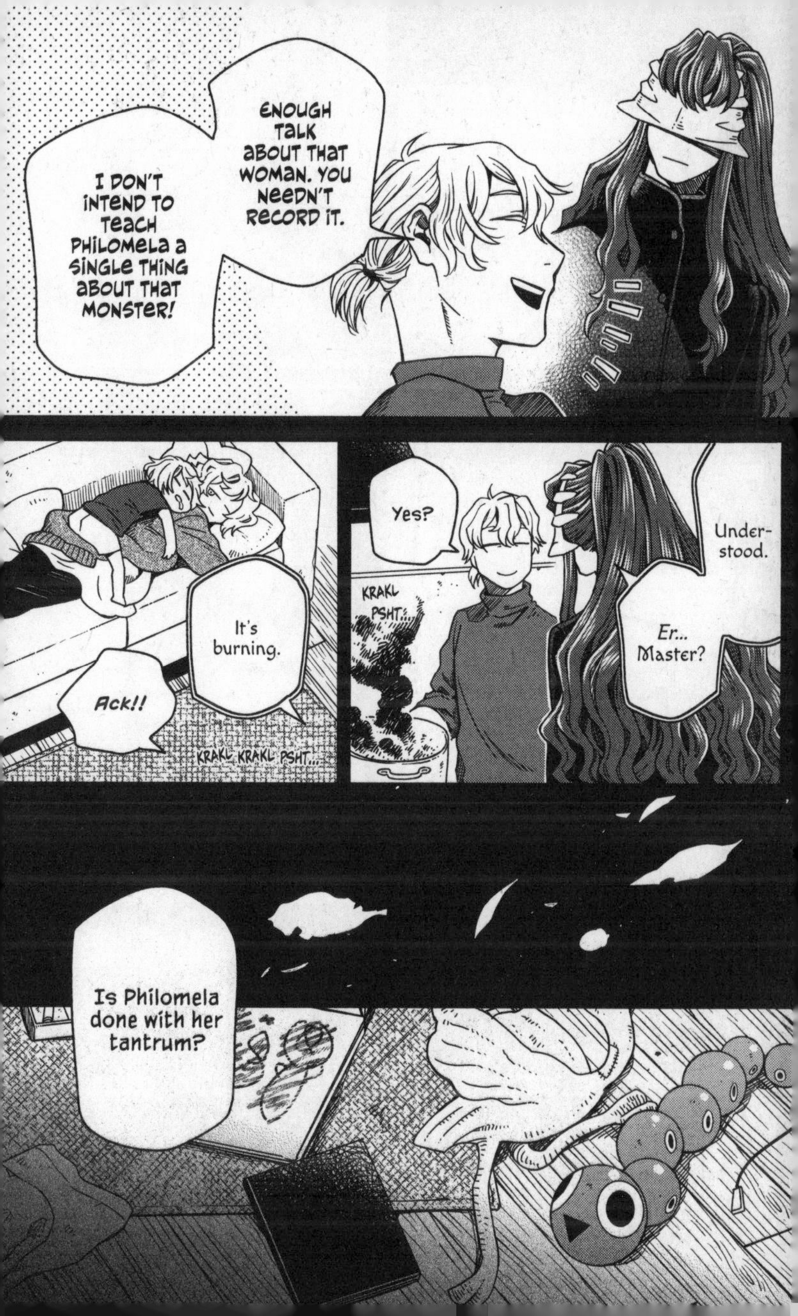
ENOUGH TALK ABOUT THAT WOMAN. YOU NEEDN'T RECORD IT.
I DON'T INTEND TO TEACH PHILOMELA A SINGLE THING ABOUT THAT MONSTER!
Understood.
Er... Master?
Yes?
KRAKL PSHT...
It's burning.
Ack!!
KRAKL KRAKL PSHT...
Is Philomela done with her tantrum?

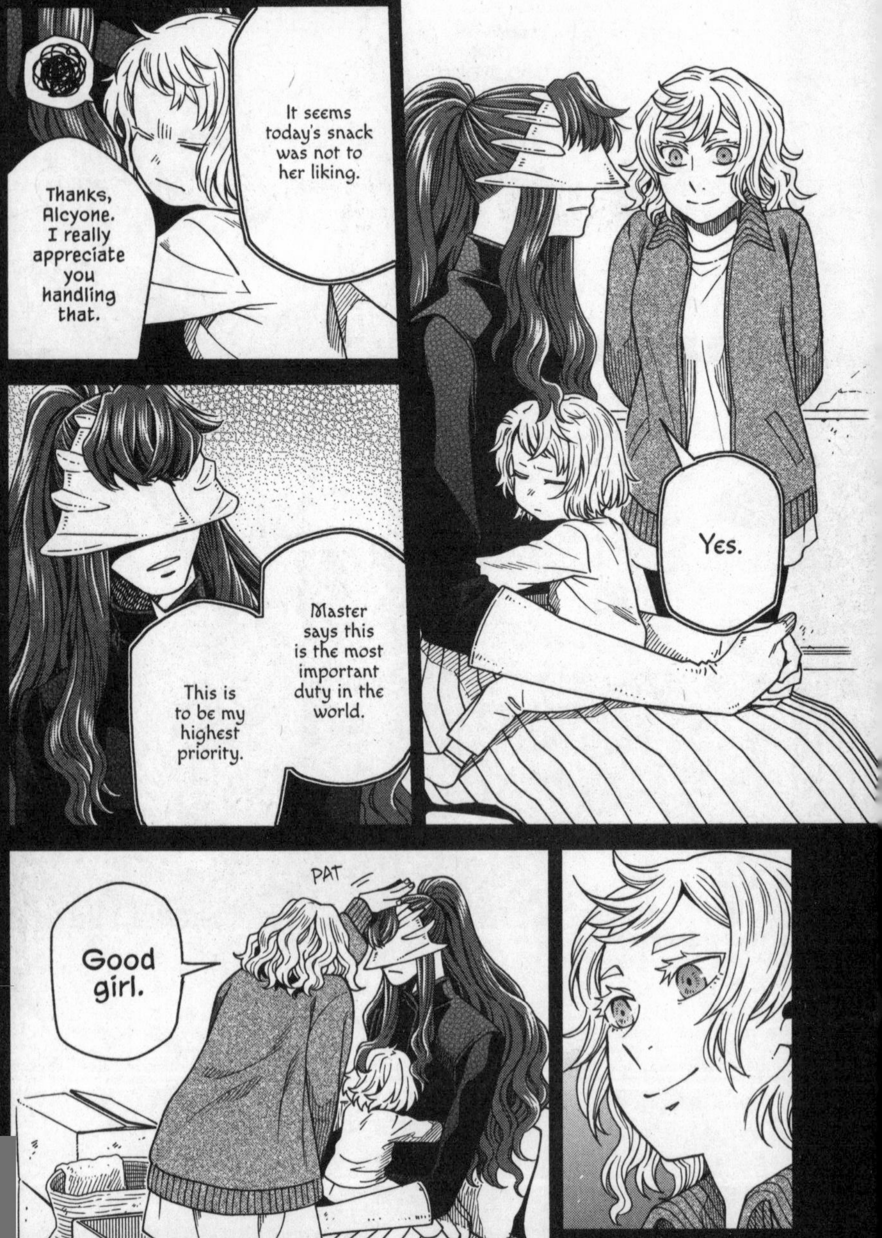
Yes.
It seems today's snack was not to her liking.
Thanks, Alcyone. I really appreciate you handling that.
Master says this is the most important duty in the world.
This is to be my highest priority.
PAT
Good girl.

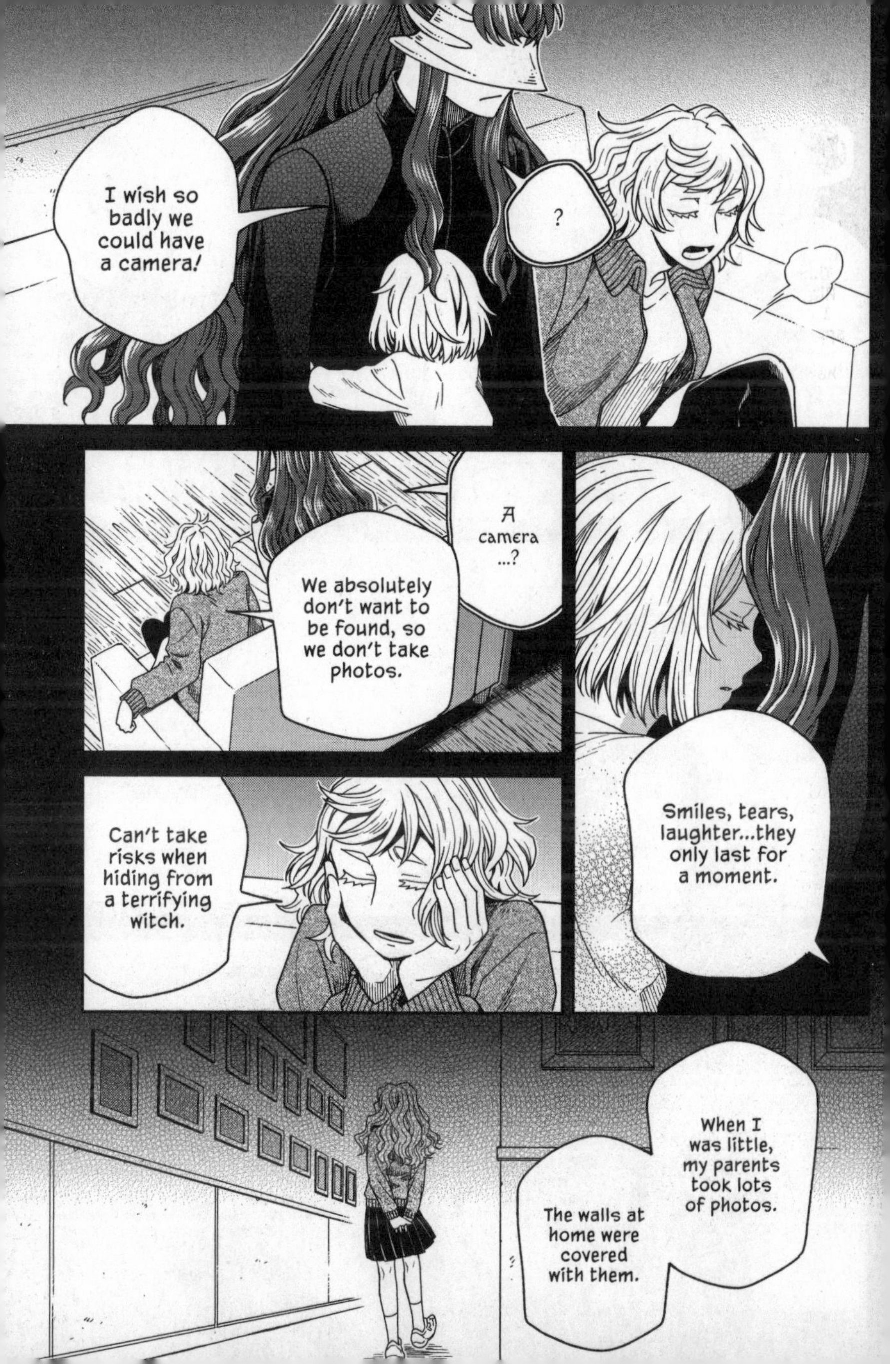
I wish so badly we could have a camera!
?
A camera ...?
We absolutely don't want to be found, so we don't take photos.
Can't take risks when hiding from a terrifying witch.
Smiles, tears, laughter...they only last for a moment.
When I was little, my parents took lots of photos.
The walls at home were covered with them.

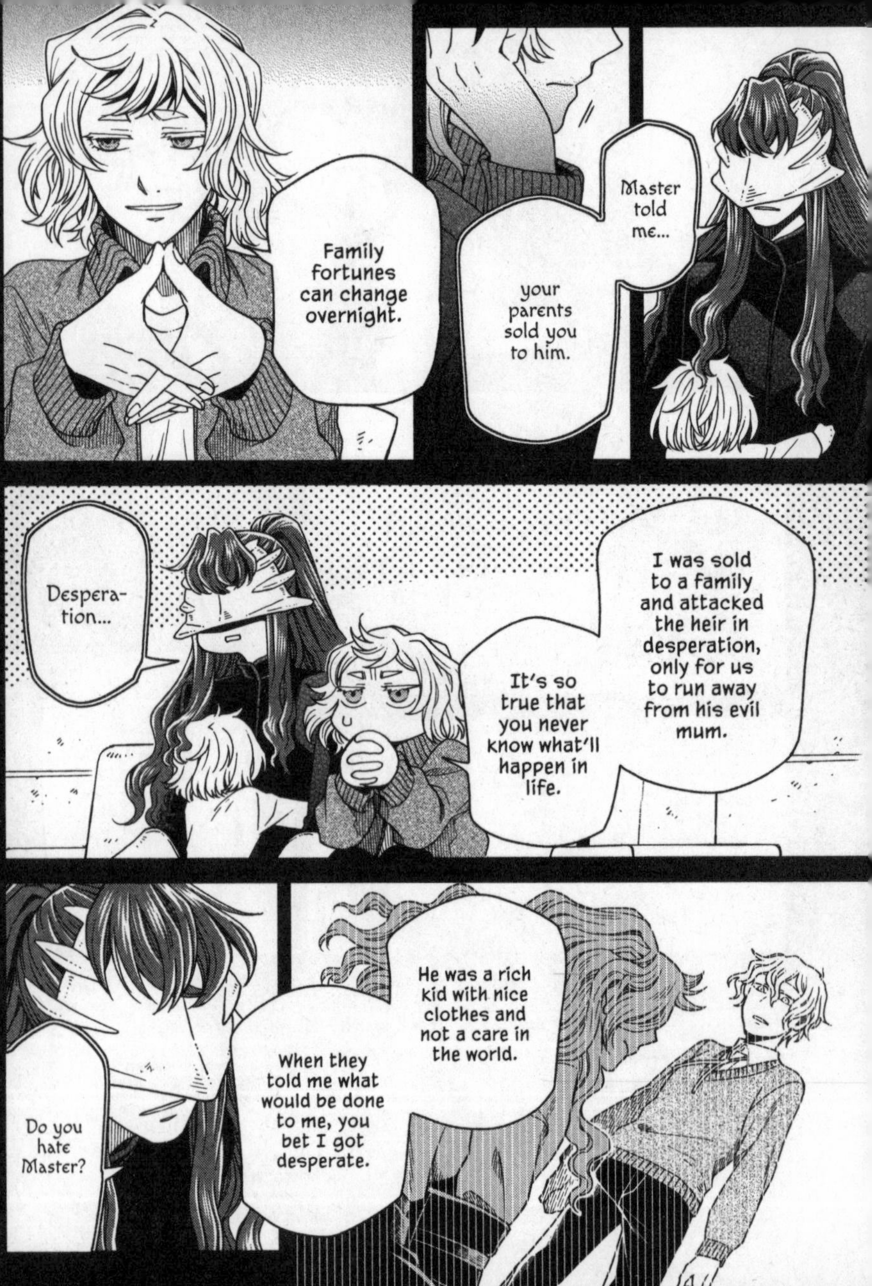
Master told me...
your parents sold you to him.
Family fortunes can change overnight.
I was sold to a family and attacked the heir in desperation, only for us to run away from his evil mum.
It's so true that you never know what'll happen in life.
Desperation...
He was a rich kid with nice clothes and not a care in the world.
When they told me what would be done to me, you bet I got desperate.
Do you hate Master?

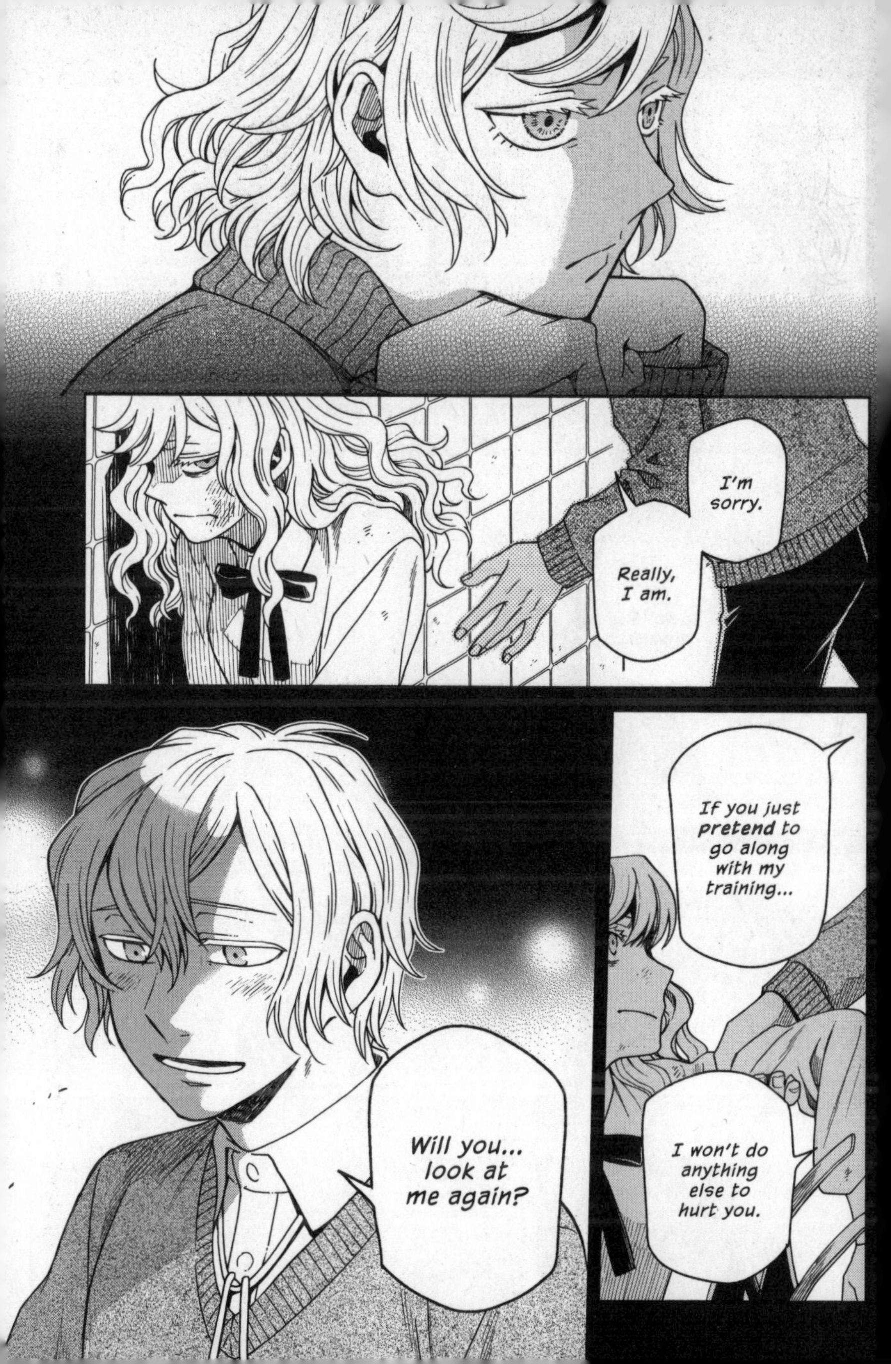
I'm sorry.
Really, I am.
If you just pretend to go along with my training...
I won't do anything else to hurt you.
Will you... look at me again?

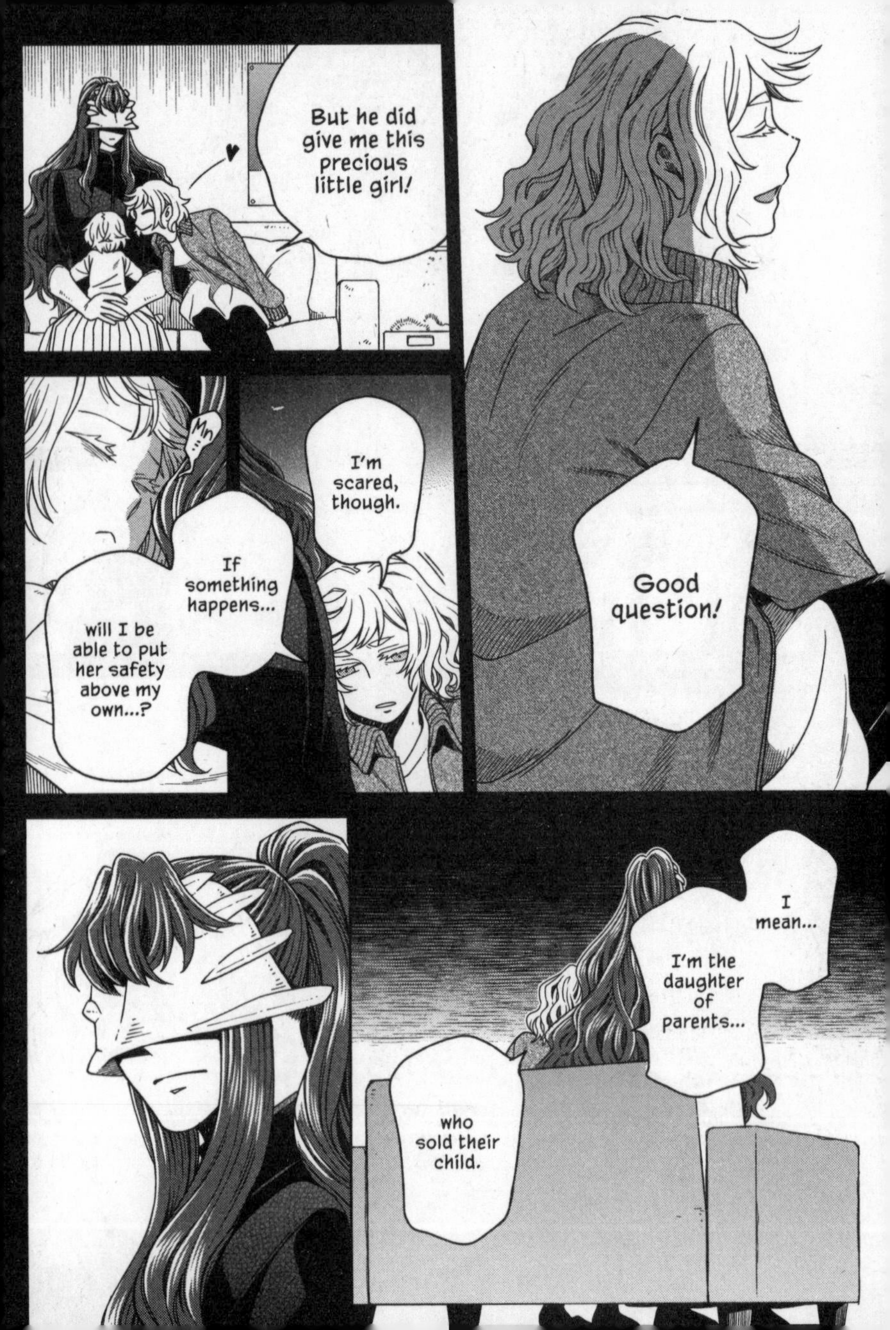
Good question!
But he did give me this precious little girl!
I'm scared, though.
If something happens...
will I be able to put her safety above my own...?
I mean...
I'm the daughter of parents...
who sold their child.

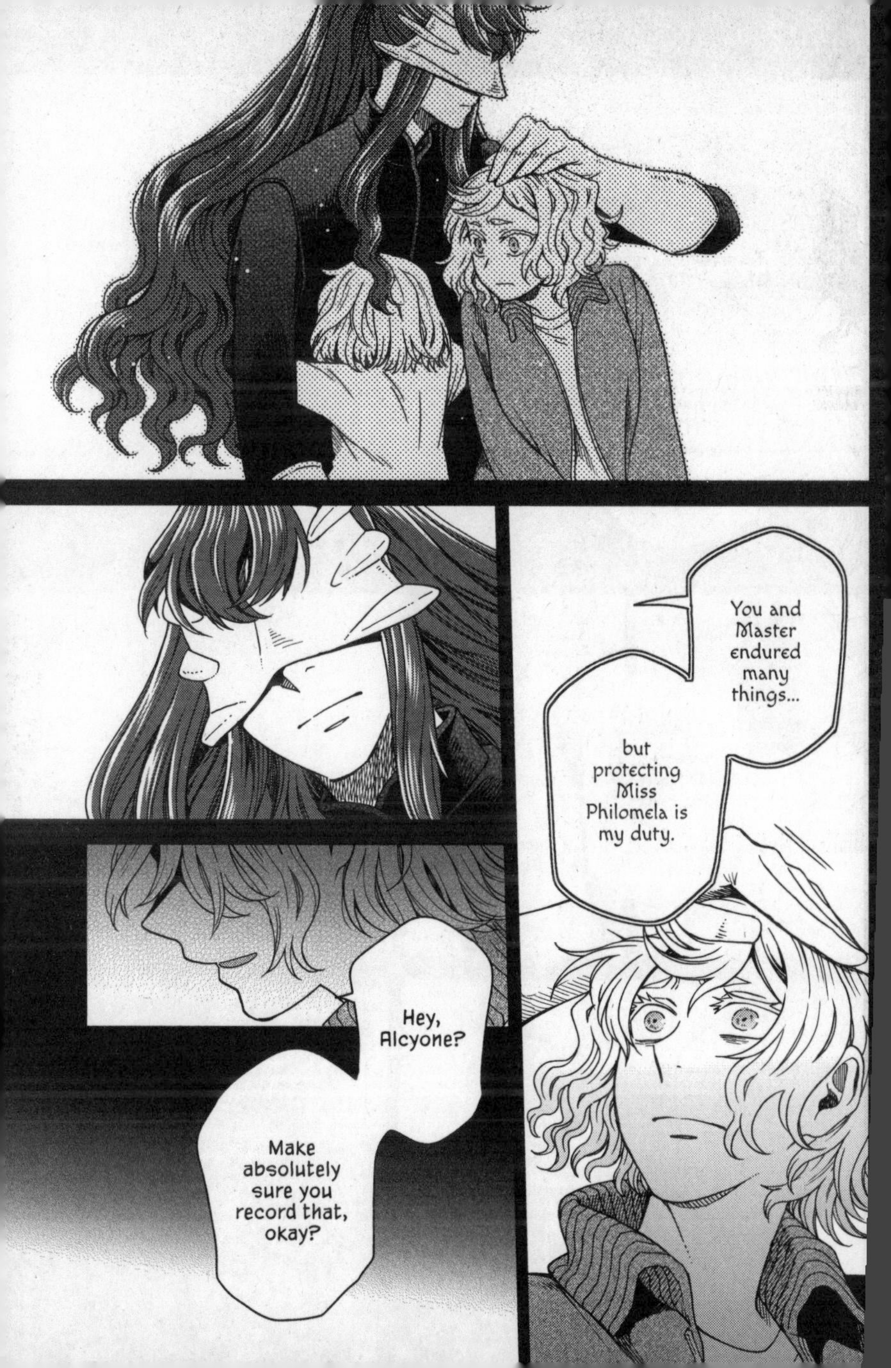

You and Master endured many things...
but protecting Miss Philomela is my duty.
Hey, Alcyone?
Make absolutely sure you record that, okay?

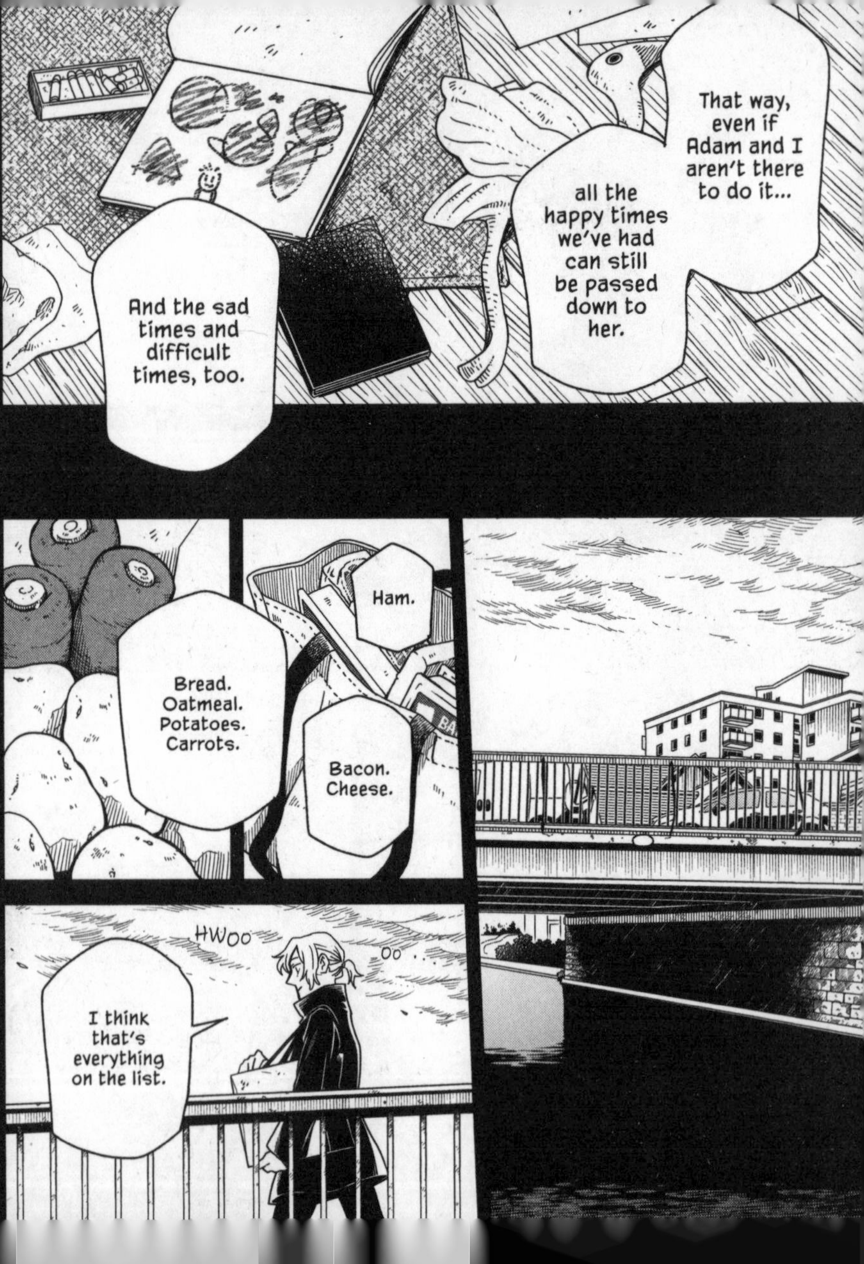
That way, even if Adam and I aren't there to do it...
all the happy times we've had can still be passed down to her.
And the sad times and difficult times, too.
Ham.
Bacon. Cheese.
Bread. Oatmeal. Potatoes. Carrots.
HWOO
OO
I think that's everything on the list.

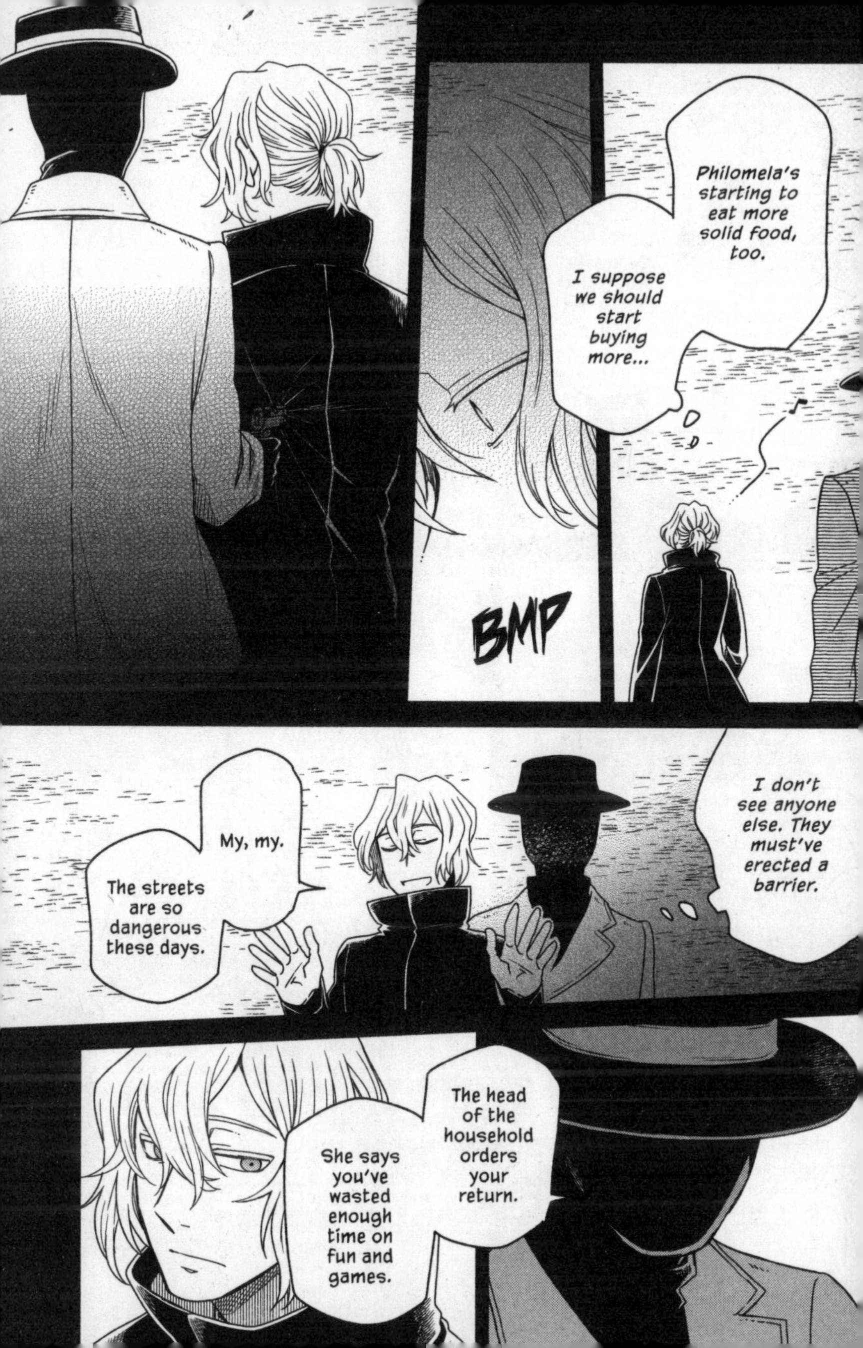
Philomela's starting to eat more solid food, too.
I suppose we should start buying more...
BMP
I don't see anyone else. They must've erected a barrier.
My, my.
The streets are so dangerous these days.
The head of the household orders your return.
She says you've wasted enough time on fun and games.

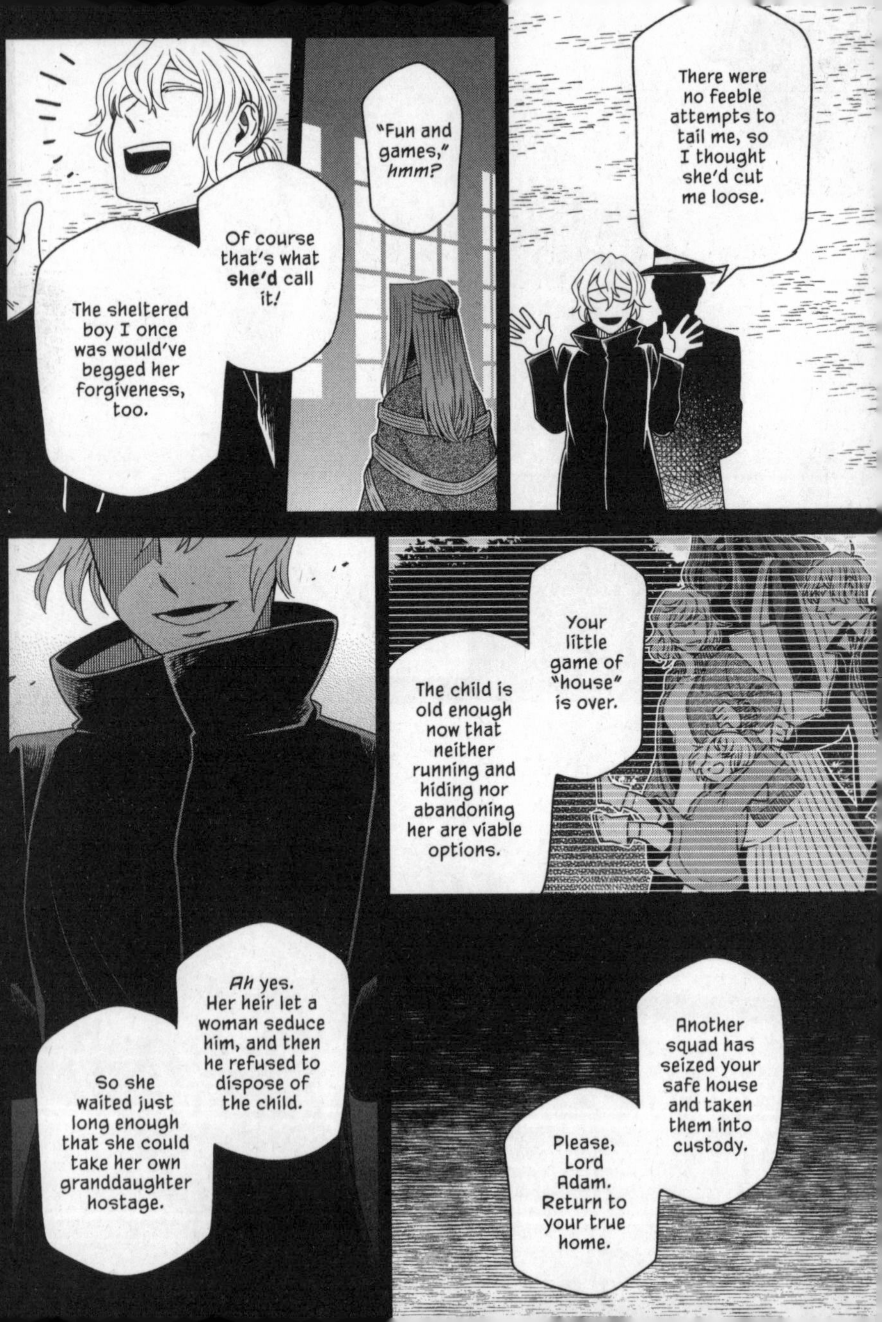

There were no feeble attempts to tail me, so I thought she'd cut me loose.
"Fun and games," *hmm?*
Of course that's what **she'd** call it!
The sheltered boy I once was would've begged her forgiveness, too.
Your little game of "house" is over.
The child is old enough now that neither running and hiding nor abandoning her are viable options.
Another squad has seized your safe house and taken them into custody.
Please, Lord Adam. Return to your true home.
Ah yes. Her heir let a woman seduce him, and then he refused to dispose of the child.
So she waited just long enough that she could take her own granddaughter hostage.

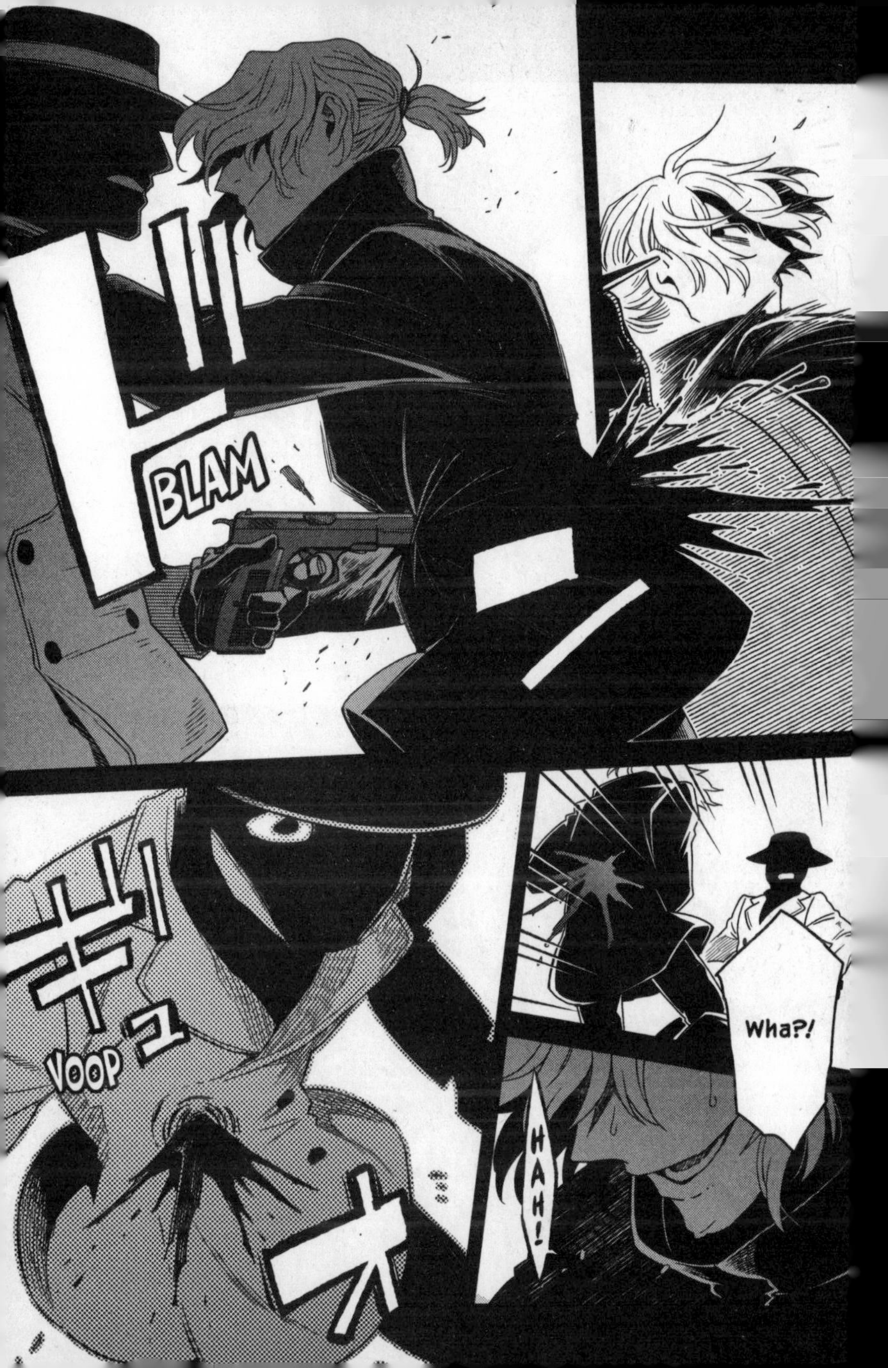
BLAM
Wha?!
HAH!
VOOP

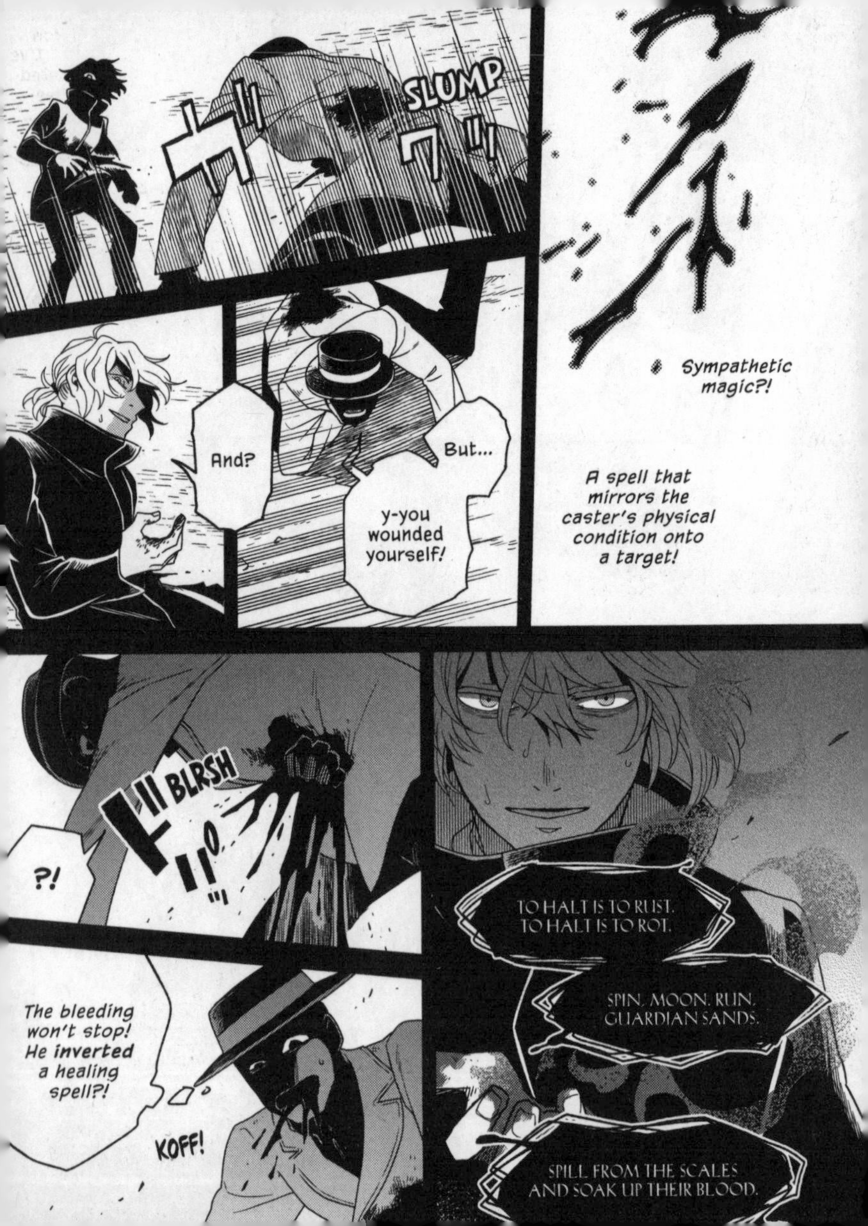
Sympathetic magic?!
A spell that mirrors the caster's physical condition onto a target!
SLUMP
But...
y-you wounded yourself!
And?
TO HALT IS TO RUST. TO HALT IS TO ROT.
SPIN, MOON. RUN, GUARDIAN SANDS.
SPILL FROM THE SCALES AND SOAK UP THEIR BLOOD.
BLRSH
?!
The bleeding won't stop! He inverted a healing spell?!
KOFF!

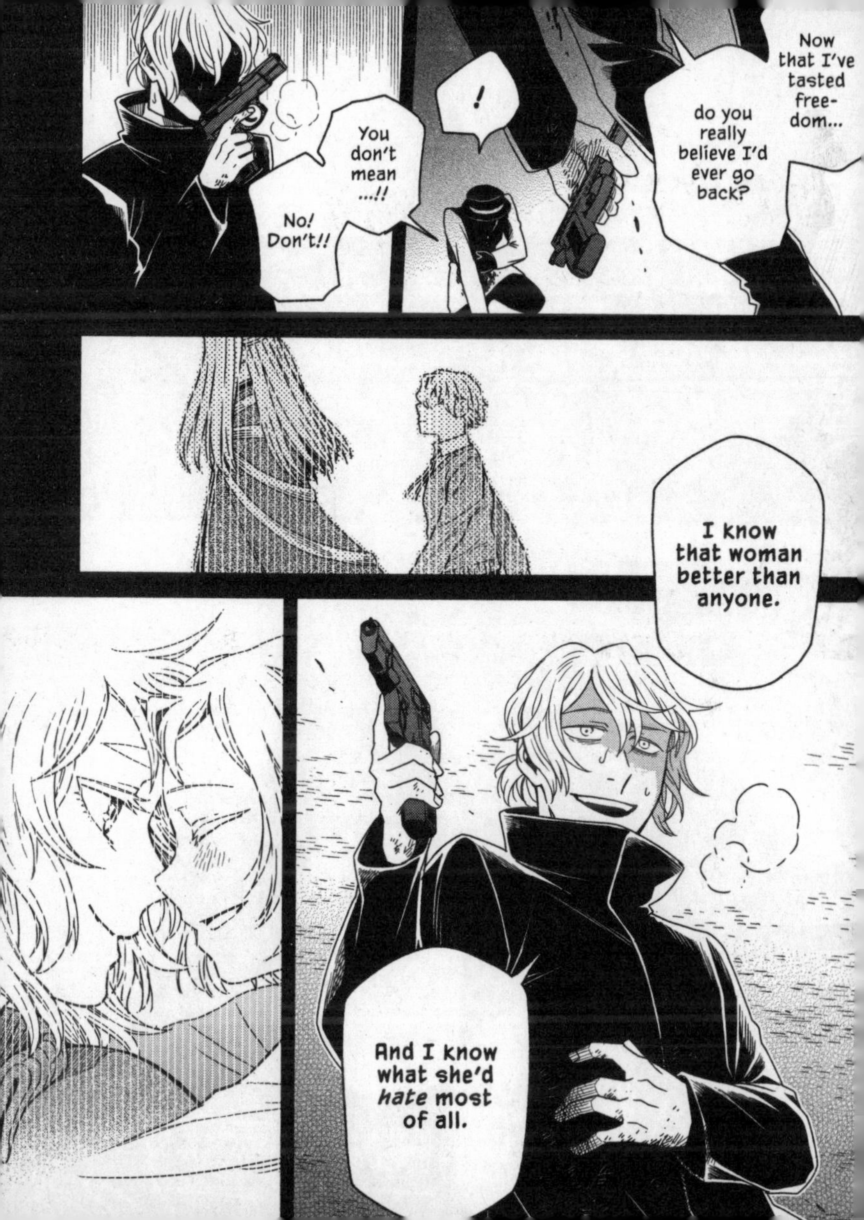

Now that I've tasted free-dom...
do you really believe I'd ever go back?
!
You don't mean ...!!
No! Don't!!
I know that woman better than anyone.
And I know what she'd *hate* most of all.

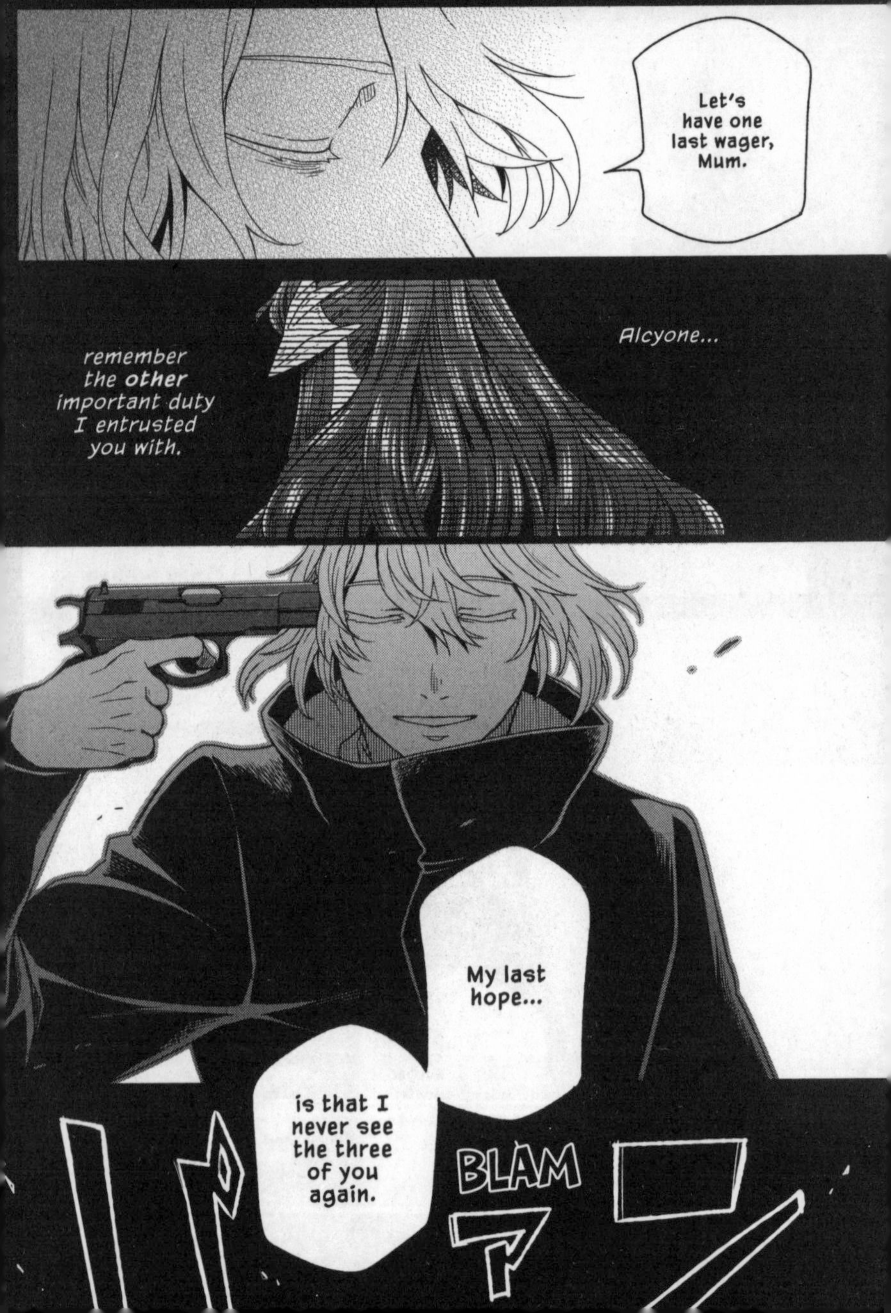
Let's have one last wager, Mum.
Alcyone...
remember the other important duty I entrusted you with.
My last hope...
is that I never see the three of you again.
BLAM

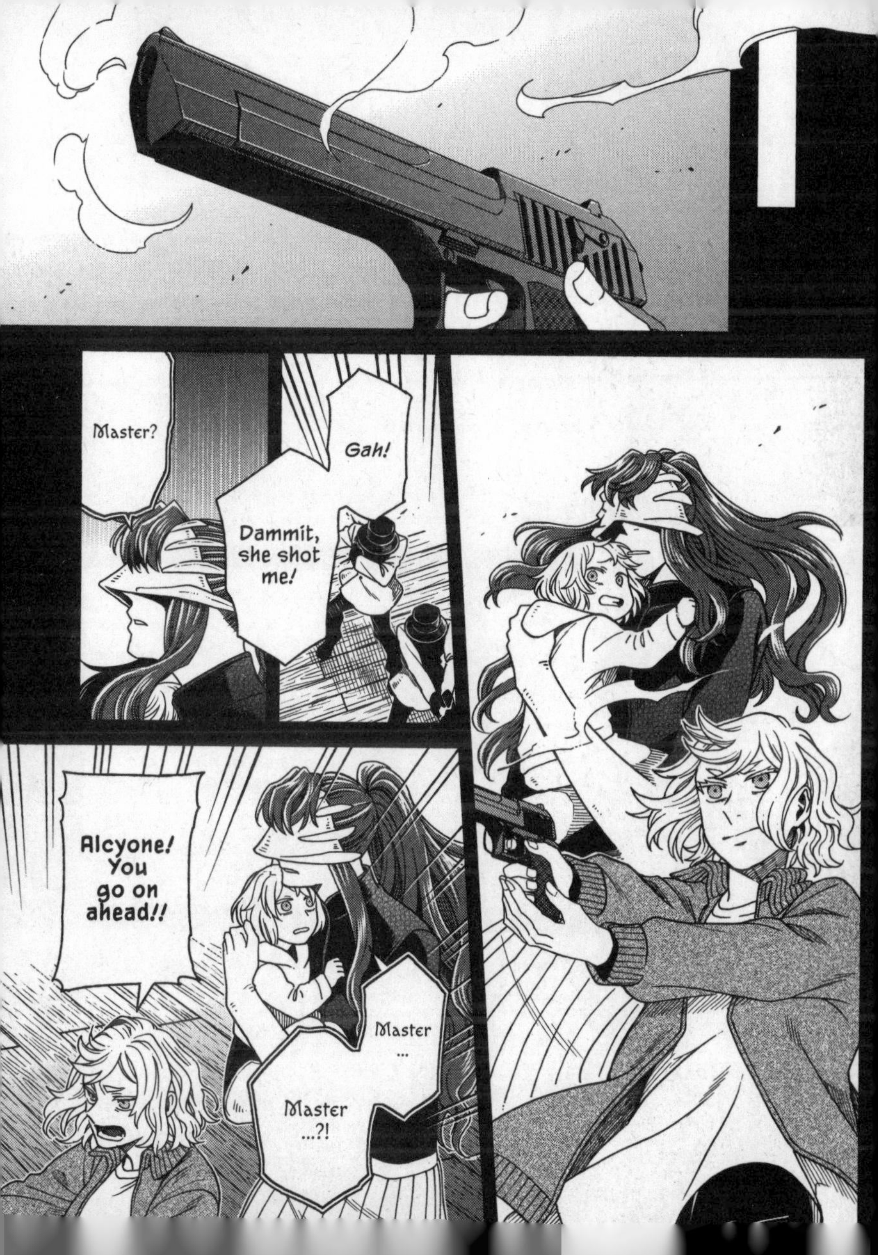
Gah!
Dammit, she shot me!
Master?
Alcyone! You go on ahead!!
Master ...
Master ...?!

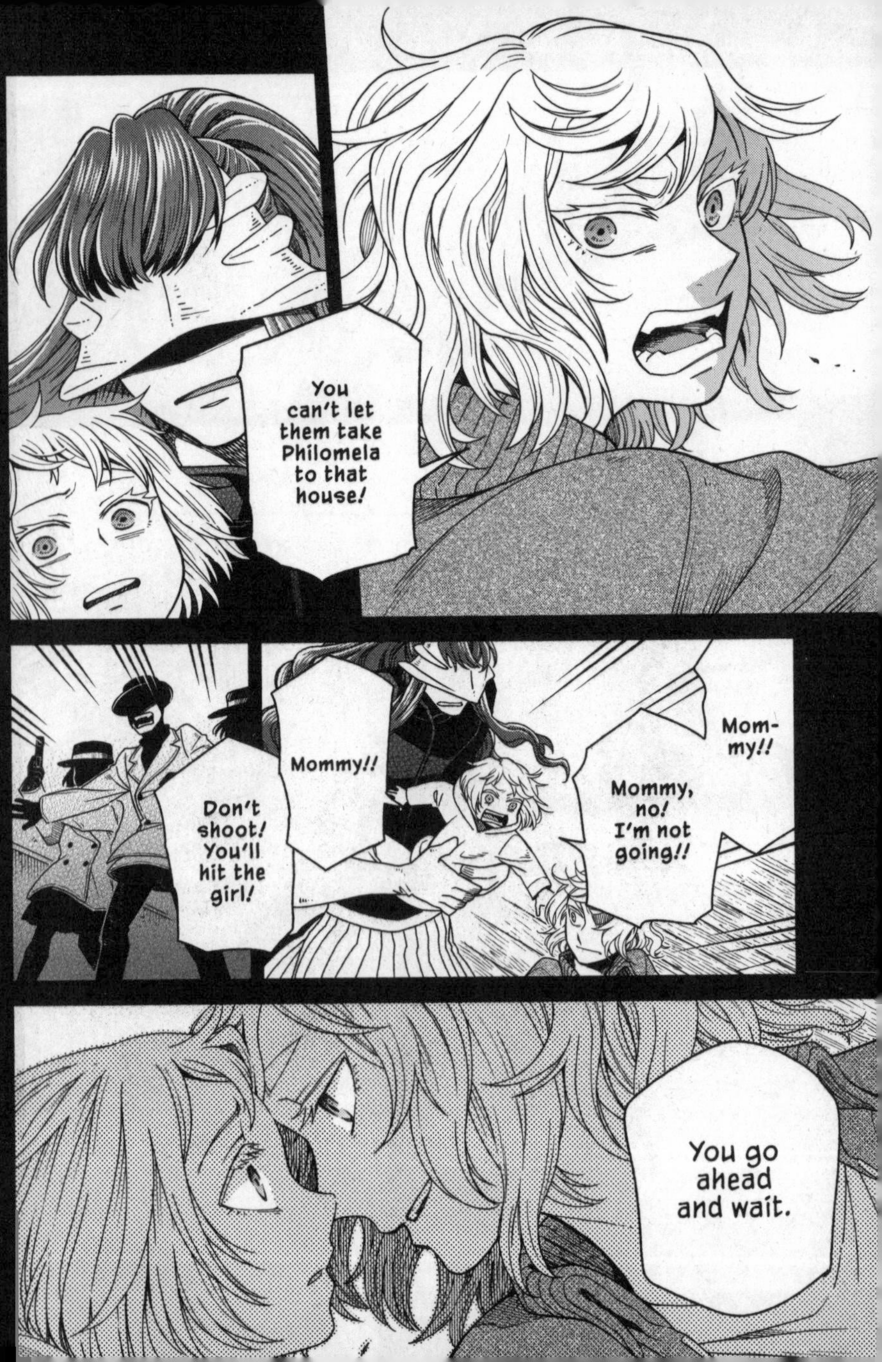
You can't let them take Philomela to that house!
Mom-my!!
Mommy, no! I'm not going!!
Mommy!!
Don't shoot! You'll hit the girl!
You go ahead and wait.

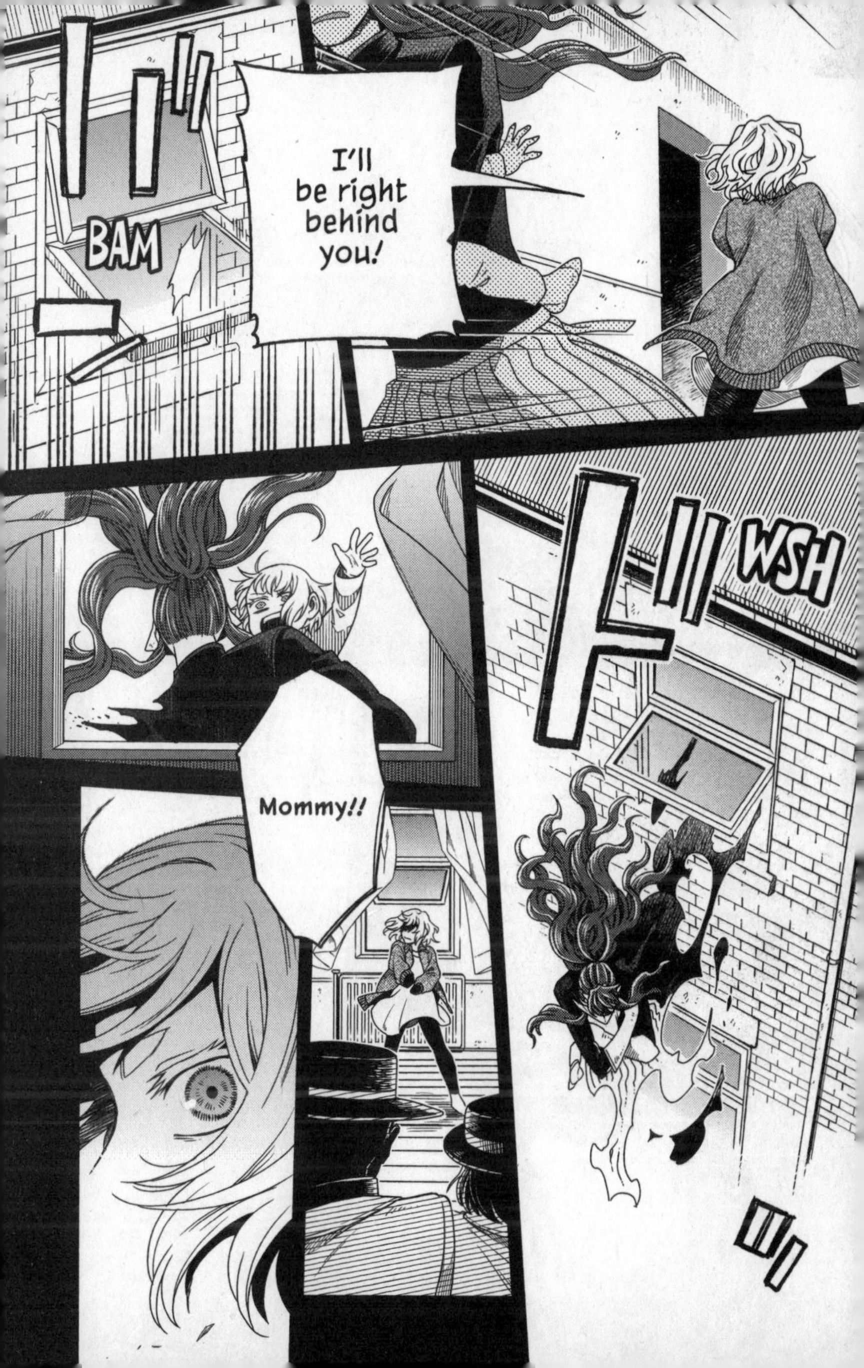

BAM
I'll be right behind you!
WSH
Mommy!!

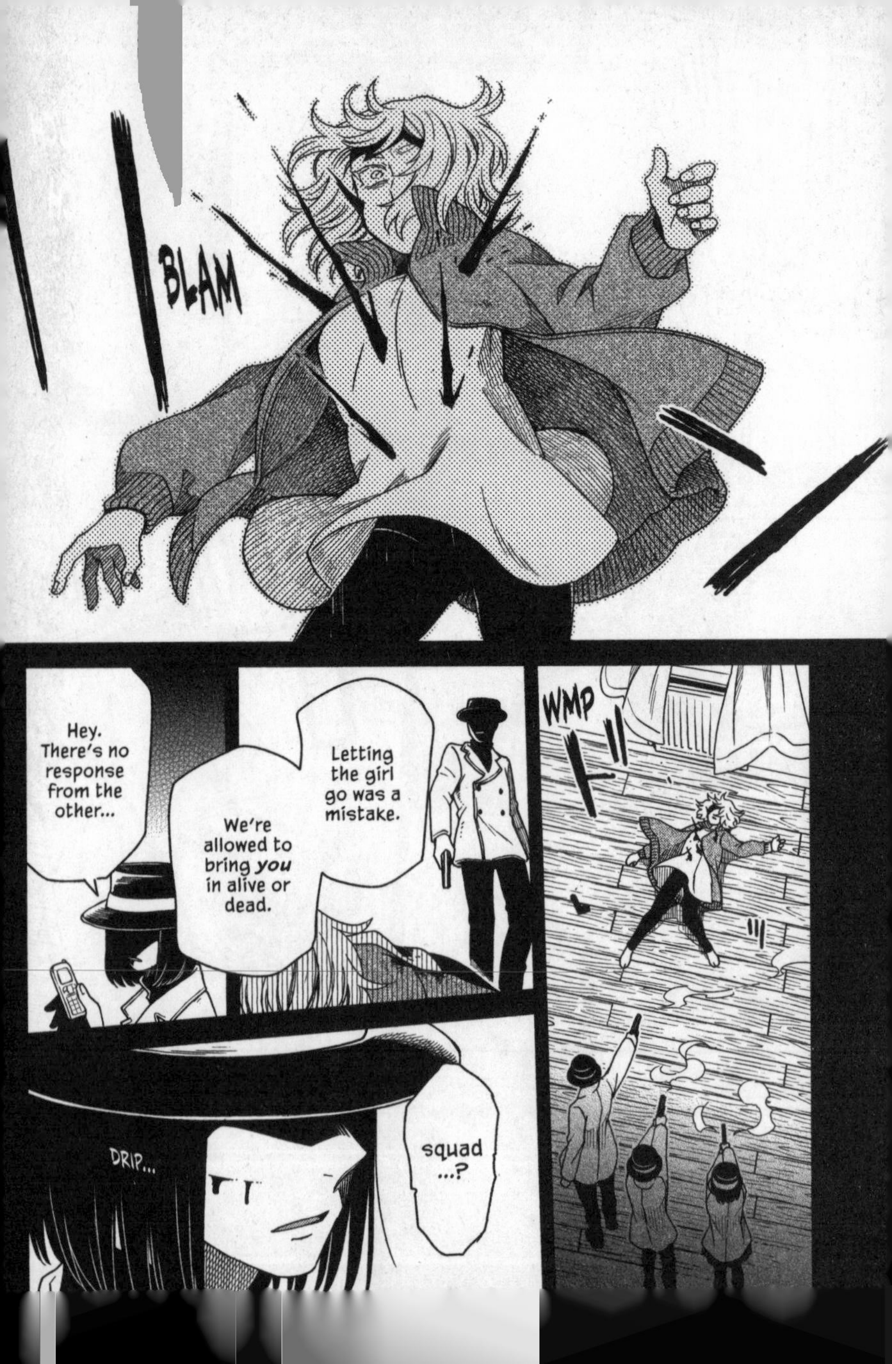
BLAM
WMP
Letting the girl go was a mistake.
We're allowed to bring *you* in alive or dead.
Hey. There's no response from the other...
squad ...?
DRIP...

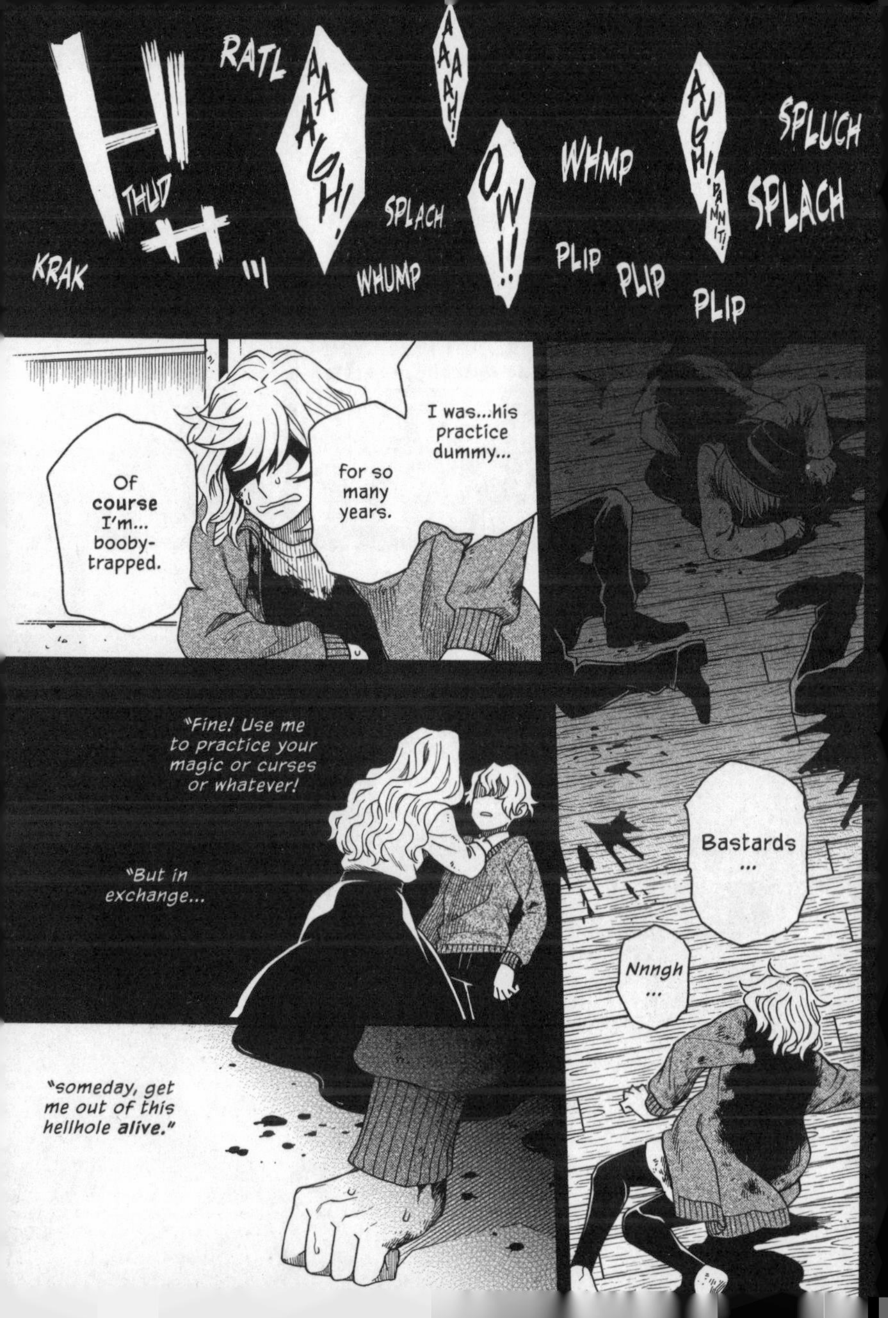
HI
THUD
KRAK
RATL
AAAGH!
AAAAH!
SPLACH
WHUMP
OW!!
WHMP
PLIP
PLIP
AUGH!
DAMMIT!
SPLUCH
SPLACH
PLIP
Bastards...
Nnngh...
I was...his practice dummy...
for so many years.
Of course I'm... booby-trapped.
"Fine! Use me to practice your magic or curses or whatever!
"But in exchange...
"someday, get me out of this hellhole alive."

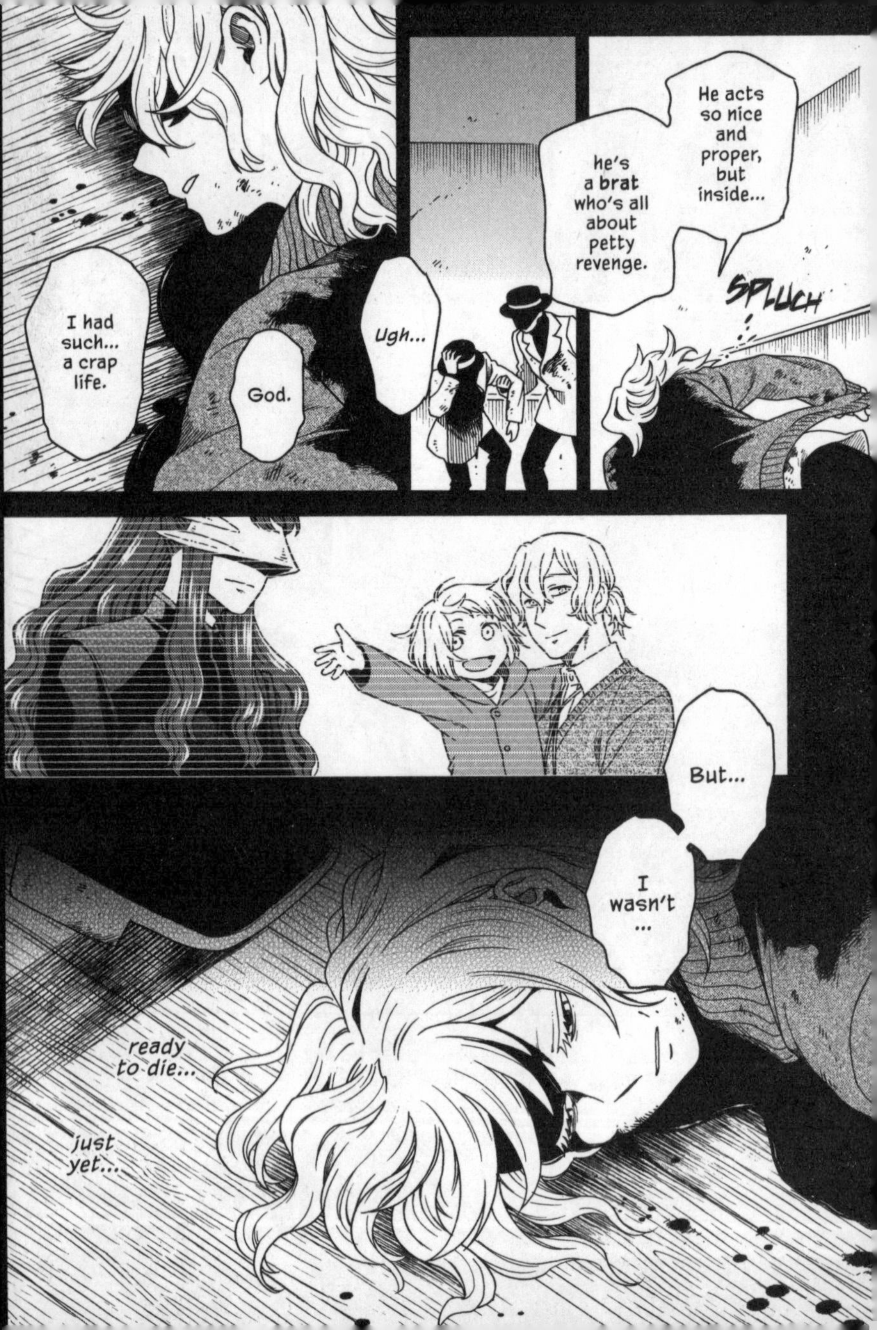
He acts so nice and proper, but inside...
he's a brat who's all about petty revenge.
SPLUCH
Ugh...
God.
I had such... a crap life.
But...
I wasn't ...
ready to die...
just yet...

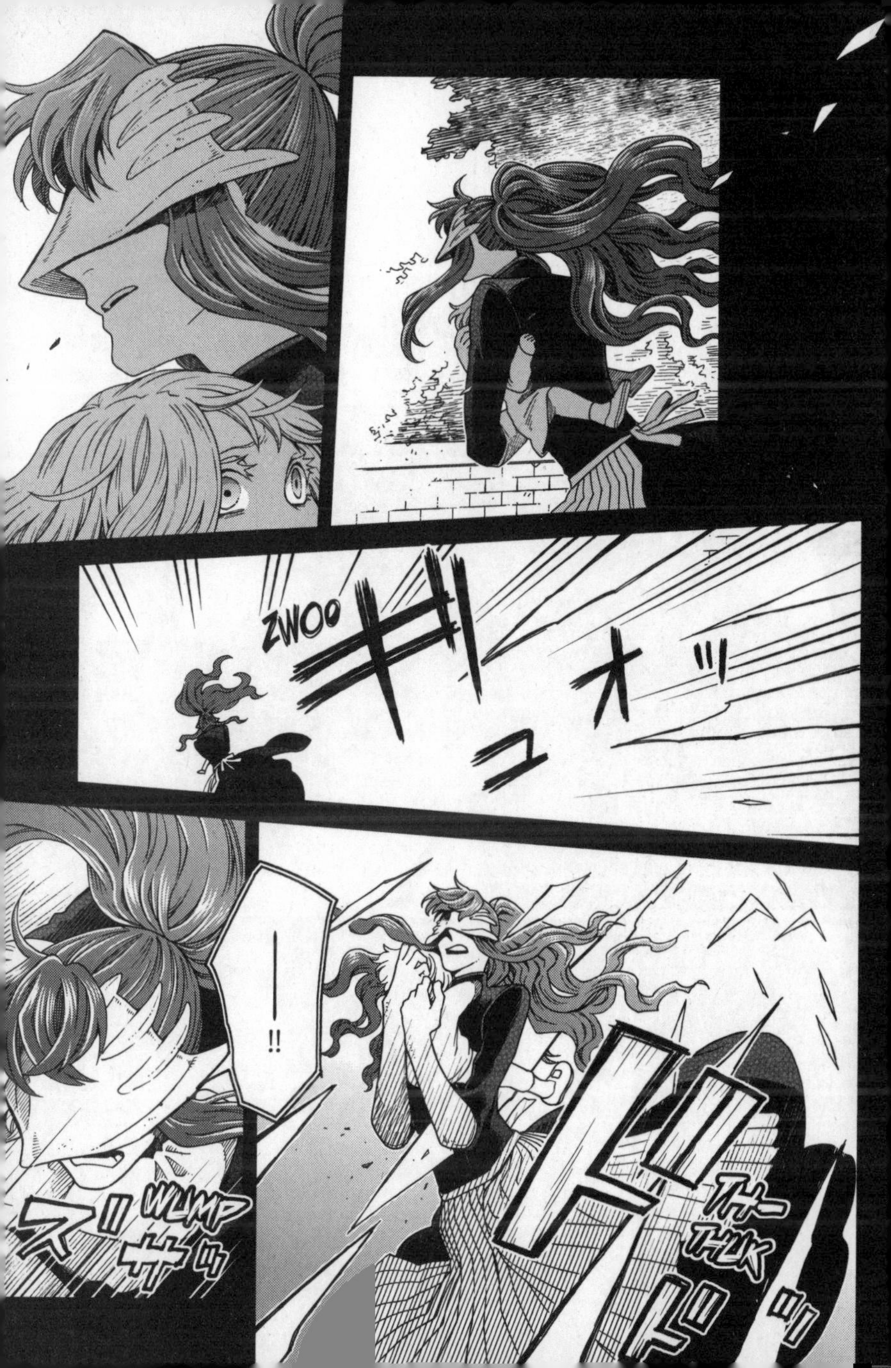
ZWOO
ギュオッ
—!!
TH-THUK
ドドッ
WUMP
ズサッ

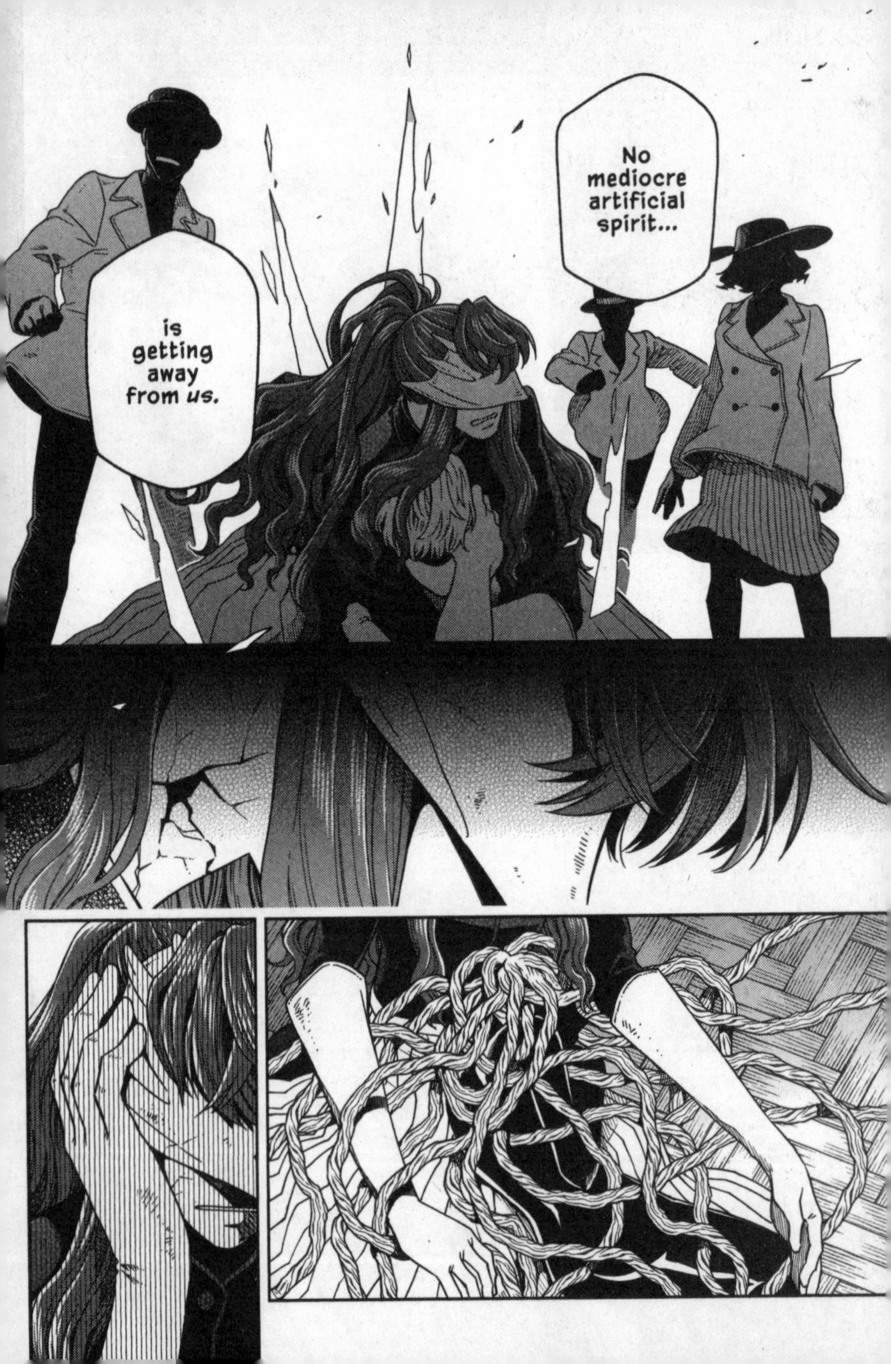
No mediocre artificial spirit...
is getting away from us.

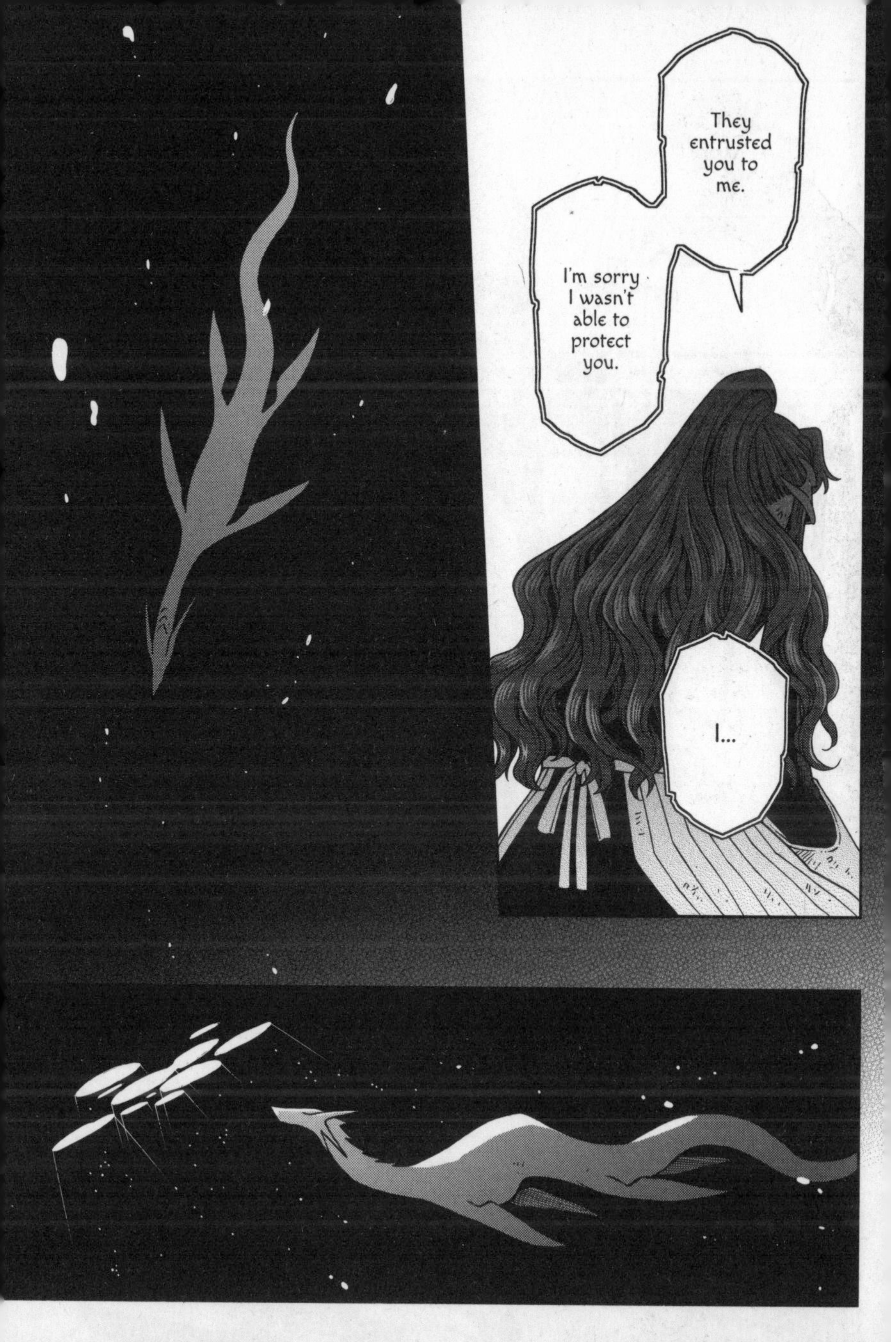
They entrusted you to me.
I'm sorry I wasn't able to protect you.
I...

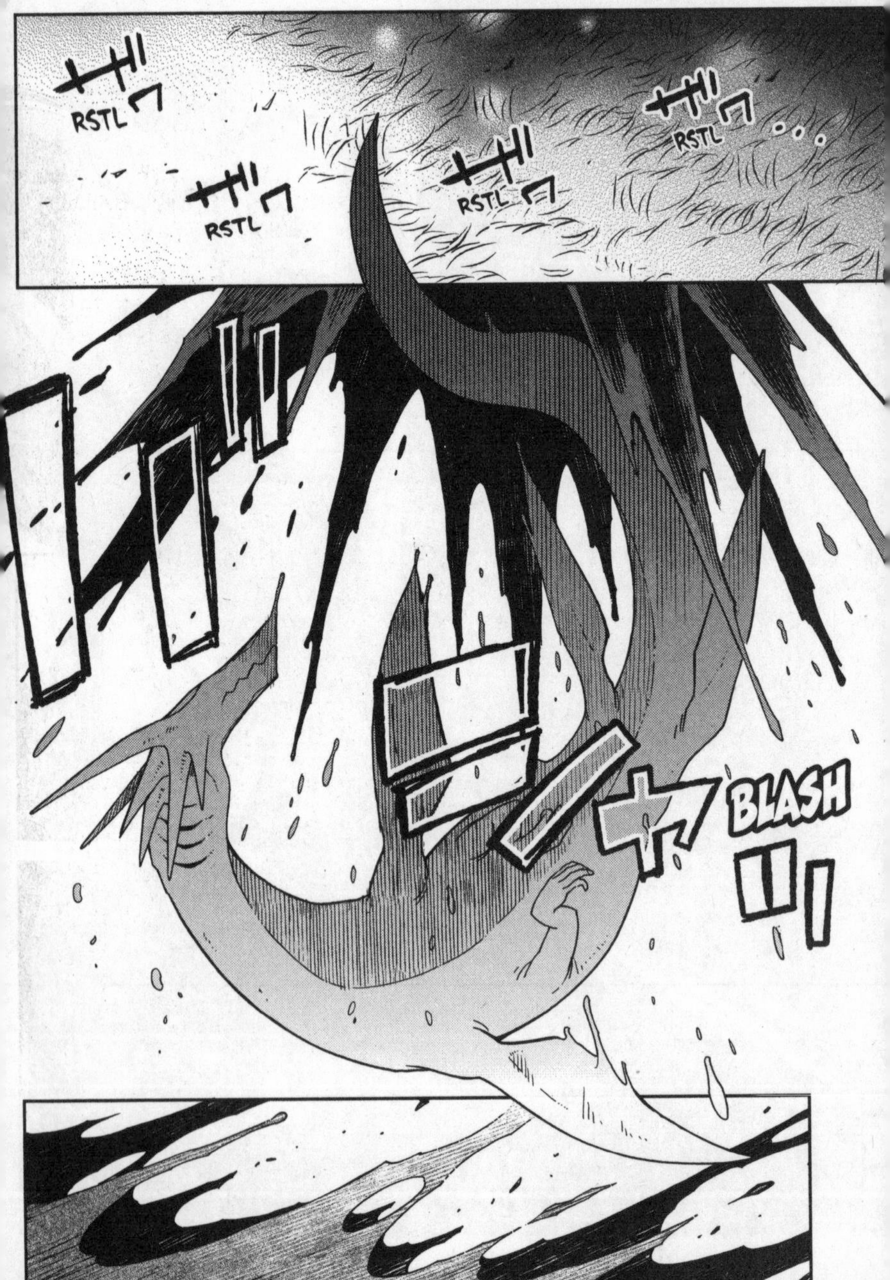
RSTL
RSTL
RSTL
RSTL...
BLASH

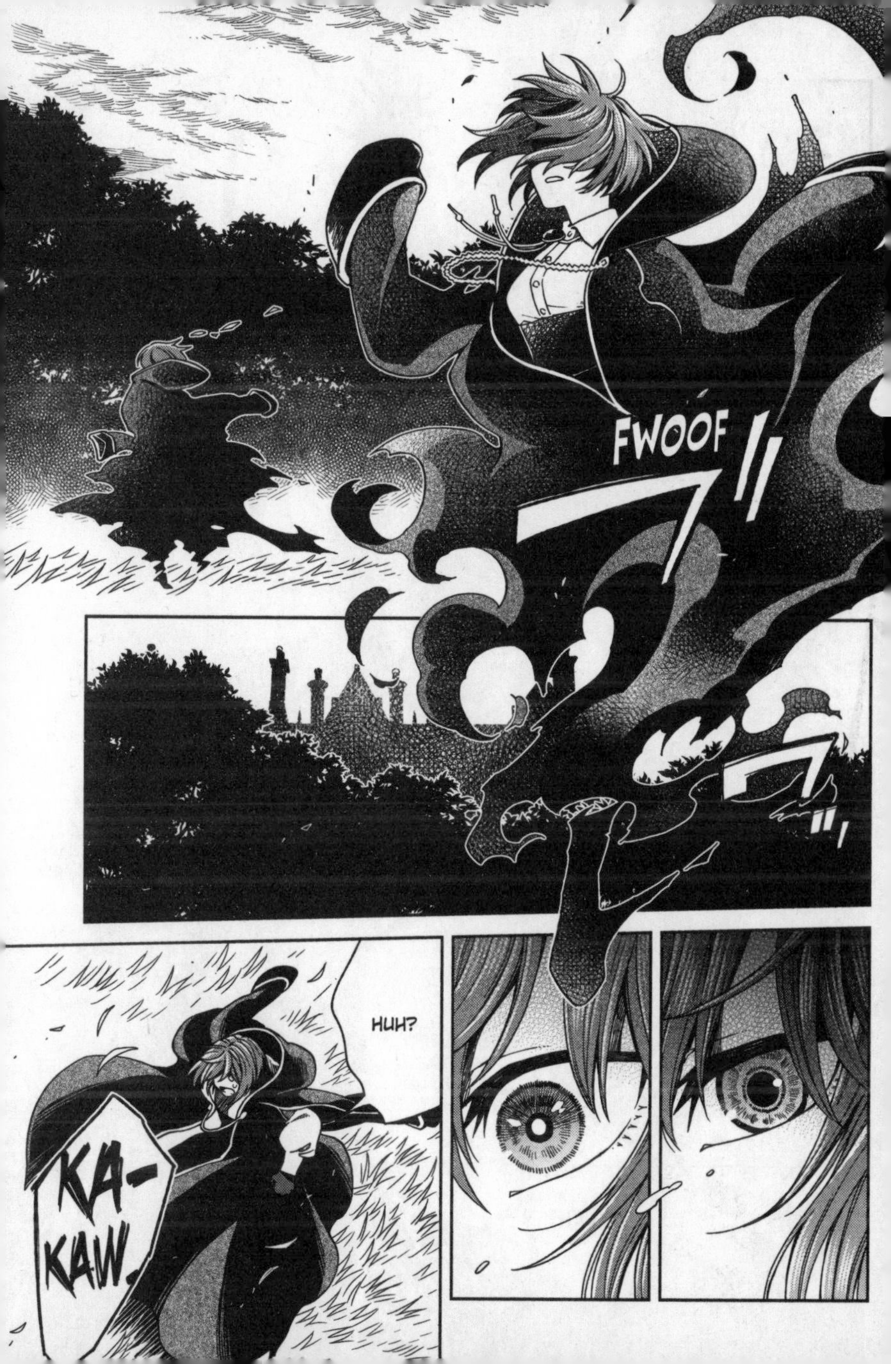
FWOOF
HUH?
KA-
KAW.

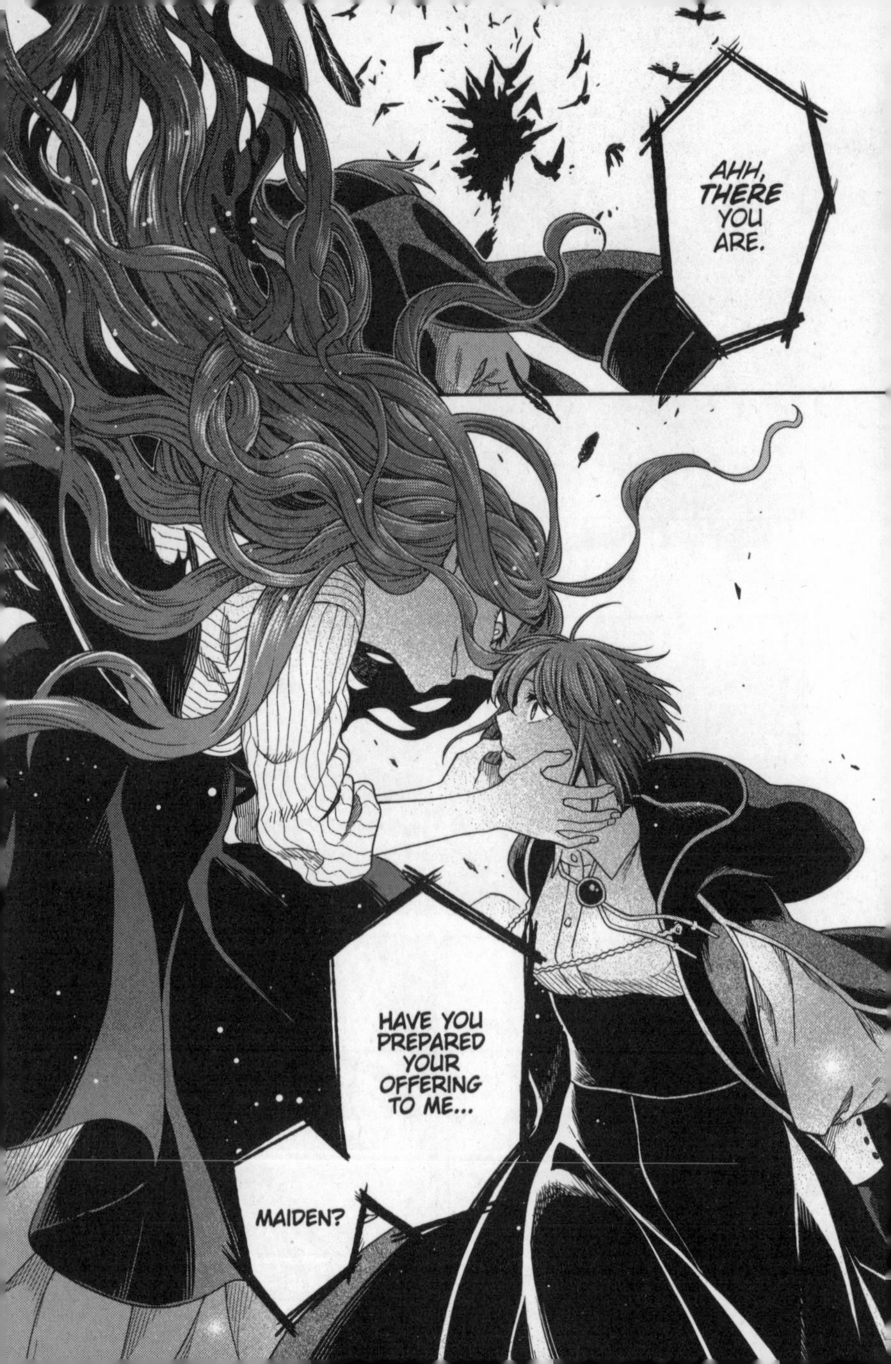
AHH, THERE YOU ARE.
HAVE YOU PREPARED YOUR OFFERING TO ME...
MAIDEN?

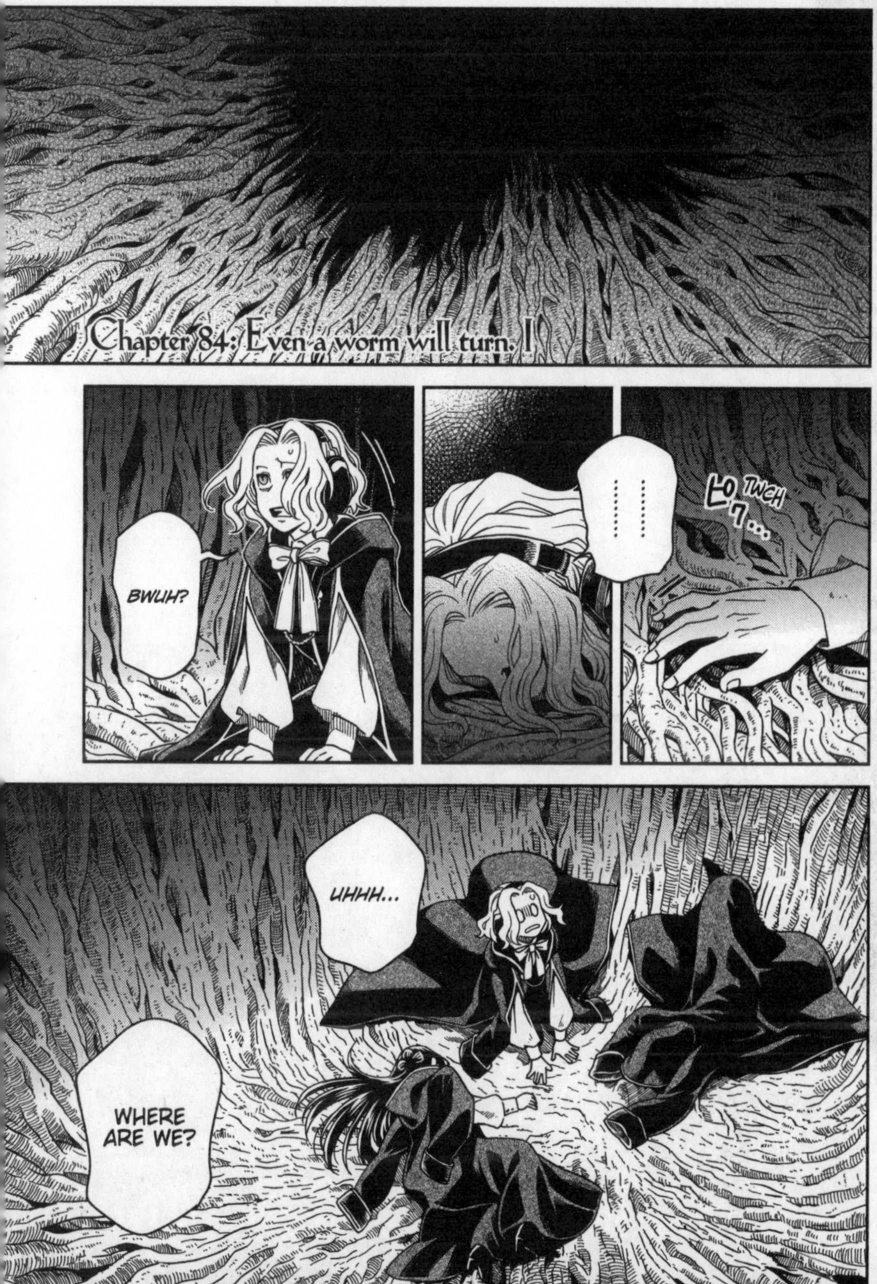
Chapter 84: Even a worm will turn. I
TWCH
......
BWUH?
UHHH...
WHERE ARE WE?

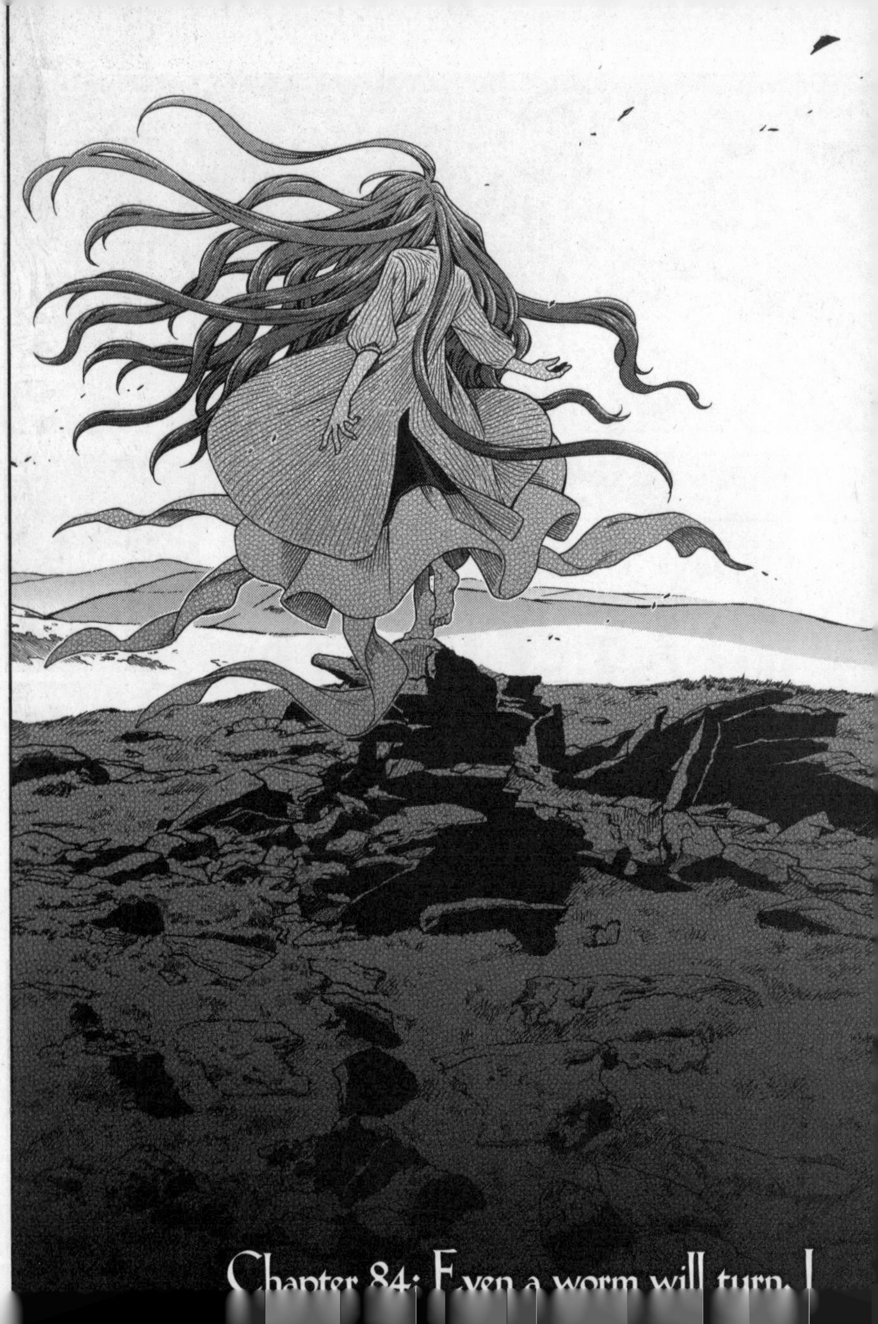
Chapter 84: Even a worm will turn. I

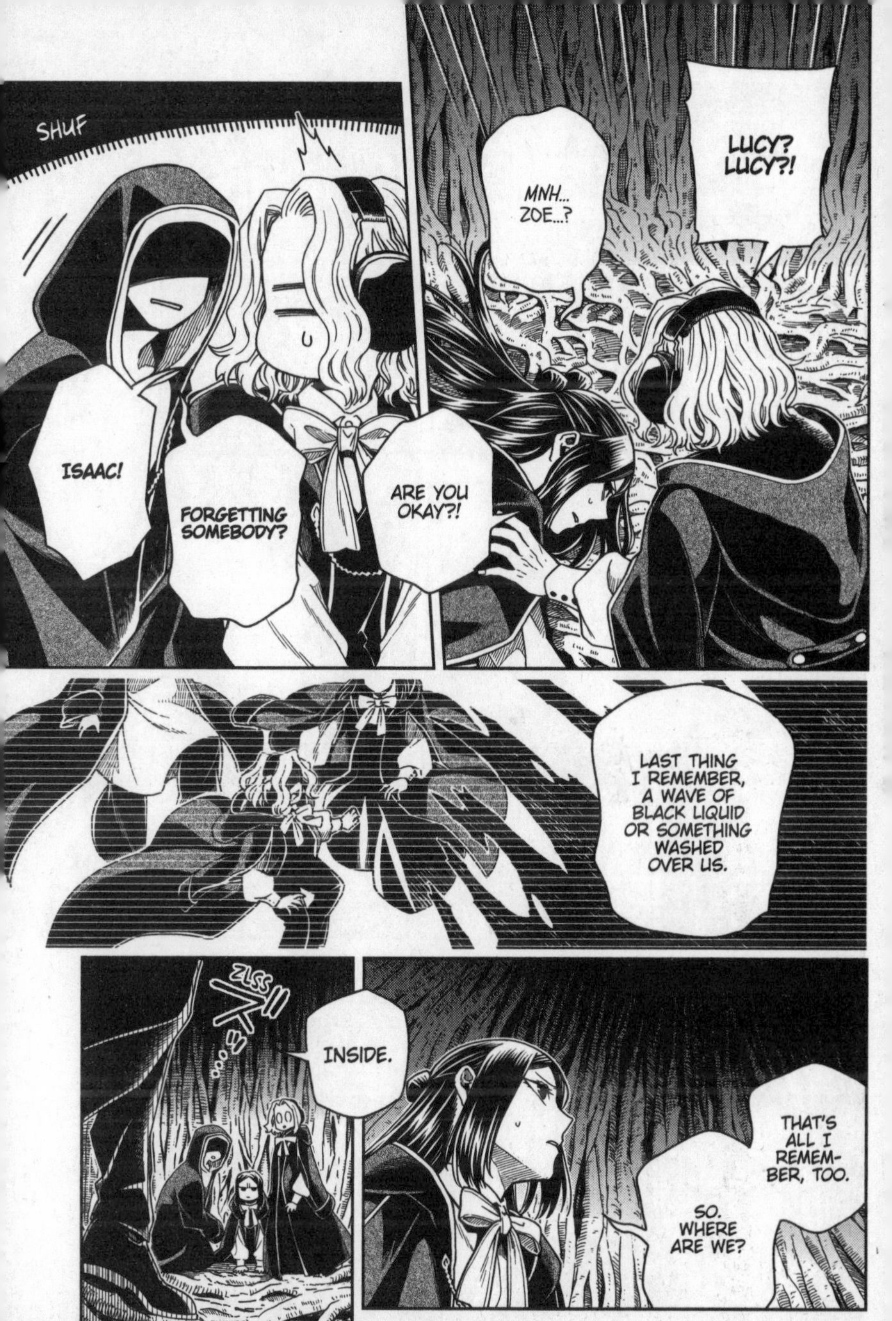
LUCY? LUCY?!
MNH... ZOE...?
SHUF
ISAAC!
FORGETTING SOMEBODY?
ARE YOU OKAY?!
LAST THING I REMEMBER, A WAVE OF BLACK LIQUID OR SOMETHING WASHED OVER US.
ZLSS
INSIDE.
THAT'S ALL I REMEMBER, TOO.
SO. WHERE ARE WE?

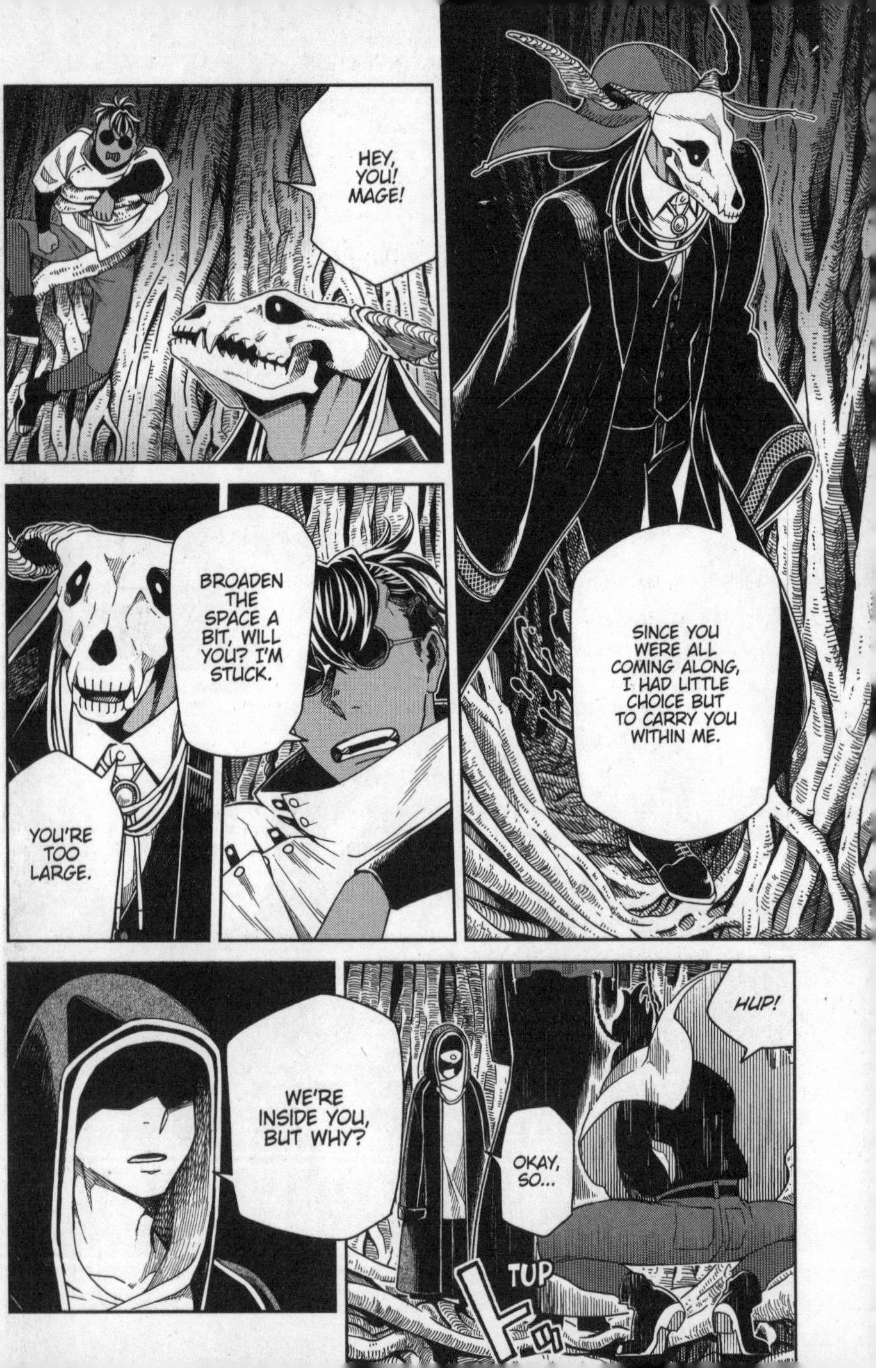

HEY, YOU! MAGE!
BROADEN THE SPACE A BIT, WILL YOU? I'M STUCK.
YOU'RE TOO LARGE.
SINCE YOU WERE ALL COMING ALONG, I HAD LITTLE CHOICE BUT TO CARRY YOU WITHIN ME.
HUP!
TUP
OKAY, SO...
WE'RE INSIDE YOU, BUT WHY?

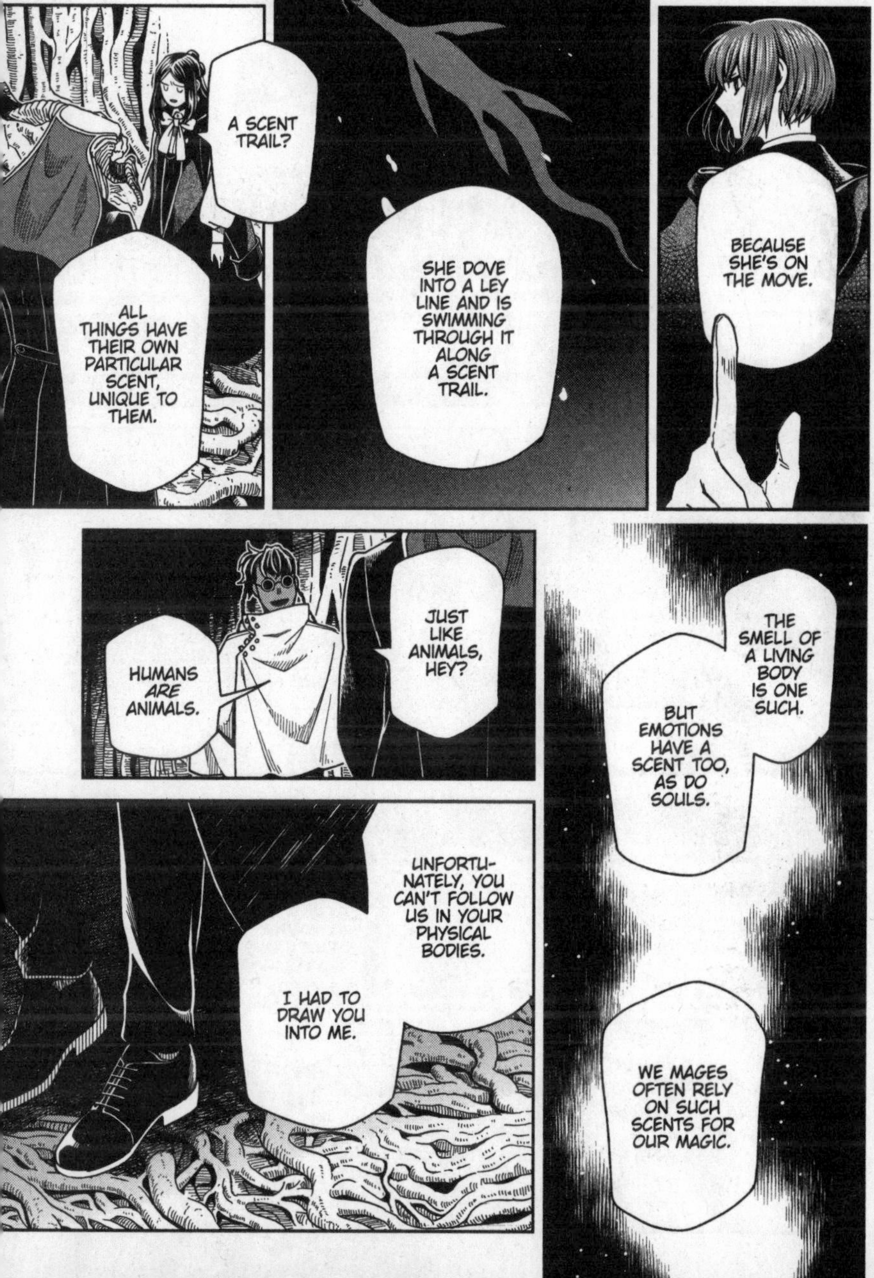
BECAUSE SHE'S ON THE MOVE.
SHE DOVE INTO A LEY LINE AND IS SWIMMING THROUGH IT ALONG A SCENT TRAIL.
A SCENT TRAIL?
ALL THINGS HAVE THEIR OWN PARTICULAR SCENT, UNIQUE TO THEM.
THE SMELL OF A LIVING BODY IS ONE SUCH.
BUT EMOTIONS HAVE A SCENT TOO, AS DO SOULS.
JUST LIKE ANIMALS, HEY?
HUMANS *ARE* ANIMALS.
WE MAGES OFTEN RELY ON SUCH SCENTS FOR OUR MAGIC.
UNFORTUNATELY, YOU CAN'T FOLLOW US IN YOUR PHYSICAL BODIES.
I HAD TO DRAW YOU INTO ME.

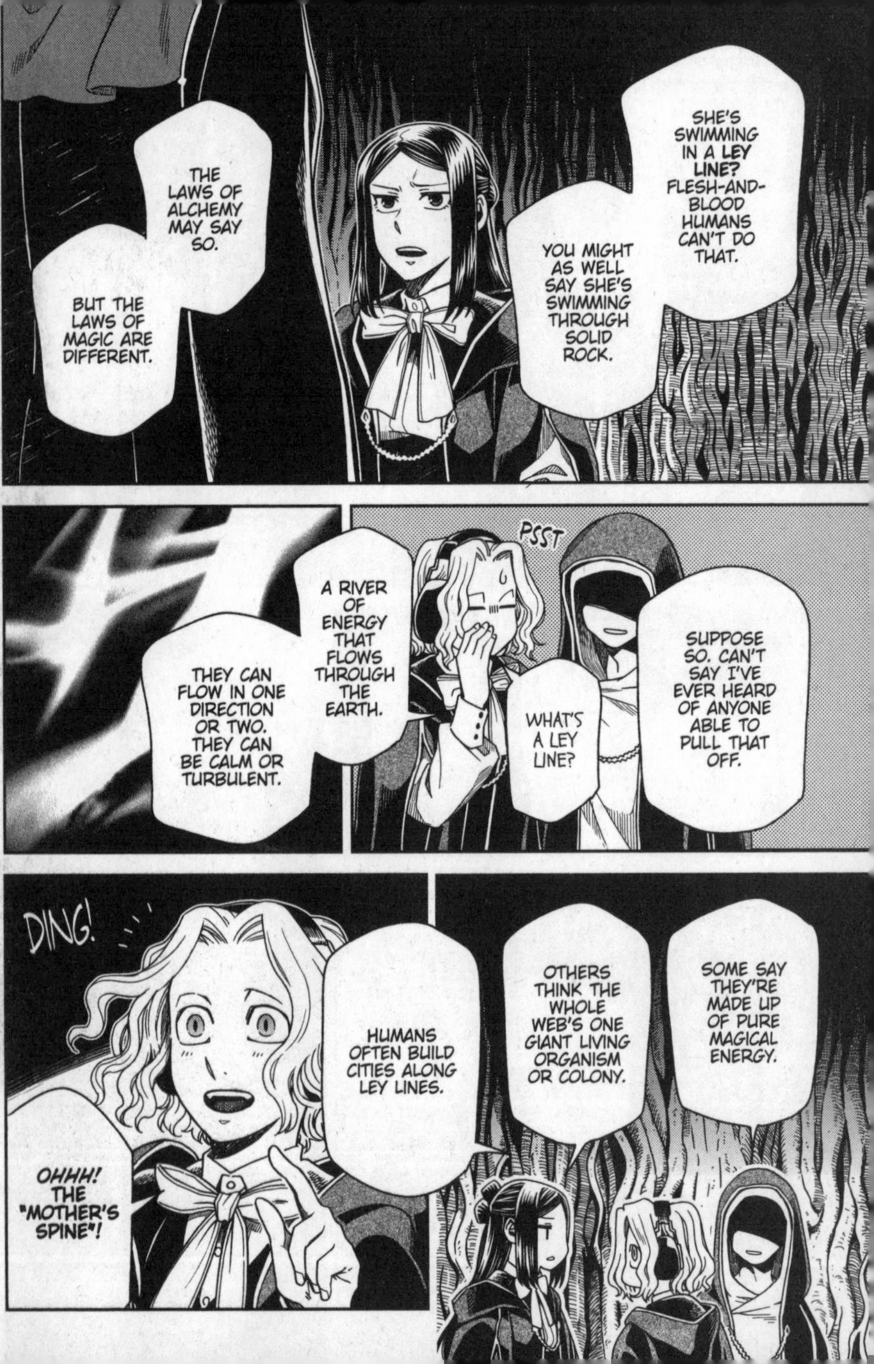
SHE'S SWIMMING IN A LEY LINE? FLESH-AND-BLOOD HUMANS CAN'T DO THAT.
YOU MIGHT AS WELL SAY SHE'S SWIMMING THROUGH SOLID ROCK.
THE LAWS OF ALCHEMY MAY SAY SO.
BUT THE LAWS OF MAGIC ARE DIFFERENT.
SUPPOSE SO. CAN'T SAY I'VE EVER HEARD OF ANYONE ABLE TO PULL THAT OFF.
PSST
WHAT'S A LEY LINE?
A RIVER OF ENERGY THAT FLOWS THROUGH THE EARTH.
THEY CAN FLOW IN ONE DIRECTION OR TWO. THEY CAN BE CALM OR TURBULENT.
SOME SAY THEY'RE MADE UP OF PURE MAGICAL ENERGY.
OTHERS THINK THE WHOLE WEB'S ONE GIANT LIVING ORGANISM OR COLONY.
HUMANS OFTEN BUILD CITIES ALONG LEY LINES.
DING!
OHHH! THE "MOTHER'S SPINE"!

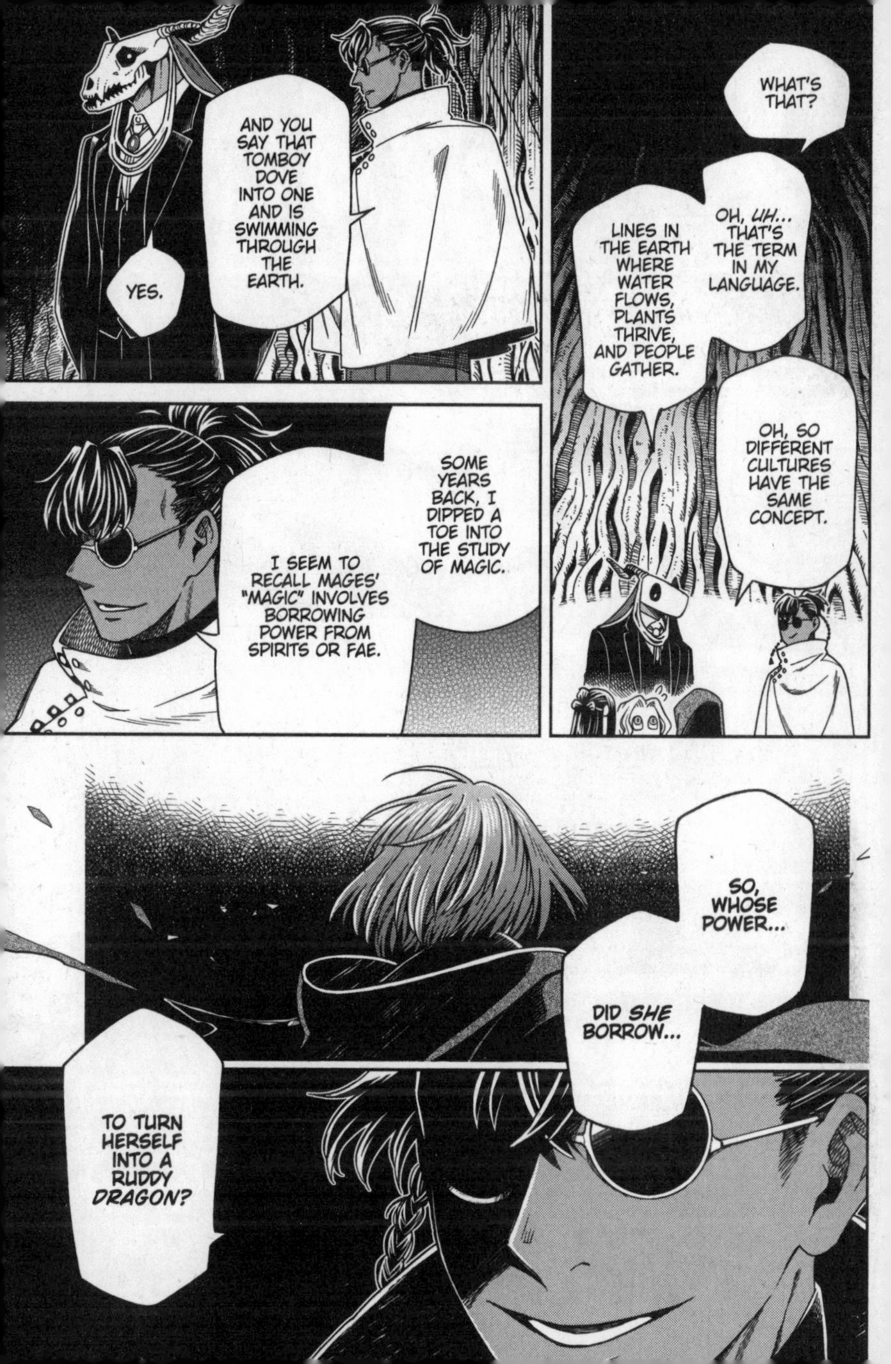
WHAT'S THAT?
OH, UH... THAT'S THE TERM IN MY LANGUAGE.
LINES IN THE EARTH WHERE WATER FLOWS, PLANTS THRIVE, AND PEOPLE GATHER.
OH, SO DIFFERENT CULTURES HAVE THE SAME CONCEPT.
AND YOU SAY THAT TOMBOY DOVE INTO ONE AND IS SWIMMING THROUGH THE EARTH.
YES.
SOME YEARS BACK, I DIPPED A TOE INTO THE STUDY OF MAGIC.
I SEEM TO RECALL MAGES' "MAGIC" INVOLVES BORROWING POWER FROM SPIRITS OR FAE.
SO, WHOSE POWER...
DID *SHE* BORROW...
TO TURN HERSELF INTO A RUDDY *DRAGON*?

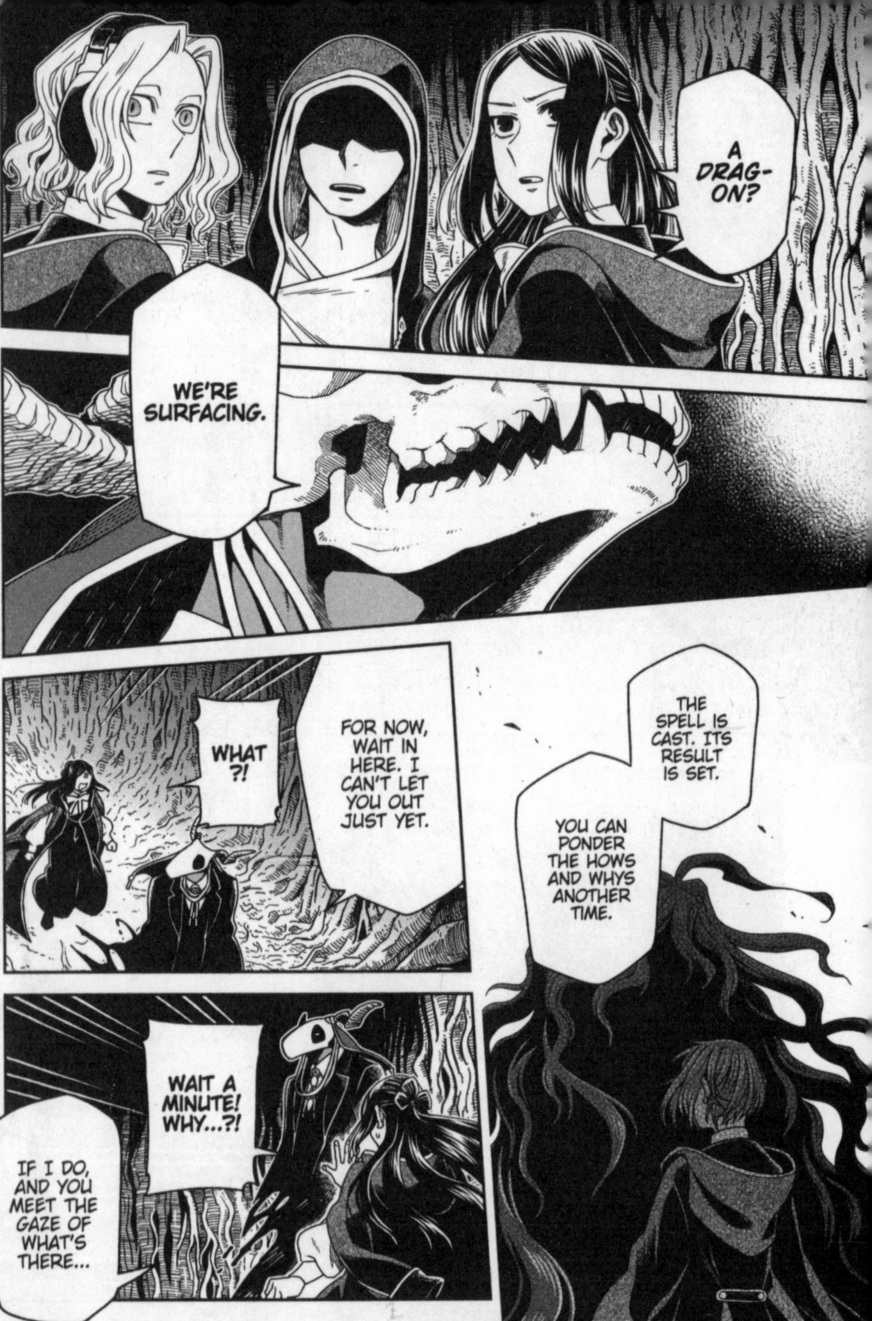
A DRAG-ON?
WE'RE SURFACING.
THE SPELL IS CAST. ITS RESULT IS SET.
YOU CAN PONDER THE HOWS AND WHYS ANOTHER TIME.
FOR NOW, WAIT IN HERE. I CAN'T LET YOU OUT JUST YET.
WHAT?!
WAIT A MINUTE! WHY...?!
IF I DO, AND YOU MEET THE GAZE OF WHAT'S THERE...

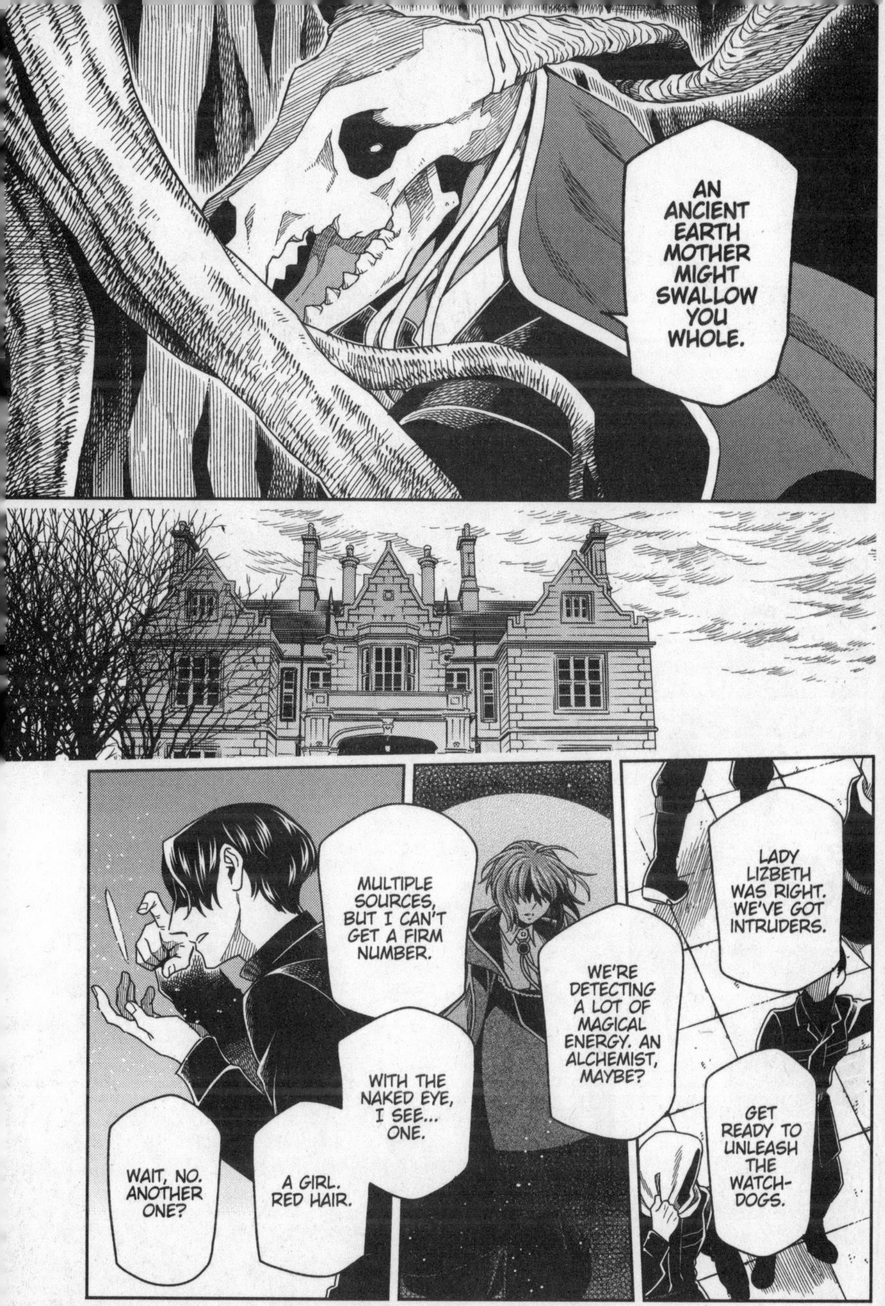
AN ANCIENT EARTH MOTHER MIGHT SWALLOW YOU WHOLE.
LADY LIZBETH WAS RIGHT. WE'VE GOT INTRUDERS.
GET READY TO UNLEASH THE WATCH-DOGS.
WE'RE DETECTING A LOT OF MAGICAL ENERGY. AN ALCHEMIST, MAYBE?
MULTIPLE SOURCES, BUT I CAN'T GET A FIRM NUMBER.
WITH THE NAKED EYE, I SEE... ONE.
A GIRL. RED HAIR.
WAIT, NO. ANOTHER ONE?

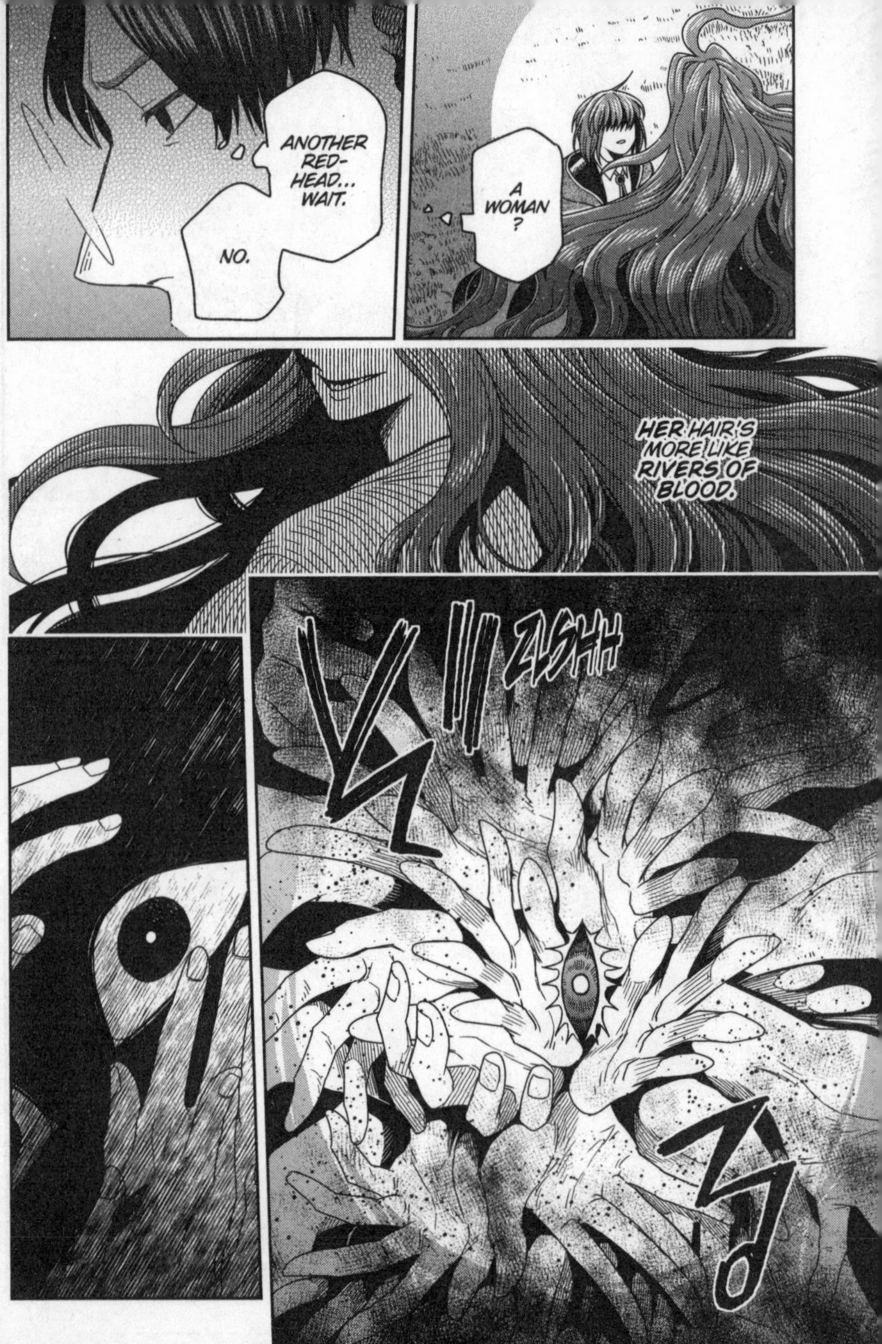
A WOMAN?
ANOTHER RED-HEAD... WAIT.
NO.
HER HAIR'S MORE LIKE RIVERS OF BLOOD.
ZLSHH

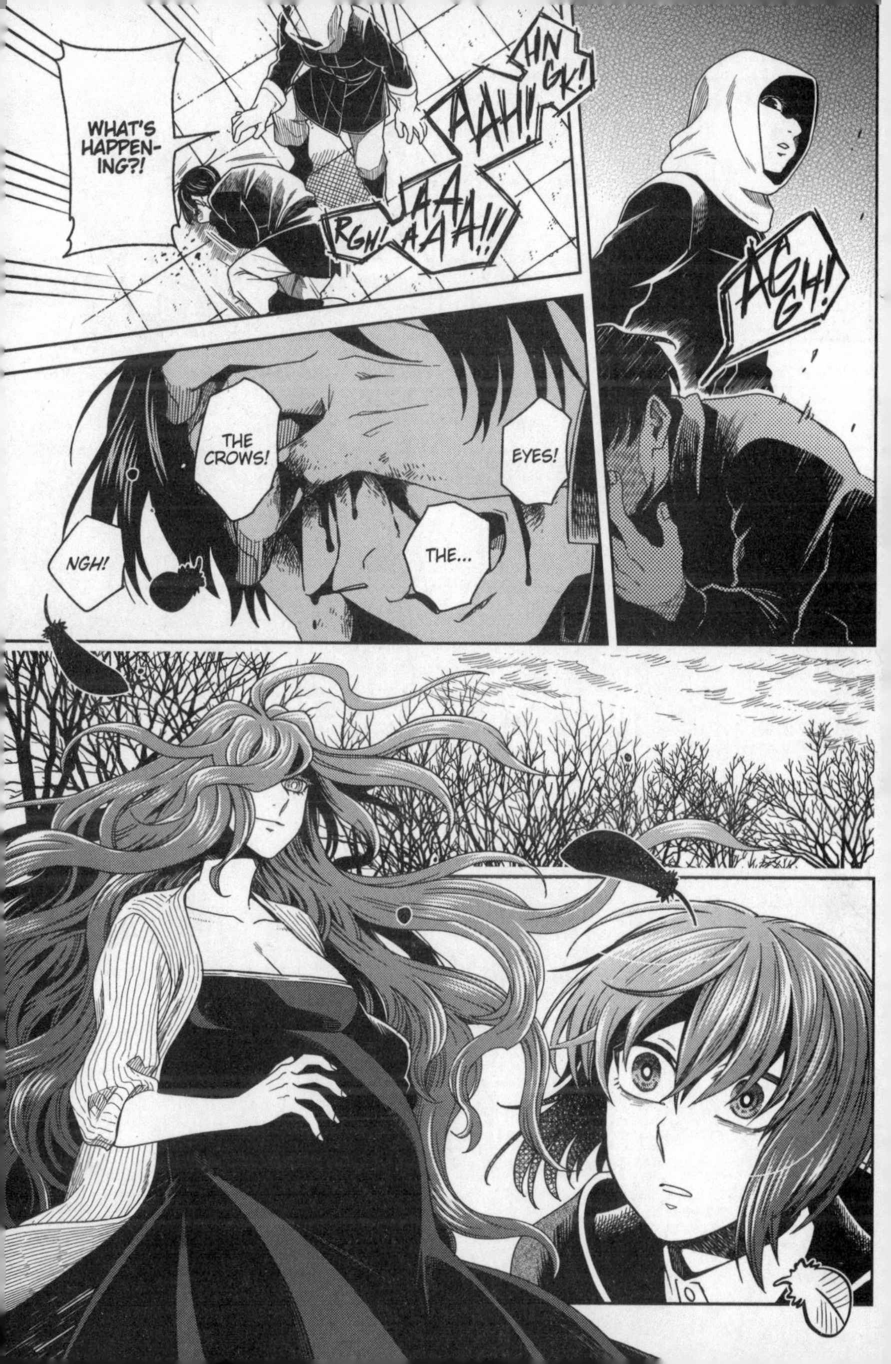
AGGH!
AAH!
HNGK!
AAAAA!!
RGH!
WHAT'S HAPPENING?!
EYES!
THE...
THE CROWS!
NGH!

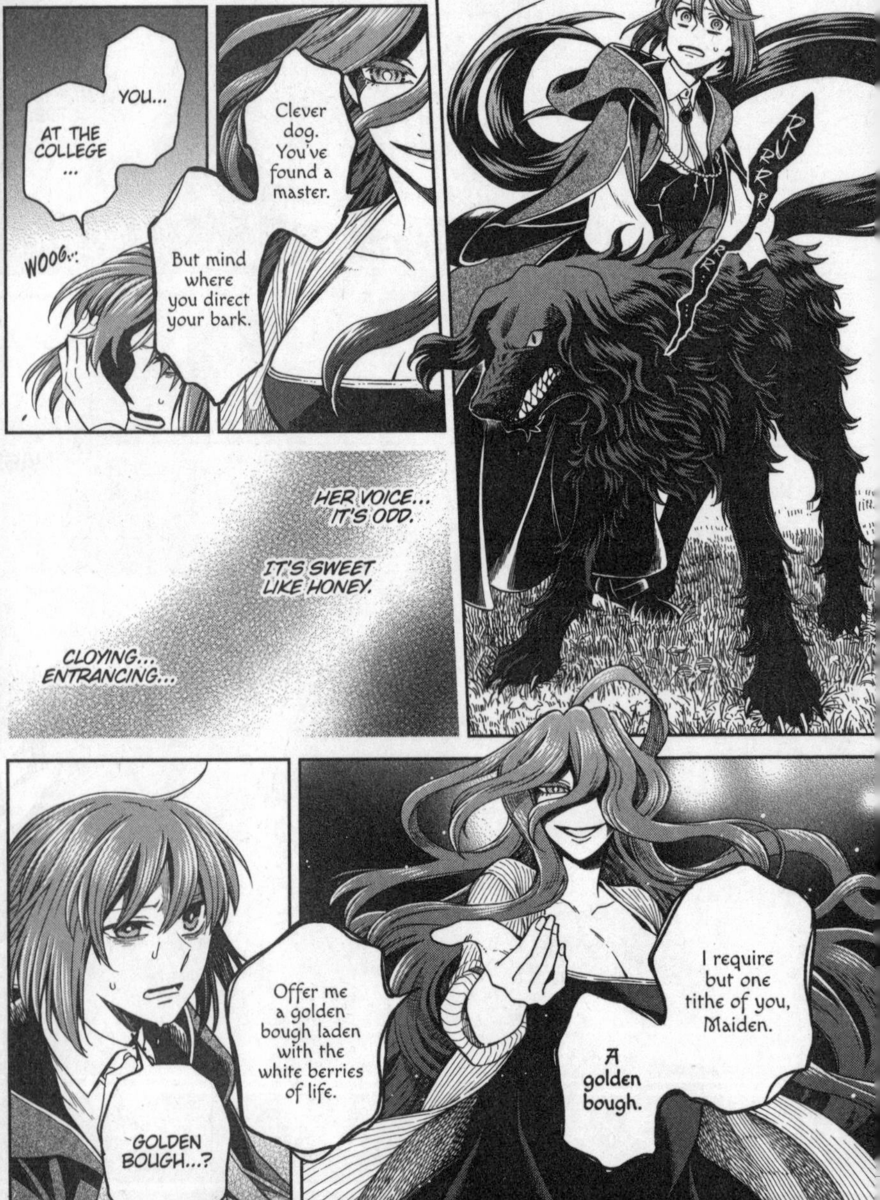
RRRRRR
Clever dog. You've found a master.
But mind where you direct your bark.
YOU... AT THE COLLEGE...
WOOG...
HER VOICE... IT'S ODD.
IT'S SWEET LIKE HONEY.
CLOYING... ENTRANCING...
I require but one tithe of you, Maiden.
A golden bough.
Offer me a golden bough laden with the white berries of life.
GOLDEN BOUGH...?

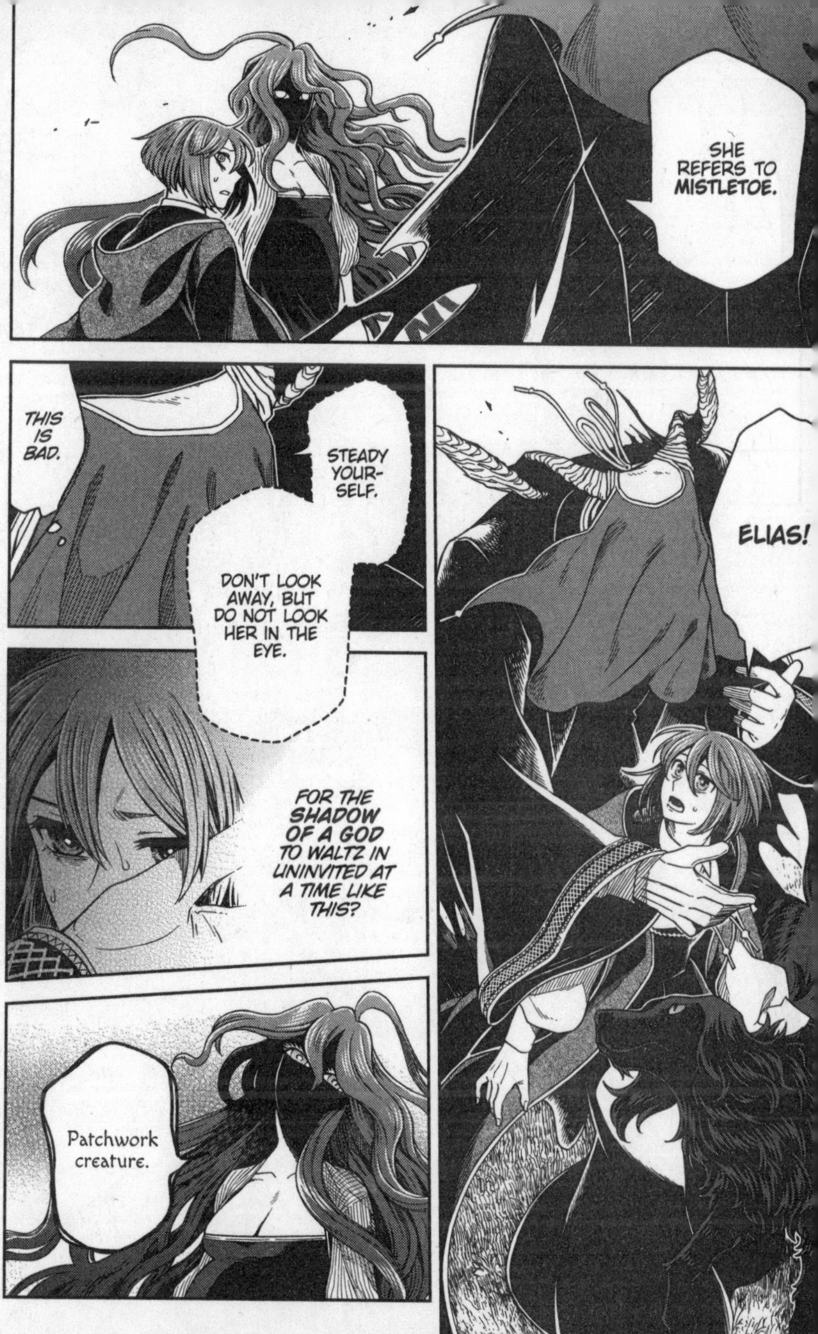
SHE REFERS TO MISTLETOE.
ELIAS!
THIS IS BAD.
STEADY YOURSELF.
DON'T LOOK AWAY, BUT DO NOT LOOK HER IN THE EYE.
FOR THE SHADOW OF A GOD TO WALTZ IN UNINVITED AT A TIME LIKE THIS?
Patchwork creature.

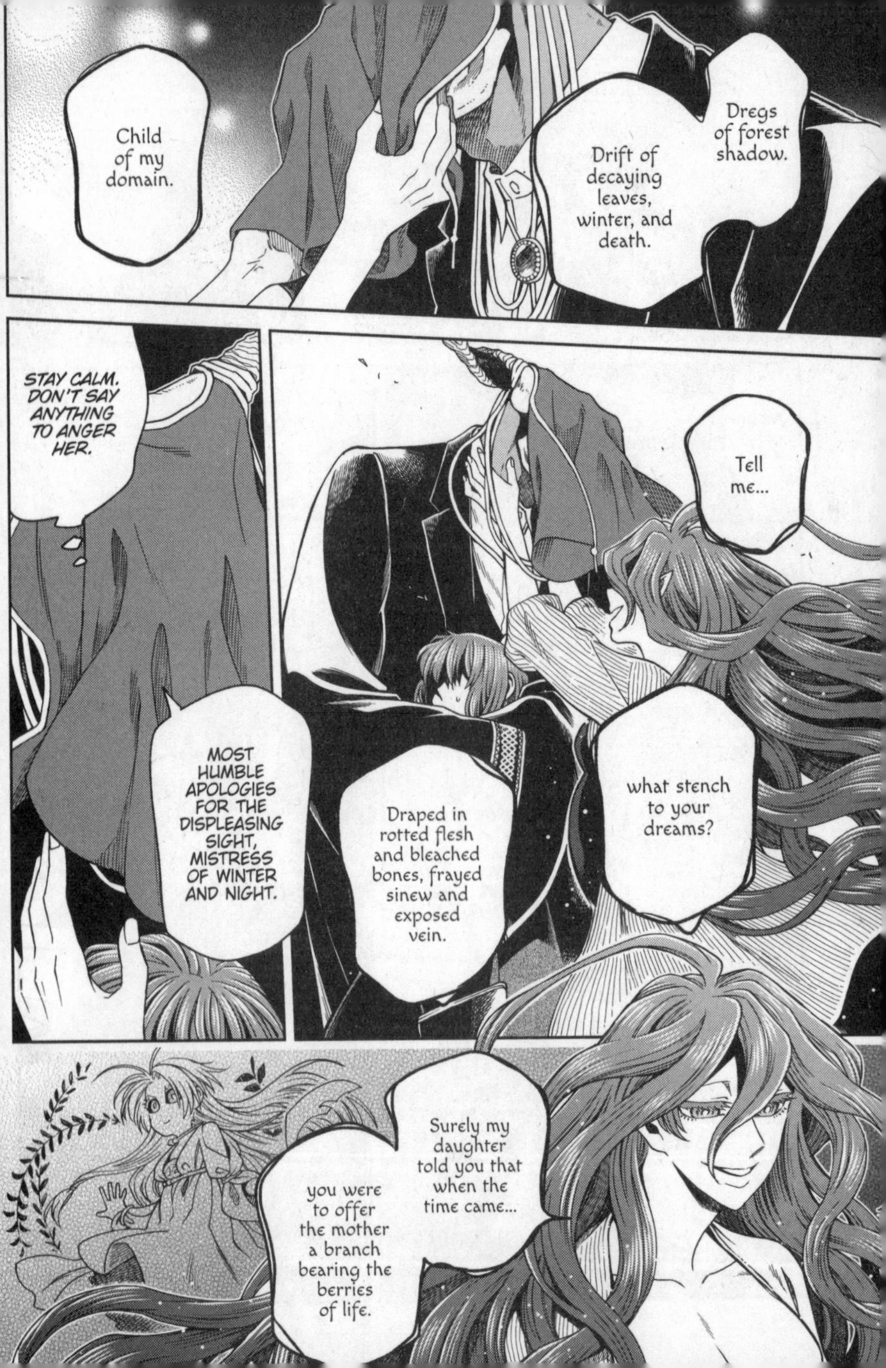
Dregs of forest shadow.
Drift of decaying leaves, winter, and death.
Child of my domain.
Tell me...
what stench to your dreams?
Draped in rotted flesh and bleached bones, frayed sinew and exposed vein.
STAY CALM. DON'T SAY ANYTHING TO ANGER HER.
MOST HUMBLE APOLOGIES FOR THE DISPLEASING SIGHT, MISTRESS OF WINTER AND NIGHT.
Surely my daughter told you that when the time came...
you were to offer the mother a branch bearing the berries of life.

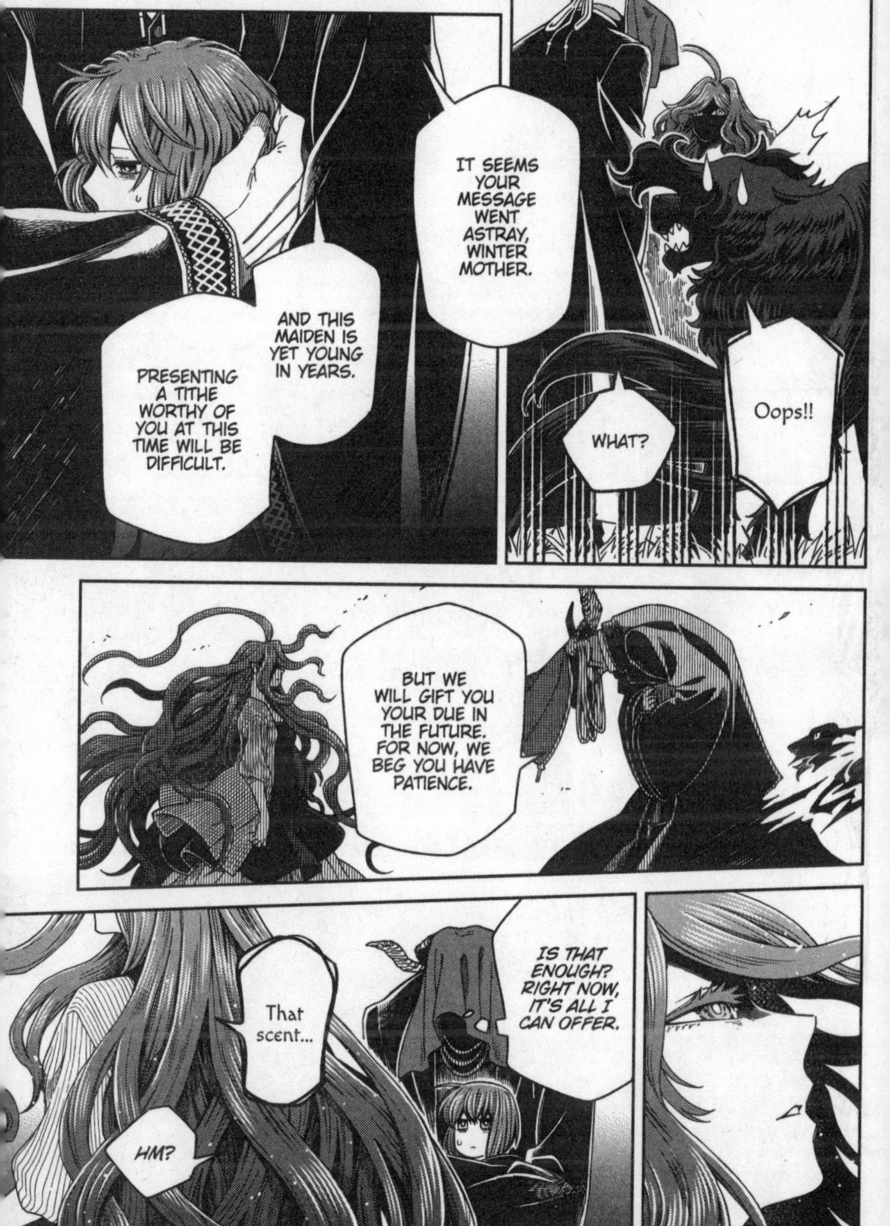

Oops!!
WHAT?
IT SEEMS YOUR MESSAGE WENT ASTRAY, WINTER MOTHER.
AND THIS MAIDEN IS YET YOUNG IN YEARS.
PRESENTING A TITHE WORTHY OF YOU AT THIS TIME WILL BE DIFFICULT.
BUT WE WILL GIFT YOU YOUR DUE IN THE FUTURE. FOR NOW, WE BEG YOU HAVE PATIENCE.
IS THAT ENOUGH? RIGHT NOW, IT'S ALL I CAN OFFER.
That scent...
HM?

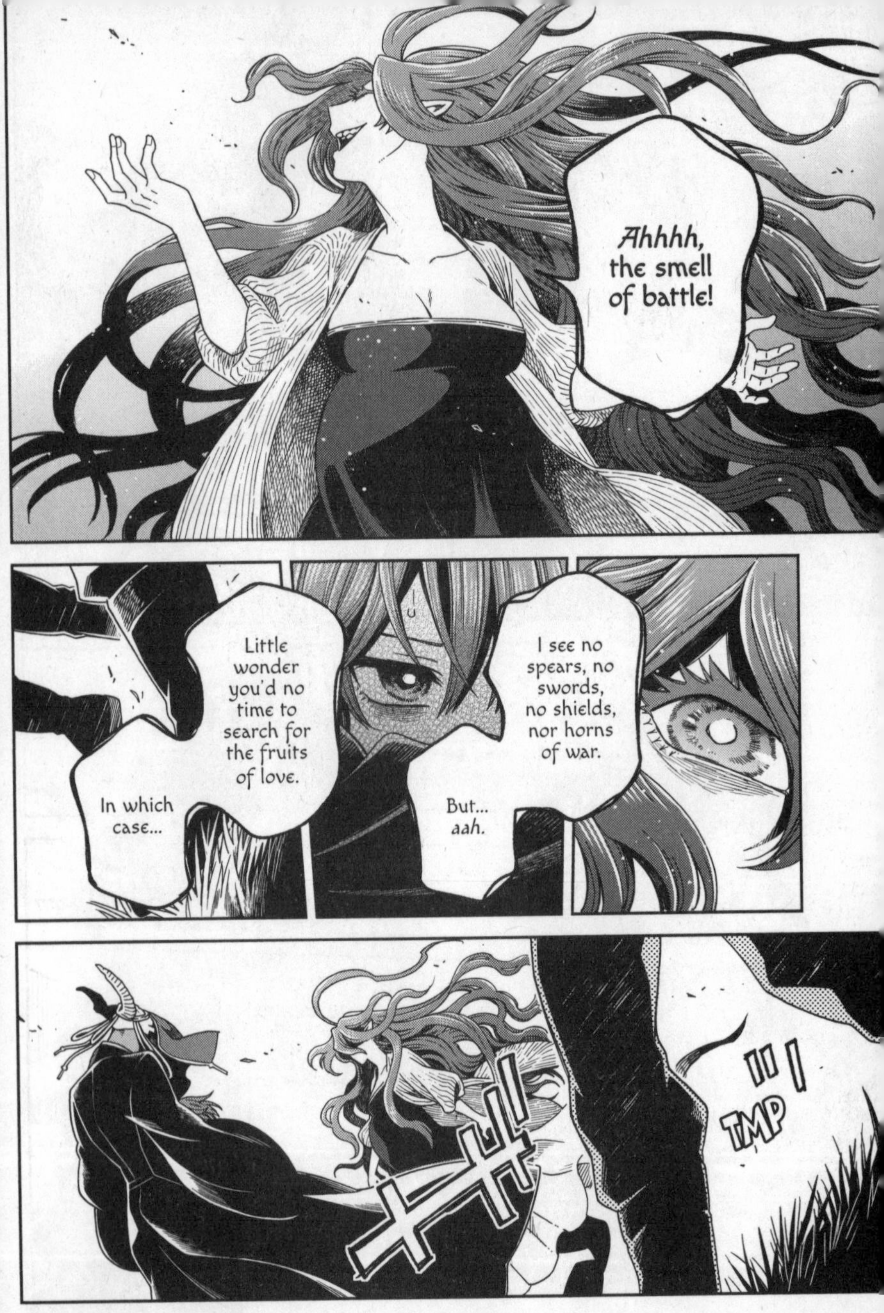
Ahhhh, the smell of battle!
I see no spears, no swords, no shields, nor horns of war.
But... aah.
Little wonder you'd no time to search for the fruits of love.
In which case...
TMP

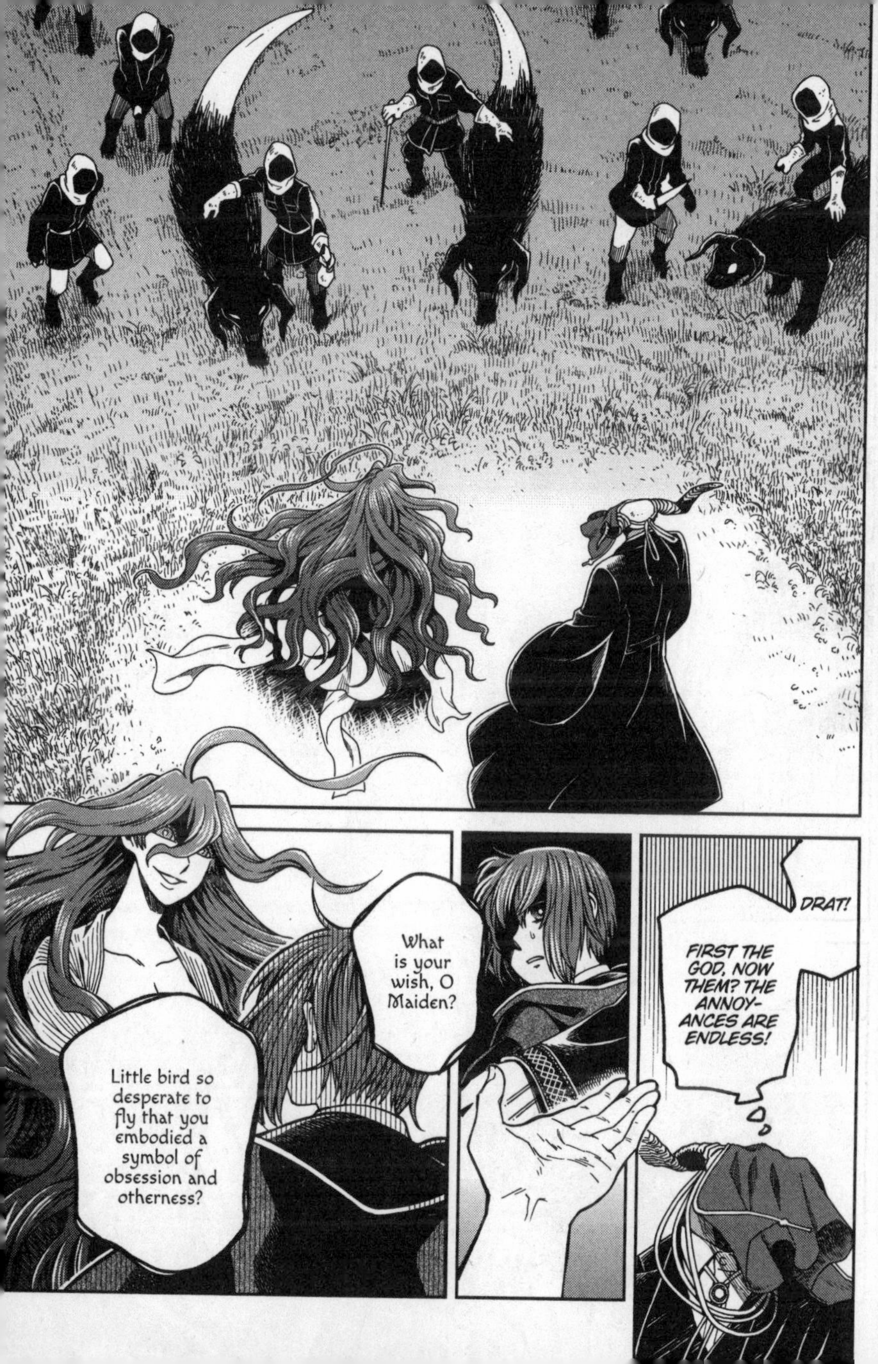

DRAT!
FIRST THE GOD, NOW THEM? THE ANNOY-ANCES ARE ENDLESS!
What is your wish, O Maiden?
Little bird so desperate to fly that you embodied a symbol of obsession and otherness?

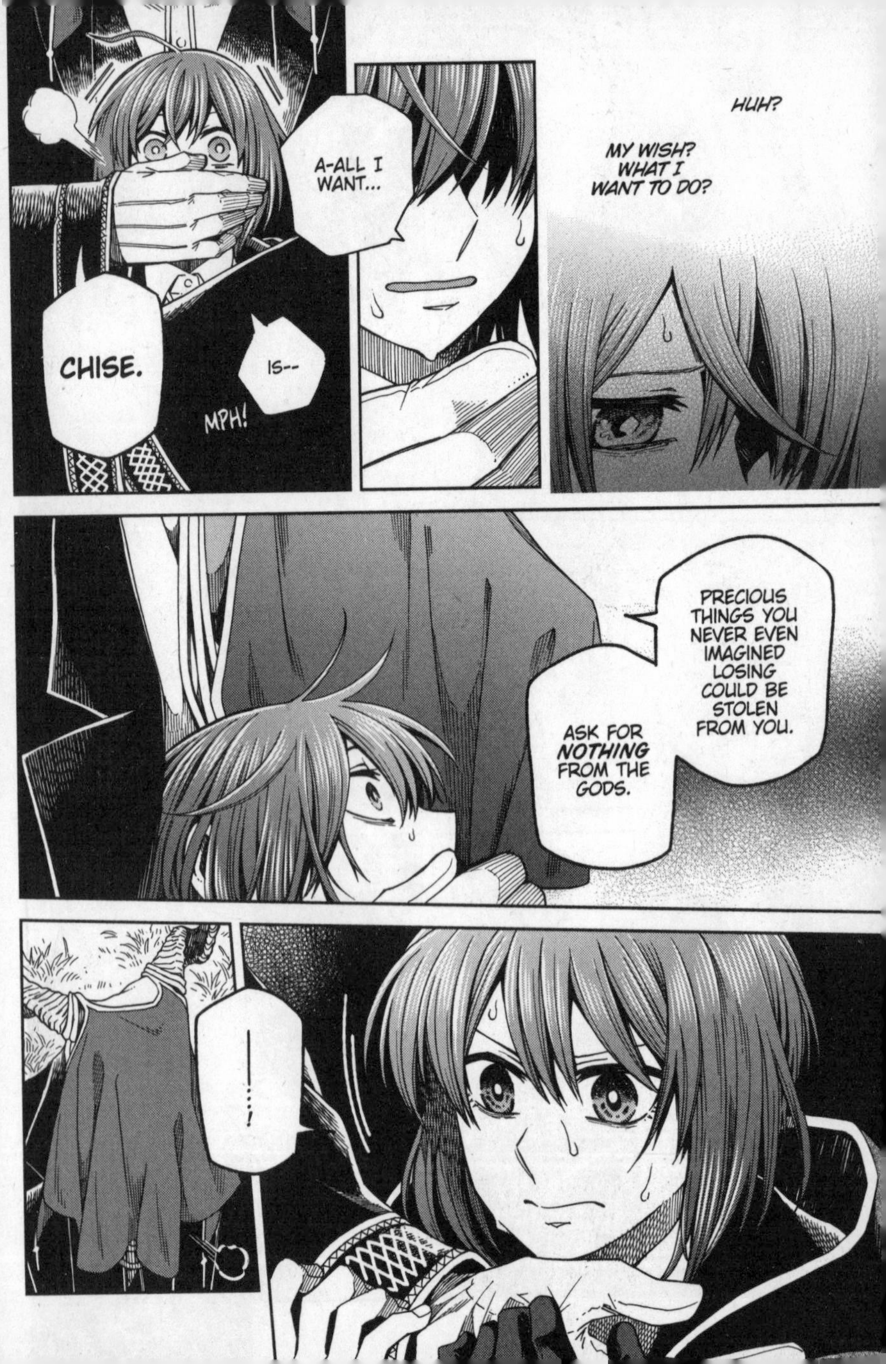
HUH?
MY WISH? WHAT I WANT TO DO?
A-ALL I WANT...
IS--
CHISE.
MPH!
PRECIOUS THINGS YOU NEVER EVEN IMAGINED LOSING COULD BE STOLEN FROM YOU.
ASK FOR NOTHING FROM THE GODS.
...!

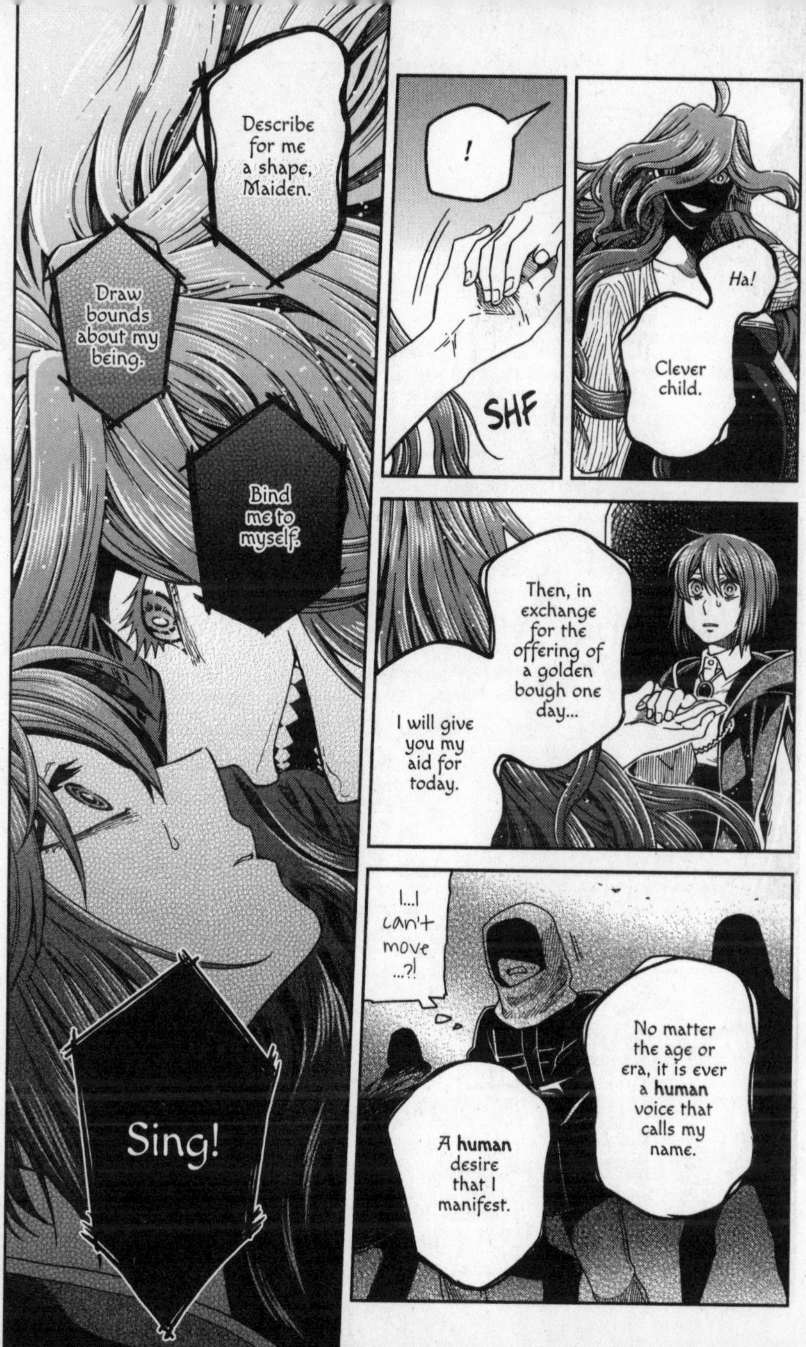
Ha!
Clever child.
!
SHF
Then, in exchange for the offering of a golden bough one day...
I will give you my aid for today.
No matter the age or era, it is ever a **human** voice that calls my name.
A **human** desire that I manifest.
I...I can't move ...?!
Describe for me a shape, Maiden.
Draw bounds about my being.
Bind me to myself.
Sing!

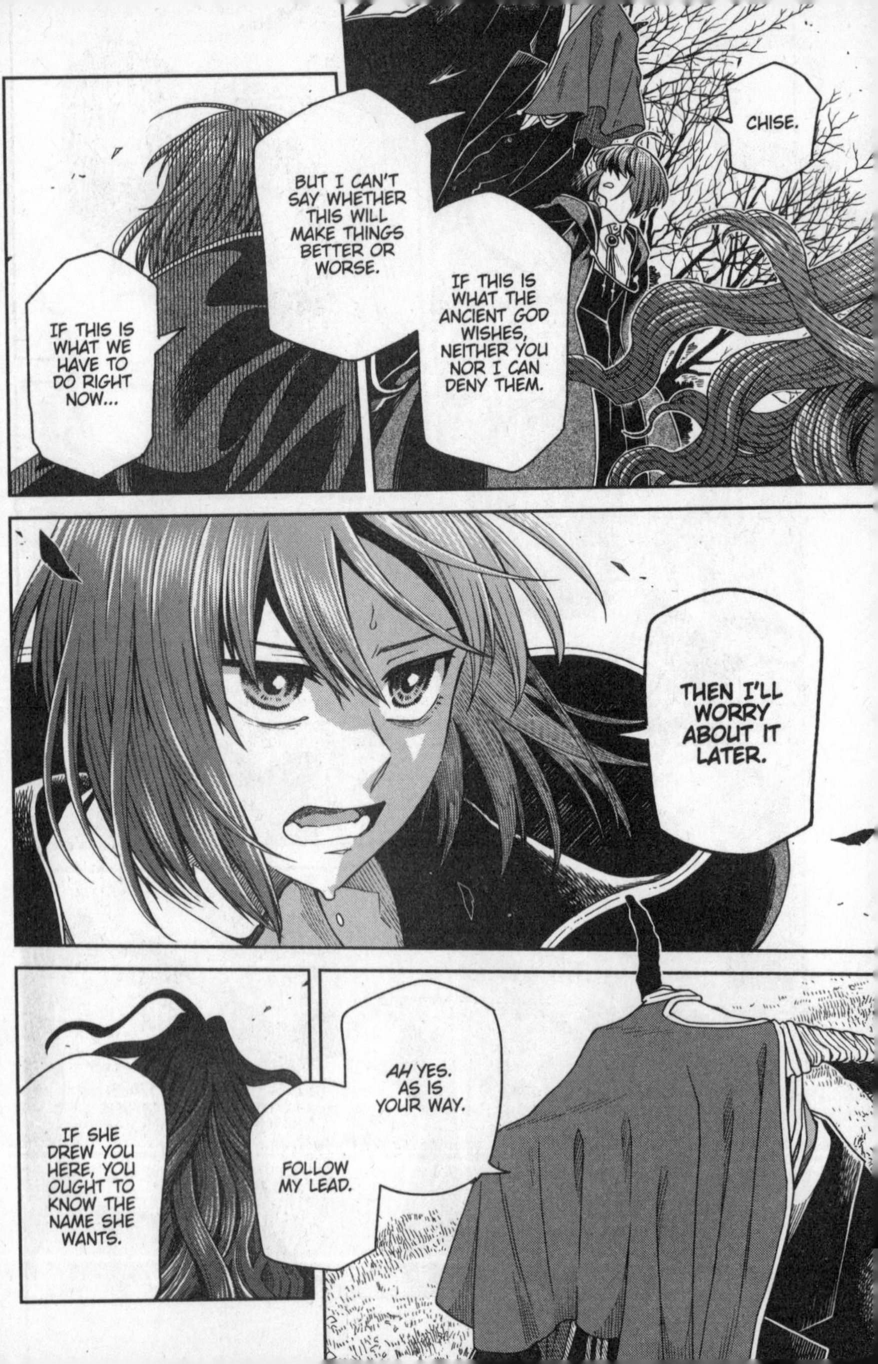
CHISE.
IF THIS IS WHAT THE ANCIENT GOD WISHES, NEITHER YOU NOR I CAN DENY THEM.
BUT I CAN'T SAY WHETHER THIS WILL MAKE THINGS BETTER OR WORSE.
IF THIS IS WHAT WE HAVE TO DO RIGHT NOW...
THEN I'LL WORRY ABOUT IT LATER.
AH YES. AS IS YOUR WAY.
FOLLOW MY LEAD.
IF SHE DREW YOU HERE, YOU OUGHT TO KNOW THE NAME SHE WANTS.

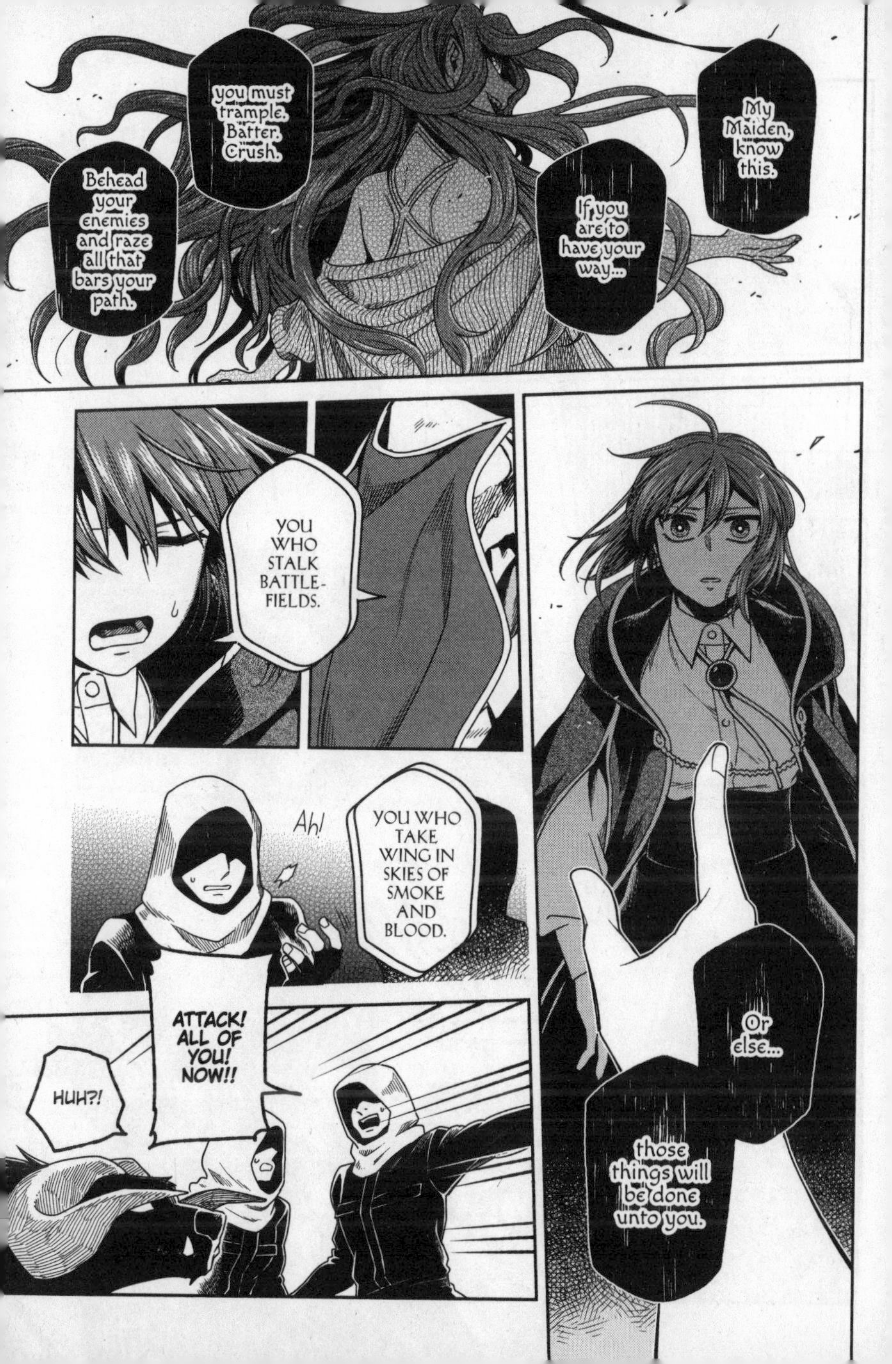

My Maiden, know this.
If you are to have your way...
you must trample. Batter. Crush.
Behead your enemies and raze all that bars your path.
Or else...
those things will be done unto you.
YOU WHO STALK BATTLE-FIELDS.
YOU WHO TAKE WING IN SKIES OF SMOKE AND BLOOD.
Ah!
ATTACK! ALL OF YOU! NOW!!
HUH?!

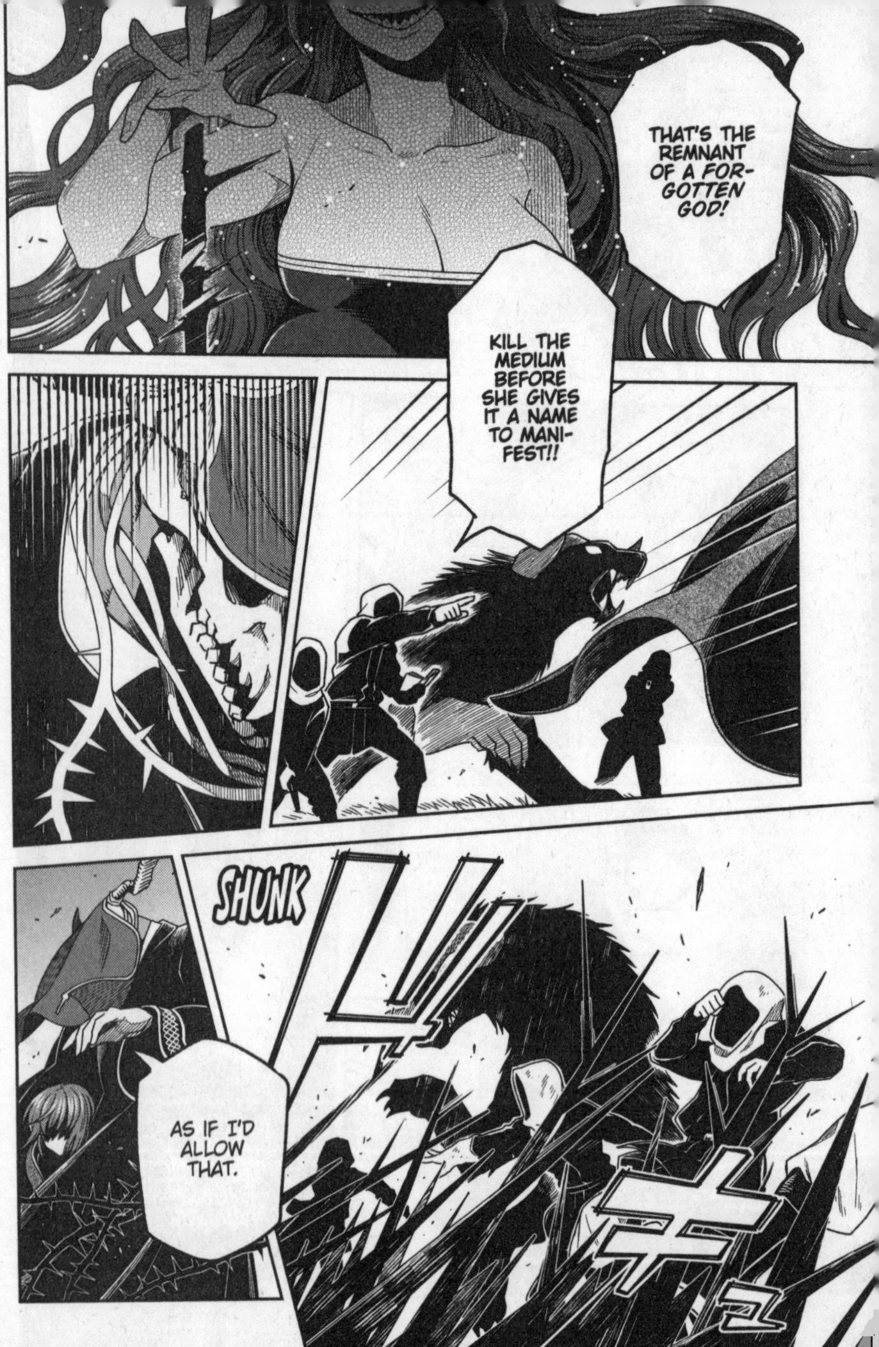

THAT'S THE REMNANT OF A FOR-GOTTEN GOD!
KILL THE MEDIUM BEFORE SHE GIVES IT A NAME TO MANI-FEST!!
SHUNK
AS IF I'D ALLOW THAT.

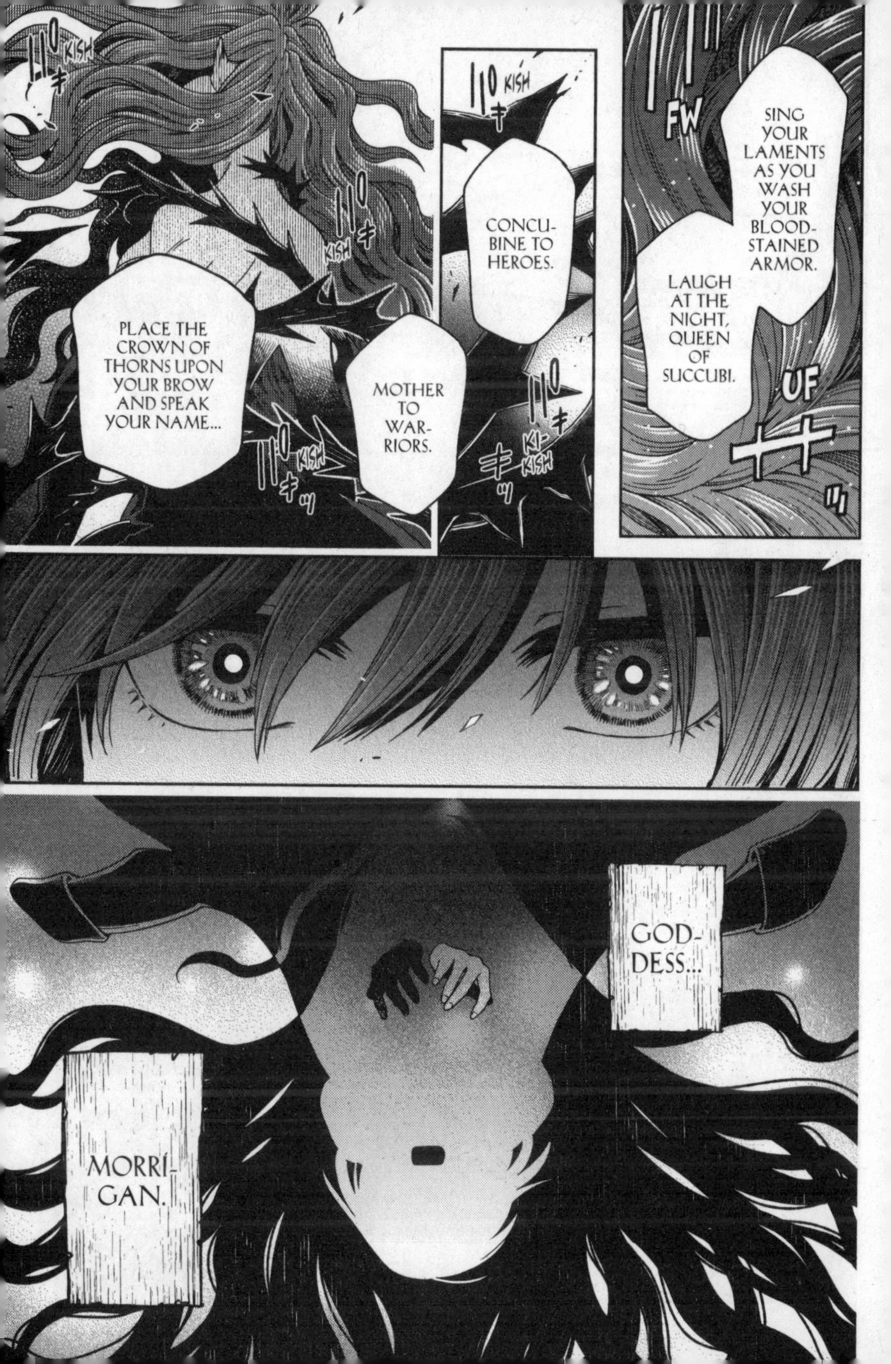
FW
SING YOUR LAMENTS AS YOU WASH YOUR BLOOD-STAINED ARMOR.
LAUGH AT THE NIGHT, QUEEN OF SUCCUBI.
UF
KISH
CONCUBINE TO HEROES.
KI-KISH
KISH
KISH
PLACE THE CROWN OF THORNS UPON YOUR BROW AND SPEAK YOUR NAME...
MOTHER TO WARRIORS.
KISH
GOD-DESS...
MORRÍ-GAN.

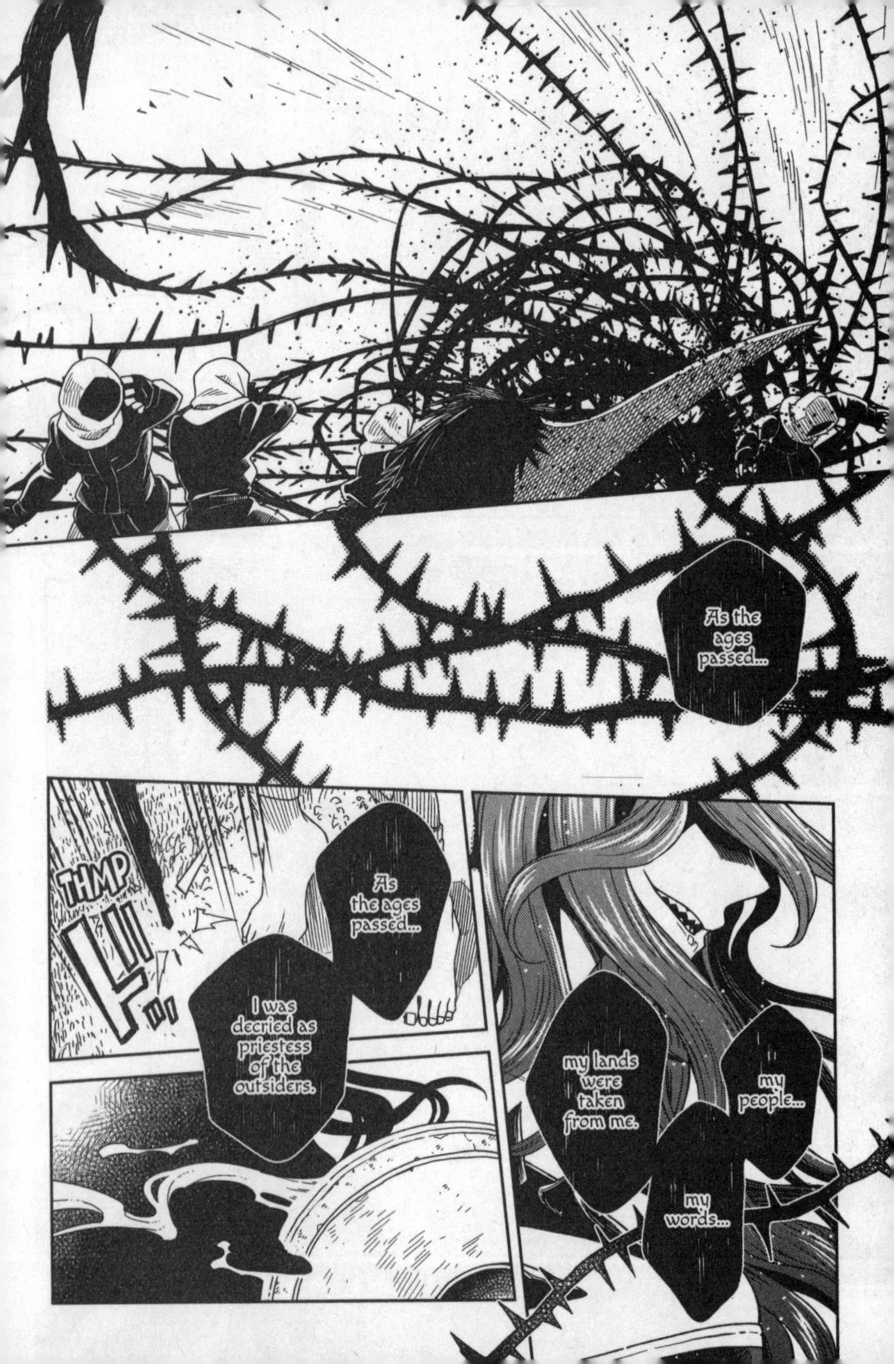

As the ages passed...
my people...
my words...
my lands were taken from me.
As the ages passed...
I was decried as priestess of the outsiders.
THMP

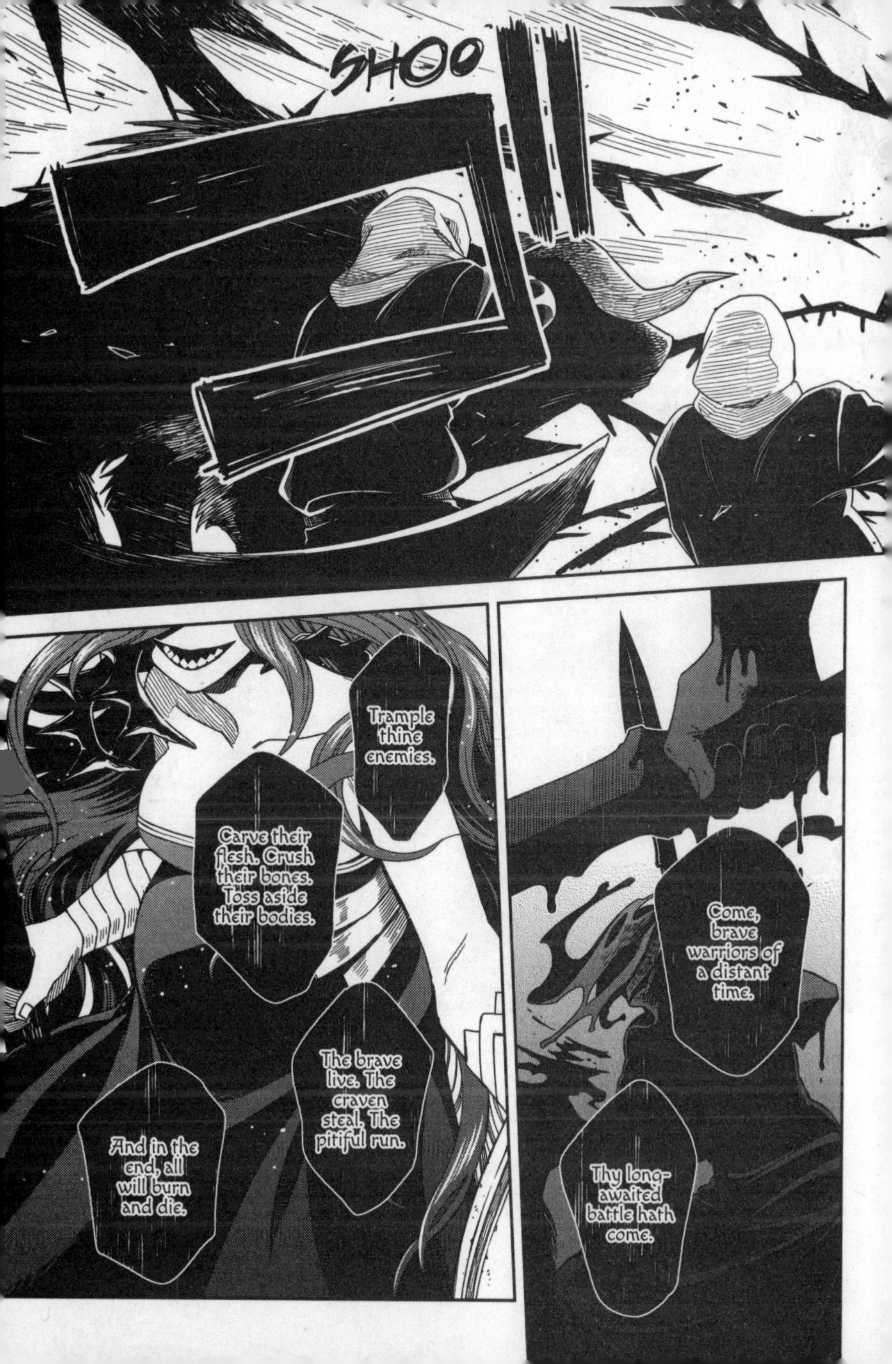
SHOO
Come, brave warriors of a distant time.
Thy long-awaited battle hath come.
Trample thine enemies.
Carve their flesh. Crush their bones. Toss aside their bodies.
The brave live. The craven steal. The pitiful run.
And in the end, all will burn and die.

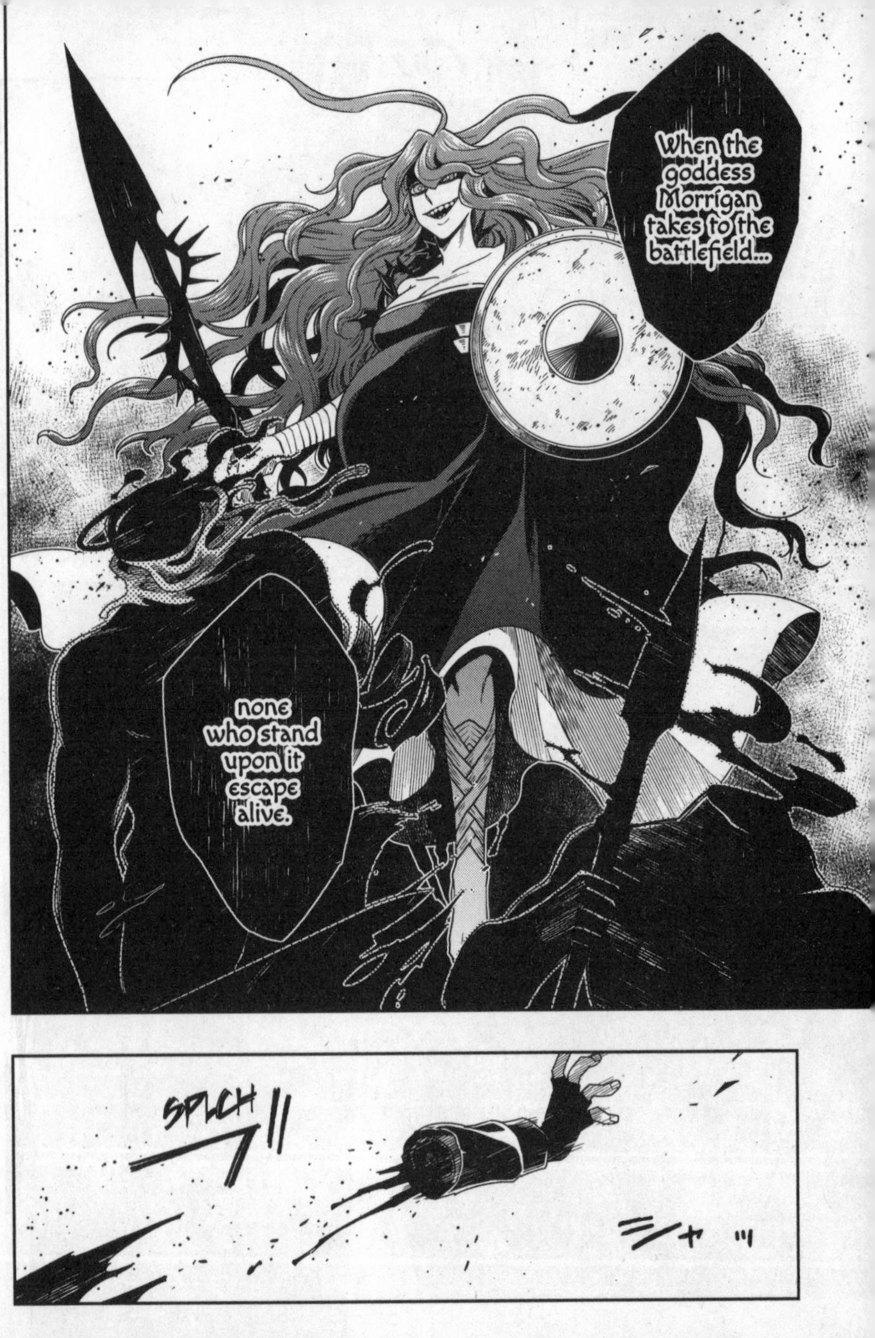
When the goddess Morrígan takes to the battlefield...
none who stand upon it escape alive.
SPLCH

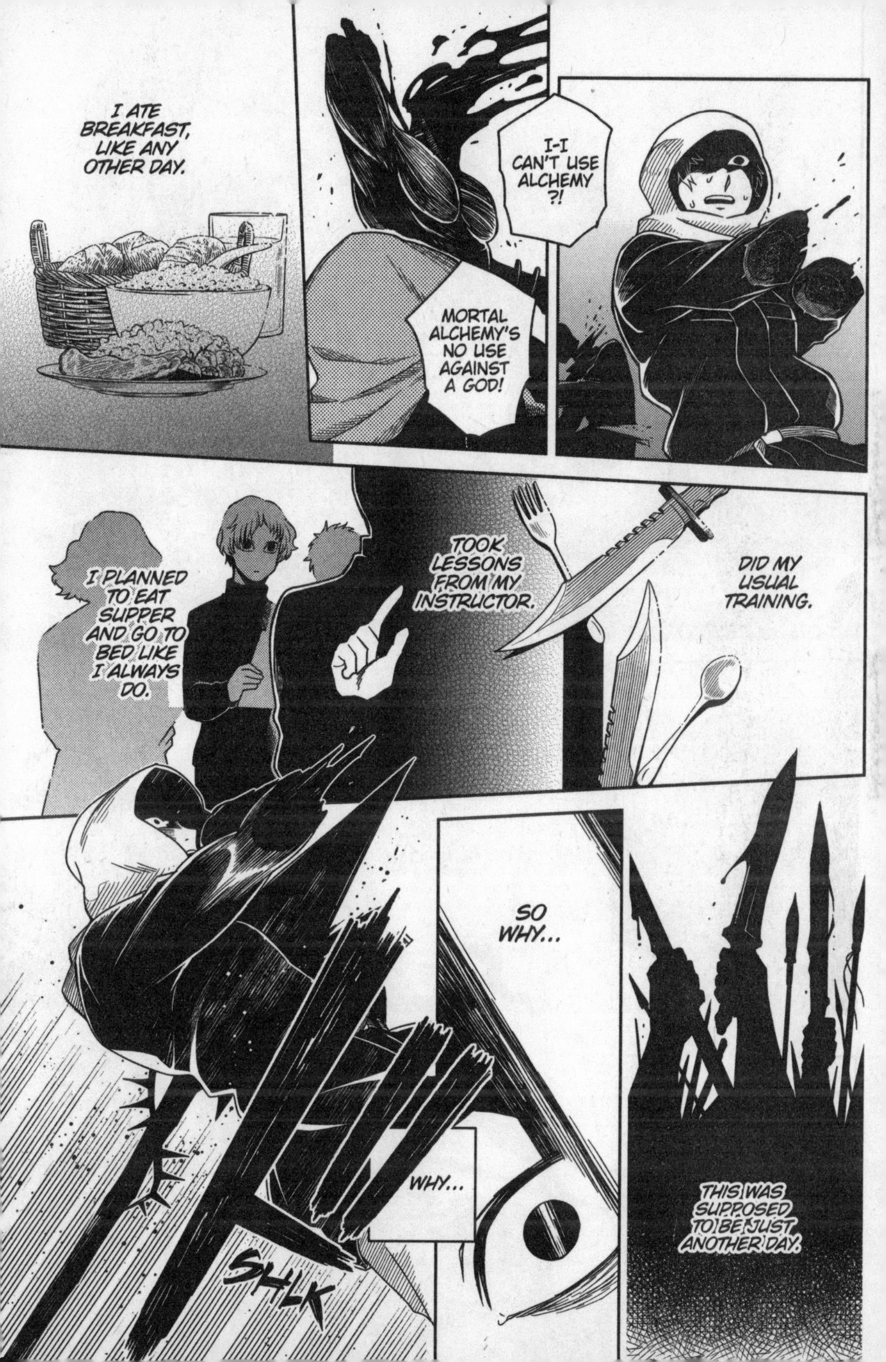
I-I CAN'T USE ALCHEMY ?!
MORTAL ALCHEMY'S NO USE AGAINST A GOD!
I ATE BREAKFAST, LIKE ANY OTHER DAY.
DID MY USUAL TRAINING.
TOOK LESSONS FROM MY INSTRUCTOR.
I PLANNED TO EAT SUPPER AND GO TO BED LIKE I ALWAYS DO.
THIS WAS SUPPOSED TO BE JUST ANOTHER DAY.
SO WHY...
WHY...
SHLK

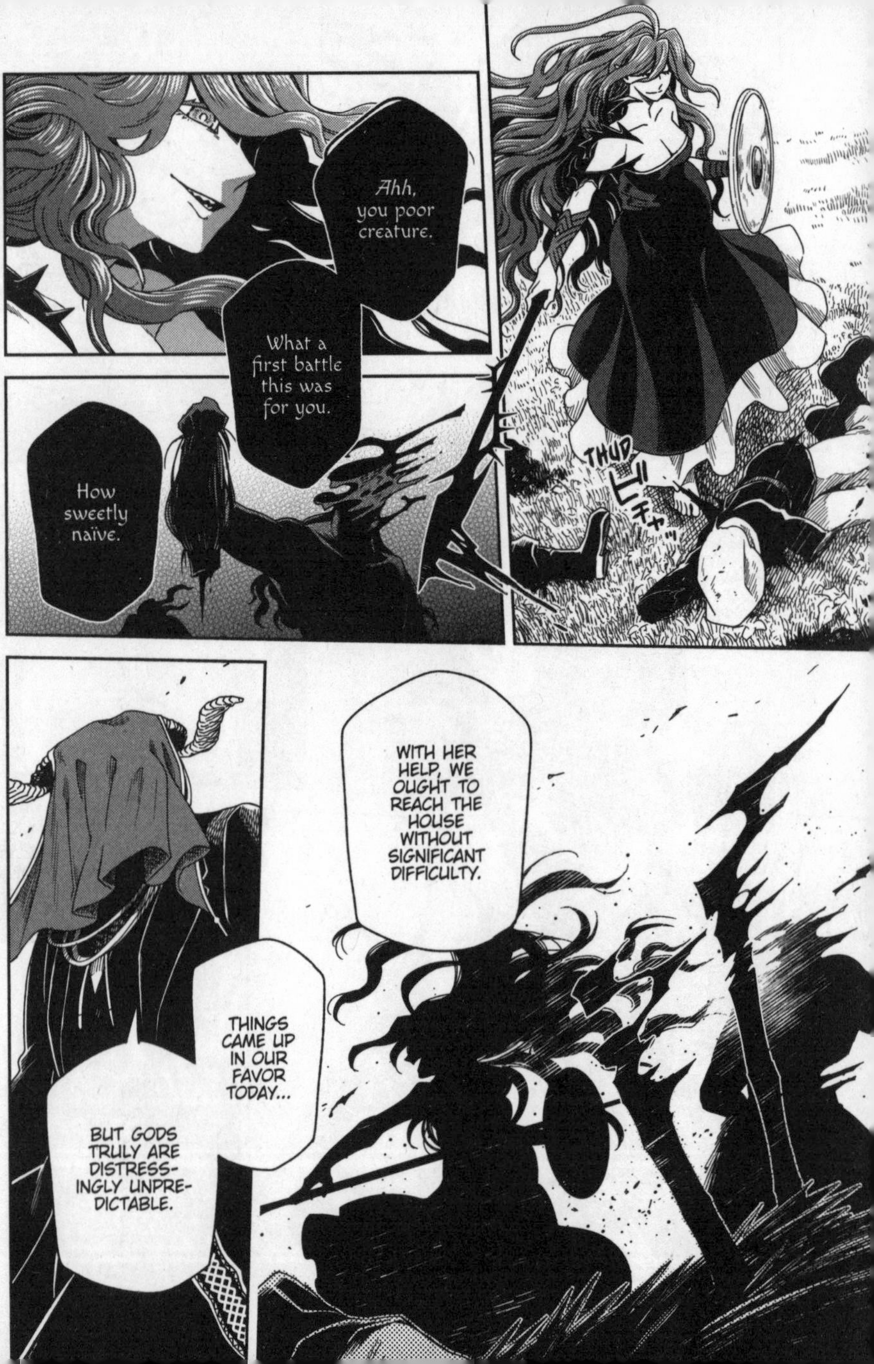
THUD
ビチャッ
Ahh, you poor creature.
What a first battle this was for you.
How sweetly naïve.
WITH HER HELP, WE OUGHT TO REACH THE HOUSE WITHOUT SIGNIFICANT DIFFICULTY.
THINGS CAME UP IN OUR FAVOR TODAY...
BUT GODS TRULY ARE DISTRESSINGLY UNPREDICTABLE.

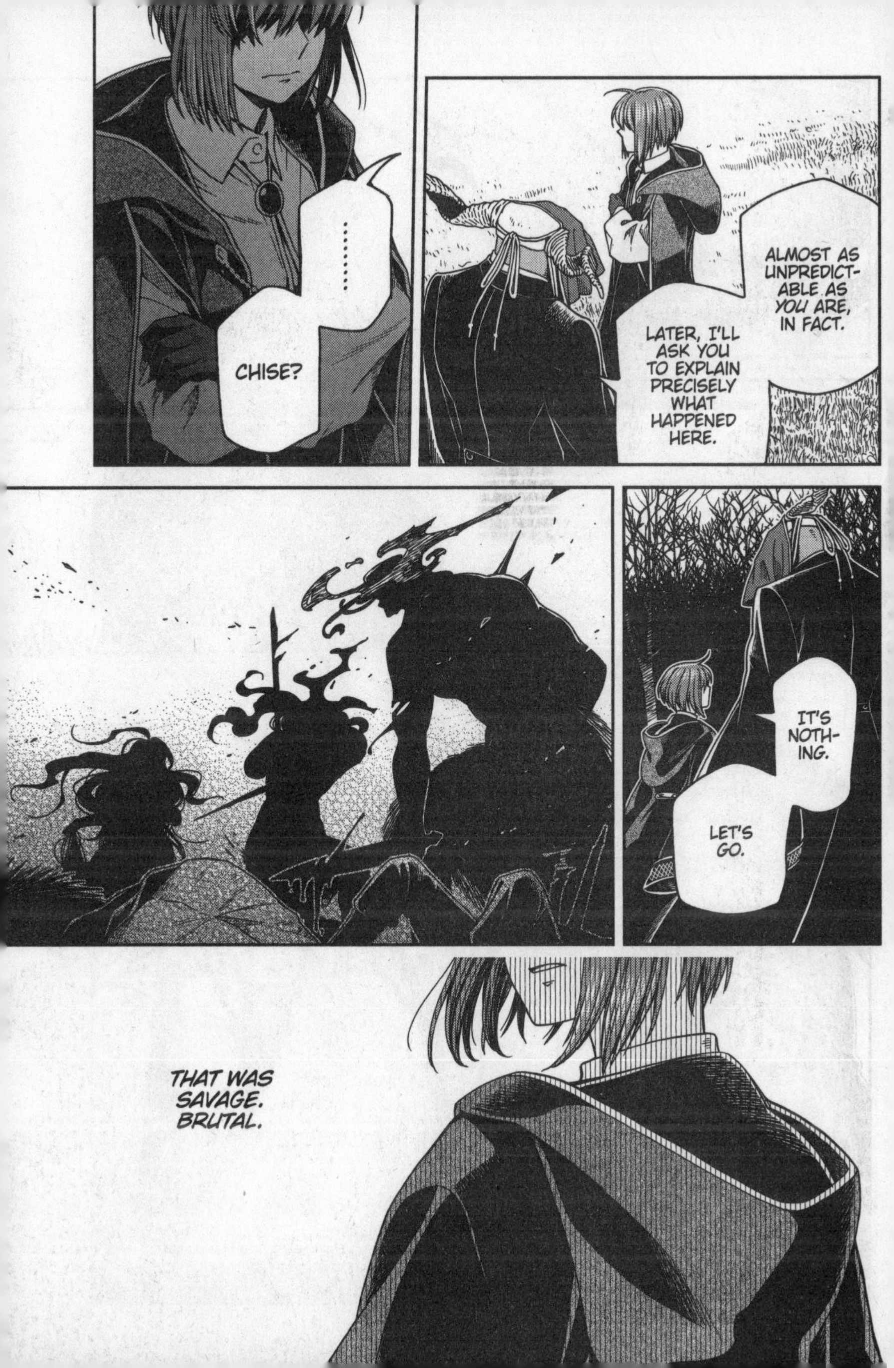
ALMOST AS UNPREDICTABLE AS *YOU* ARE, IN FACT.
LATER, I'LL ASK YOU TO EXPLAIN PRECISELY WHAT HAPPENED HERE.
......
CHISE?
IT'S NOTHING.
LET'S GO.
THAT WAS SAVAGE. BRUTAL.

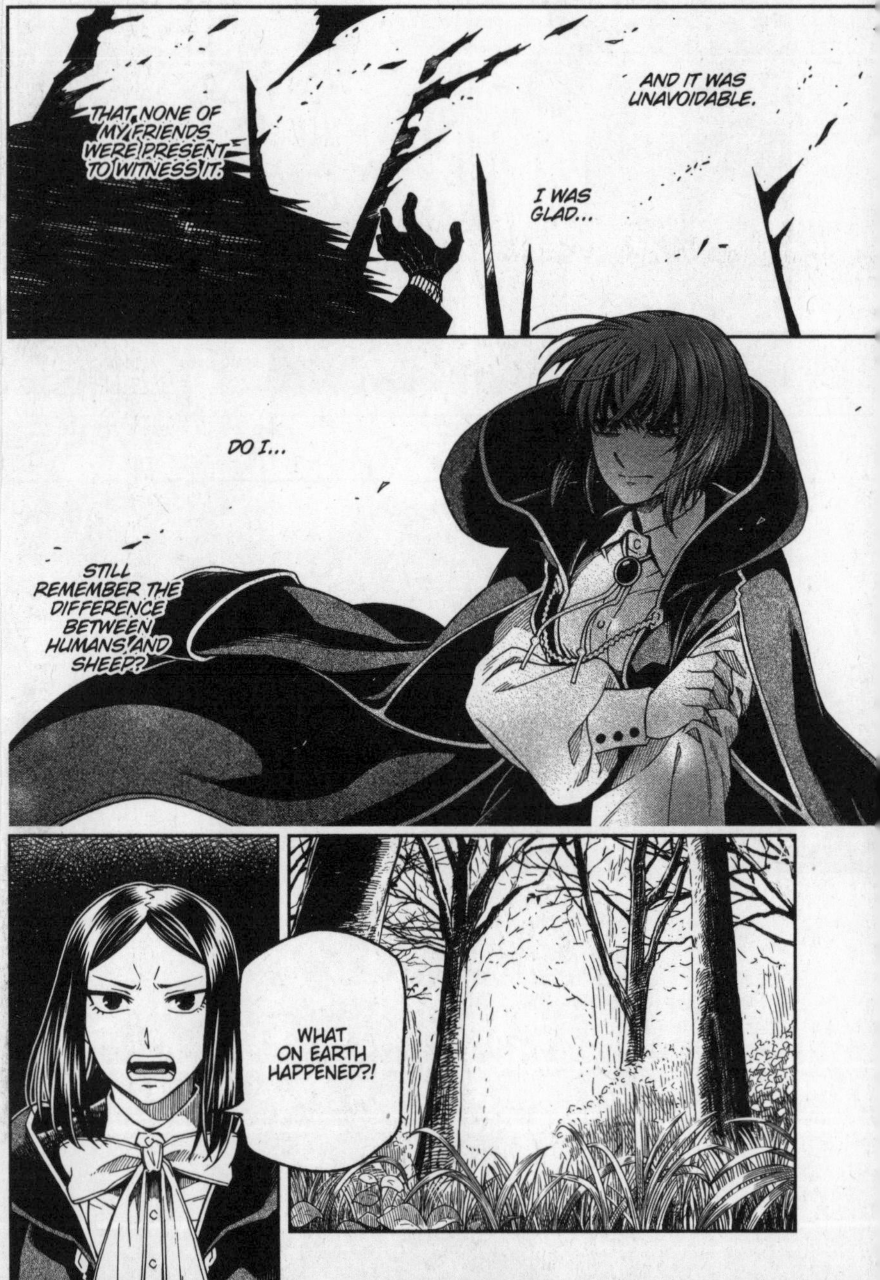
AND IT WAS UNAVOIDABLE.
I WAS GLAD...
THAT NONE OF MY FRIENDS WERE PRESENT TO WITNESS IT.
DO I...
STILL REMEMBER THE DIFFERENCE BETWEEN HUMANS AND SHEEP?
WHAT ON EARTH HAPPENED?!

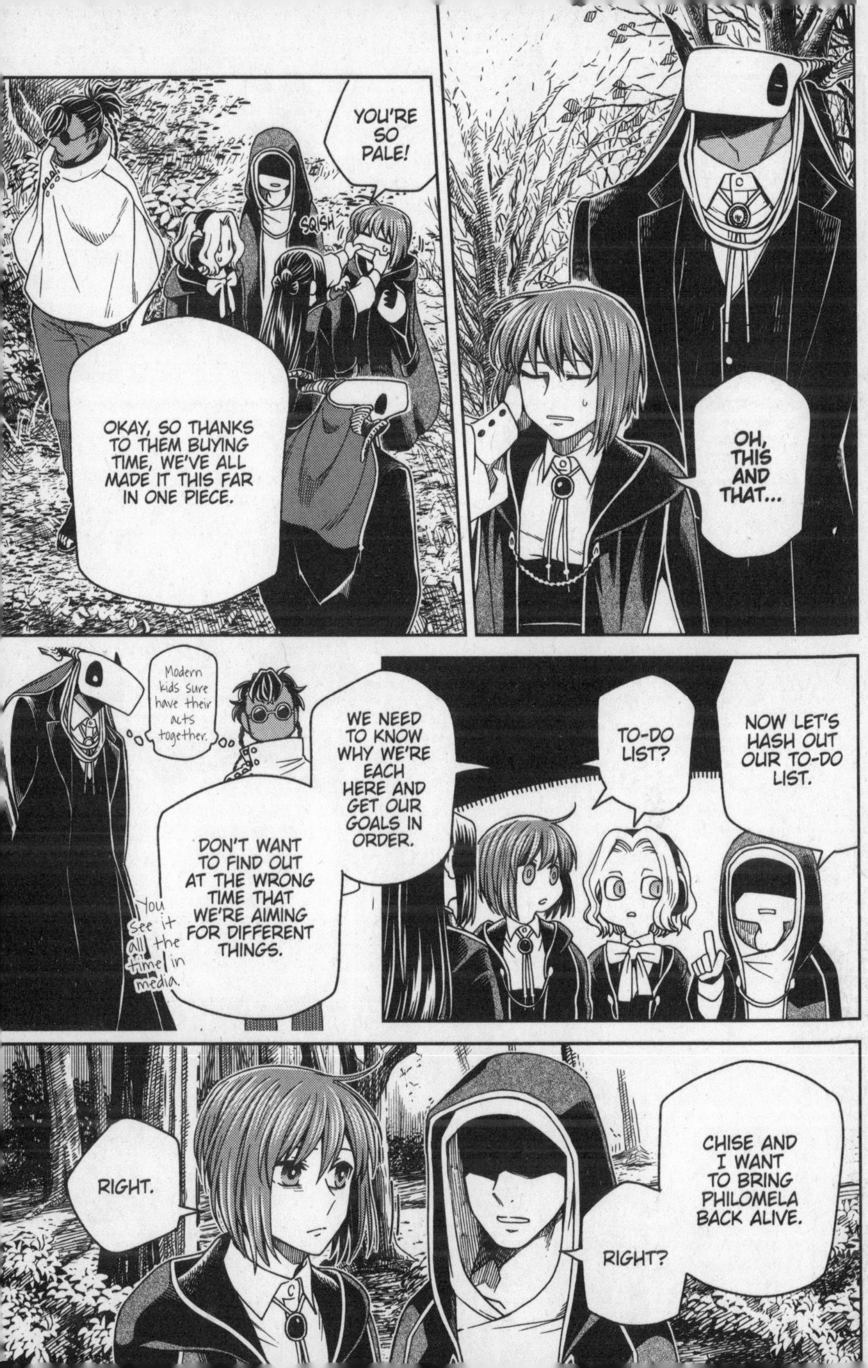
OH, THIS AND THAT...
YOU'RE SO PALE!
SQISH
OKAY, SO THANKS TO THEM BUYING TIME, WE'VE ALL MADE IT THIS FAR IN ONE PIECE.
NOW LET'S HASH OUT OUR TO-DO LIST.
TO-DO LIST?
WE NEED TO KNOW WHY WE'RE EACH HERE AND GET OUR GOALS IN ORDER.
DON'T WANT TO FIND OUT AT THE WRONG TIME THAT WE'RE AIMING FOR DIFFERENT THINGS.
Modern kids sure have their acts together.
You see it all the time in media.
CHISE AND I WANT TO BRING PHILOMELA BACK ALIVE.
RIGHT?
RIGHT.

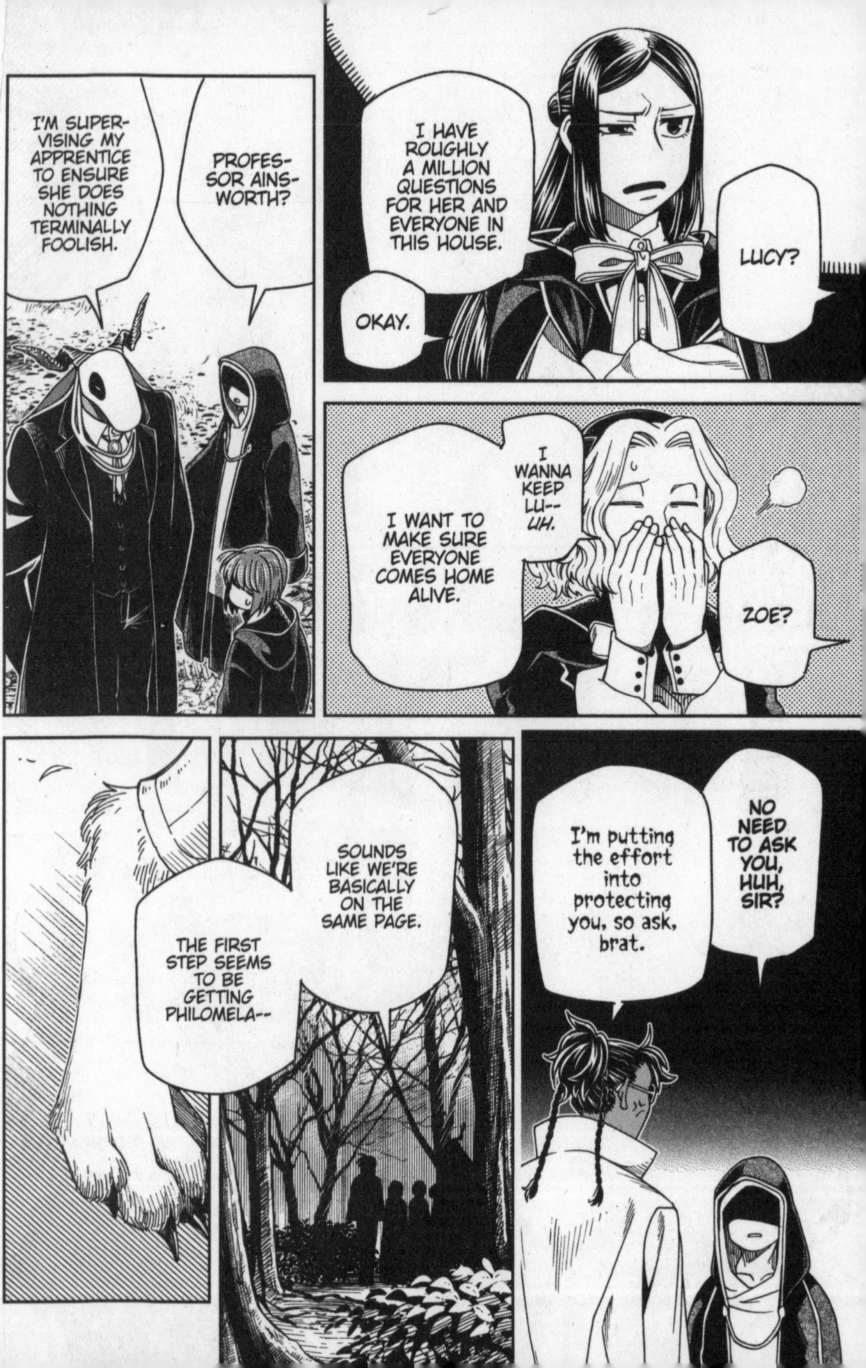
LUCY?
I HAVE ROUGHLY A MILLION QUESTIONS FOR HER AND EVERYONE IN THIS HOUSE.
OKAY.
ZOE?
I WANNA KEEP LU-- UH.
I WANT TO MAKE SURE EVERYONE COMES HOME ALIVE.
PROFESSOR AINSWORTH?
I'M SUPERVISING MY APPRENTICE TO ENSURE SHE DOES NOTHING TERMINALLY FOOLISH.
NO NEED TO ASK YOU, HUH, SIR?
I'm putting the effort into protecting you, so ask, brat.
SOUNDS LIKE WE'RE BASICALLY ON THE SAME PAGE.
THE FIRST STEP SEEMS TO BE GETTING PHILOMELA--

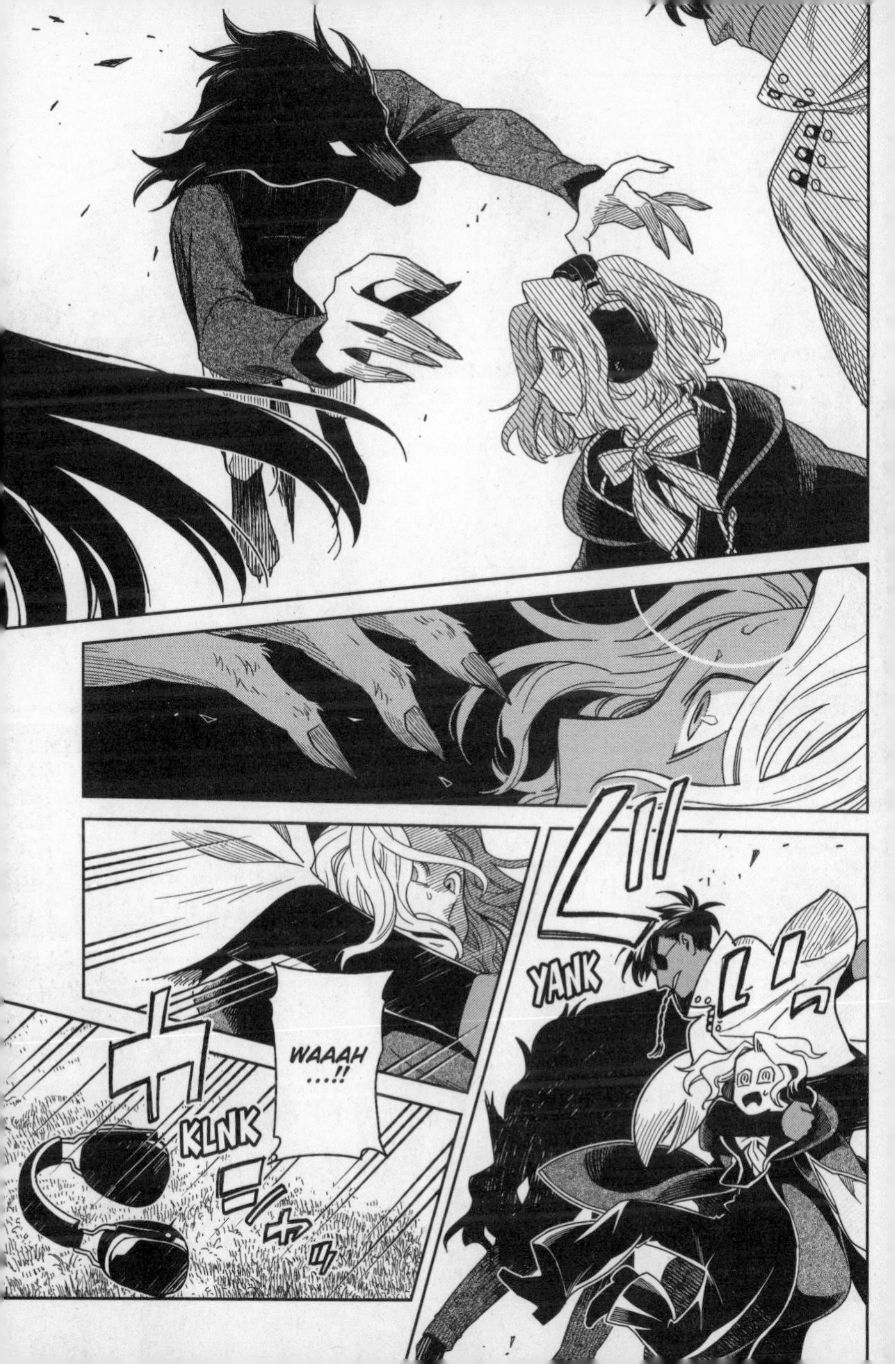
WAAAH ...!!
KLNK
YANK

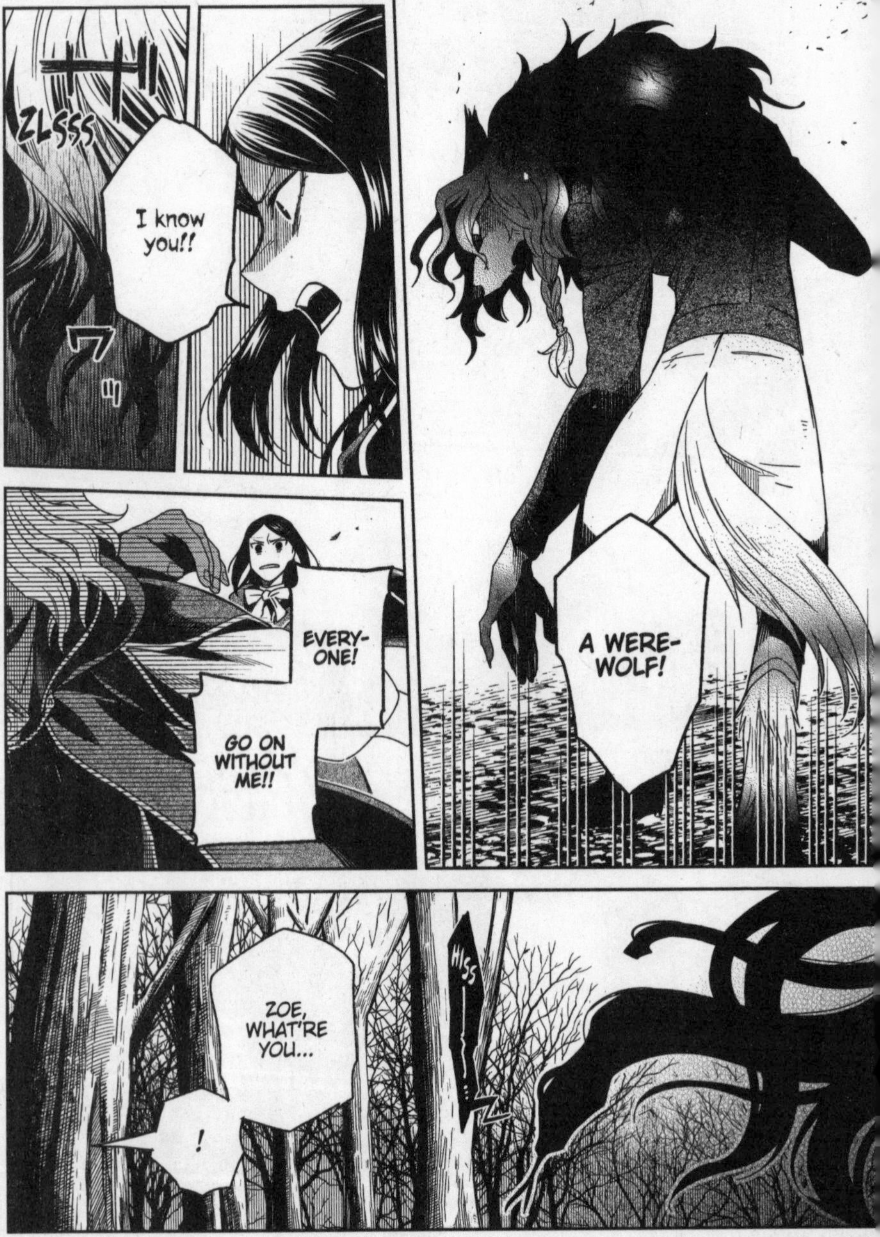
A WERE-WOLF!
ZLSSS
I know you!!
EVERY-ONE!
GO ON WITHOUT ME!!
HISS
ZOE, WHAT'RE YOU...
!

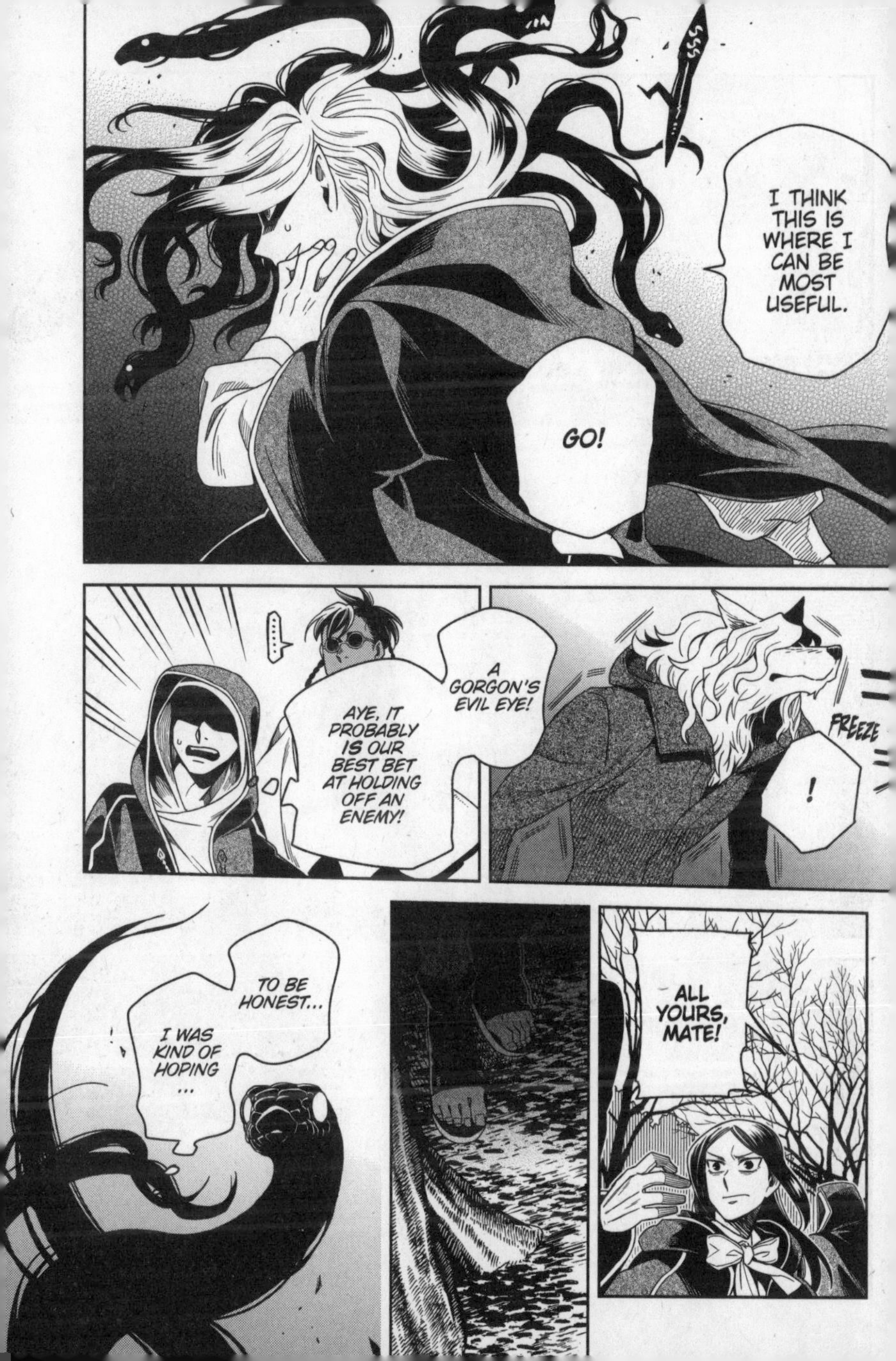
I THINK THIS IS WHERE I CAN BE MOST USEFUL.
GO!
FREEZE
!
A GORGON'S EVIL EYE!
AYE, IT PROBABLY IS OUR BEST BET AT HOLDING OFF AN ENEMY!
......
ALL YOURS, MATE!
TO BE HONEST...
I WAS KIND OF HOPING ...

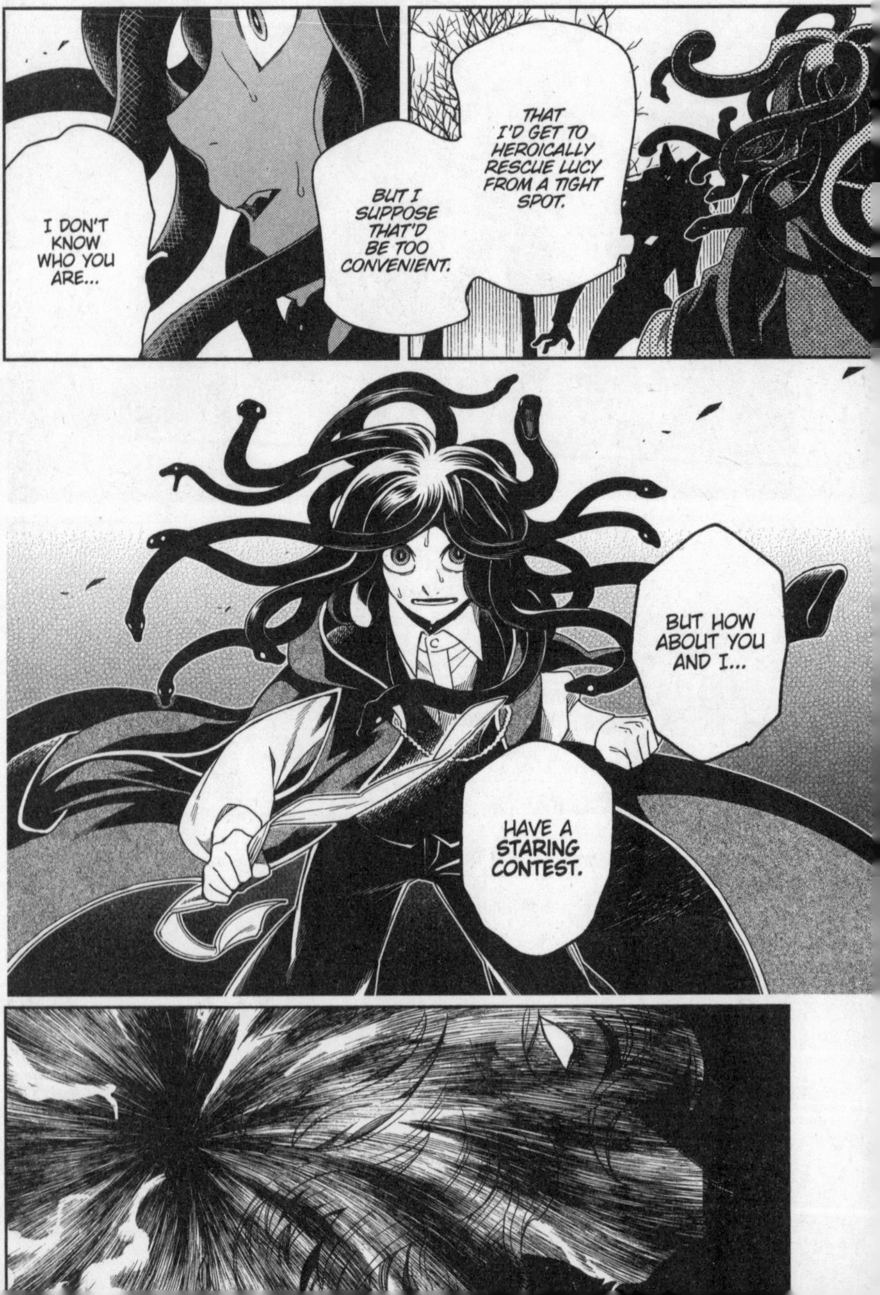
THAT I'D GET TO HEROICALLY RESCUE LUCY FROM A TIGHT SPOT.
BUT I SUPPOSE THAT'D BE TOO CONVENIENT.
I DON'T KNOW WHO YOU ARE...
BUT HOW ABOUT YOU AND I...
HAVE A STARING CONTEST.

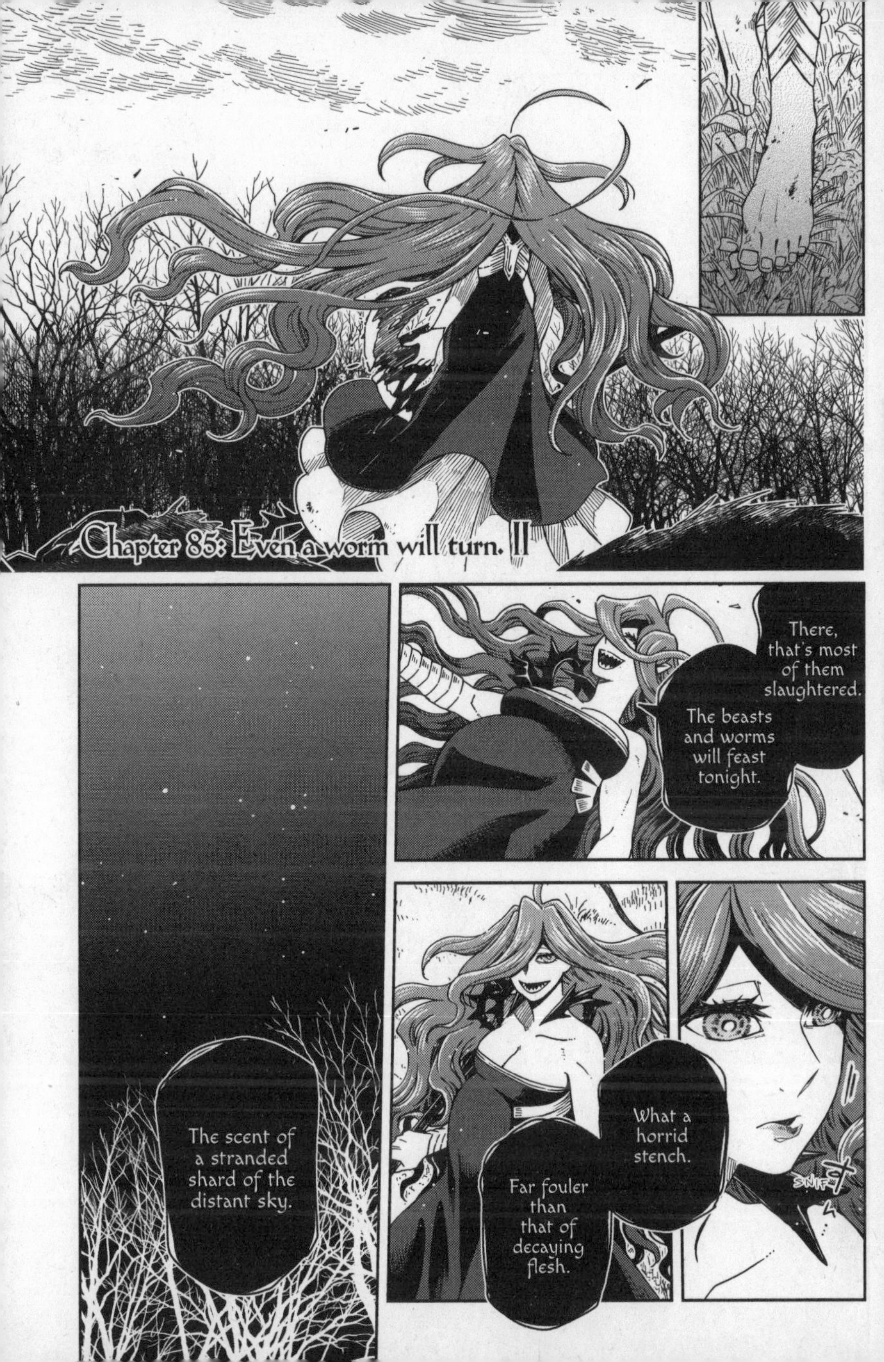
Chapter 85: Even a worm will turn. II
There, that's most of them slaughtered.
The beasts and worms will feast tonight.
The scent of a stranded shard of the distant sky.
What a horrid stench.
Far fouler than that of decaying flesh.
SNIFF

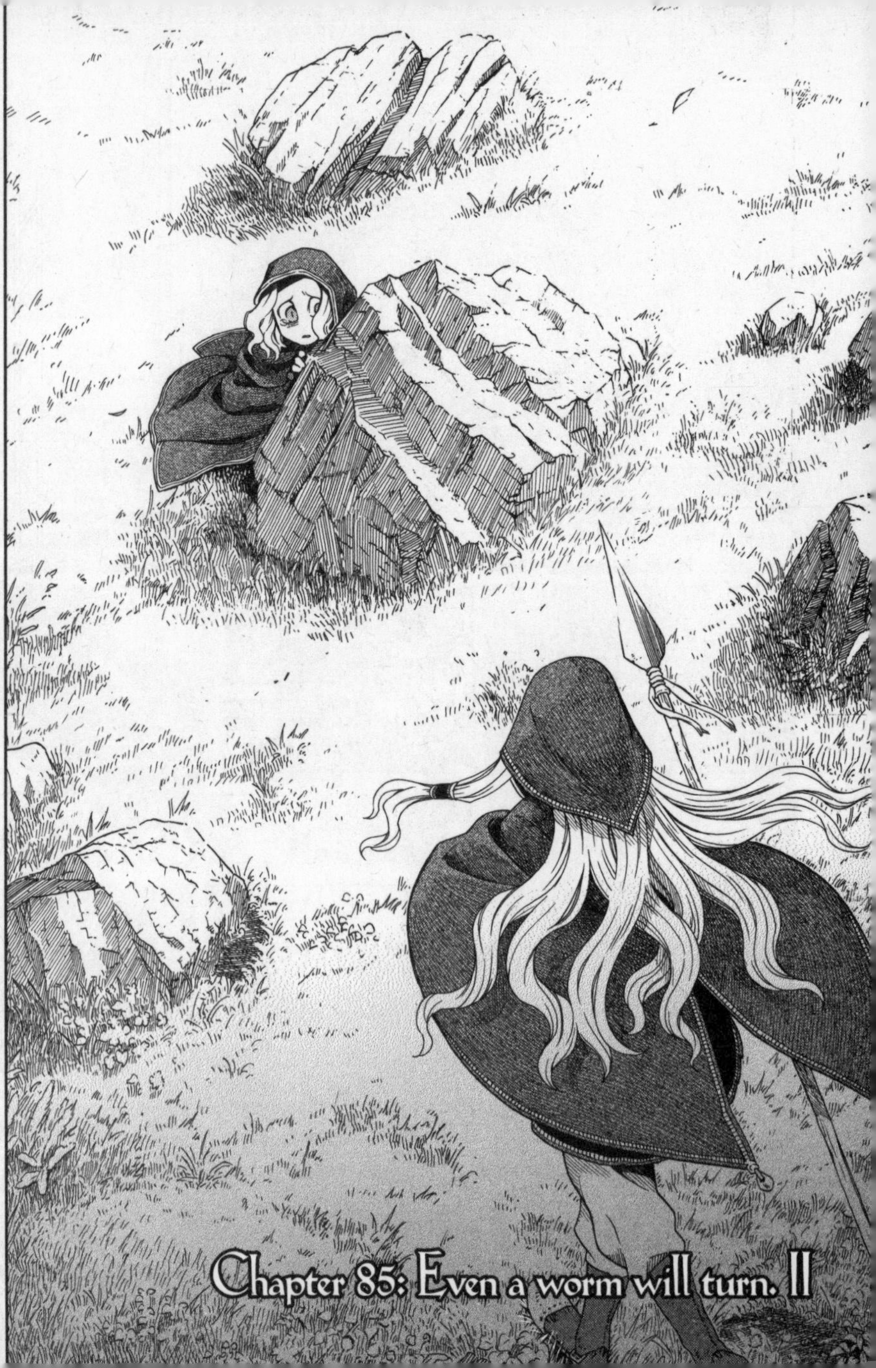
Chapter 85: Even a worm will turn. II

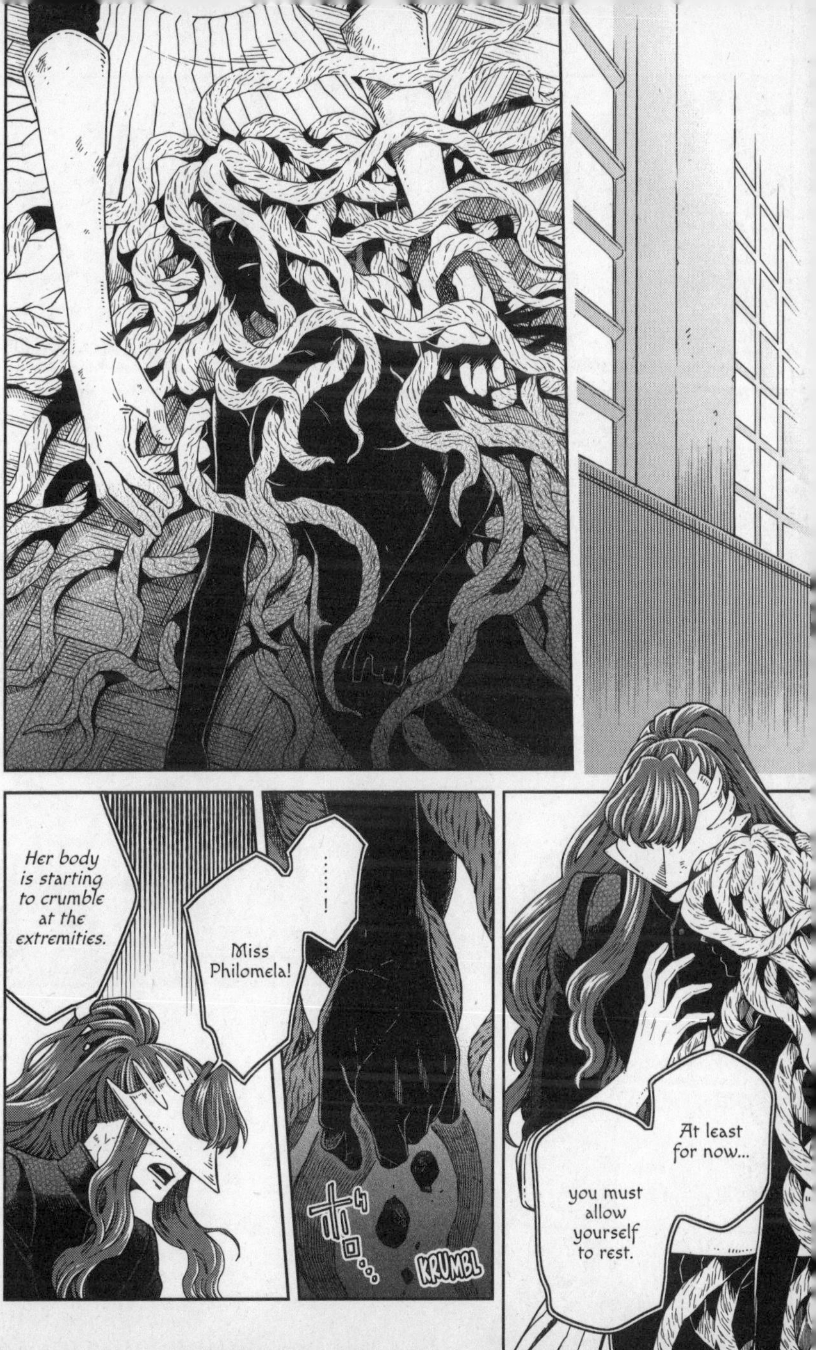
At least for now...
you must allow yourself to rest.
......!
Miss Philomela!
KRUMBL
Her body is starting to crumble at the extremities.

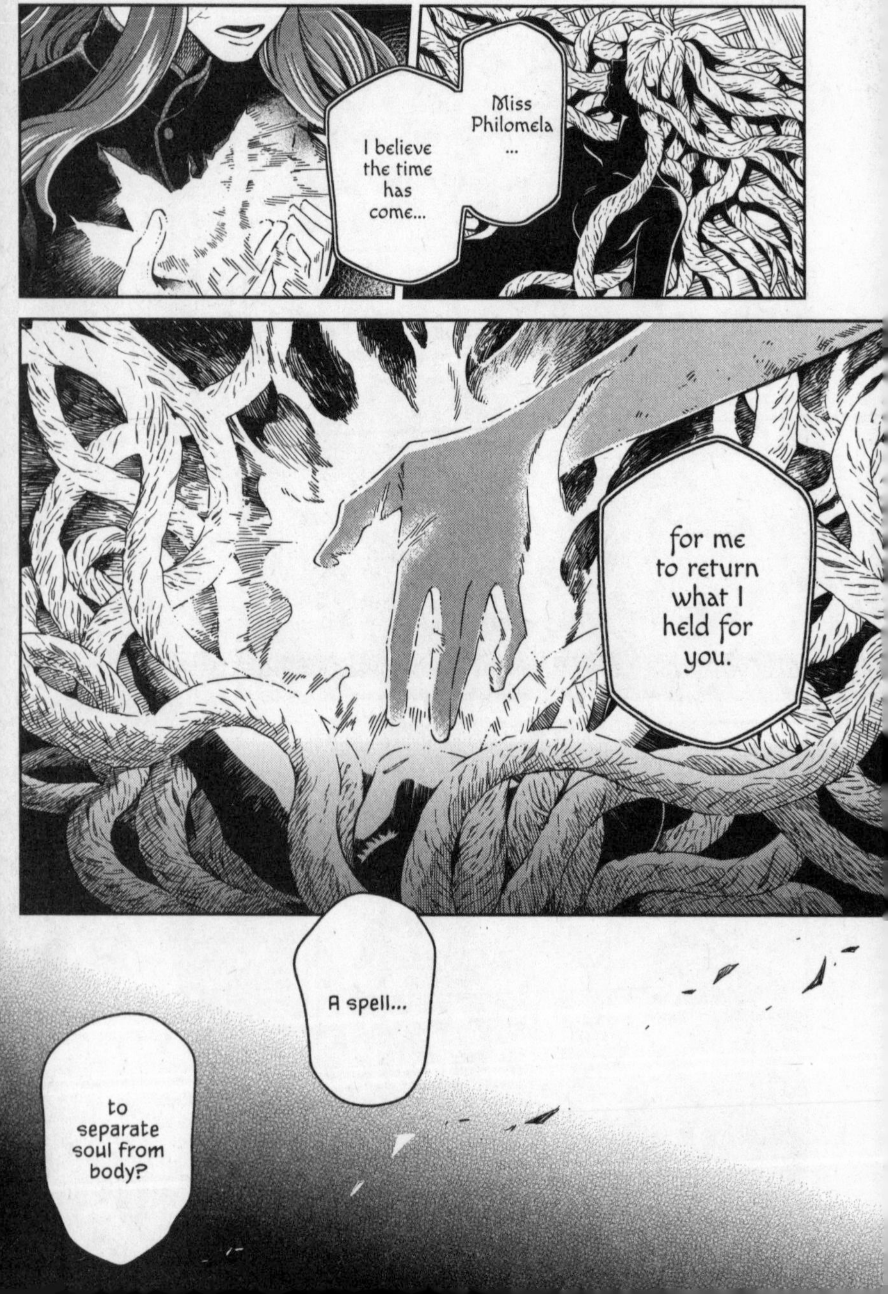
Miss Philomela ...
I believe the time has come...
for me to return what I held for you.
A spell...
to separate soul from body?

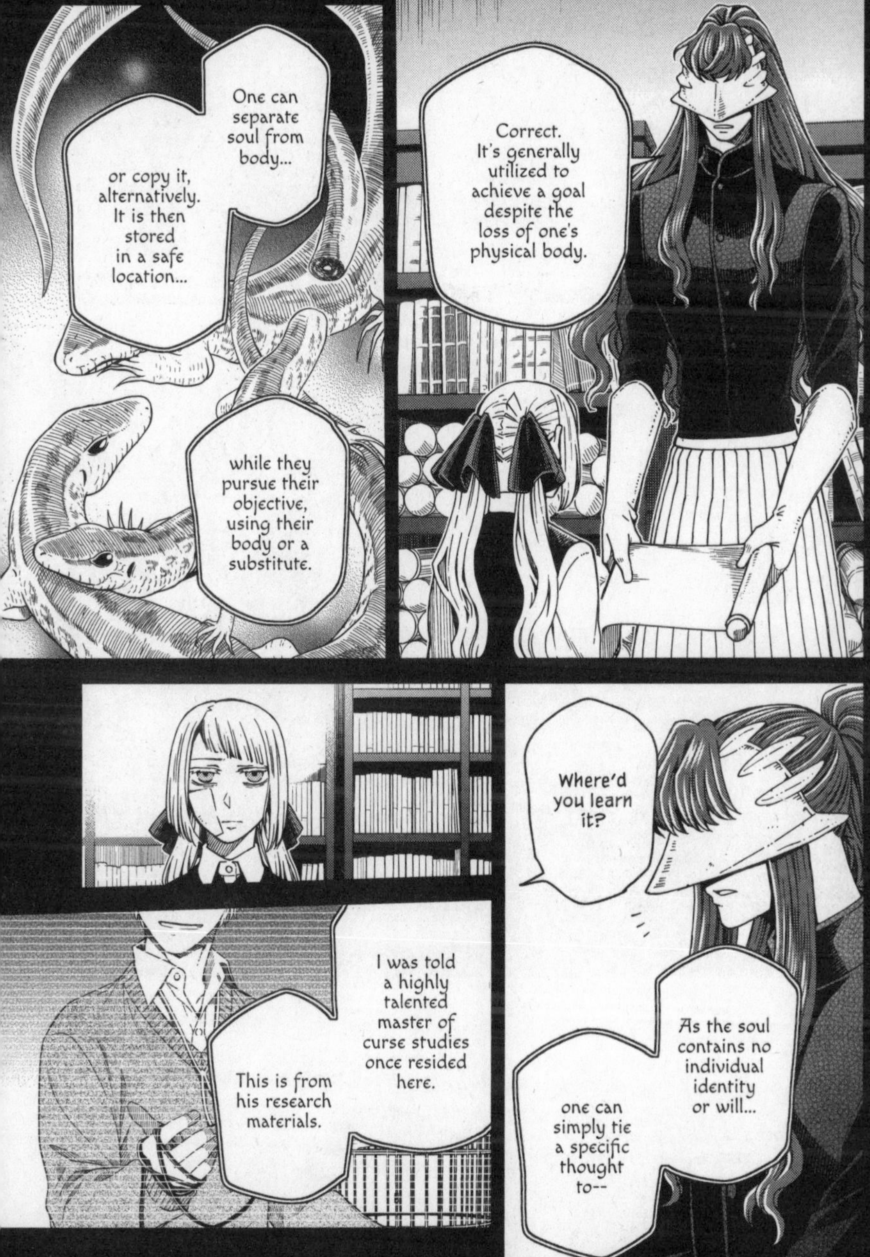
Correct. It's generally utilized to achieve a goal despite the loss of one's physical body.
One can separate soul from body...
or copy it, alternatively. It is then stored in a safe location...
while they pursue their objective, using their body or a substitute.
Where'd you learn it?
I was told a highly talented master of curse studies once resided here.
This is from his research materials.
As the soul contains no individual identity or will...
one can simply tie a specific thought to--

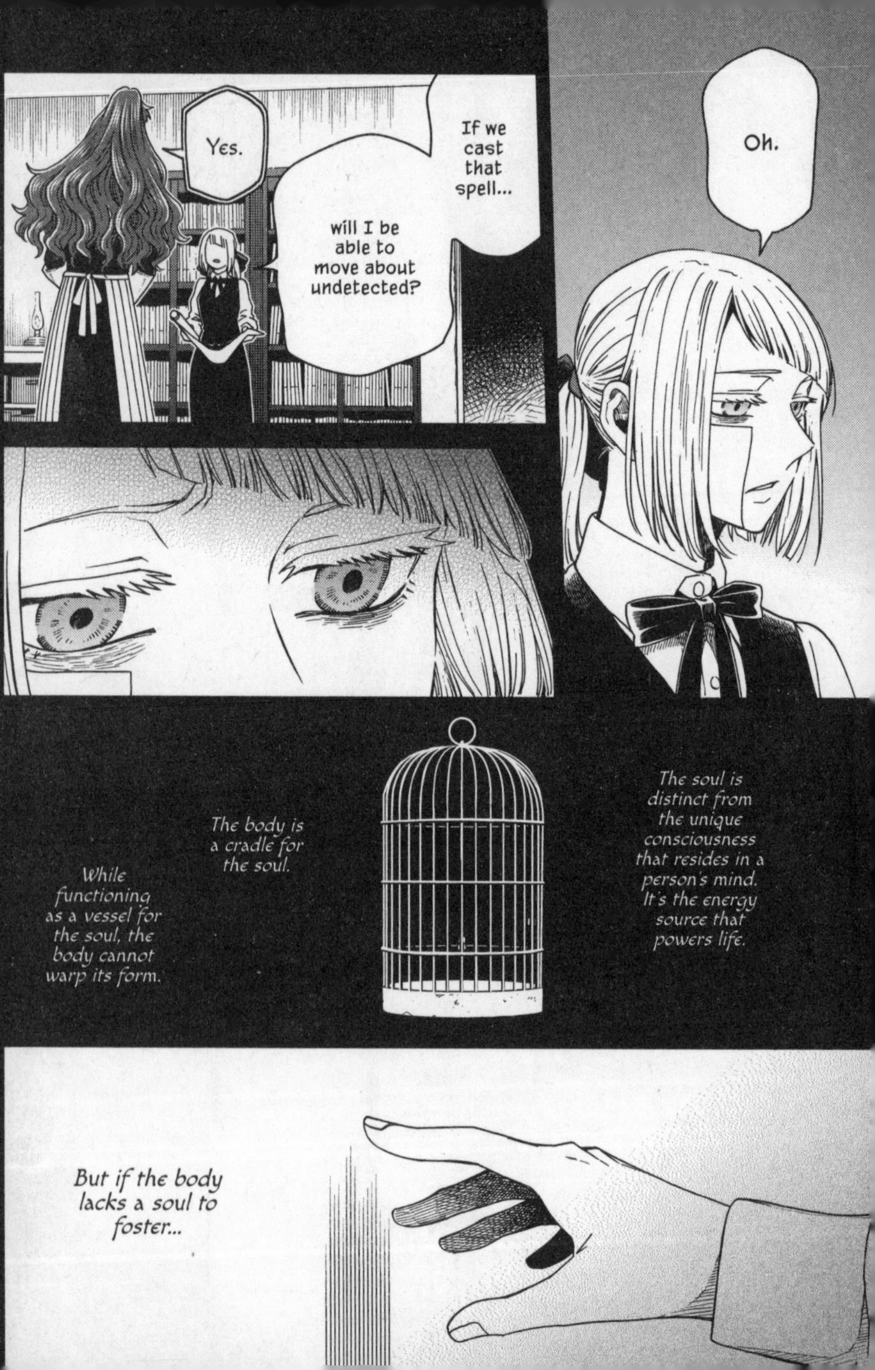
Yes.
If we cast that spell...
will I be able to move about undetected?
Oh.
The body is a cradle for the soul.
While functioning as a vessel for the soul, the body cannot warp its form.
The soul is distinct from the unique consciousness that resides in a person's mind. It's the energy source that powers life.
But if the body lacks a soul to foster...

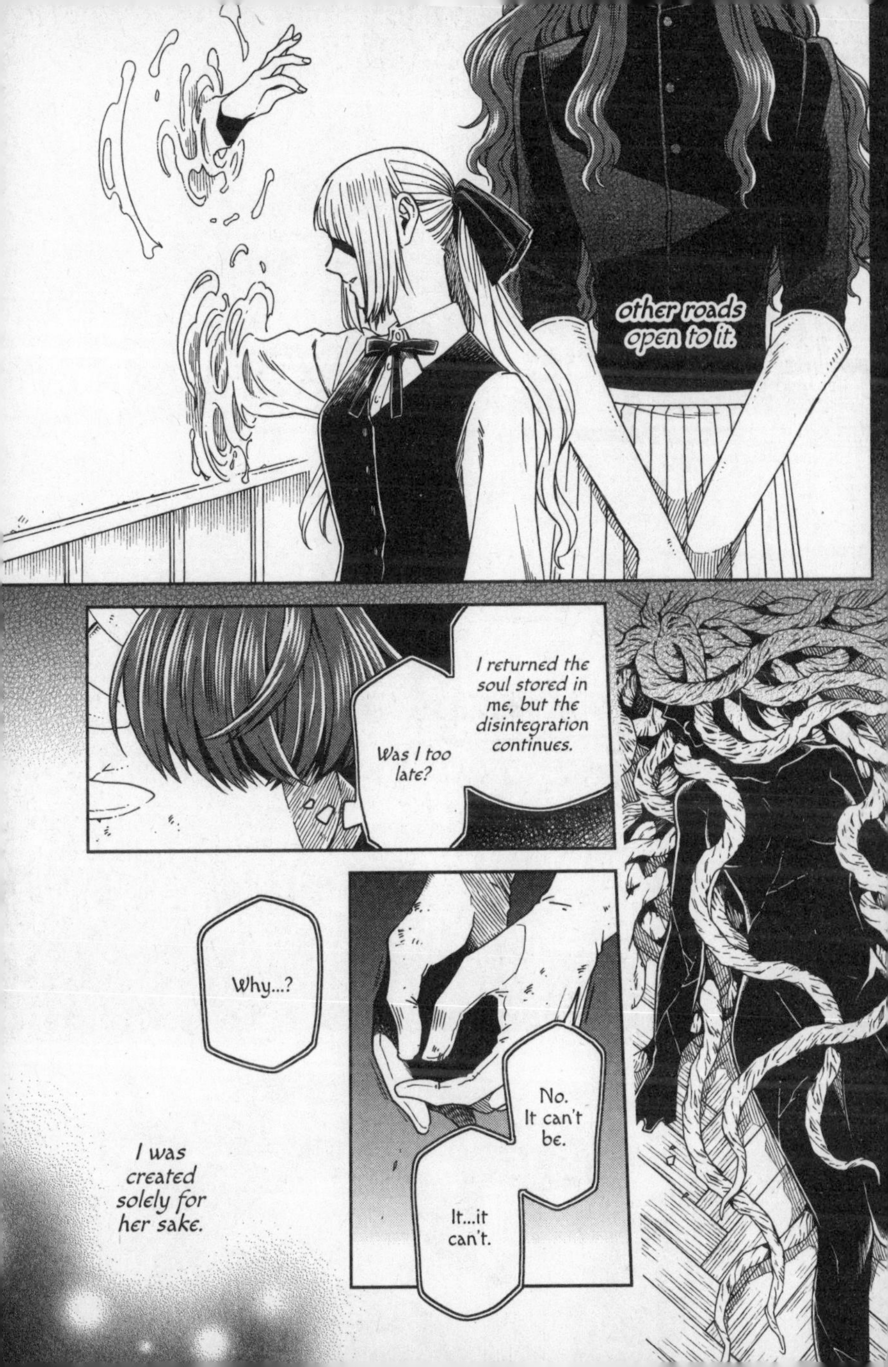
other roads open to it.
I returned the soul stored in me, but the disintegration continues.
Was I too late?
No. It can't be.
It...it can't.
Why...?
I was created solely for her sake.

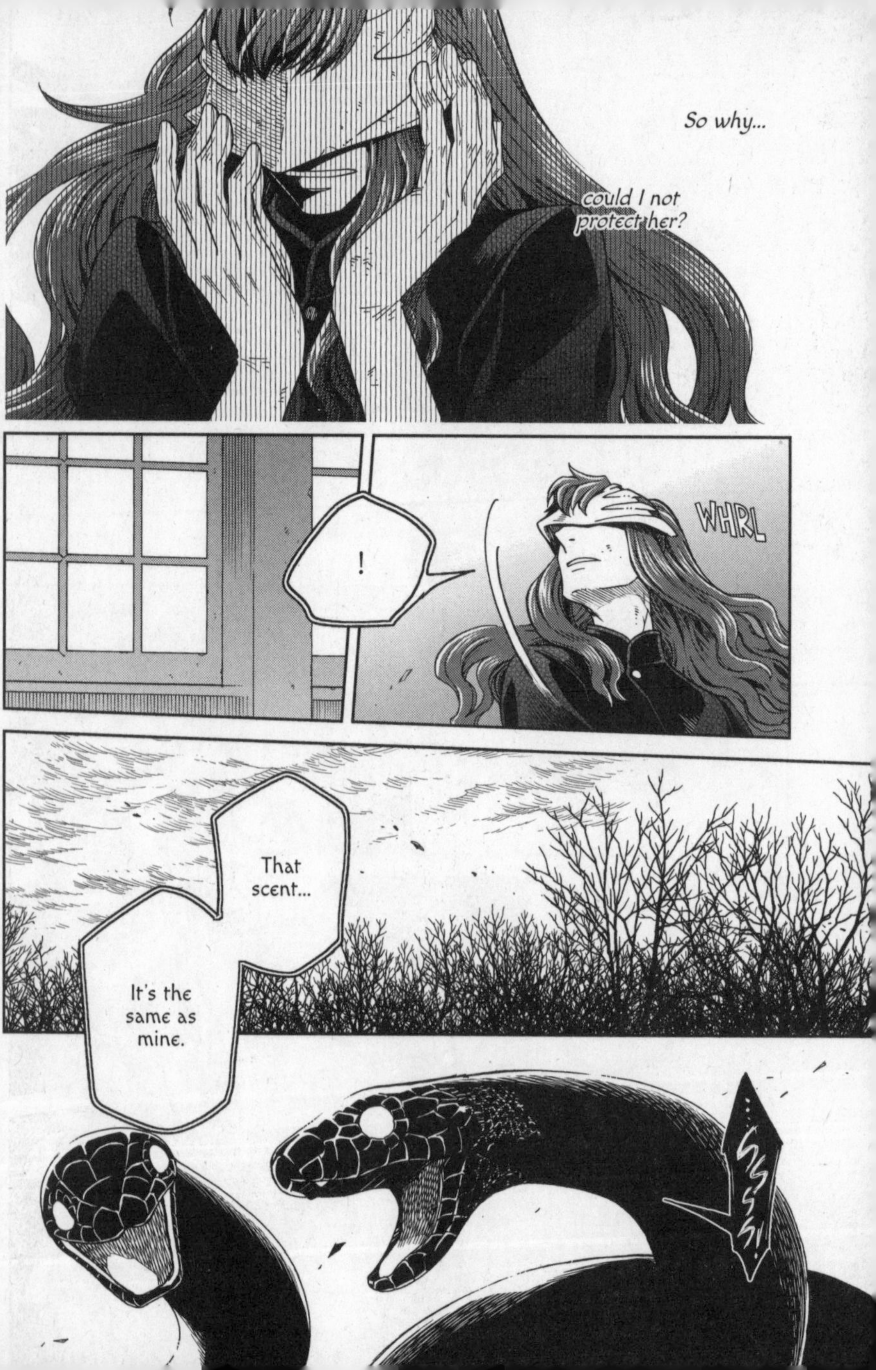
So why...
could I not protect her?
!
WHRL
That scent...
It's the same as mine.
SSS

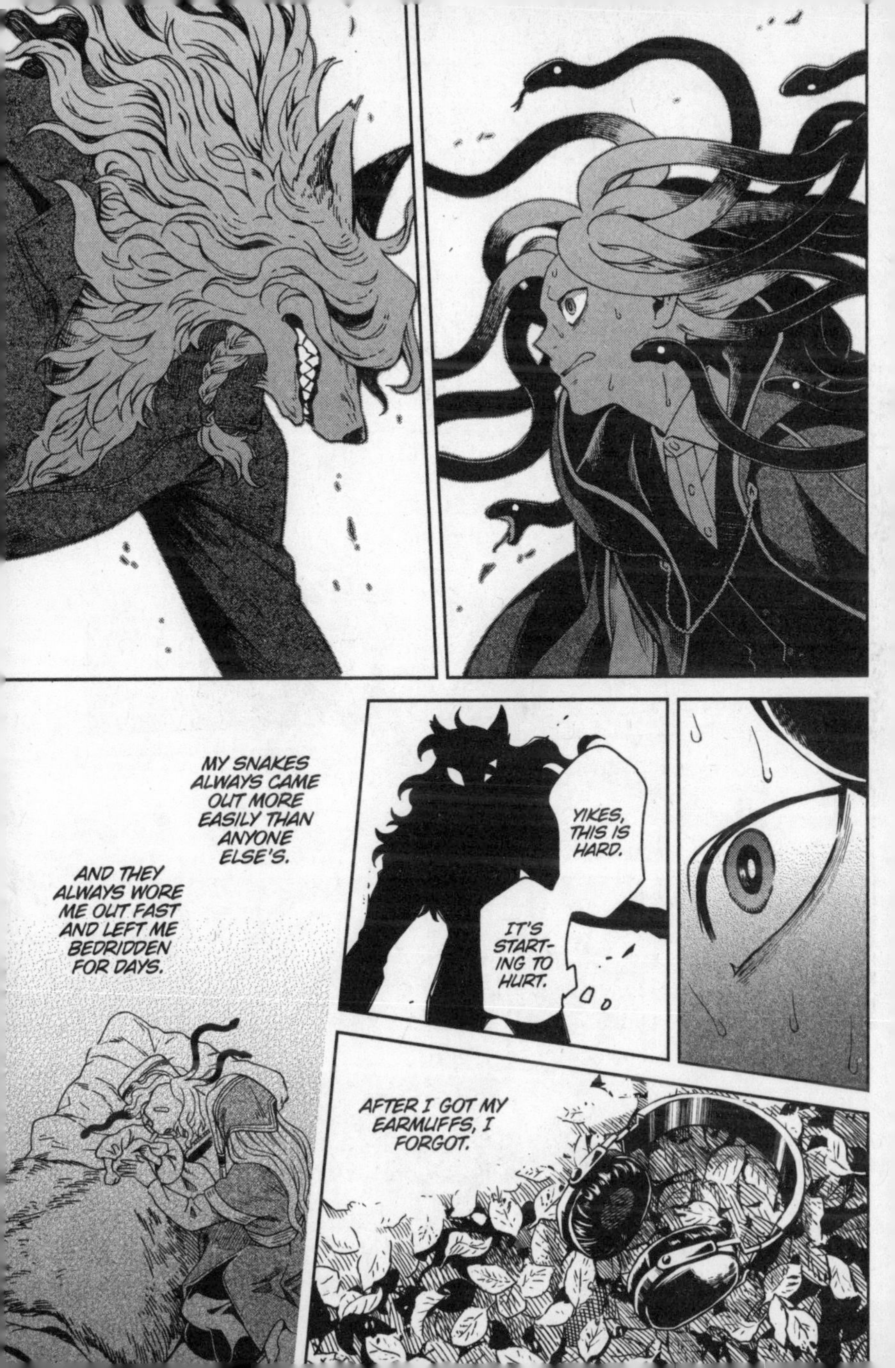
YIKES, THIS IS HARD.
IT'S STARTING TO HURT.
MY SNAKES ALWAYS CAME OUT MORE EASILY THAN ANYONE ELSE'S.
AND THEY ALWAYS WORE ME OUT FAST AND LEFT ME BEDRIDDEN FOR DAYS.
AFTER I GOT MY EARMUFFS, I FORGOT.

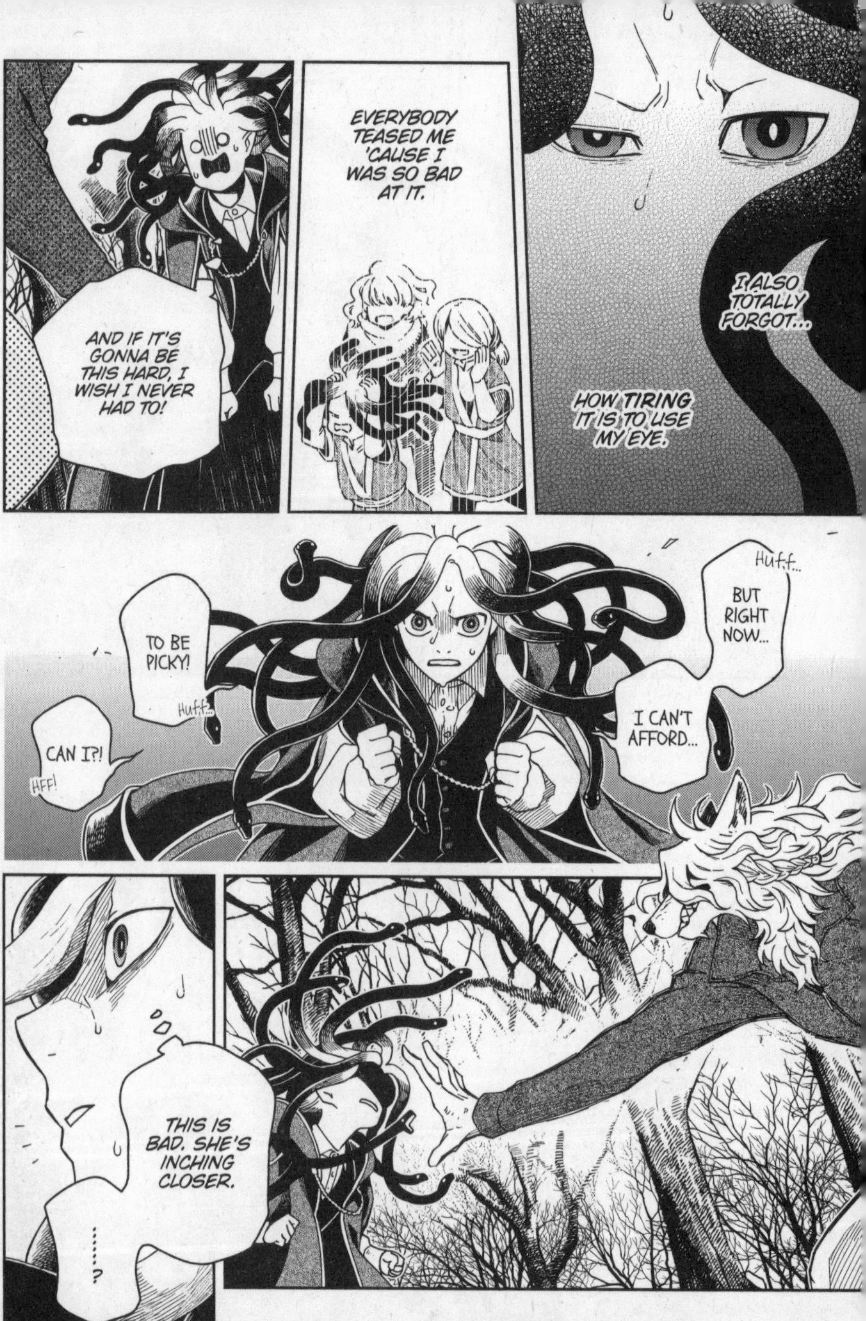
I ALSO TOTALLY FORGOT...
HOW TIRING IT IS TO USE MY EYE.
EVERYBODY TEASED ME 'CAUSE I WAS SO BAD AT IT.
AND IF IT'S GONNA BE THIS HARD, I WISH I NEVER HAD TO!
Huff...
BUT RIGHT NOW...
I CAN'T AFFORD...
TO BE PICKY!
Huff...
CAN I?!
HFF!
THIS IS BAD. SHE'S INCHING CLOSER.
......?

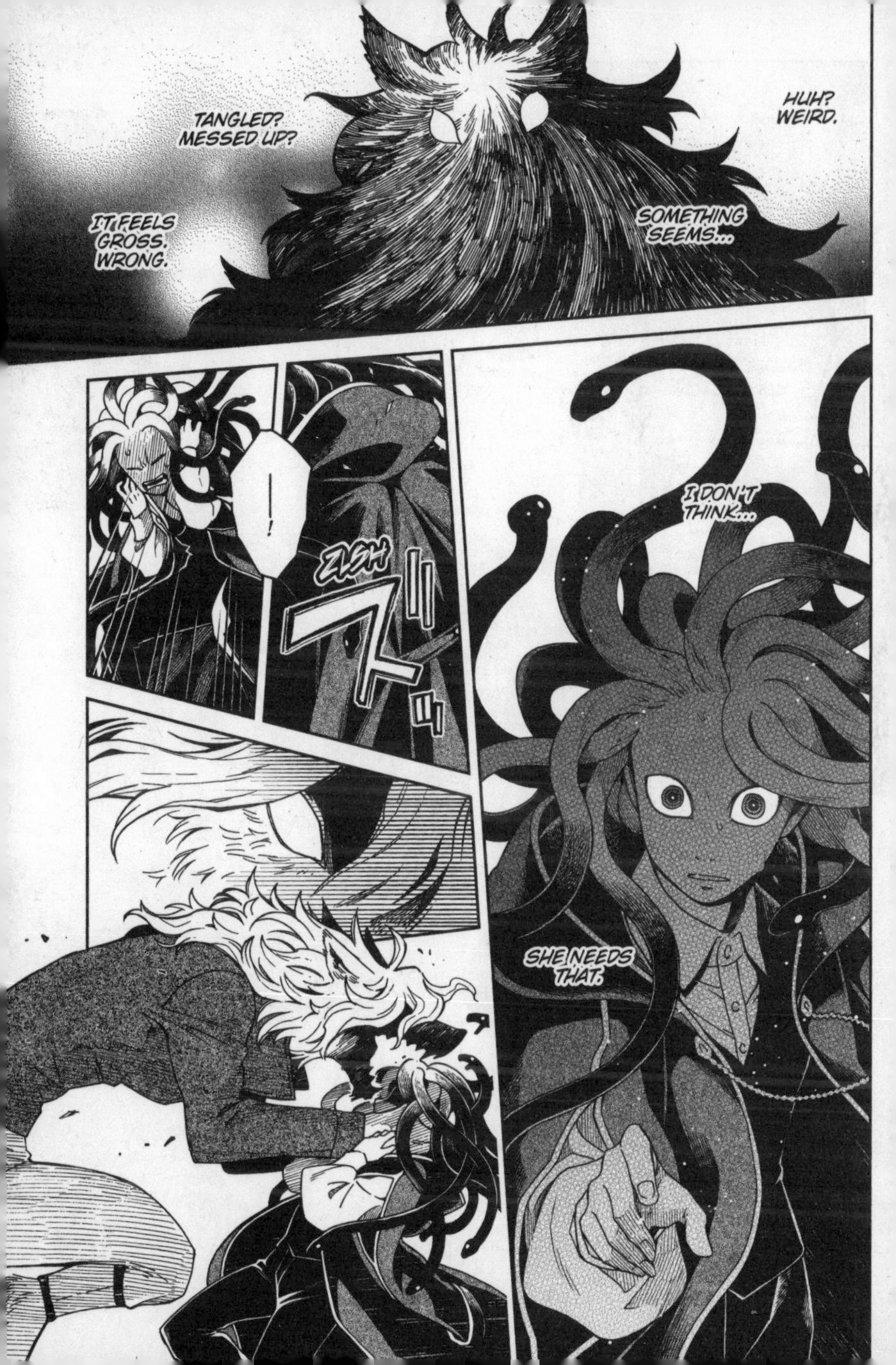
HUH? WEIRD.
SOMETHING SEEMS...
TANGLED? MESSED UP?
IT FEELS GROSS. WRONG.
!
ZUSH
I DON'T THINK...
SHE NEEDS THAT.

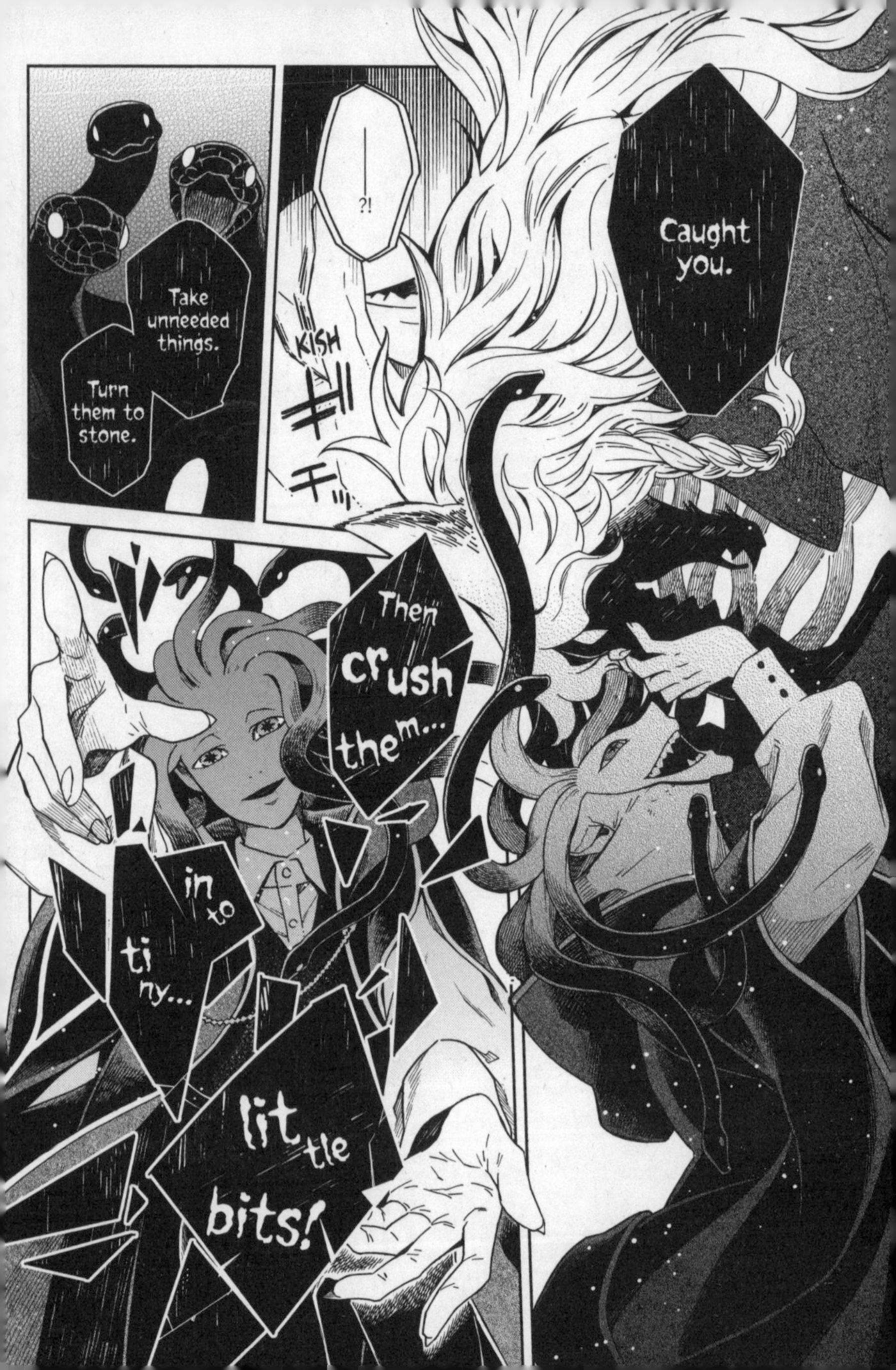
Caught you.
?!
KISH
Take unneeded things.
Turn them to stone.
Then crush them...
into tiny...
little bits!

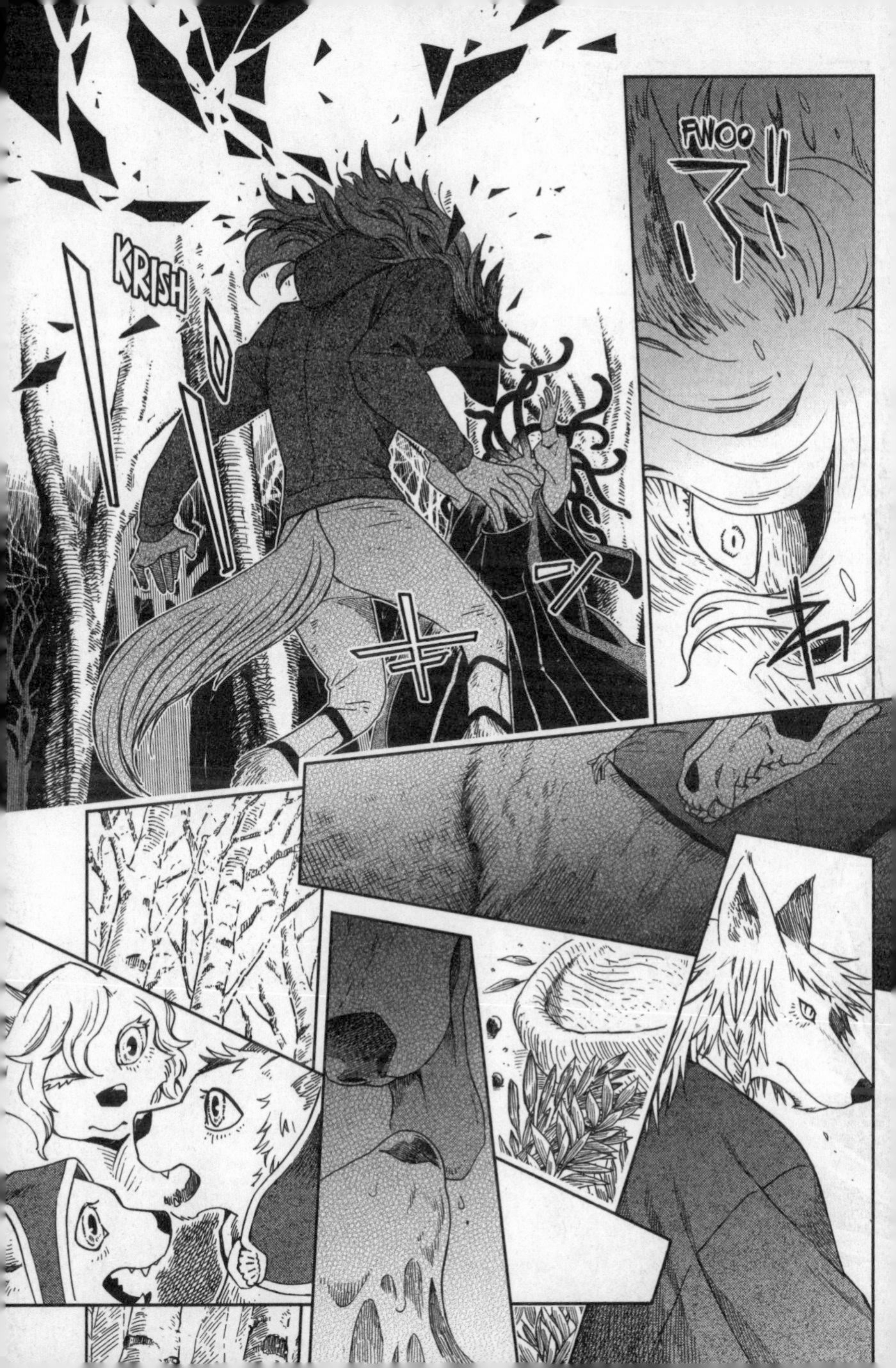
FWOO
KRISH

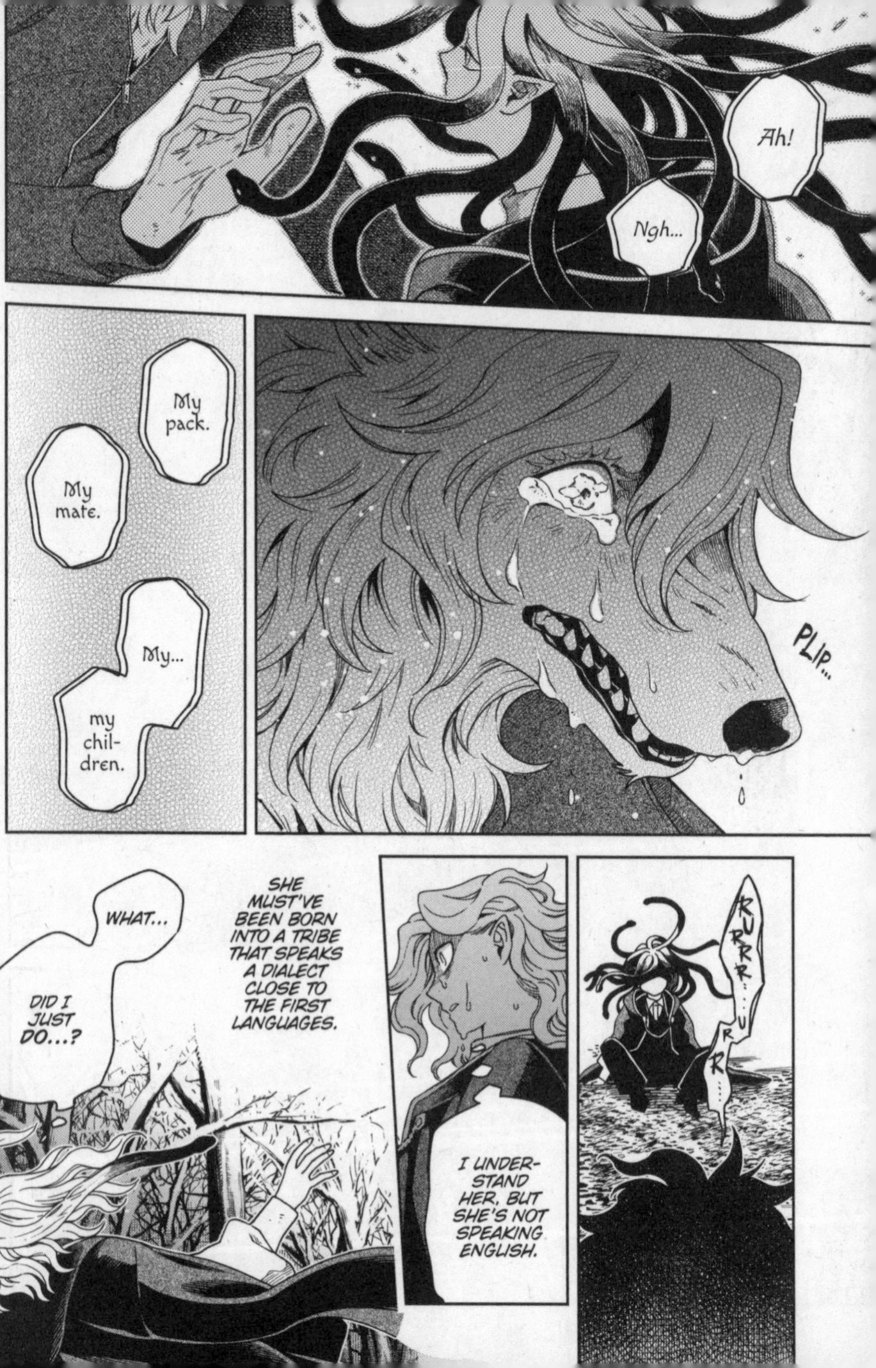
Ah!
Ngh...
PLIP...
My pack.
My mate.
My...
my children.
RURRR...URRR...
I UNDERSTAND HER, BUT SHE'S NOT SPEAKING ENGLISH.
SHE MUST'VE BEEN BORN INTO A TRIBE THAT SPEAKS A DIALECT CLOSE TO THE FIRST LANGUAGES.
WHAT...
DID I JUST DO...?

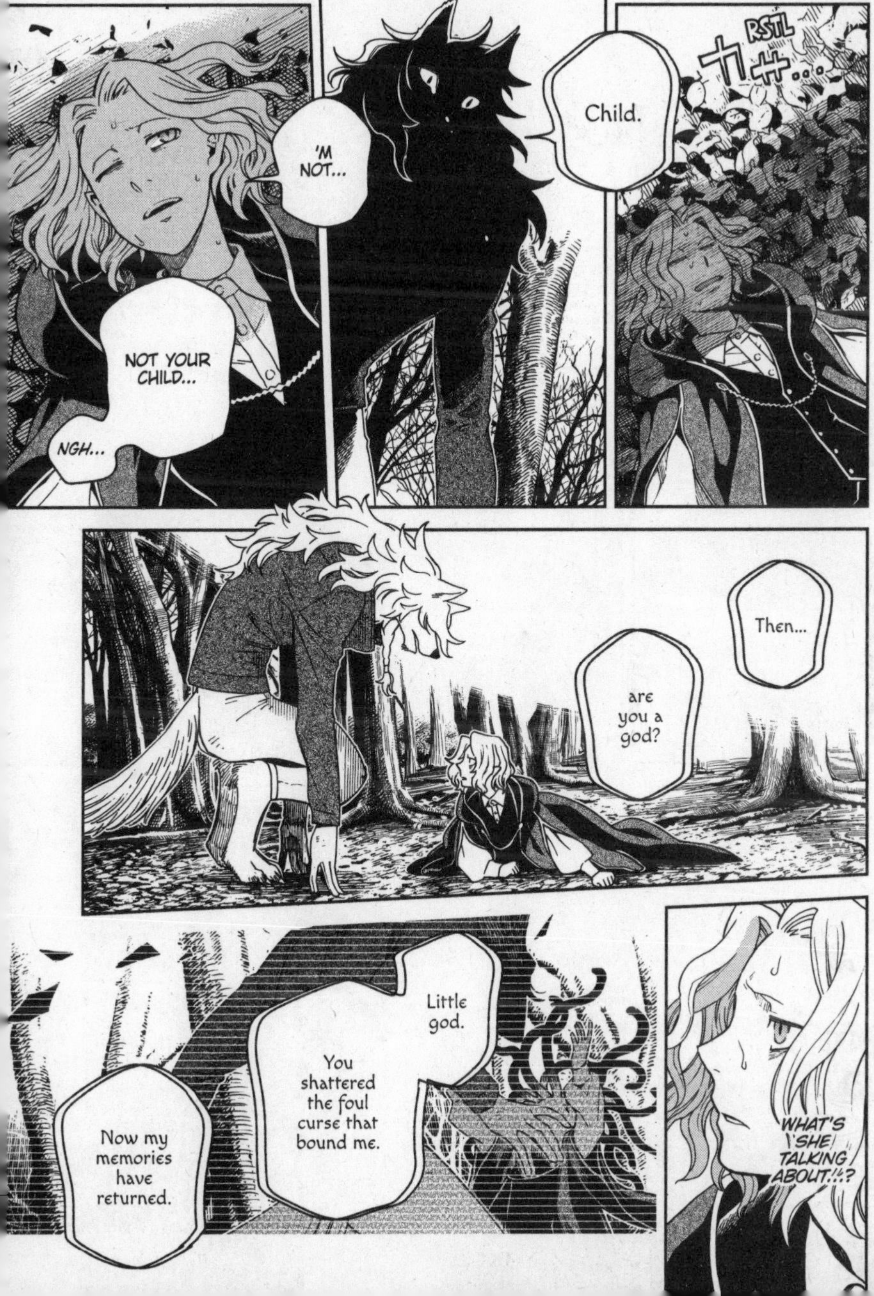
RSTL
Child.
'M NOT...
NOT YOUR CHILD...
NGH...
Then...
are you a god?
WHAT'S SHE TALKING ABOUT!?
Little god.
You shattered the foul curse that bound me.
Now my memories have returned.

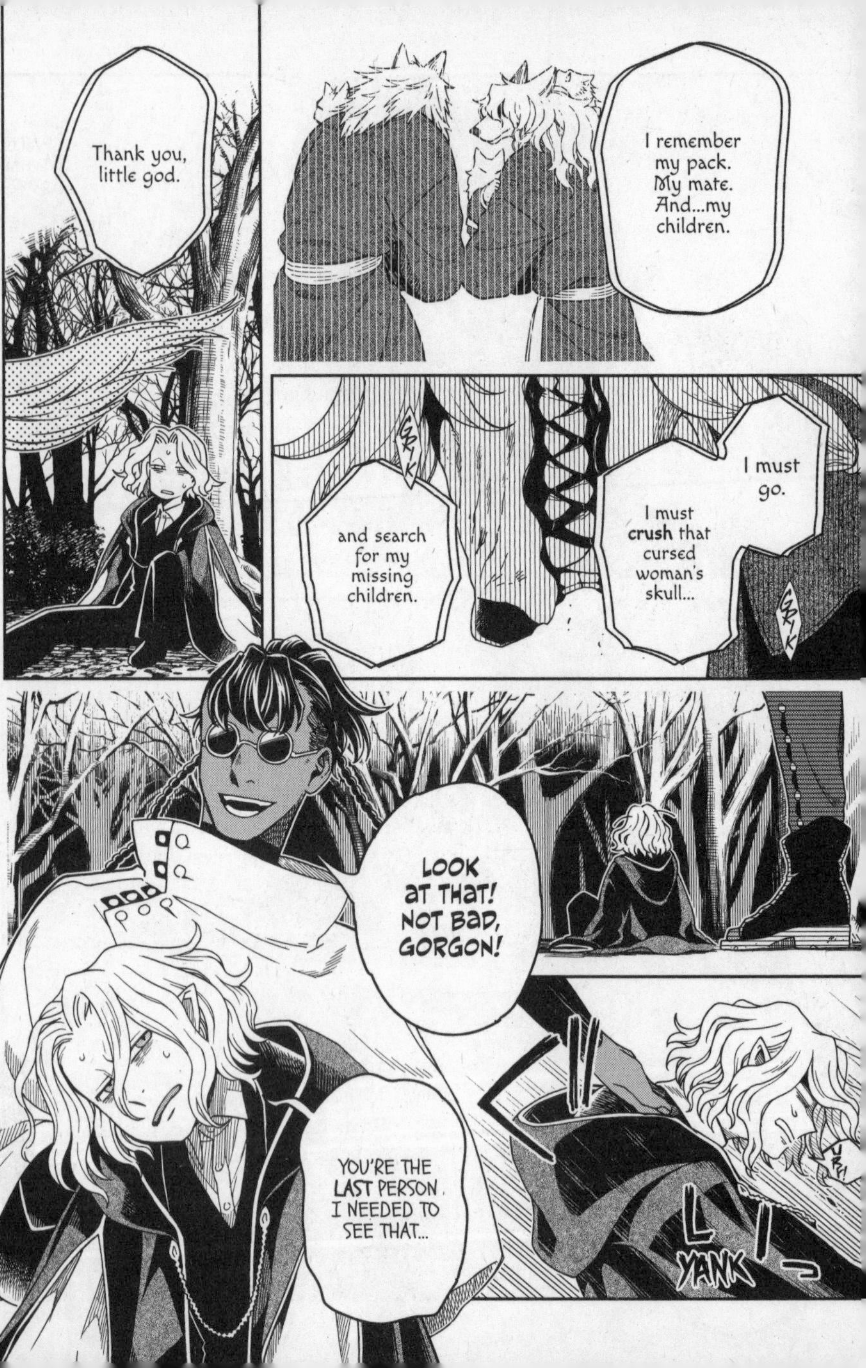
I remember my pack. My mate. And...my children.
Thank you, little god.
I must go.
I must crush that cursed woman's skull...
GRIK
and search for my missing children.
GRIK
LOOK AT THAT! NOT BAD, GORGON!
YANK
URK!
YOU'RE THE LAST PERSON I NEEDED TO SEE THAT...

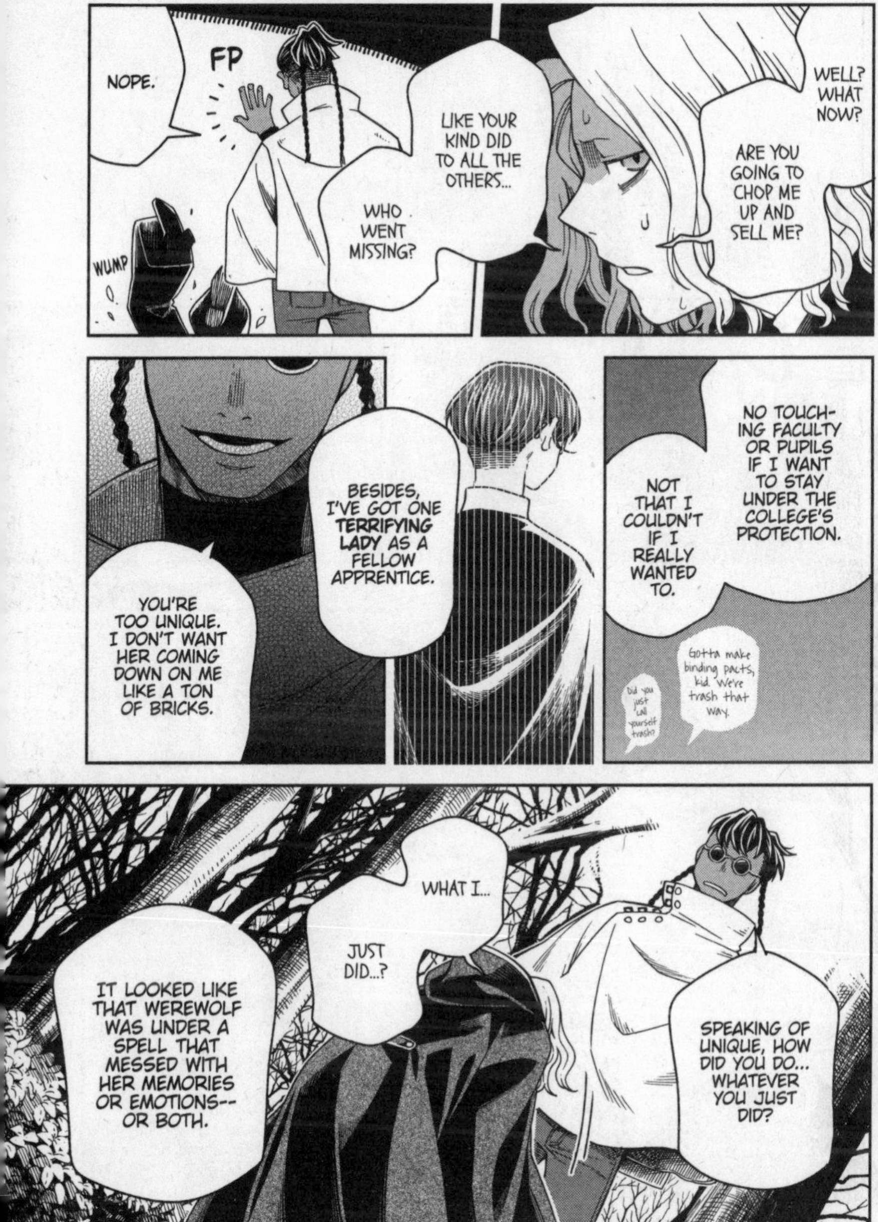
WELL? WHAT NOW?
ARE YOU GOING TO CHOP ME UP AND SELL ME?
LIKE YOUR KIND DID TO ALL THE OTHERS...
WHO WENT MISSING?
NOPE.
FP
WUMP
BESIDES, I'VE GOT ONE **TERRIFYING LADY** AS A FELLOW APPRENTICE.
YOU'RE TOO UNIQUE. I DON'T WANT HER COMING DOWN ON ME LIKE A TON OF BRICKS.
NO TOUCHING FACULTY OR PUPILS IF I WANT TO STAY UNDER THE COLLEGE'S PROTECTION.
NOT THAT I COULDN'T IF I REALLY WANTED TO.
Gotta make binding pacts, kid. We're trash that way.
Did you just call yourself trash?
SPEAKING OF UNIQUE, HOW DID YOU DO... WHATEVER YOU JUST DID?
WHAT I...
JUST DID...?
IT LOOKED LIKE THAT WEREWOLF WAS UNDER A SPELL THAT MESSED WITH HER MEMORIES OR EMOTIONS--OR BOTH.

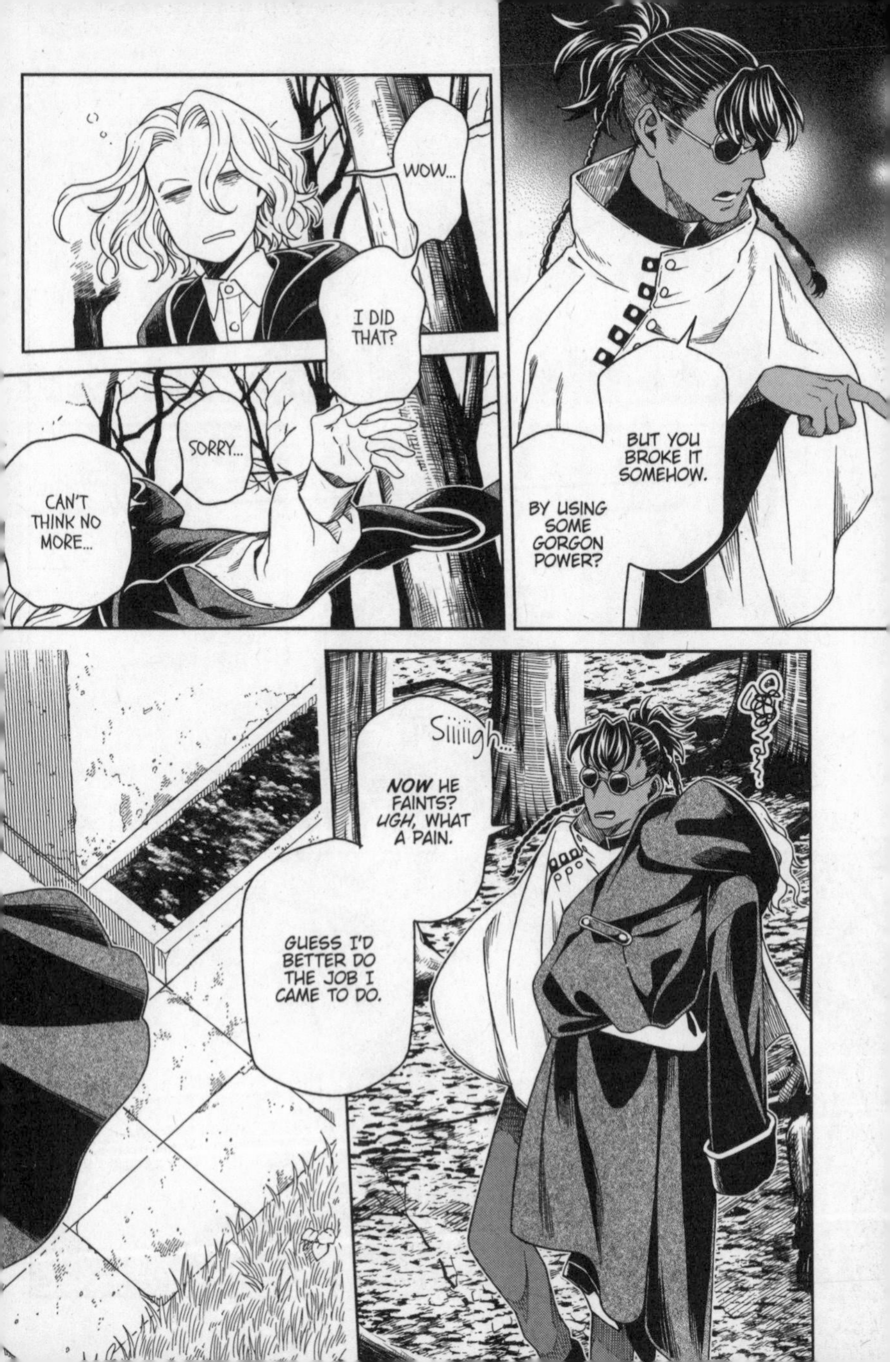
BUT YOU BROKE IT SOMEHOW.
BY USING SOME GORGON POWER?
WOW...
I DID THAT?
SORRY...
CAN'T THINK NO MORE...
Siiiiigh...
NOW HE FAINTS? *UGH*, WHAT A PAIN.
GUESS I'D BETTER DO THE JOB I CAME TO DO.

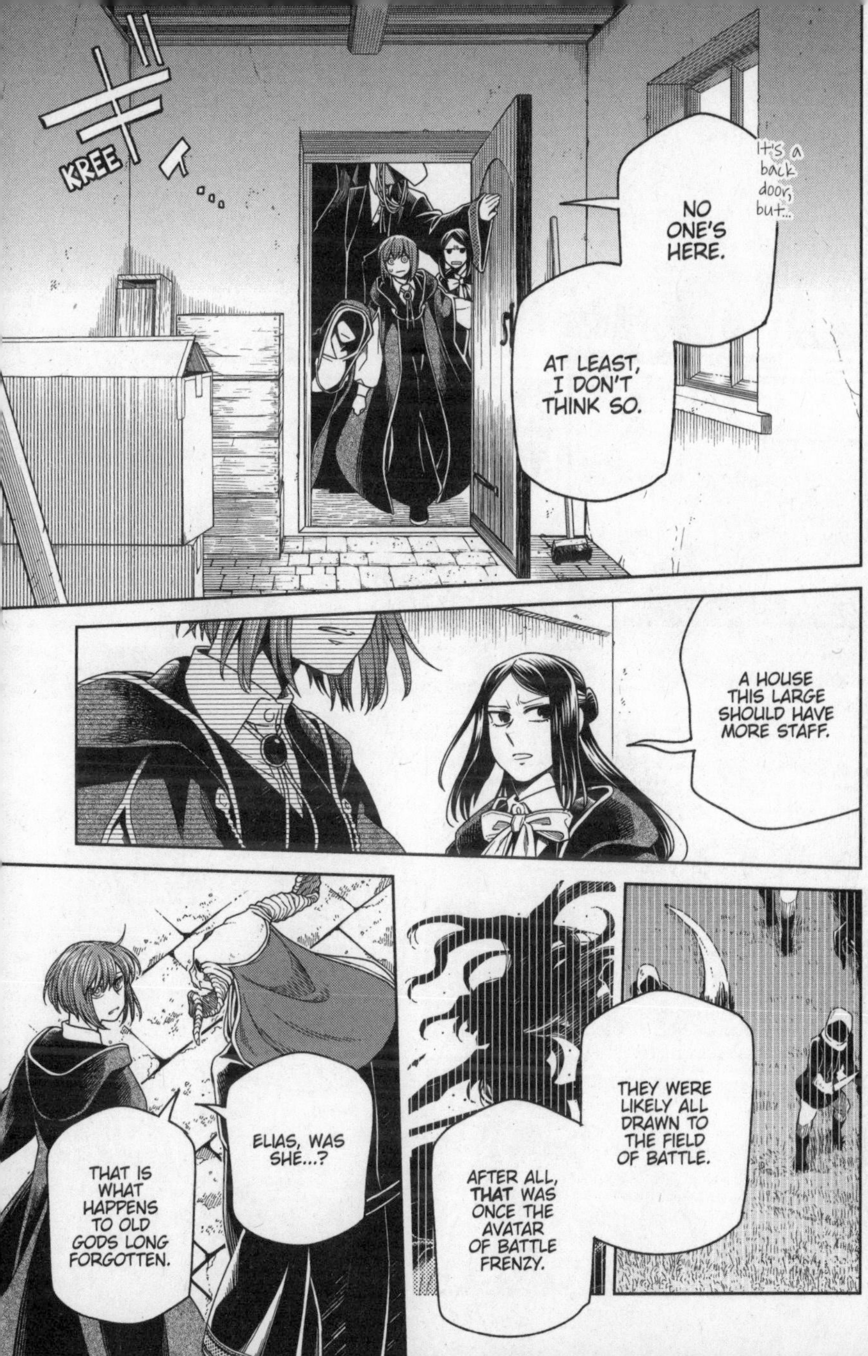
KREE
It's a back door, but...
NO ONE'S HERE.
AT LEAST, I DON'T THINK SO.
A HOUSE THIS LARGE SHOULD HAVE MORE STAFF.
THEY WERE LIKELY ALL DRAWN TO THE FIELD OF BATTLE.
AFTER ALL, THAT WAS ONCE THE AVATAR OF BATTLE FRENZY.
ELIAS, WAS SHE...?
THAT IS WHAT HAPPENS TO OLD GODS LONG FORGOTTEN.

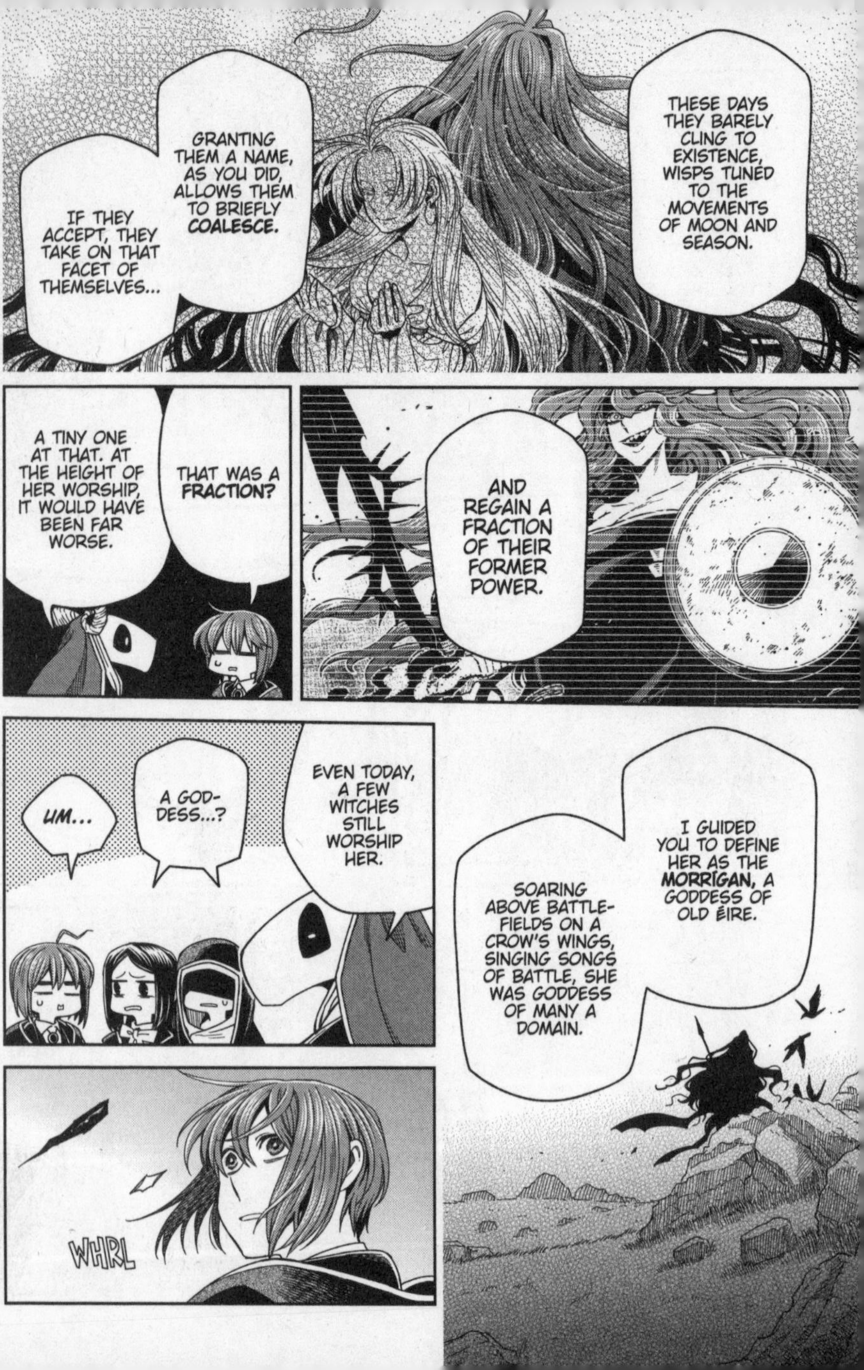
THESE DAYS THEY BARELY CLING TO EXISTENCE, WISPS TUNED TO THE MOVEMENTS OF MOON AND SEASON.
GRANTING THEM A NAME, AS YOU DID, ALLOWS THEM TO BRIEFLY **COALESCE.**
IF THEY ACCEPT, THEY TAKE ON THAT FACET OF THEMSELVES...
AND REGAIN A FRACTION OF THEIR FORMER POWER.
THAT WAS A **FRACTION?**
A TINY ONE AT THAT. AT THE HEIGHT OF HER WORSHIP, IT WOULD HAVE BEEN FAR WORSE.
I GUIDED YOU TO DEFINE HER AS THE **MORRIGAN,** A GODDESS OF OLD ÉIRE.
SOARING ABOVE BATTLE-FIELDS ON A CROW'S WINGS, SINGING SONGS OF BATTLE, SHE WAS GODDESS OF MANY A DOMAIN.
EVEN TODAY, A FEW WITCHES STILL WORSHIP HER.
A GOD-DESS...?
UM...
WHRL

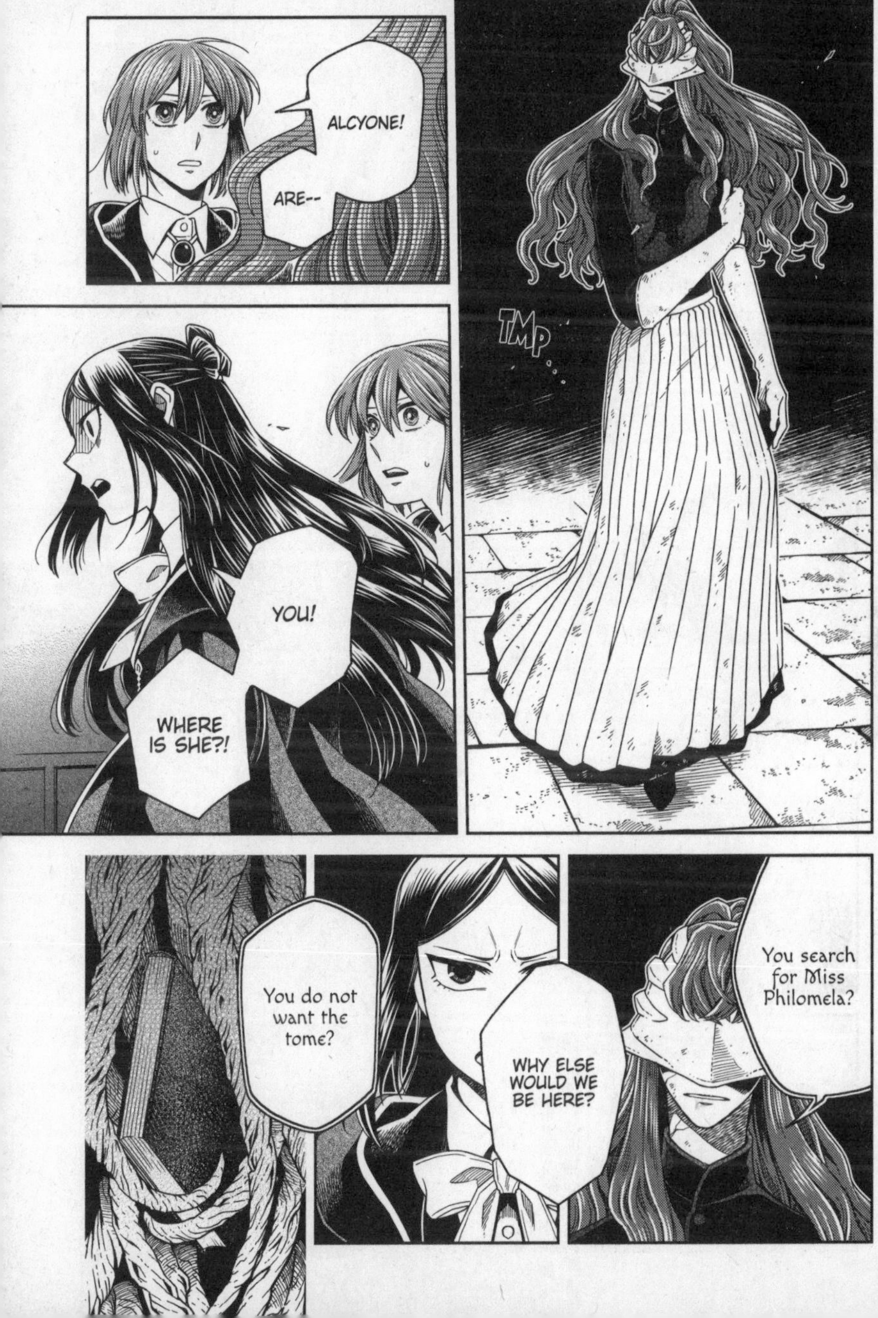
TMP
ALCYONE!
ARE--
YOU!
WHERE IS SHE?!
You search for Miss Philomela?
WHY ELSE WOULD WE BE HERE?
You do not want the tome?

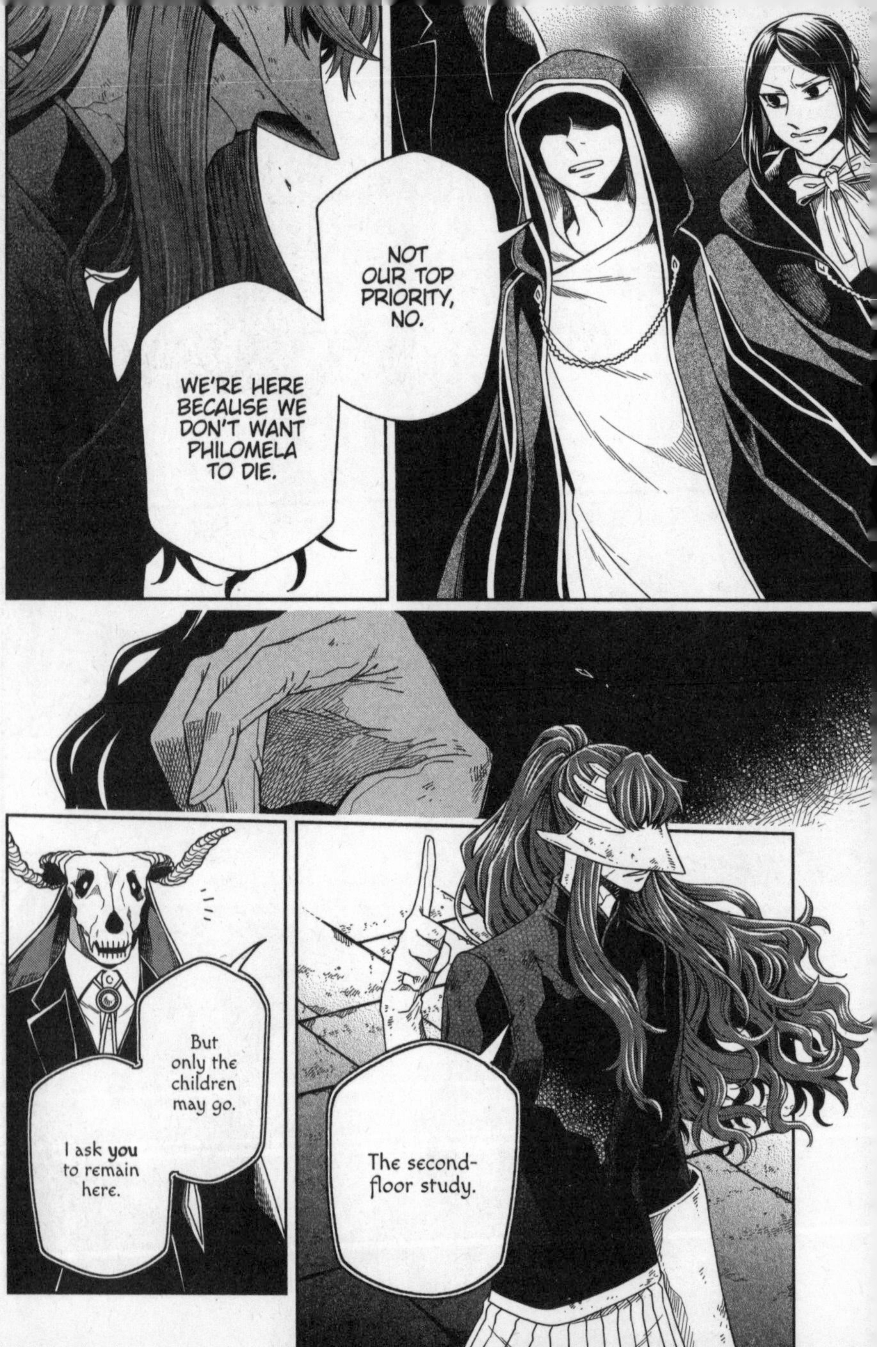
NOT OUR TOP PRIORITY, NO.
WE'RE HERE BECAUSE WE DON'T WANT PHILOMELA TO DIE.
The second-floor study.
But only the children may go.
I ask you to remain here.

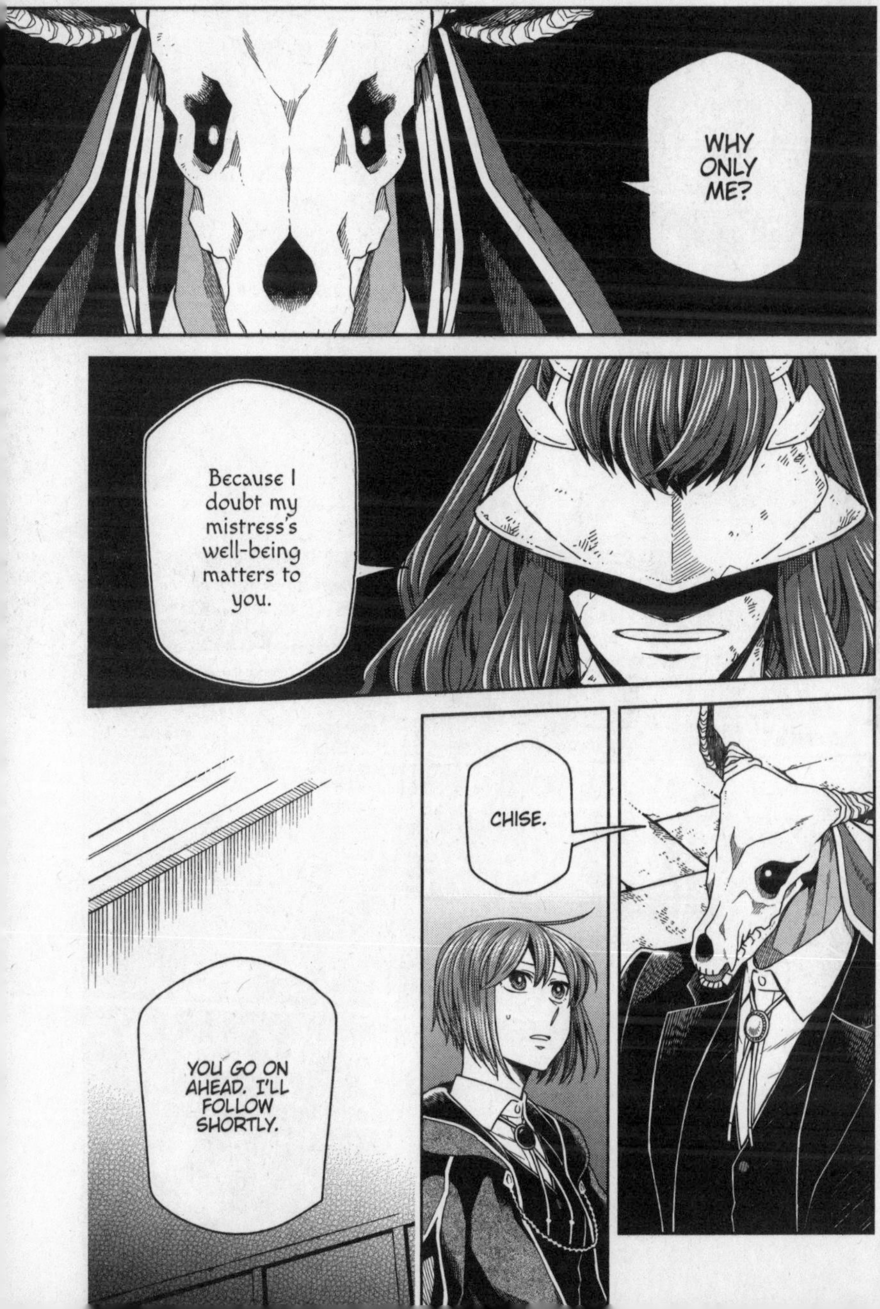
WHY ONLY ME?
Because I doubt my mistress's well-being matters to you.
CHISE.
YOU GO ON AHEAD. I'LL FOLLOW SHORTLY.

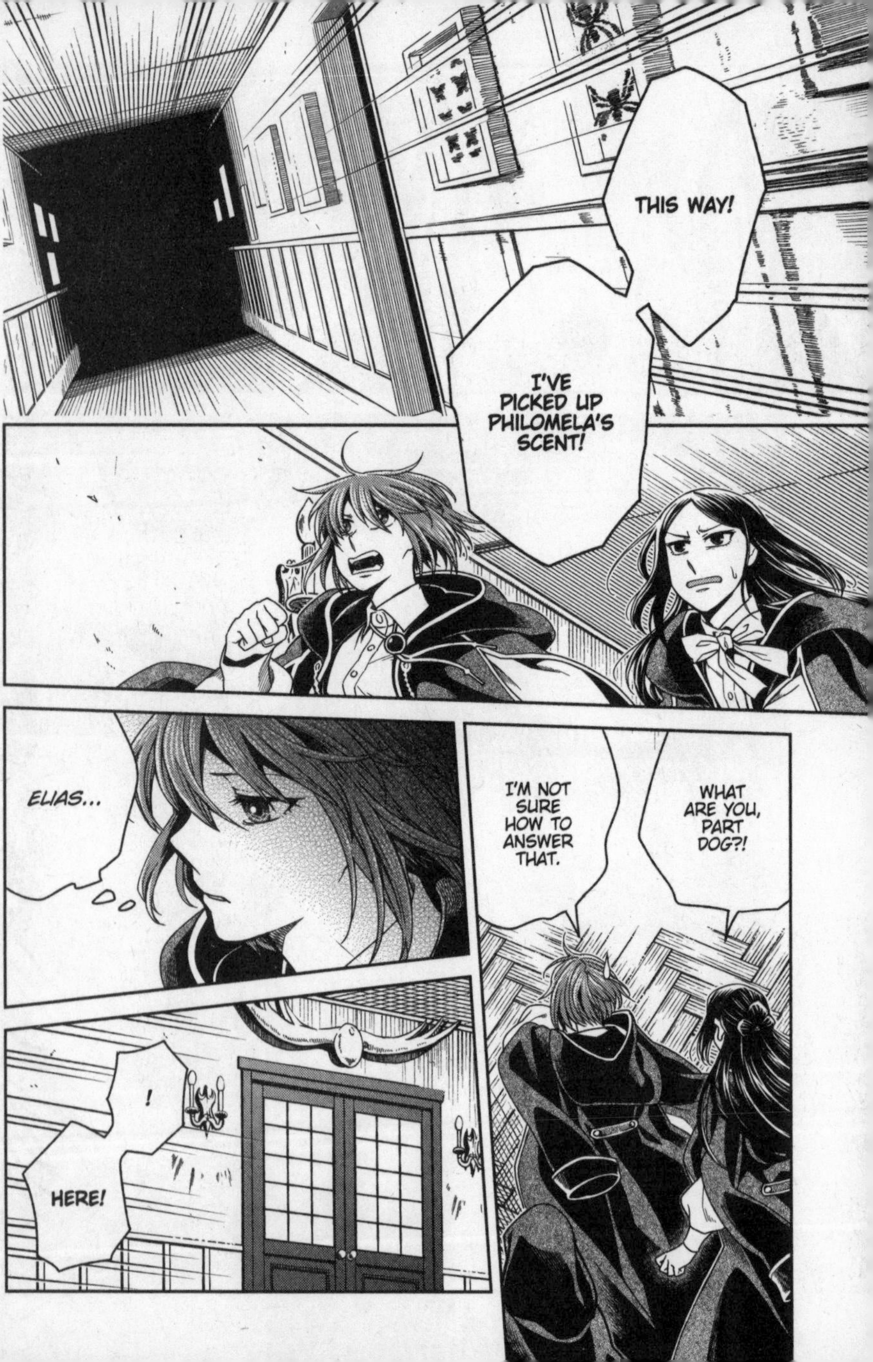
THIS WAY!
I'VE PICKED UP PHILOMELA'S SCENT!
WHAT ARE YOU, PART DOG?!
I'M NOT SURE HOW TO ANSWER THAT.
ELIAS...
!
HERE!

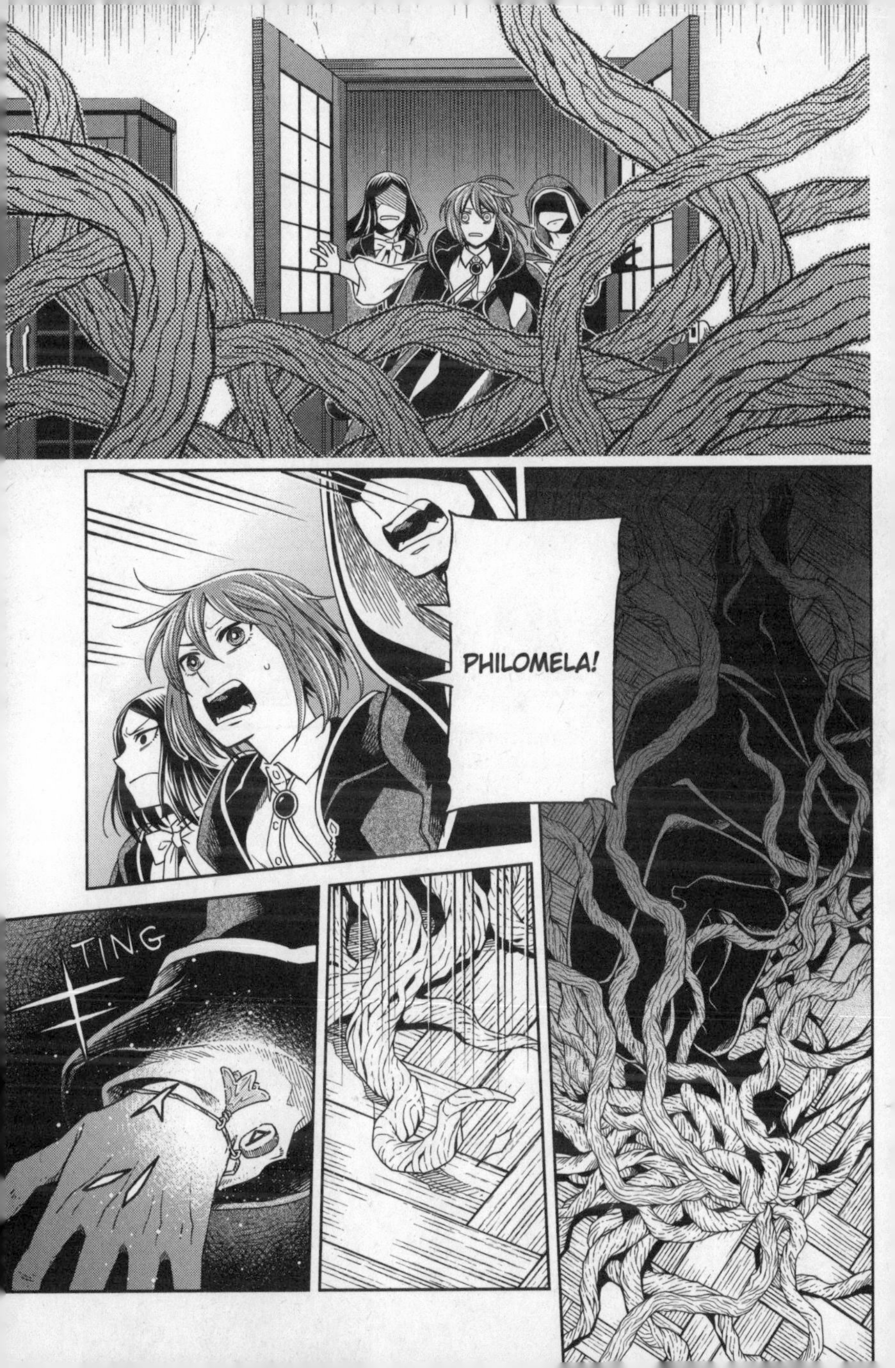
PHILOMELA!
TING

PHILO-
MELA!

Phew!

THE
CHARMS
...

ARE
WORKING
LIKE I'D
HOPED.

GAH?!

PASH

CHISE!

Not...

enough
...

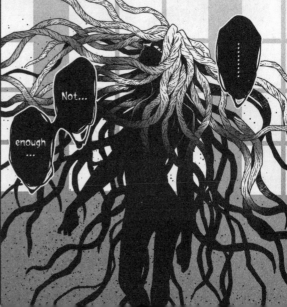

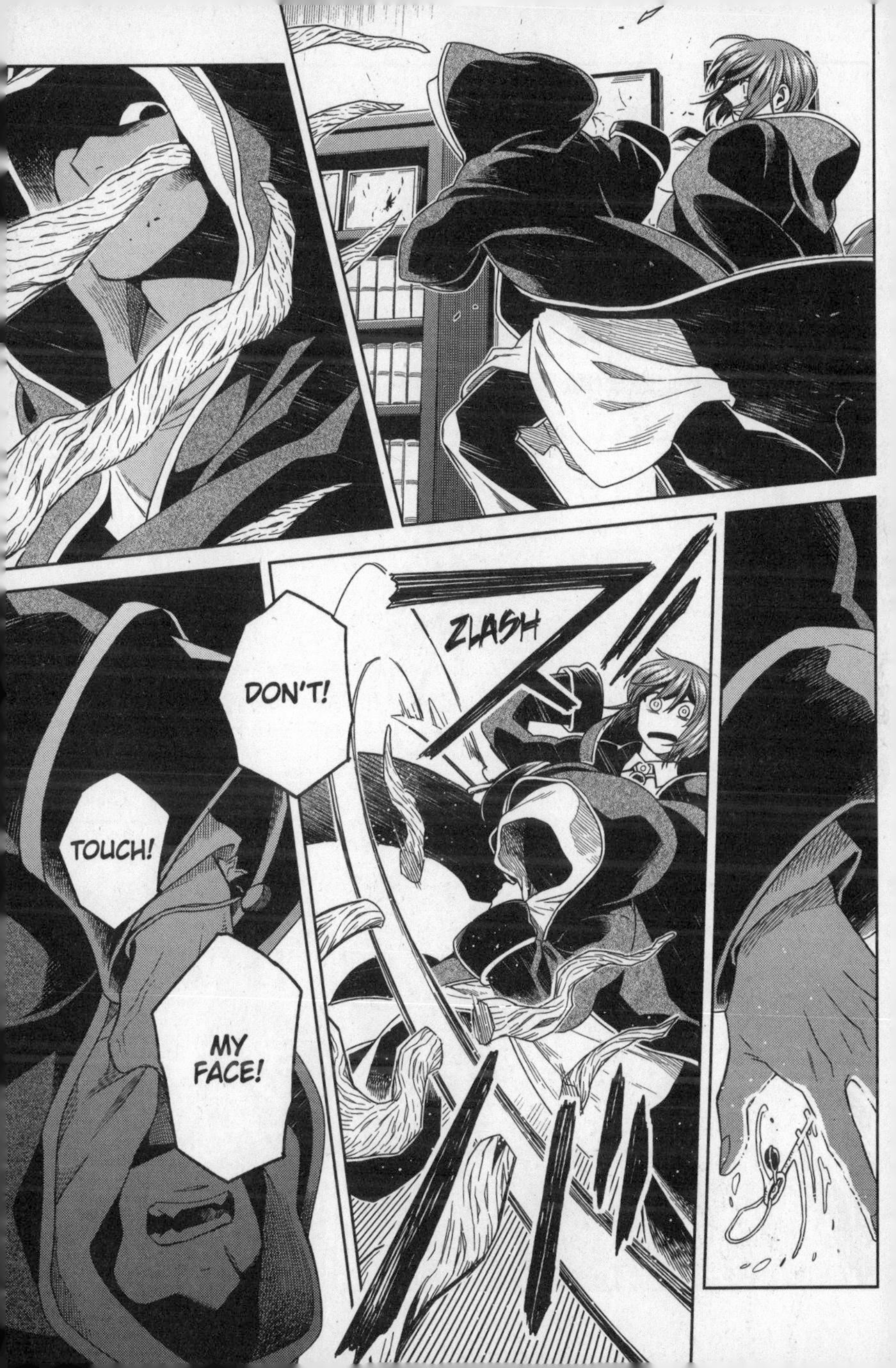
ZLASH
DON'T!
TOUCH!
MY FACE!

THANKS, ISAAC!

HIS FACE? SO THERE IS SOMETHING GOING ON THERE.

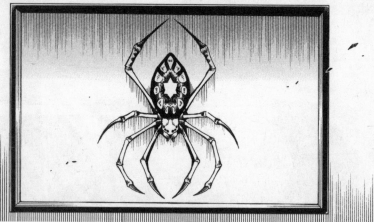

YANK

LUCY?

LUCY!

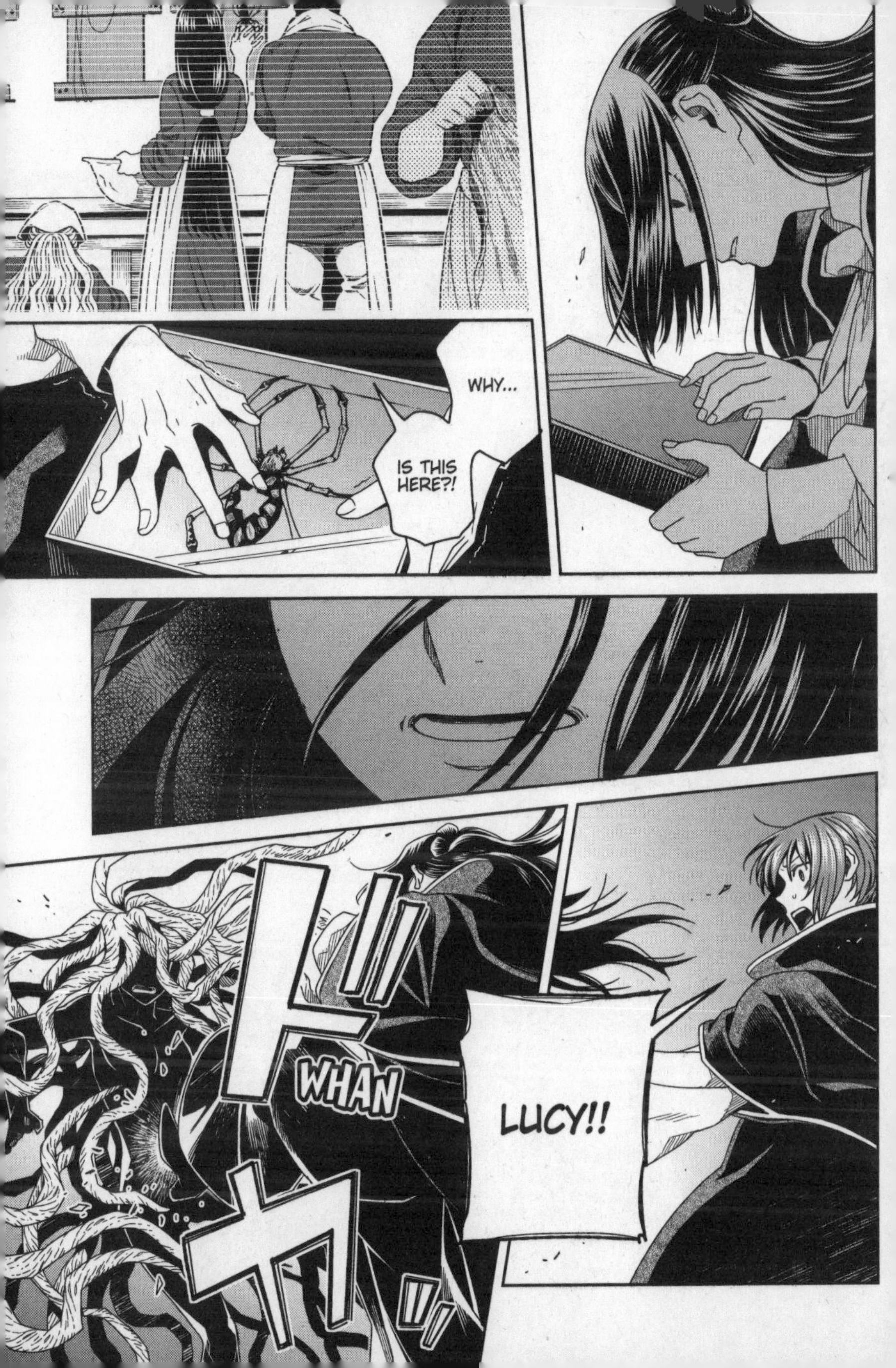
WHY...
IS THIS HERE?!
LUCY!!
WHAN

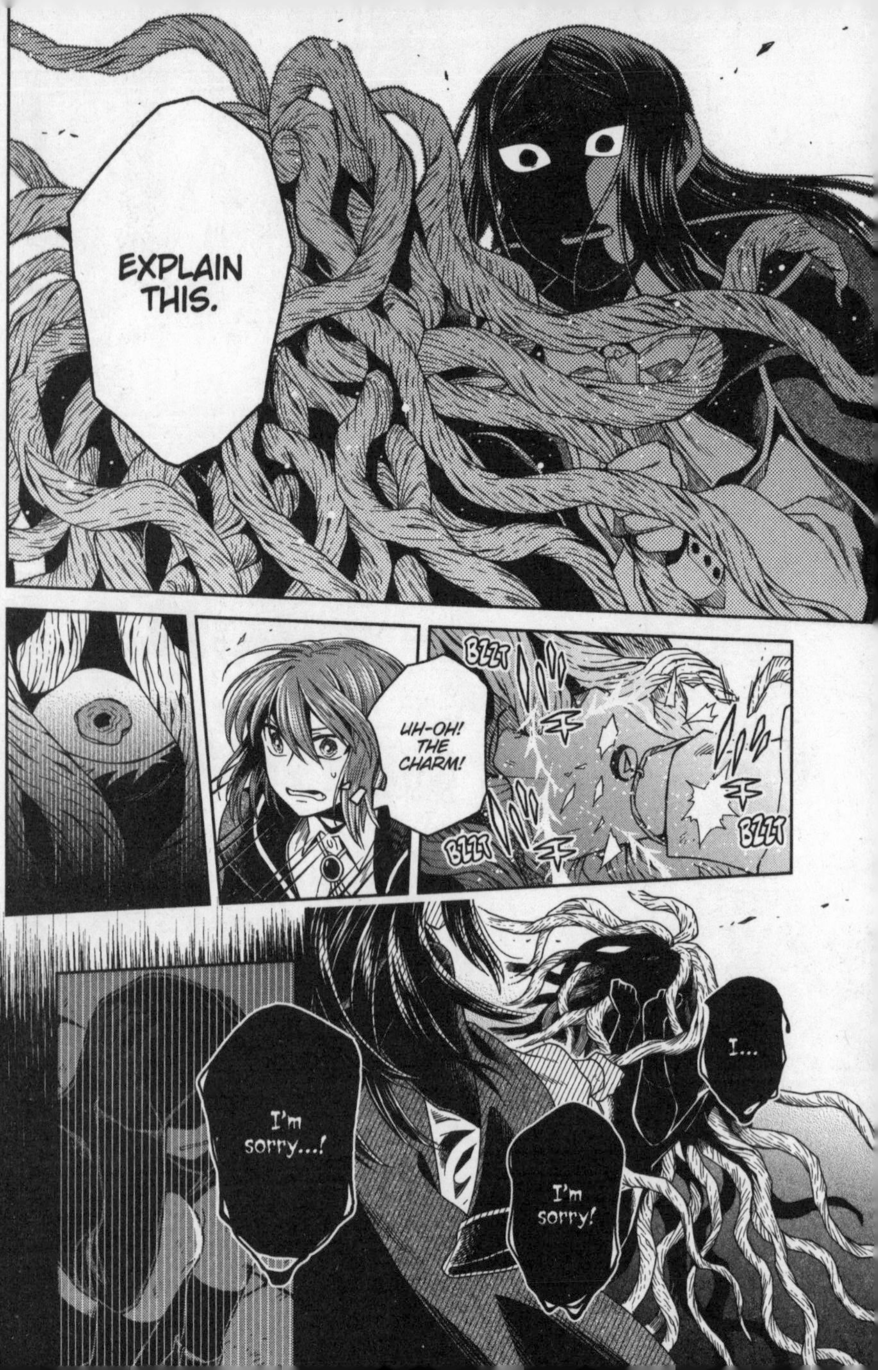
EXPLAIN THIS.
UH-OH! THE CHARM!
BZZT
BZZT
BZZT
I...
I'm sorry...!
I'm sorry!

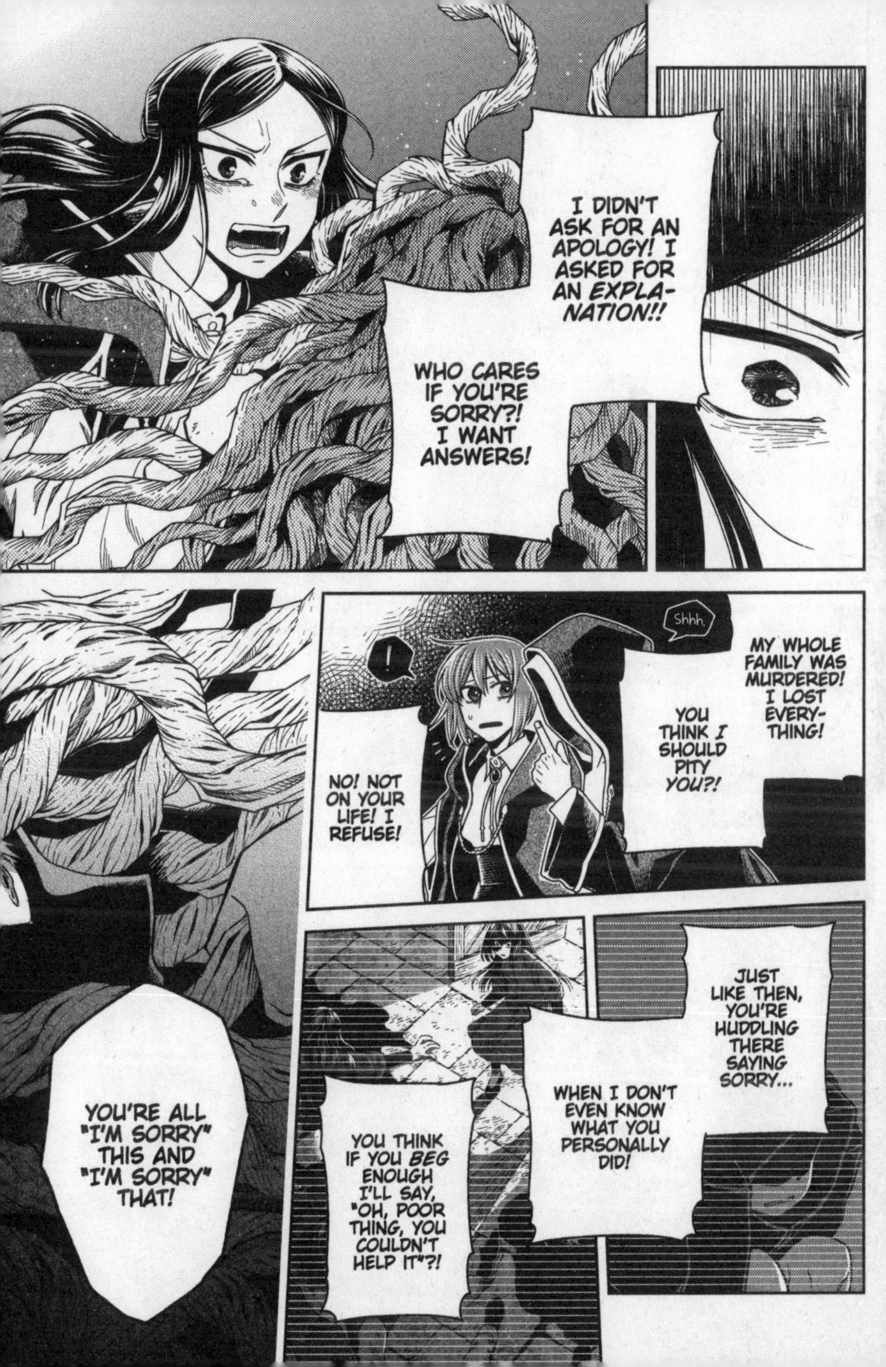
I DIDN'T ASK FOR AN APOLOGY! I ASKED FOR AN *EXPLA-NATION!!*
WHO CARES IF YOU'RE SORRY?! I WANT ANSWERS!
Shhh.
!
MY WHOLE FAMILY WAS MURDERED! I LOST EVERY-THING!
YOU THINK *I* SHOULD PITY *YOU?!*
NO! NOT ON YOUR LIFE! I REFUSE!
JUST LIKE THEN, YOU'RE HUDDLING THERE SAYING SORRY...
WHEN I DON'T EVEN KNOW WHAT YOU PERSONALLY DID!
YOU THINK IF YOU *BEG* ENOUGH I'LL SAY, "OH, POOR THING, YOU COULDN'T HELP IT"?!
YOU'RE ALL "I'M SORRY" THIS AND "I'M SORRY" THAT!

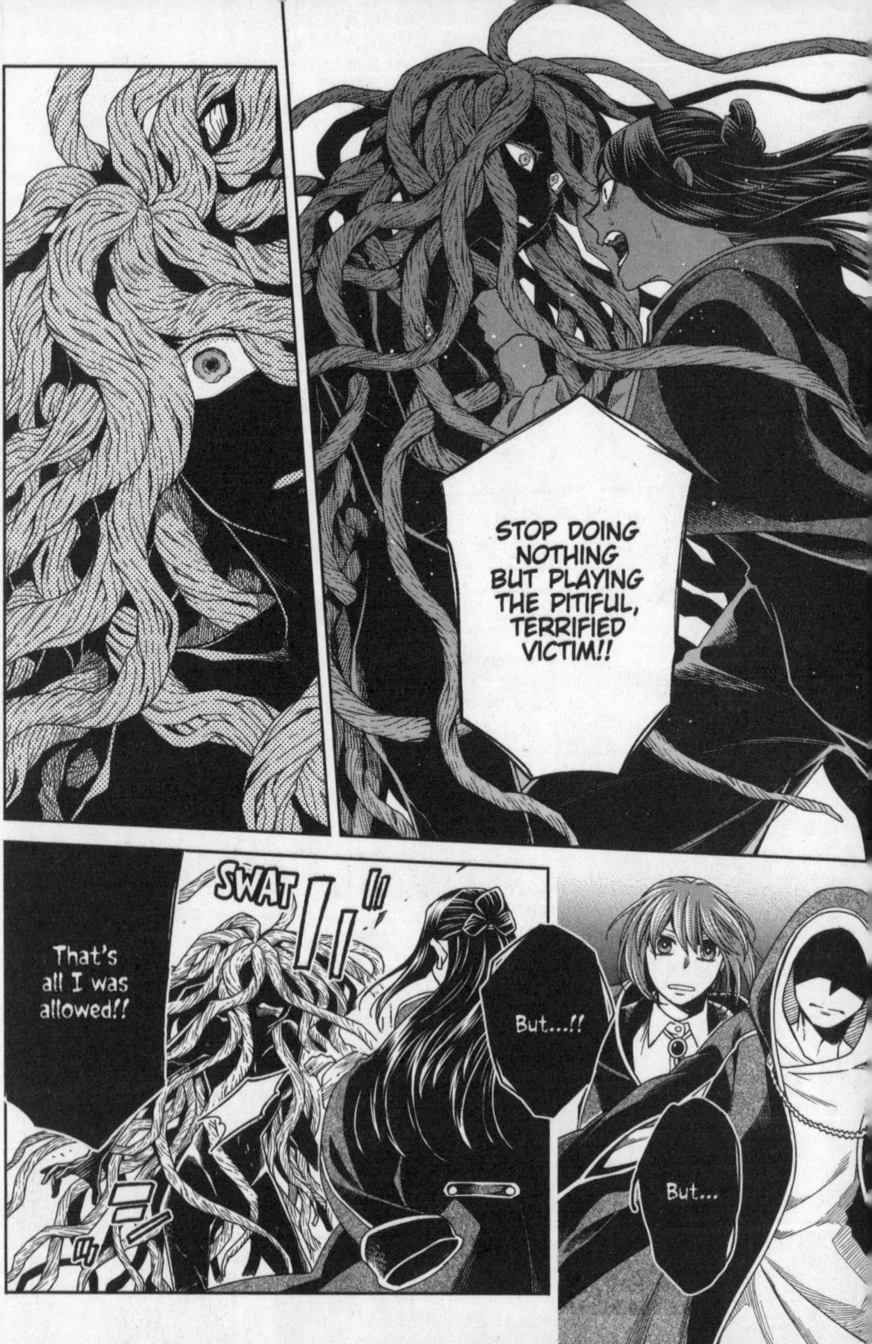
STOP DOING NOTHING BUT PLAYING THE PITIFUL, TERRIFIED VICTIM!!
But...!!
But...
SWAT
That's all I was allowed!!

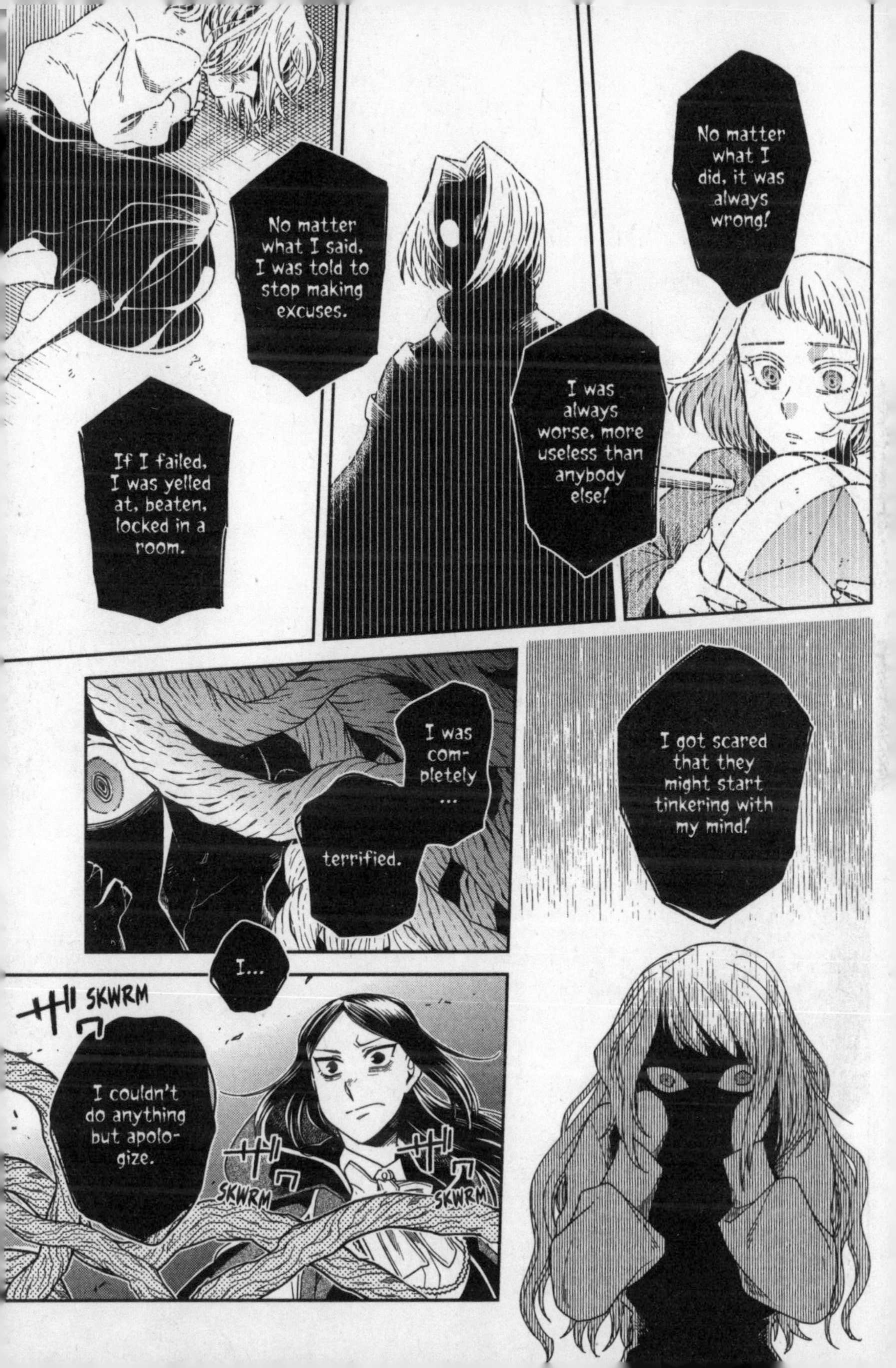
No matter what I did, it was always wrong!
I was always worse, more useless than anybody else!
No matter what I said, I was told to stop making excuses.
If I failed, I was yelled at, beaten, locked in a room.
I got scared that they might start tinkering with my mind!
I was completely ...
terrified.
I...
SKWRM
SKWRM
SKWRM
I couldn't do anything but apologize.

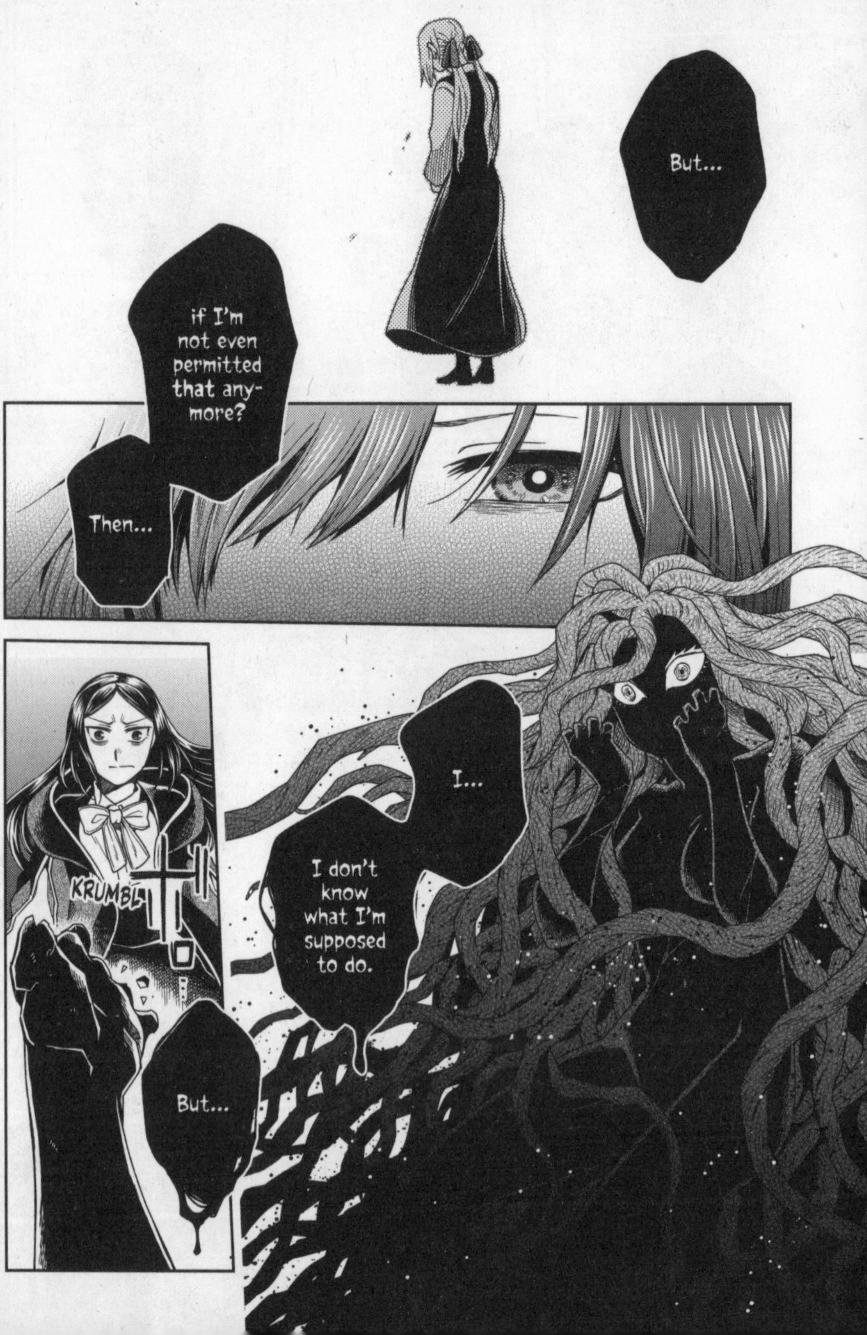
But...
if I'm not even permitted that any-more?
Then...
I...
I don't know what I'm supposed to do.
KRUMBL
But...

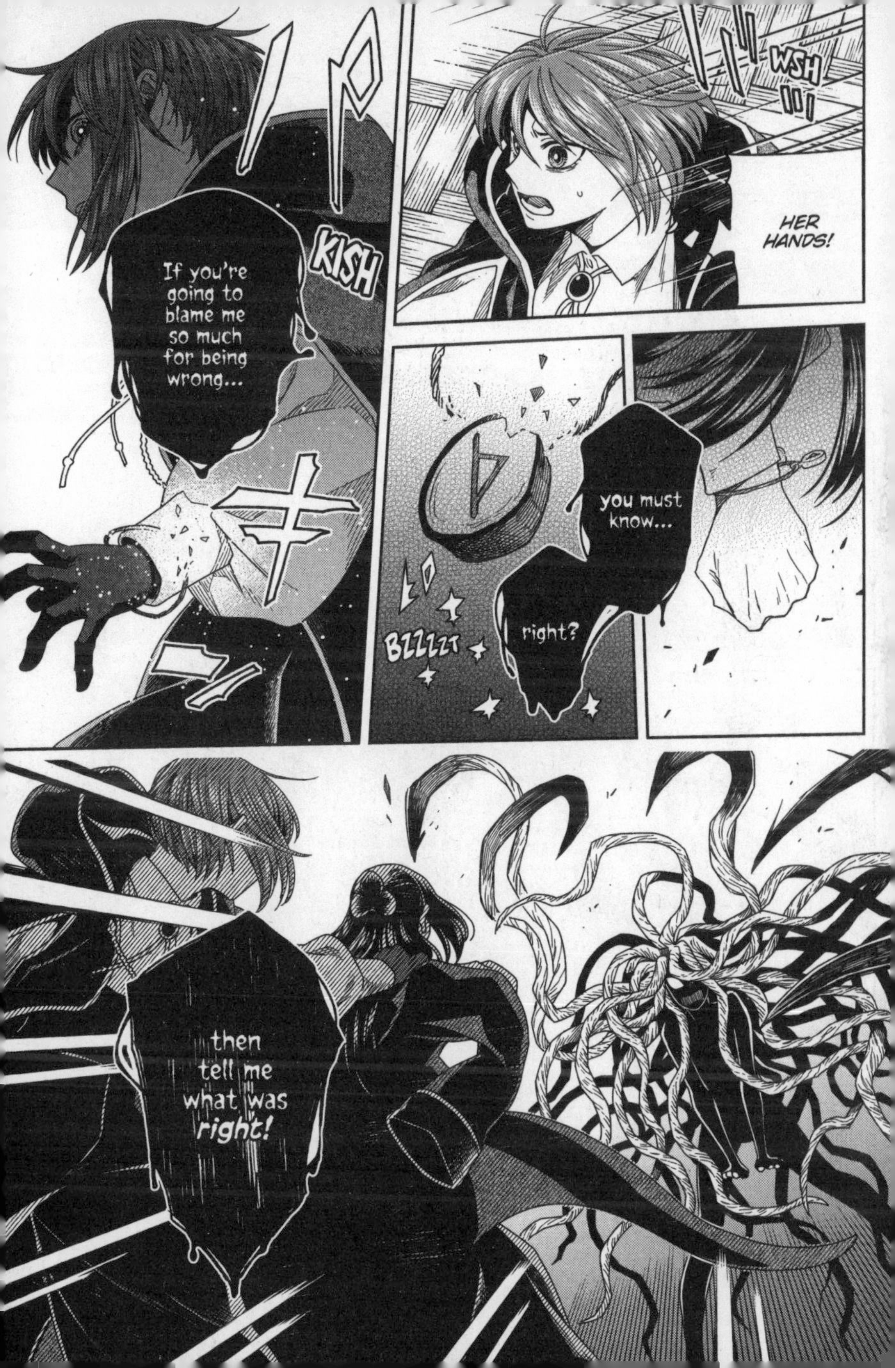
WSH
HER HANDS!
KISH
If you're going to blame me so much for being wrong...
you must know...
right?
BZZZZT
then tell me what was *right!*

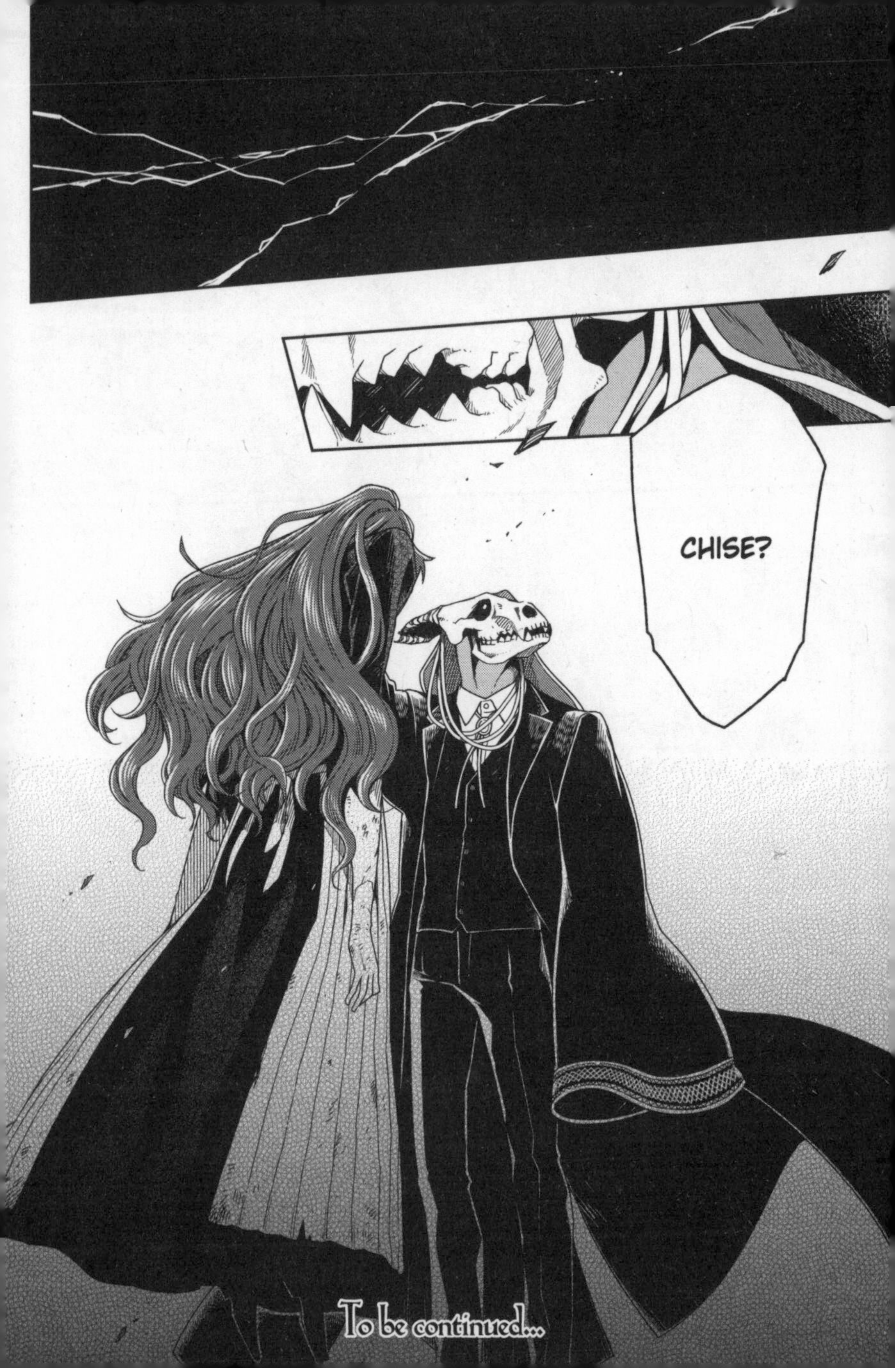
CHISE?
To be continued...

The Ancient Magus' Bride

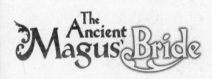

The Ancient Magus' Bride

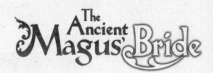

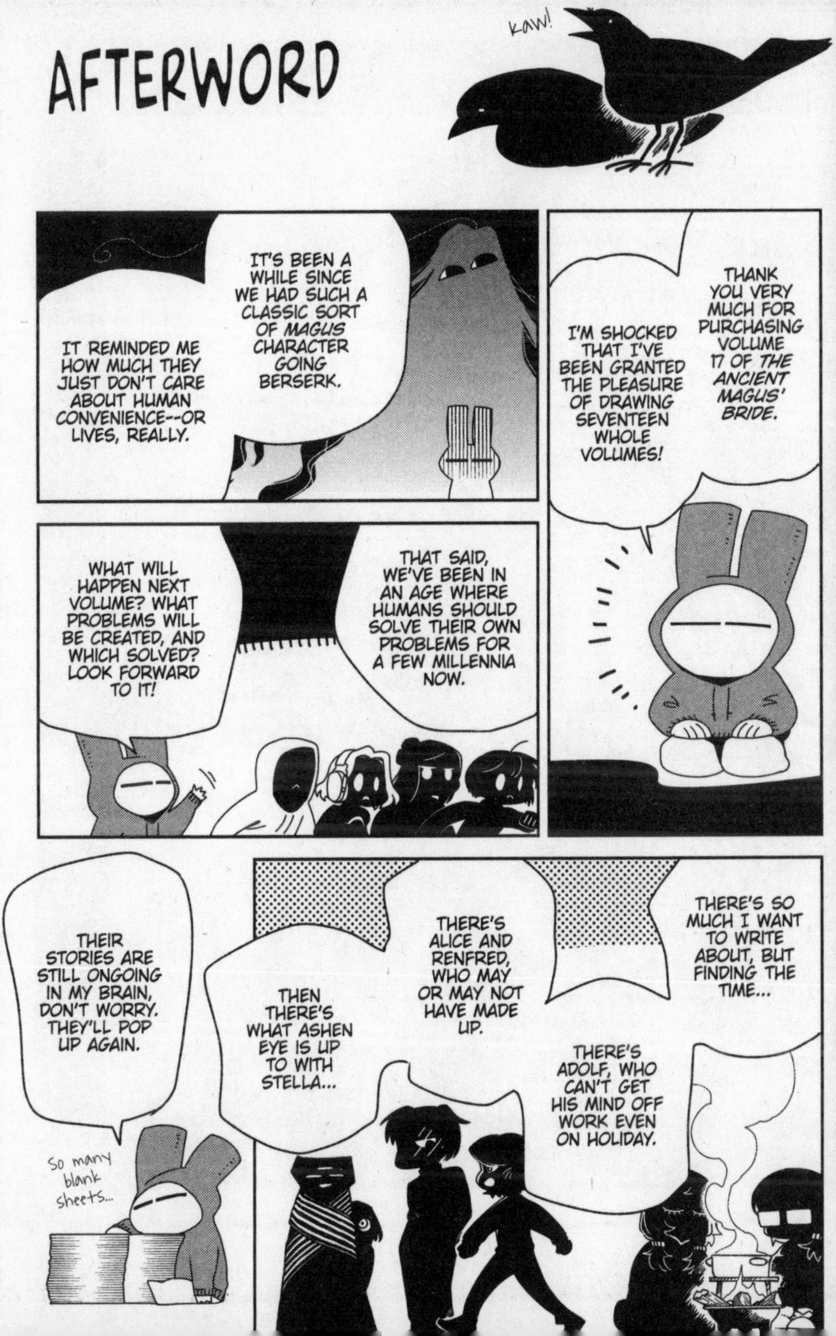
AFTERWORD
kaw!
THANK YOU VERY MUCH FOR PURCHASING VOLUME 17 OF *THE ANCIENT MAGUS' BRIDE.*
I'M SHOCKED THAT I'VE BEEN GRANTED THE PLEASURE OF DRAWING SEVENTEEN WHOLE VOLUMES!
IT'S BEEN A WHILE SINCE WE HAD SUCH A CLASSIC SORT OF *MAGUS* CHARACTER GOING BERSERK.
IT REMINDED ME HOW MUCH THEY JUST DON'T CARE ABOUT HUMAN CONVENIENCE--OR LIVES, REALLY.
THAT SAID, WE'VE BEEN IN AN AGE WHERE HUMANS SHOULD SOLVE THEIR OWN PROBLEMS FOR A FEW MILLENNIA NOW.
WHAT WILL HAPPEN NEXT VOLUME? WHAT PROBLEMS WILL BE CREATED, AND WHICH SOLVED? LOOK FORWARD TO IT!
THERE'S SO MUCH I WANT TO WRITE ABOUT, BUT FINDING THE TIME...
THERE'S ALICE AND RENFRED, WHO MAY OR MAY NOT HAVE MADE UP.
THERE'S ADOLF, WHO CAN'T GET HIS MIND OFF WORK EVEN ON HOLIDAY.
THEN THERE'S WHAT ASHEN EYE IS UP TO WITH STELLA...
THEIR STORIES ARE STILL ONGOING IN MY BRAIN, DON'T WORRY. THEY'LL POP UP AGAIN.
So many blank sheets...

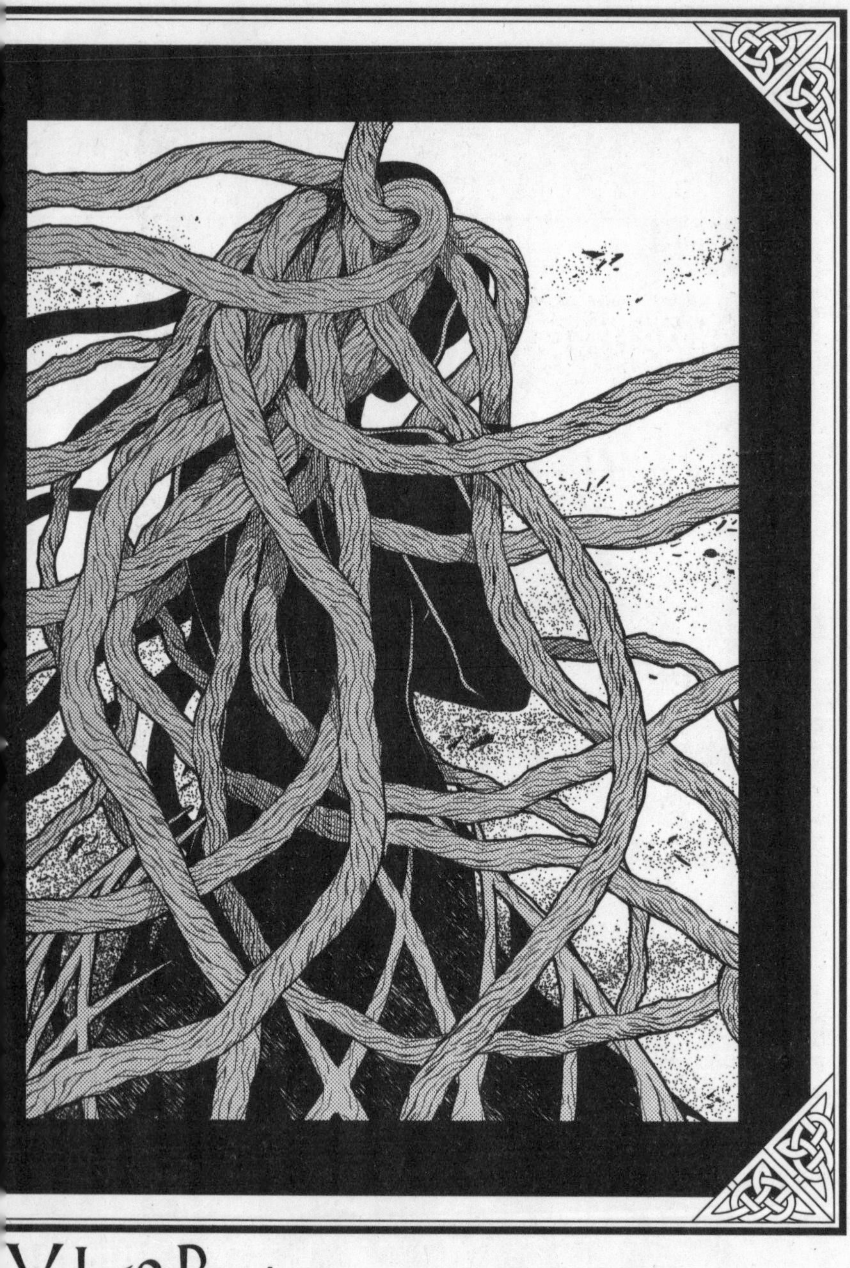

Vol. 18 Preview

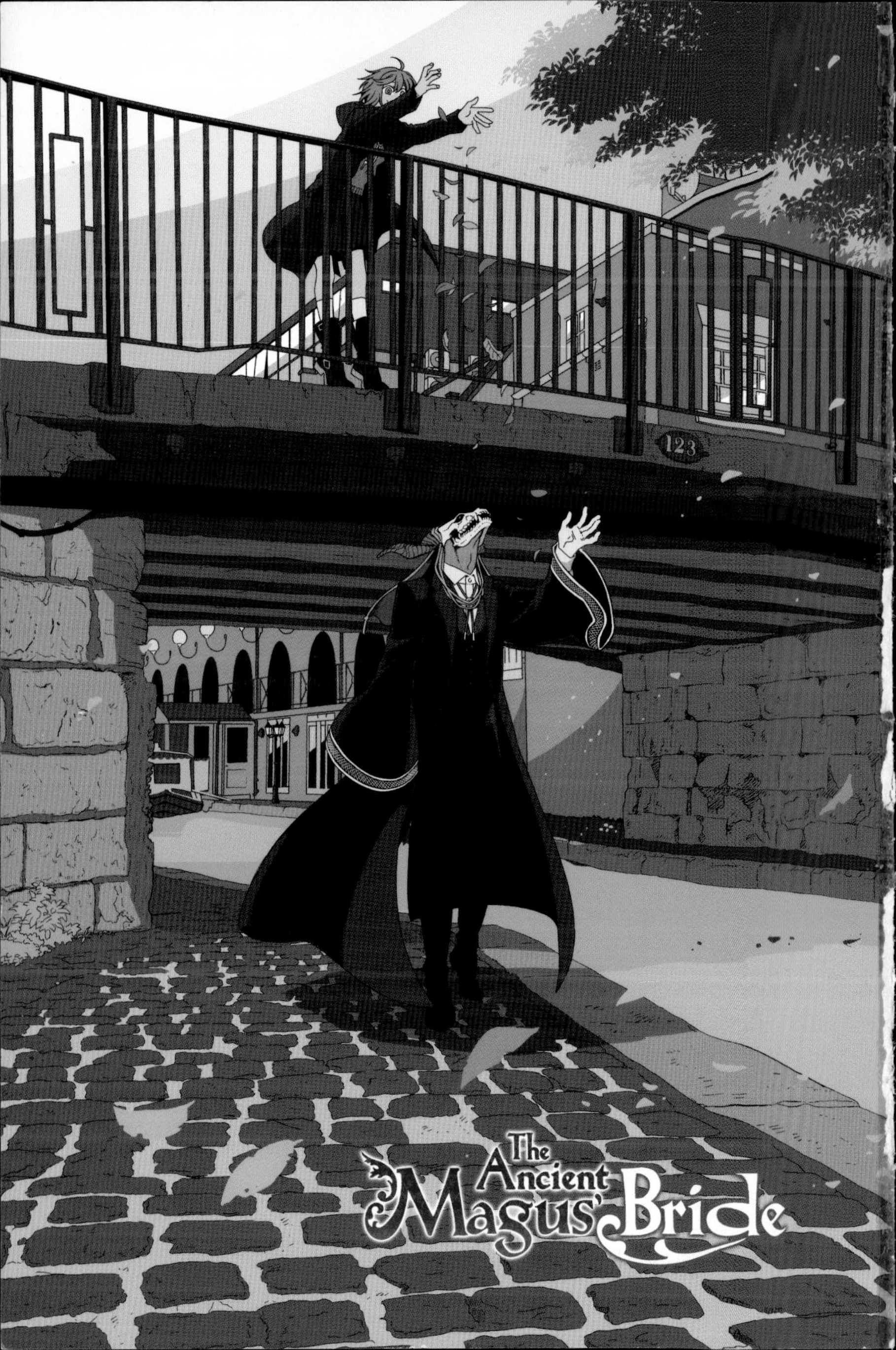

123
The Ancient Magus' Bride

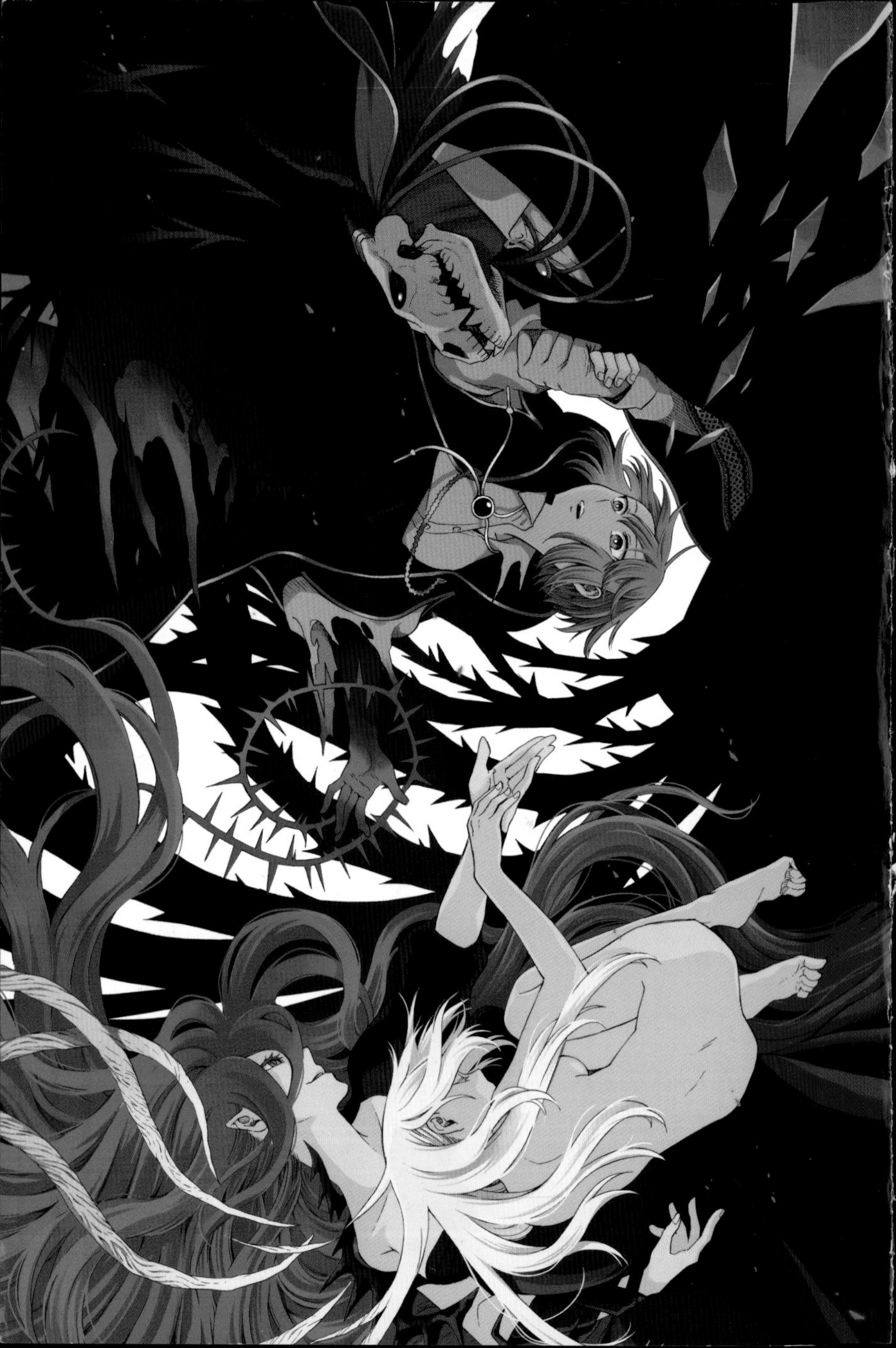